MARKET DOMINANCE

How Firms Gain, Hold, or Lose It and the Impact on Economic Performance

Edited by
DAVID I. ROSENBAUM

Westport, Connecticut
London

Library of Congress Cataloging-in-Publication Data

Market dominance : how firms gain, hold, or lose it and the impact on
  economic performance \ edited by David I. Rosenbaum.
    p.   cm.
  Includes bibliographical references and index.
  ISBN 0–275–95604–0 (alk. paper)
  1. Market share—United States. 2. Industrial concentration—
United States. 3. Big business—United States. 4. Competition—
United States. 5. Success in business—United States.
  I. Rosenbaum, David Ira.
  HD2757.15.M37   1998
  338.8′0973—dc21   97–27004

British Library Cataloguing in Publication Data is available.

Library of Congress Catalog Card Number: 97–27004
ISBN: 0–275–95604–0

First published in 1998

Praeger Publishers, 88 Post Road West, Westport, CT 06881
An imprint of Greenwood Publishing Group, Inc.

Printed in the United States of America

The paper used in this book complies with the
Permanent Paper Standard issued by the National
Information Standards Organization (Z39.48–1984).

10 9 8 7 6 5 4 3

CONTENTS

ILLUSTRATIONS

1

INTRODUCTION

David I. Rosenbaum

A competitive market system creates incentives for firms to vie for large market shares. Sometimes one firm is so successful in this fight, it acquires a dominant position in a market. From the firm's point of view, a large market share is good. After all, dominance implies power and control. It creates a real potential to increase profits. From society's point of view, however, dominance may not be quite so desirable. For the power that goes with dominance can be acquired and used in a number of ways. While some of these ways may promote economic welfare, others might reduce it. If the reductions are large and long-lived, we may want to reconsider whether dominance should be affirmed in all cases.

Among economists, there is no consensus on the allocative consequences of market dominance. Some argue that the process of gaining and holding a dominant position naturally improves economic welfare. Under this school of thought, firms become dominant because they are doing something better than their competitors. It may be managing better or producing a better product or even producing more efficiently. Whatever the specific source, the general foundation for dominance is being "more efficient" than competing firms. The argument continues that once dominance is attained, it is then maintained only through efficient pricing and continuing efforts to remain more efficient than competitors. Hence, dominant firms act to improve economic welfare.

Other economists argue that efficiency is neither the requisite source nor the mandated consequence of market dominance. Firms can become dominant through actions that will eventually decrease economic welfare. Predatory behavior is an example. Furthermore, the power that comes with market dominance arguably can have inefficient consequences. Prices, for example, may remain persistently above competitive levels. Dominance possibly can be used to forestall the smooth flow of re sources between markets. A dominant firm may be able either to delay exit or hinder entry that would naturally occur under more competitive conditions. This reduces economic welfare.

The welfare impacts of market dominance have a direct bearing on the policy toward dominant firms. If the sources and consequences of dominance are efficiency, then reliance on a market system is a sufficient policy. On the other hand, if the sources and/or consequences of power reduce welfare, then direct intervention either to forestall or disrupt power may, at times, be necessary.

This book is an attempt to shed further light on market dominance and its economic consequences. Ten industries are examined. Each has been controlled at one time by either a dominant firm or a group of firms acting as a dominant unit. The sources, methods of maintenance, and ramifications of dominance are examined in each. The studies seek to determine whether efficiency was the source and result of dominance, or whether dominance was acquired and extended through inefficient means. Looking across the studies should help in drawing further-reaching conclusions. It should reveal whether certain factors or actions are typically associated with acquiring and maintaining power, or, alternatively, if a variety of factors might evolve that could lead to these outcomes.

The implications of this review may help in forming an economic policy toward dominant firms. In the 1960s and 1970s, merger policy, for example, was heavily oriented toward concentration. More current research has shown that concentration is not always the compelling factor in merger analysis. Several other factors affect oligopoly performance as well. Recognition of these factors has broadened the focus of merger evaluation. The studies in this book will broaden the focus of any dominant-firm policy. Dominance itself may not be the defining element of any policy. Rather, other structural and behavioral characteristics may also be important in determining the best policies for dealing with the issue of market dominance.

EFFICIENCY AND DOMINANCE

One of the major concerns of microeconomics is resource allocation. In a world of limited resources, getting the right amount and type of inputs into various markets can help optimize production and maximize welfare. The notion of efficient resource allocation, however, really occurs within two time-related dimensions: the static dimension, which examines allocations at a point in time, and the dynamic dimension, which looks at allotments over time. The two are interconnected. Efficiency over time suggests the need for a smooth transition from any current situation of inefficient allocation to a future situation of more efficient allocation. For example, chronic losses in one market should provoke an exodus of resources to other markets. Excess profits, on the other hand, should attract new resources into a market. Dynamic efficiency also suggests the steady flow of new technologies into markets.

Static inefficiencies can occur even in smooth-running economic systems. Monopoly is a classic example. This potential for static misallocations calls for an understanding of how resources are reallocated. If the process of moving inputs from one market to another over time works fairly well, then static misallocations should be of secondary concern. If, however, reallocation does not always work well, static misallocations can be long-lived and of significant concern. In the United States, we rely on the market system and its "invisible hand" to carry out this allocation and reallocation process. Such a reliance requires a conviction that competition is enough to bring about an efficient reallocation of resources. This may not always be the case.

Beginning in the late 1800s, antitrust laws were established in the United States to allow intervention into markets. Their adoption was based, in part, on the belief that competition alone could not always ensure the free flow of capital across markets. It was argued that certain market structures or certain types of firm activities could inhibit the flow of capital. The laws were designed to prevent either those structures or those activities from occurring. Contracts in restraint of trade (price fixing), for example, were thought to lead to static misallocations. Predation was seen as a problem in that one firm could acquire and maintain market power, leading to both static underallocation and ineffective reallocation over time.

The need for most antitrust laws, however, has remained debatable among economists. The foundation for the debate hinges, to a large degree, on faith in the market system to allocate resources efficiently. On the one side, the Chicago school or New Learning eschews government intervention in almost all cases. The Structuralist school, on the other side, acknowledges that in some situations, government intervention to force reallocation may be required.

The Chicago approach argues that firms gain market share because they are efficient.[1] This efficiency may allow a firm to raise prices above its own marginal costs in the short run. However, to maintain that ability, the firm will have to invest continually in new technologies and other things that keep it efficient over time and satisfy consumers' wants. If the firm does not, the resulting supra-normal profits will create an incentive for smaller competitors to grow and for new firms to enter the market. This will precipitate resource reallocation.

A good example of the Chicago approach comes from the writings of Robert Bork. He posits that a "large firm may be able to restrict market output and raise market price. But as it raises price (relative to its own cost) an equally efficient entrant should have an incentive to enter the market. Only a large firm that benefits from efficient production should be able to raise prices without attracting higher cost entrants. If all firms are equally efficient, the exercise of power will lead to its erosion."[2] Yale Brozen mirrors this opinion in arguing that "dominant firms may initially control a market. But if they are very profitable and the pioneering firms fail to expand rapidly and provide a sufficient supply to depress price and drive profits down to the long-run equilibrium level, entry soon diffuses them."[3] Brozen writes later, "only if leading firms continually improve processes and products to preserve their relative efficiency, and only if they price competitively, do they succeed in maintaining their positions."[4] In effect, static inefficiencies must be small in that firms that price inefficiently or fall behind in technology enjoy only short-term excess profits.

Actually Brozen's predictions seem more extreme than Bork's. Brozen would have us believe that a dominant firm must be efficient in terms of progressiveness and technology, and must price efficiently. Bork would allow that if a firm becomes and remains dominant because it is relatively more efficient than its competitors, the firm could raise price above marginal cost without attracting entry. Two caveats prevail: the dominant firm would have to price at cost to discourage an equally efficient rival, and if it could price above cost, this would create all the more incentive for others to enter.

The Structuralist view is quite different. It argues that a firm or group of firms can acquire power in a market. That power can be used to price above marginal cost in the short run and to prevent the reallocation of resources in the long run within a market system. On the issue of short-run pricing, Leonard Weiss put together an impressive book analyzing the link between concentration and pricing in a number of industries and over several different time periods. His hypothesis is that concentration creates market power. The exercise of that power leads to short-run pricing distortions. The results are quite unequivocal and "seem to give overwhelming support to the concentration-price hypothesis."[5] Other studies have shown a positive link between brand market share and prices, again indicating that large firms can acquire market power.[6]

On the issue of dynamic efficiency, the Structuralist school points to entry barriers as conditions that allow firms persistently to raise prices above competitive levels without attracting new firms into markets. Entry barriers can be a problem in that they may either prevent or significantly retard the flow of resources into markets where they may otherwise naturally go. Bain's seminal work examined the extent of structural barriers across twenty different industries.[7] He broke the barriers into four categories and found that in some industries they can be rather significant.

In another study, Shepherd identified eight structural and six behavioral categories of entry barriers.[8] The behavioral barriers encompassed a variety of pre-emptive and retaliatory actions by existing firms against new firms. These actions included pricing, marketing, and product differentiation schemes. Other research has shown that behavioral barriers can include strategic patenting (including sleeping patents), resource control, and brand proliferation. Behavioral barriers are particularly interesting in that they are explicit actions undertaken by firms to prevent the flow of resources into markets.

Following the Structuralist train of thought, actions that allow a firm either to acquire or maintain power do not necessarily have to be blatantly anticompetitive. Pricing below marginal cost with the intent of excluding a rival and recovering profits at a later date is classic, anticompetitive predation. Yet one could argue that less severe price-setting can have the same impact without meeting the controversial marginal cost test.[9] First-mover advantages are another area where actions that are not considered "anti-competitive" in and of themselves can help create or maintain dominance. If a first-mover advantage is long lived, it may allow a firm to price above cost without quickly inducing entry. The firm is not engaging in anticompetitive behavior. But competition may not work as quickly as free market proponents predict.

Whether firms can create long-term advantages for themselves seems to be an issue that divides the Structuralist school from the Chicago school. Following the reasoning of Bork and Brozen, static advantages, whether tangible or intangible should be reproducible in a working competitive marketplace. Lower costs can be replicated, unless the source is a scarce resource or a government-endorsed advantage like a patent. Better managers can always be bought away from successful companies. A "superior" product or reputation can be reproduced.[10] So in a smoothly working market system, even non-predatory types of advantages should dissipate. The key issue then is whether these firm-specific advantages dissipate in a timely manner, or remain for long periods of time.

The resulting policies of the two schools are quite different. The Structuralist school argues for potential intervention to control both market conditions and behaviors. Merger policy would limit market concentration. Other policies would prevent monopolization or abusive practices more generally. The Chicago policy prescription is to leave the market system alone. The policy debate, however, raises the crux of the issue: must society be prepared to intervene in markets, or is the market system vigorous enough to respond on its own to short-run resource misallocation problems?

This book should provide some insights into the dynamic workings of the market system. It consists of ten studies, each of an industry controlled at one time by a dominant firm. The focal point is on dominant firms for two reasons. Dominance itself is engaging. It is interesting to understand how firms acquire and maintain dominance, and in some cases, how that dominance is lost. More important, though, is the link between dominance and dynamic market efficiency. Preventing the smooth flow of resources into and out of markets requires power. The most likely place to find that power is in industries with dominant firms.

THE EXTENT OF DOMINANCE

Webster's dictionary defines dominance as "being commanding, controlling, or prevailing over all others."[11] Shepherd defines market dominance as having "a majority of the market and no close rival."[12] Carlton and Perloff define a dominant firm as "one with a large share of the market."[13] Beyond largess, dominance implies power. Dominant firms control markets. That control gives them power to influence competition and pricing–at least in the short term.

Dominance is neither vacant nor overwhelming in the U.S. economy. The 1992 Census of Manufacturers shows that the twelve four-digit industries with the highest levels of concentration had Herfindahl indices ranging from 2549 to 2999.[14] These Herfindahls generate leading firms with from 25 to 55 percent of the market. While 25 percent may be too small to qualify for dominance, 55 percent is ample.[15] Another eleven industries had either such high concentration or one potentially identifiable firm so that their Herfindahl Indices were not disclosed.[16] Non-disclosure suggests leading firms as well. These twenty-three industries generated about 8 percent of manufacturing value of shipments in 1992. A look at concentration figures over time shows that most of these industries have been highly concentrated for a number of years.

Given the broadness of both product and geographic markets at the census four-digit level, the 8 percent of value of shipments probably underestimate the extent of dominance across markets. Film is not included as a concentrated industry. Yet one of the chapters in this book shows that Kodak has been dominant in that market for decades. As another example of underrepresentation of dominance, consider the four-digit industry "Pharmaceutical Preparations." This industry is defined broadly enough to include preparations for the central nervous system, heart, and lungs. It also includes fertility and birth-control preparations. It has a 1992 Herfindahl Index of only 341, suggesting the leading firm had at most a market share of from 3 to 18 percent. But concentration is surely considerably higher among markets for specific pharmaceuticals.

The national cement industry is fairly unconcentrated. Its 1992 Herfindahl equaled 472, suggesting the largest national firm had no more than 20 percent of the market. However, a regional market can be quite concentrated. One recent study shows that across a sample of twenty-five cities in 1989, the Herfindahl Index averaged 3,300.[17] Some cities have even experienced monopoly control for a number of years. All of this suggests that dominance occurs with at least some regularity.

ECONOMIC ANALYSIS OF DOMINANCE

Two methodologies have seen extensive use in examining the link between dominance and dynamic economic efficiency. The first methodology follows the work of Dennis Mueller.[18] He models firms as earning a return equal to the competitive return plus a long-run rent peculiar to the firm itself and a short run rent also peculiar to the firm but that varies over time and converges to zero. If competition works, then the long-run rent should equal zero and the short-run rent should converge to zero fairly quickly.

Mueller then describes relative profits in excess of the economy norm as a function of the competitive return and the two firm-specific rents. If all profit rates converge to the norm, as would be expected under competitive conditions, excess profits should equal zero. However, he finds that for firms that start with extranormal profits (losses), excess profits are statistically greater (less) than zero, implying that their profits converge to some rate greater (less) than the economy-wide norm. Mueller concludes that "an element of profits of all firms at any point in time is a permanent rent, positive or negative, that the competitive process fails to erode."[19]

He goes on to examine the sources of excess profits or losses. In the case of profits, he finds a link with market share. Market leaders are much more likely to exhibit persistent excess profits than excess losses. He also finds that small firms should never experience persistent excess profits.[20] These results suggest that persistent excess profits may be tied to market power.

Mueller then goes on to explore the persistence of leading positions. He looks at the leading firms in markets that maintain their definition between 1950 and 1972 and finds "fairly persistent stability in the identities of the leaders in those industries."[21] A reasonable conclusion to draw from this work is that leading firms can hold a leading position for a long period of time—in this case at least twenty-two years. Interestingly, the probability of retaining leadership increases as the leaders become more dominant (concentration increases). The probability is not a function of two firm-specific investments that could create rents: namely advertising and patents. Rather, Mueller concludes that the data "reveal an inherent stickiness in market shares and market leadership positions that reflects an attenuated working of the competitive process. Moreover, the bigger—that is, economically more important—the industry, the more stability one observes."[22]

Analyses like Mueller's are important. They suggest that competition may not quickly erode excess profits. They show that leading positions can be maintained for significant periods of time. However, this does not tell us what makes a firm a leader or why it is able to maintain either its leadership or its excess profits. Consider the issue of excess profits. Mueller finds that excess profits can be long-lived and attributes it to a long-run, firm-specific rent. This very much supports a Structuralist view. But another explanation comes to mind. If a firm remains progressive, it could have persistent above-normal returns, not because it earns long-run rents, but because it keeps getting a new positive short-run rent through its progressiveness. Suppose, for example that a firm invents a new product. This invention gives it a short-term advantage over its competitors and allows it to earn excess profits. As its competitors develop the same product, this firm may lose its initial advantage. But if this firm develops a better second generation of the product, it may again acquire a short-term advantage over its competitors. As this process progresses over time, the firm may exhibit persistent excess profits, not as a result of a long-term advantage, but as a result of successive short-term advantages.

The inconclusiveness of these results with respect to the sources of maintaining dominance is frustrating. It would be nice to have better results. Perhaps another method of analysis would provide more satisfying answers. This leads to a second major technique used to examine market dynamics, simultaneous equation modeling.[23] The simultaneous equation literature focuses on the flow of resources across markets over time and the implications for transitions from short-run inefficient states to long-run efficient states. The results, however, can be used to see whether competition expeditiously erodes either dominance itself, or the advantages that may blossom from a dominant position.

The models are divided into two categories: structural models and reduced-form models. The structural models fashion causal links between indicators of current economic conditions (such as profits or concentration), measures of transition (such as entry or changes in concentration), and indicators of future economic conditions. Geroski and Masson, for example, link profit to entry. Another structural model links concentration to profits, which are then linked to entry, which itself influences future concentration.[24] This latter model forms a recursive system. The reduced-form models are not so causally oriented. Rather, reduced-form models specify simultaneous equation systems with each endogenous variable a function of some subset of the other endogenous variables and a group of exogenous variables.[25]

A common result of these models is that markets move slowly. Geroski and Masson, for example, find that it takes almost seventy years for excess profits to move only half way from some mean excess level to the competitive level. They conclude that "the picture of the competitive process . . . is, to say the least, sluggish in the extreme. Any modest departure from equilibrium caused for whatever reason gives rise to an extremely persistent departure from anywhere close to their long run levels."[26] Other studies find similarly slow adjustment.

With regard to dominance, this implies that excess profits are not quickly eroded and that dominant market shares are not quickly lost. Another common feature of these models, however, is that the results are not very robust. Levels of statistical significance and explanatory power tend to be low. Further, in the recursive models that use large data sets, some of the ending equations have notoriously poor fits. This is undoubtedly due, in part, to the problems of large cross-sectional data sets.[27] Again, we are left with unsatisfying answers.

Froeb and Geweke develop an interesting variation on the standard reduced-form models.[28] They develop a two-equation model that describes structure (measured by concentration) and performance (measured by profits) as functions of lagged values of both variables and variance terms. They use the variance structure of the model to develop measures of periodicity which, in turn, allow them to estimate whether the structure has short-term and/or long-term effects on performance. In essence, they are looking for a result qualitatively similar to Mueller's. Their model is further enhanced in that they plausibly remove some of the noise inherent in cross-sectional multi-equation models by looking at only one industry over time.

The Froeb and Geweke results portray a more resilient market system. They "find that structure affects performance in the short run . . . but not in the long run . . . [and that] performance affects structure in the long run but not in the short run."[29] In other words, power may influence profits in the short run (six years in their analysis) and entry eventually erodes power. But the long-run effect can take twenty years or more.

Geroski also reviews several studies using either structural or reduced-form models to examine market dynamics.[30] Some of the studies look at cross-sectional data sets. Others focus on particular industries. Geroski describes mixed results where some models predict very slow evolution, others predict fairly rapid movement from some disequilibrium position to a steady state and still others predict movement in the wrong direction. On the whole, this area of research does not produce conclusive results.

The plethora of results precipitates the current book. Perhaps dominance is an area where returning to the methods of industry-specific analyses can provide some meaningful answers. Ten industry analyses follow. Each examines an industry that was dominated by either one firm or a group of firms acting together. While the results may not be applicable to all industries and all situations, they should shed important light on the methods of gaining, maintaining, and sometimes losing dominant positions. Furthermore, the results may also indicate whether dominance and its possible inefficient allocative effects can be long-lived. This may tell us whether the antithetical positions of either no policy or a policy never allowing dominant firms are too extreme.

ACKNOWLEDGMENTS

Many thanks to the authors participating in this project. Thanks also to Kim Largin, Donna Marvin, and Julie Schuur for their exceptional help in preparing this manuscript.

NOTES

1. This point is argued in Harold Demsetz, "Industry Structure, Market Rivalry, and Public Policy," *Journal of Law and Economics* 16 (1973).

2. Robert H. Bork, *The Antitrust Paradox: A Policy at War with Itself.* (New York: Basic Books, 1978), p. 178.

3. Yale Brozen, *Concentration, Mergers, and Public Policy* (New York: Macmillan 1982), p. 12.

4. Ibid., p. 107.

5. Leonard W. Weiss, *Concentration and Price* (Cambridge, MA: MIT Press, 1989), p. 268.

6. See, for example, Lawrence E. Haller and Ronald W. Cotterill, "Evaluating Traditional Share-Price and Residual Demand Measures of Market Power of the Catsup Industry," *Review of Industrial Organization* 11 (1996): 293-306.

7. Joe S. Bain, *Barriers to New Competition* (Cambridge, MA: Harvard University Press, 1956).

8. William G. Shepherd, *The Economics of Industrial Organization*, 3d ed. (Englewood Cliffs, NJ: Prentice Hall, 1990), pp. 273-276.

9. See, for example, Frederick M. Scherer, "Predatory Pricing and the Sherman Act: A Comment," *Harvard Law Review* 89 (1967): 868-903.

10. As Kaysen and Turner write, should any firm develop an "advantage in men and methods, rivals can and will copy the methods and hire the men away." Carl Kaysen and Donald F. Turner, *Antitrust Policy* (Cambridge, MA: Harvard University Press, 1959),

p. 9. This view is contested in Alfred Chandler, *Strategy and Structure* (New York: Doubleday, 1966).

11. *Webster's Seventh New College Dictionary* (Springfield, MA: G. & C. Mirriam Company, 1972), pp. 247-248.

12. Shepherd, *Industrial Organization*, pp. 13-14.

13. W. Carlton and Jeffrey M. Perloff, *Modern Industrial Organization* (Glenview, IL: Scott Foresman, 1990), p. 180.

14. The twelve industries with high Herfindahl indices in 1992 include potato chips and snacks, tire cord and fabrics, greeting cards, medicinals and botanicals, copper, aluminum rolling and drawing not elsewhere classified, turbines, electric lamp bulbs and tubes, batteries, cars, aircraft, and hard-surface floor coverings not elsewhere classified.

15. Williamson, in Oliver E. Williamson, *Markets and Hierarchies: Analysis and Antitrust Implications* (New York: Free Press, 1975), p. 209, defines a dominant firm as one whose market share "has persistently exceeded 60 percent of the relevant market and entry barriers are great."

16. These industries include malt beverages, cigarettes, chewing and smoking tobacco, wool mills, cellulose manmade fibers, semivitreous table and kitchenware, asbestos, malleable-iron foundries, nonferrous foundries not elsewhere classified, small-arms ammunition, and household laundry equipment.

17. See David I. Rosenbaum, "Efficiency v. Collusion: Evidence Cast in Cement," *Review of Industrial Organization* 9 (1994): 379-392.

18. See, for example, Dennis C. Mueller, *Profits in the Long Run* (Cambridge: Cambridge University Press, 1986).

19. Ibid., p. 31.

20. Mueller writes that the "odds of a company with a 1950 market share greater than 20 percent having projected long-run profits substantially above the norm were eight times better than the odds that its profits would be persistently 50 percent or more below the average. The chances that a firm with a market share of less than 1 percent in 1950 would earn profits 50 percent or more above normal were nil." Ibid., p. 38.

21. Ibid., p. 41.

22. Ibid., p. 49.

23. See, for example, Paul A. Geroski, et al., "The Dynamics of Market Structure," *International Journal of Industrial Organization* 5 (1987): 93-100; Paul A. Geroski and Robert T. Masson, "Dynamic Market Models in Industrial Organization," *International Journal of Industrial Organization* 5 (1987): 1-14, or Paul A. Geroski, *Market Dynamics and Entry* (Oxford: Blackwell, 1991).

24. David I. Rosenbaum, "Profit, Entry and Changes in Concentration," *International Journal of Industrial Organization* 11 (1993): 185-203.

25. Again, see Paul A. Geroski and Robert T. Masson, *Dynamics*, or Paul A. Geroski, *Market Dynamics and Entry*.

26. Ibid., p. 7.

27. See Richard Schmalensee, "Inter-Industry Studies of Structure and Performance," in Richard Schmalensee and Robert D. Willig (eds.), *Handbook of Industrial Organization*, vol. 2 (Amsterdam: North Holland, 1989), pp. 951-1010.

28. Luke Froeb and John Geweke, "Long Run Competition in the U.S. Aluminum Industry," *International Journal of Industrial Organization* 5 (1987): 67-78.

29. Ibid., p. 77.

30. Paul A. Geroski, *Market Dynamics and Entry*.

2

DOMINANCE IN THE OIL INDUSTRY: STANDARD OIL FROM 1865 TO 1911

Leslie D. Manns

The discovery of oil at Titusville, Pennsylvania, in 1859 would, within a few short years, result in the creation of a highly competitive, highly unstable petroleum industry in the United States. Out of this chaotic economic environment would rise one of the greatest industrial combinations the world has ever known: the Standard Oil Trust. From its ancestor's modest beginnings in 1863 until its court-ordered dissolution in 1911, Standard Oil provides an excellent case study of how a virtual monopoly was created and sustained.

In examining the rise of Standard Oil to a position of unquestioned dominance in the petroleum industry, one is struck by the deep divisions of interpretation of the facts that exist. The period in which Standard came to dominate the industry is known for populist hatred of big business, especially perceived monopolies and "yellow journalism." In such an environment it is difficult to separate fact from fiction. Even more disinterested observers arrive at radically different conclusions when examining the operations of the Standard Oil Trust.[1]

In its brief of the facts filed in 1909, the United States Department of Justice averred that Standard had engaged in the following methods to continue the monopoly and restrain interstate commerce:

Rebates, preferences, and other discriminatory practices in favor of the combination by railroad companies; restraint and monopolization by control of pipe lines, and unfair practices against competing pipe lines; contracts with competitors in restraint of trade; unfair methods of competition, such as local price cutting at the points where necessary to suppress competition; [and] espionage of the business of competitors, the operation of bogus independent companies, and payment of rebates on oil, with the like intent.[2]

The United States had also identified, in its brief, three periods over which Standard Oil had conspired to monopolize the oil industry and restrain interstate commerce. The periods identified were 1870 to 1882; 1882 to 1899; and 1899 until the filing of the government's case in 1906.[3] This chapter examines the rise of Standard Oil to dominant-firm status. Special emphasis will be placed on Standard's conduct in each of these periods as it sought to attain and maintain a position of dominance in the U.S. petroleum industry.

ROCKEFELLER AND THE EARLY OIL INDUSTRY

Only four years after the strike at Titusville, John D. Rockefeller along with four other men established the Excelsior Works refinery in Cleveland, Ohio.[4] In 1865, the firm of Rockefeller and Andrews expanded its operations by constructing the Standard refinery, also in Cleveland.[5] In that same year, William Rockefeller, Stephen Harkness, and Henry Flagler joined the firm as partners; the foundation for what was to eventually become the Standard Oil Trust had been laid.

The period from 1867 to 1869 was characterized by generally profitable conditions in the oil refining industry. As a result, existing firms expanded capacity and new firms entered, given that barriers were low and capital was relatively scarce. Refining in this period was a very competitive industry, characterized by an overabundance of relatively small firms. Entry and exit was common in response to booms and busts in the oil economy of Pennsylvania and Ohio. The period from 1869 to 1871 witnessed a severe price squeeze for refiners as crude oil prices declined 19 percent on average while kerosene prices dropped 25 percent on average.[6] Furthermore, transportation rates fell in a way that benefitted refiners located in New York and Pennsylvania but hurt the Cleveland refineries which had previously enjoyed a freight-rate advantage.[7]

Responses of existing refineries to the economic hardships of 1869 through 1871 varied greatly and included (1) remaining independent while working hard to reduce costs and expand markets, (2) joining an agency system for buying crude oil, selling refined products, and negotiating transportation rates, and (3) forming a closely held firm to control the stock of many refineries and thereby manage them as one. While Rockefeller and his partners tried both the independent and agency routes, they eventually chose to consolidate their interests by forming the Standard Oil Company of Ohio in 1870.[8] Originally capitalized at $1 million, Standard Oil of Ohio "controlled 10 percent of the nation's oil-refining capacity" at its founding in 1870.[9]

STANDARD OIL FROM 1870–1882: ON THE ROAD TO DOMINANCE

The years between 1870 and 1882 would prove to be most prosperous for the Standard Oil Company of Ohio. During this period it would experience phenomenal growth which would culminate in the creation of the Standard Oil Trust of Ohio in 1882. At its birth the Trust would control 90 to 95 percent of the refining capacity of the United States.[10] Thus, by the end of this period Standard Oil had become a truly dominant firm.

The year 1870 found the refining industry with capacity capable of refining three times as much oil as was produced.[11] While Standard was hurt by this overcapacity, it saw an opportunity to consolidate and expand its refining presence in Cleveland. The key to accomplishing this objective lay in stabilizing "the company's relation with the railroads."[12] Given Standard's relative strength in Cleveland's refining industry, it was in a strong position to demand greater-than-normal concessions from the railroads at this time. Cleveland refiners paid a non-discounted two-way rate of $2.40 per barrel, which covered $0.40 per barrel to ship crude from the oil regions of Pennsylvania to Cleveland and $2.00 per barrel to ship refined products from Cleveland to the major markets in and around New York.[13] Henry Flagler was able to negotiate with the Lake Shore-New York Central railroad a two-way rate for Standard Oil of between $1.20 and $1.60.[14] In return for the rebate Standard would guarantee year-round shipments for the railroad so that the railroad would gain both higher volume and additional regular shipments.

Such rebates put Standard in a very strong competitive position with regard to other refiners, especially in Cleveland. In response to cries of discrimination from other Cleveland refiners who demanded similar concessions, the Lake Shore-New York Central promised the same rebate "to any and all parties who would secure or guarantee a like amount of traffic."[15] None could, and, as a result, Standard gained an advantage from which it would eventually consolidate its hold on Cleveland's refining industry.

The problem of overproduction and continued price declines ravaged the oil refining industry in 1871. Many in the industry believed that some mechanism was necessary whereby production could be limited, prices stabilized, and cutthroat competition checked. Rockefeller was convinced that "the great units must combine, or their huge investment values could be wiped out."[16] Already, he was formulating a merger plan "to consolidate all oil-refining firms and corporations into one great organization which should eliminate most of the excess capacity and stop the price cutting."[17] During 1871 the number of stockholders in the Standard Oil Company of Ohio was increased and, as a result, Standard's capital was increased to $2.5 million, "an indispensable step if the Standard was to become an all-embracing organization, the core of a great merger."[18] While Rockefeller had sketched out the plan in his mind, the carrying out of the details would have to wait until it was known whether the South Improvement scheme could accomplish the same objectives.

The South Improvement scheme was an attempt by refiners to stabilize oil prices and freight rates, thereby benefiting both the refining industry and the rail industry. Alliances between refineries and railroads had been bifurcated for a long time, with the Cleveland refineries "tied" to the Pennsylvania railroad.[19] The resulting rate wars between the railroads, and the consequent effects on a refining industry recently plagued by overproduction, were disastrous. Thus, an "evening" system was sought through the South Improvement scheme. The scheme was essentially

a plan to unite the oil-carrying railroads in a pool; to unite the refiners in an association, the South Improvement Company; and to tie the two elements together by agreements which would stop destructive price-cutting and restore freight charges to profitable level. The railroads were to divide the oil-freights by a pre-arranged scale; the refiners were to act as *eveners*, insuring each road its proper share of the business from consigners; and in return the refiners were to get rate concessions which would wipe out all recalcitrant competitors.[20]

Not only would members of the South Improvement Company get larger rebates on their own oil shipments, they were also to get drawbacks on all shipments by competitors who were not members.[21] The drawbacks allowed each member of the South Improvement Company to receive money from the railroads "equal to the ordinary rebate" on each barrel of oil shipped by a non-member, so that Standard Oil, for example, got "the 40-cent rebate on crude from the regions; it [also] got 40 cents for every barrel brought to Cleveland by a competitor–that competitor paying 80."[22] It would be hard to imagine a more anticompetitive device.

The contract setting up the South Improvement Company was signed January 18, 1872, and went into effect February 26 of that year.[23] However, details of the contract leaked out, and furor and panic emanated from the independent oil companies and others not party to the South Improvement scheme. On March 25, 1872 the railroads signed an agreement with independent refiners that ended the contract with the South Improvement Company and promised perfect equality of rates to all shippers.[24] On April 6 the charter of the South Improvement Company was revoked by action of the Pennsylvania legislature.[25] The collapse of the South Improvement Company prior to the commencement of any business on its part only reaffirmed in Rockefeller's mind that one great company was the only viable solution to the problems of the refining industry.

Shortly before his involvement with the South Improvement Company, Rockefeller embarked on his plan to consolidate all the refineries in the Cleveland area. The goal of this consolidation was to eliminate overcapacity, close down smaller, less efficient refineries, and expand larger refineries thereby hoping to capture greater economies of scale. In December of 1871 Rockefeller proposed a merger with Clark, Payne and Company, his major refining competitor in Cleveland; the proposal was accepted and the owners of Clark, Payne and Company were well compensated with Standard Oil stock.[26] Having swallowed his largest competitor, Rockefeller turned his attention toward the remaining Cleveland refineries.

The troubled economic times of the early 1870s meant that most, if not all, refineries were losing money; thus, Rockefeller's task was made easier by these depressed conditions. The economic clout of Standard Oil, particularly because of its huge advantage in rail shipping terms, and the knowledge of Standard's involvement in the South Improvement Company made smaller companies "fear that competition would be impossible."[27] Rockefeller's connections with both the railroads and major banks in Cleveland led smaller rivals to the conclusion, sometimes reinforced by Standard Oil representatives, that the only options were to either sell out to or be crushed by Standard.[28] Rockefeller, forty years after the fact, denied that threats were ever made; he also claimed that all the mergers were completed on generous terms.[29] Those who sold out, particularly the owners of the smaller refineries, claimed they were usually offered "from 45 to 65 percent of their value."[30] Regardless of the degree of threat and the amount paid for the acquired firms, the fact remains that by April of 1872 "all but five of the twenty-six Cleveland refineries" had sold out to Standard Oil, and it "had achieved a practical monopoly of production in the principal refining center of the country."[31] Furthermore, Rockefeller's Cleveland refineries "were consolidated into one six-plant organization, by far the most efficient in the country."[32] With Cleveland as a base, Rockefeller was ready to extend his control over the oil industry by seeking alliances with other refiners, particularly those in the eastern United States.

Following the collapse of the South Improvement Company, a decentralized refiners' pool was established under the auspices of the National Refiners Association.[33] The pool sought to reduce the nation's refining capacity, fix prices, and divide up the nation's refining business. Lacking any enforcement mechanism, the pool agreement broke down, and the National Refiners Association was disbanded in June 1873. The failure of this latest pool served to reinforce in Rockefeller's mind that the only mechanism through which the refining industry could be stabilized was through the creation of one company that would control everything. In a small way, the National Refiners Association aided Rockefeller as he moved toward this objective. Through the association Rockefeller both collected and disseminated information: collected information about his competitors and disseminated information to his rivals attesting to the power and efficiency of Standard Oil.[34]

To extend its control over the industry, Standard needed to grow, and the fastest way to grow was via merger. With better information, Rockefeller embarked on a merger binge outside of Cleveland. He targeted refineries and related companies in New York, Philadelphia, and Baltimore. A strong presence on the East coast would allow Standard to more thoroughly penetrate eastern domestic markets and begin to build export markets. Rockefeller began to diversify Standard Oil via these new acquisitions. Prior to 1873 Standard was primarily a manufacturer, but now it was moving into other areas including distribution and pipeline transportation. The acquisition of Chess, Carley and Company, the major wholesale and retail distributor in Kentucky, allowed Standard to break into the marketing end of the oil industry. The purchase of Bostwick and Company, an export marketing agency that also owned terminal and warehouse facilities in New York Harbor, proved crucial to Standard as it sought to increase its oil exports. Given the animosity that the Standard Oil name was already capable of igniting, it is noteworthy that both of these acquisitions stipulated that the acquired companies would operate under their old names.[35] The move toward vertical integration had begun.

Standard's forays into pipeline transportation were motivated by the fear that pipelines, if controlled by a competitor, could jeopardize the success of a refining monopoly by interrupting the flow of crude oil. Therefore, Standard moved quickly to buy up many existing pipelines and their storage facilities. Vandergrift and Forman, one of the oldest and largest pipeline companies in the regions, was acquired by Standard in 1873 and renamed the United Pipe Lines Company.[36] In this way, Standard hoped to guarantee a steady supply of crude oil and, eventually, lower transportation costs when the pipelines were well organized. In that same year the American Transfer Company, a Standard subsidiary, was established for the purpose of spearheading Standard's construction of additional pipelines and storage tanks in the regions.[37] Through acquiring United Pipe Lines and American Transfer, Rockefeller had "completely safeguarded the Standard against a pipe line monopoly. . . . Indeed, he was already dreaming of his own pipe line monopoly."[38] By 1874 Standard Oil was firmly on a growth path toward complete dominance of the U.S. petroleum industry.

The year 1874 also brought another round of intense competition to the railroads as they scrambled for freight. A new pool was established through which the oil traffic was to be equitably divided amongst the Pennsylvania, Erie, and New York Central; freight rates were to increase; and, most importantly, "a uniform rate . . . [was] established from this station [the oil regions] to the Eastern ports *by way of all refining points*."[39] Basically, all refining centers, regardless of location, paid the same transportation costs to ship refined oil. This equalization feature of the pool agreement, proposed and demanded by Standard Oil, severely disadvantaged the transportation advantages previously enjoyed by refineries in New York, Philadelphia, and, especially, the regions.[40] Standard was once again exerting its power with an eye toward eventually increasing its control over oil refining.

With this new pool agreement in place, Rockefeller moved to acquire the major refineries in New York, Philadelphia, and Pittsburgh. Whether undue pressure to sell was exerted on any of the owners is debatable; however, Rockefeller opened Standard's books to W. G. Warden of Philadelphia, one of his first targets, and Warden quickly concluded that Standard "could sell oil far more cheaply than he could make it."[41] Under such circumstances it was clear that a price war with Rockefeller could not be won; thus, it was easier and cheaper to sell out at or near Rockefeller's offer price. The hatred of Standard Oil by others in the oil industry caused the acquisitions to be kept secret, and the companies continued to operate as if independent, all the while spying on truly independent refiners on behalf of Standard Oil.[42] Whether Rockefeller threatened predatory competition to consummate mergers is questionable, but Standard Oil certainly had the power and resources to fight if fighting proved necessary to subdue a competitor, force him out of business, or force him to sell on terms more amenable to Standard.

The acquisition of major and minor competitors continued to build Standard's monopoly control over the refining industry; however, such control was not yet sufficient in Rockefeller's view. Another pool agreement, under the direction of the Central Refiners Association, was begun in 1875 to "apportion all refining among the various members, to control all purchases of crude oil and all sales of refined oil, to make all rate agreements with railroads and pipe lines, and to divide all profits."[43] The Central Refiners Association, while nominally a pool, was really just an organizational arm of Standard Oil. Between 1875 and 1878 Standard was on an acquisition binge. If an independent could not be induced to sell, Standard would have its secret partners propose that the independent join the Central Refiners Association and thereby, in effect, lease its facilities o Standard Oil. The prices paid for Standard's acquisitions were sometimes generous, sometimes fair, and sometimes unjust. Many of the independents that sold out between 1875 and 1878 charged that "unfair pressure of various kinds" had been brought to bear on them and that when they finally sold, "their properties had been undervalued."[44] Rockefeller, as well as some of those whose firms were acquired by Standard, vigorously denied these allegations. By 1879 Rockefeller's monopoly was well established and well organized.

The mid 1870s also saw the emergence of a new threat to Standard, namely, the Baltimore and Ohio Railroad. Rockefeller viewed it as a threat because it served a region of the country where Standard did not have much of a refinery presence. In 1875, Standard secretly acquired the J. N. Camden and Company refinery and used it to establish another company, Camden Consolidated Oil.[45] Camden Consolidated Oil was then used as a base from which to purchase additional refineries; eventually it grew large enough to demand and receive significant transportation rebates from the Baltimore and Ohio. Standard's involvement was not known in any of these activities, and by 1877 almost all of the Baltimore refineries were controlled by Standard Oil.[46] Camden Consolidated "bought up whatever refineries it could, and squeezed out those which refused to sell. . . . By purchasing large quantities of the West Virginia and Ohio crude on which they depended, and holding it out of the market" until they yielded.[47]

Standard's tactics were rarely brutally anticompetitive. It was neither difficult nor expensive to set up a small refinery in the early to mid 1870s; $50,000 to $100,000 was sufficient capital to enter.[48] However, an entrant could not survive without rebates equivalent to those enjoyed by Standard Oil; thus, effective competition was nearly impossible. Generally, Standard did not employ "the rebate to eliminate existing competitors brutally when a gentler course was possible; its preferable practice was to buy or lease by amicable arrangement."[49] But, a rival who proved annoying "was likely to encounter difficulty with his flow of crude oil, his barrel supply, or his orders for [tank] cars; he was undercut in the market, or found that his distributing agency had gone over to Standard."[50] Standard thus seemed willing and able to use its power to reign in or crush competitors if need be, but only if more agreeable means did not work.[51]

In January of 1877, the Pennsylvania Railroad and its partially owned subsidiary, the Empire Transportation Company, decided to wage war with Standard Oil in hopes of reducing its control over oil refining. These powerful firms planned to have Empire "enter the refining business [through acquisition and construction] on a large scale, and the Pennsylvania . . . [would] support it by drastic rate-cutting."[52] Rockefeller, perceiving a threat to Standard's dominance, "knew that victory depended upon immediate and crushing action."[53] Rockefeller demanded that the Pennsylvania pressure Empire to withdraw immediately from refining. The Pennsylvania refused and immediately a devastating rate war broke out among the Pennsylvania, Erie, and New York Central Railroads. Standard's response was immediately to cancel all its shipments on the Pennsylvania, an amount equal to 65 percent of the total oil carried by that railroad.[54] Also, Standard cut the price of kerosene in all markets reached by Empire, bid aggressively for crude oil, and actively sold refined products domestically and in export markets in an effort to foreclose Empire.

The war was damaging to both sides, but the Pennsylvania Railroad and Empire suffered comparatively more than did Standard Oil. Rockefeller's group was never severely hurt because they "manufactured economically, and their resources were more than equal to the temporary deficits."[55] The combination of the rate war with the Erie and New York Central and the great railroad strike of 1877 proved devastating to the Pennsylvania. Empire's success depended heavily on support from the Pennsylvania, and it was no longer in a position to fight with Standard Oil. The Pennsylvania needed Standard's freight business and so requested peace and a return to more prosperous times. Empire was completely bought out by the Pennsylvania, which proceeded to sell all the oil-related ventures of Empire to Standard Oil.[56]

The demise of Empire, which was a major pipeline owner, hastened Standard's control of the pipeline industry. Within a few months the only other major pipeline firm, Columbia Conduit Company, sold out to Standard Oil.[57] Standard's control over the pipeline industry was almost complete.

Following the Pennsylvania's surrender, a new rail pool was formed, with Standard acting as the freight evener. For its services Standard "received a commission initially fixed at 10 percent on all its own shipments *and whatever other freights it might control.*"[58] In effect, this often represented a return to the drawbacks of the South Improvement Company, that is Standard also received rebates on competitors' oil shipments. Again, its monopoly control was well protected from effective new competition.

The oil industry was racked by overproduction and low prices of crude in the period between 1877 and 1879. Standard was feverishly building pipelines and storage in an effort to accommodate all the crude that was flowing, but transportation and storage could not keep up. On December 28, 1877, Standard issued an immediate shipment order under which it "would not run more than one fourth of any man's production into tanks, and would accept the rest only on an immediate shipment basis."[59] Such immediate shipment oil basically meant forced sales, sometimes at very steep discounts from prices available for stored oil. The goal of the order was to reduce overproduction, but Standard, as the major buyer of crude, benefited greatly at the expense of crude oil producers. One side effect of this cheap crude was that Standard was able to deeply penetrate foreign markets in Europe and Russia by being able to easily undersell any competitors it encountered there.

The immediate shipment order only served to further enrage crude oil producers, who had hated Standard for years. With determination and political luck, the producers got a Pennsylvania grand jury to hand down criminal indictments against nine Standard Oil officials in 1879.[60] These officials were accused of criminal conspiracy by attempting, through various means harmful to others, to monopolize the oil industry. The indictments were damaging to Standard, and it sought to get them dropped as quickly as possible.[61] The Compromise of 1880 between Standard and the oil producers led to the suits being dropped. Under the compromise, Standard agreed to (1) end discrimination by its pipelines, (2) not oppose the end of rebates and drawbacks by the railroads, (3) not accept any rebates offered by the railroads that the railroads "were not at liberty to give to other shippers," and (4) not object to full public disclosure of shipping rates.[62] From Standard's perspective it had agreed to very little and, most importantly, the principle of "rate discrimination [by the railroads] had been preserved."[63]

The last great threat to Standard's dominance in the period between 1870 and 1882 began on May 28, 1879, when oil began flowing through the Tidewater Pipe-Line Company's newly constructed, 109-mile line connecting the Bradford, Pennsylvania oil fields with the Philadelphia and Reading Railroad's loading terminals at Williamsport.[64] From Williamsport the oil could be transported by rail directly to the Atlantic seaboard. This pipeline, by providing cheap, alternative transportation of crude oil to the remaining independent refineries on the East coast represented a serious threat to Standard Oil's monopoly in refining. If pipelines began to carry significant amounts of crude oil, "the advantages which the Standard combination had been deriving from discriminatory rates would be lost" and successful competition in refining would be very likely.[65]

Rockefeller moved swiftly to meet Tidewater's challenge, He immediately ordered the construction of additional trunk pipelines to better connect Standard's refineries with the oil fields and rail terminals. He also sought to buy an interest in the Tidewater Company but was refused, whereupon he offered to buy all the crude the new pipeline could carry; again he was refused.[66] His next move was to offer to buy up, at high prices, the existing independent coastal refineries, thereby foreclosing Tidewater of its customers. Over time, this approach was most successful.

The railroads also saw the Tidewater pipeline as a major threat to their existence and so another disastrous rate war broke out. This was the railroads' last losing gasp, because they would be unable to compete once pipelines became dominant in the transportation of oil. Standard again benefited greatly from the rate war. Eventually, however, the railroads gave in and freight rates went back up. The big pipelines would remain and prosper.

The Philadelphia and Reading went bankrupt in 1880, and this was a severe blow to Tidewater. Furthermore, by 1881, only one independent refiner remained in New York, and Tidewater was beginning to feel financially strapped.[67] Also, Standard had been able to set up some of its agents as stockholders in Tidewater, and these men did whatever they could to sow dissension among other Tidewater stockholders.[68] Also, Standard was doing its best to discourage bankers and others from lending to Tidewater. External problems, together with internal squabbles among officers and stockholders, led Tidewater to the brink. In October of 1883, Standard Oil reached a settlement with Tidewater whereby Standard got 88.5 percent of all the pipeline business east of the oil regions and Tidewater got the other 11.5 percent.[69]

During the war with Tidewater, Standard was engaged in an extensive building campaign focused on long-distance pipelines. As a result, Tidewater was less and less of a threat. The pipeline revolution ended with Standard Oil "in as strong a position as ever—even stronger, for their costs had been cheapened, and they stood more completely independent of the railroad magnates."[70]

On April 8, 1879, a committee of three trustees was established by the Standard Oil Company, its thirty-seven stockholders, and all the former individual trustees.[71] The stock of all Standard subsidiaries was pooled and transferred to the three trustees in the Cleveland office who were to "hold, control, and manage" the stocks for Standard's stockholders.[72] However, the trustees had no power to control the operations of the subsidiaries. As a result, this trustee setup, while workable, was clumsy and inefficient.

A new trust agreement was signed on January 2, 1882, by all forty-two Standard stockholders and the three former trustees under which a nine-member board of trustees was created for the newly formed Standard Oil Trust, which was initially capitalized at $70 million.[73] This board was to actively manage all properties owned or controlled by Standard. Each of the forty-two existing Standard stockholders was to receive twenty trust certificates for each share of Standard Oil of Ohio owned. The Standard Oil Trust, though not a corporation under the law, did exist, and it effectively controlled all Standard properties. Dominance had been attained and control had been consolidated in the form of the Standard Oil Trust. With dominance attained, Rockefeller transferred the headquarters of the Trust from Cleveland to New York between 1883 and 1885. It was only fitting that the hub of America's oil industry be headquartered in America's financial and business capital.

STANDARD OIL FROM 1882–1899: DOMINANCE EXTENDED

The years between 1882 and 1899 were eventful for the Standard Oil Trust. During this period Standard Oil worked hard to (1) become more vertically integrated, (2) preserve and extend its monopoly power, and (3) increase its already significant presence in the exporting of oil and related products. Even though the Trust was "dissolved" in 1892 following legal losses in Ohio, Standard

Oil continued to dominate the U.S. oil industry throughout this seventeen-year period.[74]

Given Standard's stormy relationship with oil producers over the years, the company was concerned that it not suffer a slowdown in crude oil supplies for its refineries. This concern, together with the decreasing yields from the Pennsylvania fields in the early to mid 1880s, led Standard to embark on a purchase and lease campaign of oil lands, especially in Ohio, Indiana, and West Virginia. These acquisitions and leases were "partly to insure a future supply, [and] partly to limit the number of active wells and reduce the overproduction of crude oil."[75] The most prolific fields controlled by Standard in these three states was in Lima, Ohio. However, Lima crude contained extremely high concentrations of sulfur which was, for all intents and purposes, useless as either a lubricant or an illuminant. Even though Lima crude was flowing freely, Standard had to expend huge amounts of money to build sufficient tankage to store virtually all of it until a way could be found to remove the sulfur.

Rockefeller was convinced that a way could be found to make the Lima crude valuable. To justify his belief he began to spend large sums of money to woo the top talent necessary to embark on a massive research and development program. Herman Frasch, a highly talented chemist, worked with the Imperial Oil Company in Ontario, Canada, in the mid 1880s.[76] Ontario oil was also sour, or laden with sulfur, but Frasch quickly devised a method for removing it. Upon hearing of this development, Rockefeller immediately had Standard purchase Frasch's "plant, his patents, and his services."[77] While with Standard, Frasch quickly improved his process by incorporating copper oxides, which could be recycled almost indefinitely, to precipitate the sulfur out of the Lima crude. This process was the most efficient and least expensive method for removing sulfur, and Standard had the patent. This patent, acquired by a dominant firm, served to entrench Standard's lead over its competitors, who were forced to use less efficient, more expensive methods for the next seventeen years to purify sulfur-laced crude.

Following the conquest of Lima crude, Rockefeller began construction of a new refinery at Whiting, Indiana. This refinery, when completed in 1890, temporarily was the largest in the world. Furthermore, it was constructed to handle the special problems associated with Lima crude, which comprised its primary source of crude oil between 1890 and 1906. The Whiting works constituted Standard's westernmost refinery in 1890 and, for the next fifteen years, virtually the "whole Midwest, Northwest, and Far West came to depend on the Whiting works" for refined oil products.[78]

Technological developments in other industries were also providing opportunities for Standard Oil. The invention of the gas engine in the late 1880s created a need for higher quality, specialized lubricating oils. While gas engines were primarily used as stationary sources of power in the late 1880s, the early automobile engines were making progress. In both types of engines, Standard's number 23 Red Oil was the lubricant of choice up to 1900.[79] However, "until the rise of the automobile [to widespread usage] the export market was far more important to the Standard than the home market."[80]

World demand for oil was increasing at a fast pace; however, competition to serve this demand was also increasing in the late 1880s. Standard's major competitor in world markets was always Russia, with increasing pressures from Dutch-owned companies in the 1890s.[81] Standard's forte was quality products together with great marketing ability. These attributes, together with huge supplies of Lima crude available for refining, made Standard a fierce competitor in world markets, even in the face of higher transportation costs when compared to its foreign competitors. Throughout the 1880s and 1890s and on into the early 1990s, there was considerable concern that Standard lowered its prices abroad to better compete while it raised its prices at home to compensate. Standard denied these charges, but such concerns were nevertheless strongly expressed especially in the period between 1903 and 1905.[82]

Standard's practices in the area of marketing brought close scrutiny from both competitors and customers across the nation. Because of negative publicity and ill-will leveled at monopolies in general and Standard in particular, Standard often purchased wholesalers and retailers, but retained the old firms' names and actively hid Standard's involvement in the companies. Such bogus independents made it appear as if Standard faced more competition at the wholesale and retail level than it actually did.

In the period between 1883 and 1900 Standard also used "price-cutting, espionage, and intimidation" as weapons in its fight to foreclose outlets for competitors' oil products.[83] Standard's pricing policies have been the focus of voluminous research and still a clear picture does not emerge. In 1885 Standard's Executive Committee was "advocating prices [at the wholesale and retail level] which, though low enough to discourage new competition by competitors, would be high enough to encourage outsiders to continue business without a fight."[84] Such a strategy sounds very much like limit pricing to both discourage entry and foster a live-and-let-live attitude among existing firms. However, Standard was always ready to compete on price, sometimes initiating and sometimes following price cuts, especially in localities where vigorous competition existed. Rockefeller himself stated in 1888 that Standard would pursue a pricing policy "which will give us the largest percentage of the business."[85]

Whether or not Standard employed predatory price-cutting as a business tactic is impossible to prove or disprove.[86] The vast number of charges suggest that such predatory price-cutting occurred at least occasionally during the Trust's era of dominance. T. B. Westgate, a longtime competitor of Standard, related in 1899 that whenever price wars broke out in a particular location, Standard Oil representatives would not attempt to sell below his prices nine times out of ten, as long as he remained content with his existing market share of about 10 percent.[87] If Westgate's experience was representative, then competitors could expect borderline predatory pricing by Standard's wholesalers about 10 percent of the time, even if they were content with their existing market shares. Furthermore, the implication appears to be that any attempts by a competitor to increase its market share would be quickly countered by drastic, possibly predatory, price reductions by Standard.

Predatory price-cutting was only one tactic in Standard's arsenal. In addition to purchasing the aforementioned oil-producing lands in Ohio, Indiana, and West Virginia, the Trust continued purchasing both refineries and pipelines to preserve its monopoly. In the period from 1887 through 1890, Standard purchased a number of important refineries in Philadelphia and Pittsburgh.[88] Of special importance was the purchase of the Globe refineries in each of these cities because they were owned by very wealthy men who could have spent huge sums to upgrade the plants into competition for the Standard.[89] Through these various moves the Trust was able to maintain its dominant position in the U.S. petroleum industry. The leaders of the Trust believed that it "must maintain its iron grip, for [it was felt that] any relaxation would have lost the whole battle."[90] It is not surprising that the Trust came under tighter legal scrutiny as its activities from a position of dominance were more publicized.

The most significant legal challenge to the Standard Oil Trust took the form of a *quo warranto* petition filed by Ohio Attorney General David Watson on May 8, 1890. Watson charged that Standard Oil of Ohio

had transferred substantially all of its shares to the officers of the Standard Oil Trust, most of them non-residents of Ohio, and that these trustees selected the directors of the Standard Oil of Ohio, and managed its affairs. As such management by outsiders violated the State law, he asked that the company be held to have forfeited its corporate rights and powers, and be dissolved.[91]

On March 2, 1892, the Supreme Court of Ohio decided that Standard Oil of Ohio had "exercised a power for which it had no authority under the laws of this state" when it entered into the trust agreement in 1882.[92] However, the Supreme Court did not revoke Ohio Standard's charter; instead, it commanded Ohio Standard to withdraw from the trust agreement but did not set a timetable for doing so.

In response to the Ohio Supreme Court's decision, the Standard Oil Trust was dissolved at a board of trustees meeting held in New York City on March 21, 1892.[93] The voluntary dissolution split the Trust back into its twenty principal companies. The dissolution exalted form over substance. The trustees implemented a system of dividend payments, as part of the dissolution, that discouraged liquidation. What resulted was a state of perpetual liquidation that allowed the trustees to control a voting majority (over 50 percent) of the stock of all twenty companies.[94] In effect, the trustees had the same duties, the companies had the same executives, and, most importantly, the day-to-day management of the Trust was totally unaffected by the so-called dissolution.

While Standard Oil had survived the legal challenge from Ohio, the year 1892 would witness the creation of a potentially serious rival for the Standard, namely the Producers' and Refiners' Oil Company, Ltd. This cooperative was owned by fifteen independent refiners and over 1,000 oil producers.[95] The first major undertaking of the cooperative involved the construction of two pipelines to carry both crude and refined oil from the oil fields through northern Pennsylvania and eventually, by train, to the New York Harbor.[96] Standard Oil viewed successful construction and operation of these pipelines as a significant threat to both its refining and pipeline monopolies. Standard bought small strips of land all along the right of way of the proposed pipelines in hopes of tying the cooperative up in court. However, the pipelines were completed, and by the summer of 1893 oil was flowing and the prospects for the cooperative's success looked good.

The summer of 1893 also ushered in the Panic of 1893 with its consequent deflationary effect on prices, including prices for both crude and refined oil. Crude oil prices tumbled as deflation combined with increasing production from fields in Ohio and Indiana. However, as the deflation continued into late 1893, crude oil prices began to rebound. From the fall of 1893 to the middle of 1894, crude increased from 64¢ per barrel to 83.75¢ per barrel, while refined oil decreased in price from 5.24¢ per gallon to 5.19¢ per gallon.[97] This combination of prices proved costly for all refiners, but it was especially devastating for smaller, independent refiners. While market pressures may have started these price movements, Standard Oil probably worked to reinforce these market tendencies through its purchases and sales in order to put even more pressure on independents, including the Producers' and Refiners' Oil Company, Ltd.[98] While Standard's profits were certainly reduced by these price movements, falling from $19.175 million in 1892 to $15.457 million in 1893, most of the independents either broke even or incurred losses as a result.[99]

By the spring of 1894 the Trust had purchased three independent refiners and, more importantly, as a result of these purchases, acquired stock in both the U.S. Pipe Line Co. and the Producers' and Refiners' Oil Co.[100] The Standard Oil Trust appeared to have again succeeded in wiping out a significant threat from the independents. But the remaining independents were determined to compete, albeit under a new corporate umbrella: the Pure Oil Company, incorporated in early 1895.[101] The founding of the Pure Oil Company coincided with an incredible boom in oil prices. While volatility in both crude and refined prices would eventually reappear, competition for the Standard Oil Trust had gained a foothold that would not be relinquished.

In addition to the emergence of competition in the form of the Pure Oil Company, the Standard Oil Trust came under a barrage of journalistic attacks in the mid 1890s. The first of these attacks came in 1894 with the publication of Henry Demarest Lloyd's *Wealth Against Commonwealth*. This book contained some truth together with large amounts of unsubstantiated rumors, misinterpretations, distortions, and allegations, the net effect being to implant "an ugly stereotype of Rockefeller and the Standard Oil Trust upon the public mind."[102] Again the Trust chose to ignore the negative publicity generated by Lloyd's book, even though silence was interpreted by the public as evidence that Lloyd's charges were true.

As the 1890s came to a close, Rockefeller began to relinquish control over day-to-day operations of the Trust. While he was still occasionally consulted, he turned over the reins of the Trust to John D. Archbold in 1897.[103] Following the formation of Standard Oil of New Jersey holding company in 1899, Rockefeller's involvement ended.

The decision to reorganize into the holding company form in New Jersey was motivated by two conditions: First, Ohio's legislature had passed the Valentine-Stewart Antitrust Act in April of 1898 and Frank Monnett, Ohio's attorney general, had brought suit under that act against Standard Oil of Ohio in January of 1899.[104] Monnett was convinced that Standard Oil of Ohio "had conspired to evade the court decree of 1892" which had supposedly dissolved the Trust.[105] Thus, Standard Oil wanted to find a more hospitable climate in which to concentrate all of its businesses. Second, Rockefeller and his associates saw the holding company as an advantageous form of business organization. It was "simpler and less expensive for one central corporation to acquire stock control . . . in other companies than to buy the properties of these companies."[106] Furthermore, action via the holding company form usually involved less publicity and "a great combination based on holding-company control might be less exposed to anti-trust attacks than a monopolistic consolidation."[107]

In June of 1899 the charter of Standard Oil of New Jersey was amended to allow the establishment of a holding company that would control all Standard Oil properties. As part of this reorganization the capital of Standard Oil of New Jersey was increased from $10 million to $110 million and the number of shares of common stock was set at one million, while the number of preferred shares was set at 100,000.[108] This stock was exchanged for the certificates of the old Standard Oil Trust and its twenty "subsidiaries." In 1900, Standard Oil of New Jersey controlled total net assets of $205,480,000, with total net earnings of $55,500,000.[109] At the end of the nineteenth century, Standard Oil of New Jersey controlled 82 percent of the refinery capacity and sold 85 percent of all the kerosene, fuel oil, and gasoline in the United States; thus, it was clearly still the dominant firm in the petroleum industry.[110] However, a combination of factors, not the least of which would be significant legal entanglements, would change the competitive landscape of the U.S. petroleum industry over the next decade.

STANDARD OIL FROM 1899–1911: DOMINANCE CHALLENGED

The years between 1899 and 1911 saw the emergence of numerous credible threats to Standard Oil's continued dominance of the U.S. petroleum industry. Discovery of oil in areas of the country where Standard had little, if any, presence, together with the rise of significant new competition continued to erode Standard's market share, particularly in refining. Rough estimates put Standard's share of refining at 76 percent in 1904 and 66 percent in 1909.[111] In addition to the new sources of supplies of crude oil, there were significant increases and changes in demand for manufactured petroleum products. Demand for kerosene, long a Standard stronghold, was declining in the face of growing use of electricity. Furthermore, improvements in gasoline engines generated a burgeoning demand for gasoline, a market in which Standard lagged behind many of its newer competitors. Standard met these market-driven challenges head on and vigorously; however, the days of its unquestioned dominance were coming to a close. Notably, the most significant threat to Standard's dominant position resulted, not from market forces that would slowly erode its position, but from direct legal action by the U.S. government seeking the dissolution of the holding company monopoly known as Standard Oil of New Jersey.

The accession of John D. Archbold to the leadership of Standard Oil in 1897 resulted, almost immediately, in greater aggressiveness in Standard's tactics to extend where possible and protect where necessary its market position.[112] Among the changes that eventually followed Archbold's taking of the reins were sharply higher prices for refined oil, a wider margin between the cost of crude oil and the cost of refined oil, harsher competitive tactics to deal with domestic marketing rivals, and a vicious price war overseas as Standard sought to entrench and extend its position in world markets.[113]

The 1880s and 1890s had seen Standard Oil increase its presence in the marketing of petroleum products directly to retailers through the construction of bulk storage stations at strategic locations throughout the United States. By 1900, Standard's bulk station network was so well organized that Standard only had to worry about constructing smaller bulk substations where necessary to meet competition. Standard's use of the tank-wagon method of distributing oil to retailers, especially in more concentrated population areas, significantly reduced both Standard's marketing costs and the retailer's losses resulting from leakage when compared to barrel distribution.[114] The cost savings enjoyed by Standard enabled it to hold prices and increase profits where possible or decrease prices and hopefully increase profits where necessary to meet competition. The tank-wagon system of marketing made it possible for Standard to adjust local prices to competitive conditions "without disturbing its prices over any large section of its trade."[115]

Accusations of predatory pricing continued to be leveled at the Standard in the 1900s. Price discrimination on the part of Standard Oil in the form of "rebates to favored retailers and cutting prices in one locality while charging exorbitant prices in other areas" was also a constant rallying cry of Standard's competitors in marketing.[116] Standard's pricing policy in the early 1900s was best expressed by Livingston Roe, a top Standard Oil executive, in 1902 when he stated that we "regulate our selling prices in the various territories in the United States with regard to the competition we are meeting in each particular place, and to make up in one place for the sacrifices we are obliged to make in others."[117] Standard's usual practice was to sell below prevailing prices when it wished to enter a market, a tactic also practiced by most other firms. However, such price-cutting by a firm as dominant as Standard Oil could quickly lead to ruin for smaller, established competitors. Also, effective price discrimination by a dominant firm like Standard Oil could have severe anticompetitive consequences.

Even though Standard had the power to drive out competitors by using tactics like predatory pricing, available evidence does not suggest that such power was used in any systematic fashion. Whenever price wars broke out, Standard's general policy "was to be the last down and the first up" since any "losses" would generally be greater for Standard than its competitors.[118] However, a long-run profit-maximization strategy of limit pricing could be enhanced if Standard selectively made examples of bothersome competitors. While Standard's pricing strategy may have been predatory at times, generally it sought maintenance of market shares by using sophisticated limit pricing and selective price discrimination. Even though designed to protect its market share, these pricing strategies alone could not stem the erosion in Standard's market share in most markets because of the discovery of new sources of crude oil and the consequent emergence of significant new competition.

One of the most significant factors in eroding Standard's market share involved changing sources of crude oil supplies. The output of crude oil doubled between 1900 and 1905 with major discoveries in Kansas, Illinois, Oklahoma, Texas, and California.[119] Of these states, Standard only had a relatively notable presence in Illinois and California. It did not operate a refinery in Kansas, Oklahoma, or Texas, nor did it have a refinery close to these areas. As a result, new refineries sprang up, especially in the Gulf region, owned by firms such as Sun Oil Gulf, Union Oil, and Texas Oil.[120] Since these firms were located very close to supplies of crude and good water transportation, their costs were low, which allowed them to compete very effectively with Standard Oil. Also, the ever expanding auto industry created a huge demand for gasoline and many other petroleum-related products. Standard had greatly underestimated the demand for gasoline; thus, a large market was available for competitors to fill as Standard scrambled to increase its output of gasoline and other products for the auto industry. While Standard's share of crude oil production fell precipitously and its share of refining fell slowly, it did not sit idly by while new competitors entered. It held many strategic advantages given its considerable time in the industry and its well-functioning organizational structure. Additionally, its pipeline monopoly was still virtually unchallenged. Thus, its competitive response to market challenges was carefully conceived and executed.

By the turn of the century oil refining was a capital-intensive industry; the era of small-scale refineries was coming to a close. Standard was well positioned to embark on a massive refinery construction campaign, especially in the new producing areas. In fact, Standard increased its refining capacity tremendously by building eight new plants between 1899 and 1911.[121] Because of its strong capitalization and huge profits Standard was able to obtain the best locations and build the most efficient plants possible. Since its founding in 1870, Standard had carefully planned the construction and expansion of its refining network. By 1899, its refineries were very strategically located so as to capture economies in transportation of crude oil to the refineries and of finished products to the wholesale and retail markets.[122] It also had the best locations with respect to water supplies, availability of inputs, and land area available for expansion.[123] Even the strongest of the new competitors found it very difficult to meet Standard's total cost of transportation from well to consumer. A large part of the reason for competitors' inability to get their transportation costs as low as those of Standard Oil resulted directly from Standard's pipeline monopoly.

The massive discoveries of crude in the Mid-Continent field in Oklahoma and Kansas and at Spindletop in Texas meant that the oil either had to be refined and then transported, transported and then refined, or stored. Refinery capacity was lacking in these areas for a few years following the strikes, so transportation to existing refineries or storage became critical. Both transportation via pipeline and an extensive storage network allowed Standard to exert limited influence over its competitors in these areas while it undertook its refinery construction campaign.

Under both various state laws and the Hepburn Act, pipelines were designated as common carriers. Thus, Standard's pipelines, in theory, could also be used by independent refiners to ship oil. Standard's pipeline companies filed tariffs as required by law, "but the tariffs were so filed as to prevent any independent company from shipping thereunder, for three reasons: First, the point of delivery was named at places where there were no independent refineries; second, the rates were excessive; and third, the minimum amount of oil that would be transported was so large that no independent refiner could use them."[124] It is noteworthy that most of the other larger oil companies "joined Standard Oil in the contention that pipelines were private property, not public service units, engaged in transporting petroleum."[125] This issue would not be settled until 1914 when the Supreme Court declared that pipelines were involved in interstate commerce; thus, federal regulation was constitutional.

As of 1904, Standard-owned pipelines transported about 90 percent of the crude oil from the older fields and about 9 percent of Kansas crude.[126] In this same year, Standard's pipeline system totaled 40,000 miles in length, and through it Standard was "capable of transporting crude from the Oklahoma territory to the Atlantic."[127] "Standard has control of about 95 percent of the transportation of crude oil to the Atlantic seaboard, which by reason of the large percentage of oil exported gives it a tremendous advantage."[128] However, Standard's influence in the Mid-Continent field declined significantly after 1905 "when two other pipelines were built from that field to Port Arthur [Texas], one by the Texas company and the other by the Gulf Refining Company."[129] The construction of these lines made Standard's newer competitors even stronger, particularly in the Gulf Coast region. Standard's dominance was coming to an end; however, it was still a very powerful firm that would do what it could to maintain its market position. In the early years of the twentieth century the focus of these efforts was on the discovery and integration of new technology to reduce costs.

By the end of the 1890s Standard had probably achieved the lowest costs possible given its manufacturing processes in use at the time. However, its foreign competition enjoyed lower manufacturing costs, primarily because of cheaper labor, lower crude oil costs, and lower transportation costs.[130] If Standard wanted to maintain its export markets, it needed to upgrade its manufacturing processes in order to drive its costs lower. Standard's response was to adopt "two major technological changes in the first decade of the twentieth century": continuous distillation and Van Dyke tower stills.[131]

The idea of a continuous-refining process had been around since 1860. Other competitors of Standard, mostly foreign, had employed such processes for years, but only for producing certain products. Standard's dominant position at home and its superior marketing techniques abroad allowed it to continue using the higher cost batch system while it waited for the problems associated with continuous processing to be worked out.[132]

In 1899 Max Livingston, a refinery superintendent for Standard Oil, applied for a patent for a continuous process that "accomplished fractionation of petroleum by selective distillation."[133] The Livingston process would dominate the oil industry's use of continuous distillation for the next decade. Advantages associated with the process included more efficient use of capacity and labor, less wear and tear on the stills resulting from temperature maintenance, and fuel savings as high as 25 percent.[134] One major problem associated with the Livingston process was its limited range in fractionating all the various products that could be made from petroleum. This problem, combined with the discovery of new sources of crude, all of which required special handling in refining, greatly complicated the distillation process.[135]

J. W. Van Dyke and W. M. Irish, two key Standard employees and inventors, had an experimental plant operating with the Van Dyke tower stills in 1904.[136] By 1909 they had applied for a patent and Standard was converting two of its larger refineries over to the tower stills. The Van Dyke still "concentrated upon separation of components by selective condensation under the batch system."[137] Such close control of fractionation allowed a refinery using these stills to maintain very high quality while responding to various market niches quickly and efficiently. Such economies could not be effectively matched by smaller, less capitalized competitors.

Standard's funding of research and development and its construction of state-of-the-art testing and research laboratories allowed it to garner numerous patents through its employees. These patents allowed Standard to remain on the cutting edge of technology related to petroleum refining. Furthermore, Standard Oil executives were always interested in any new inventions by outsiders. The company often purchased patents from outsiders that it felt it could use. The triple check for every new invention was "economy, effectiveness, and commercial possibilities."[138] Standard's dedication to research and development enabled it to "control" its loss of market share to its new competitors; however, two factors that Standard could not control were negative publicity and ever increasing attention from state and federal legal authorities.

Ida M. Tarbell's *The History of the Standard Oil Company*, published in 1904, although incomplete and contradictory, was the first "readable, coherent exposition of the main lines of development of the Standard Oil combination and of the leading controversies connected with its history."[139] While purporting to be an unbiased examination of the Standard Oil Company, Tarbell's book allocates fifteen out of eighteen chapters to a detailed reiteration of all the allegations leveled against the company from its inception. Tarbell's book served to reinforce in the public's mind the view of Standard Oil as a menace to free competition and a monopoly of the worst kind. As a result, public furor over the Trust and its activities reached new heights.

Public indignation regarding the Standard Oil Company provided fertile political ground from which to launch attacks against the Trust. Various states, including Kansas, Texas, and Missouri, capitalized on this public outrage by filing antitrust cases against numerous Standard subsidiaries and/or affiliates between 1905 and 1906. The publication, on May 2, 1906, of the Bureau of Corporations' *Report on the Transportation of Petroleum* proved particularly helpful to the states and damaging to Standard Oil.[140] The report pointedly claimed that Standard owed its dominant position in the oil industry to the secret and discriminatory shipping rates it received from the railroads. More importantly, the publication of this report energized President Theodore Roosevelt to demand antitrust action against Standard Oil. The U.S. Justice Department launched a preliminary investigation into the organization activities of the Standard Oil Company of New Jersey.[141] The cases filed by the various states were only precursors to the main attack on Standard Oil which would come form the federal government. On November 15, 1906, the U.S. Justice Department filed "a suit in equity . . . , under sections 1 and 2 of the Sherman antitrust act, against seven individuals and about seventy-five corporations, limited partnerships, and co-partnerships"; in other words, against the Standard Oil Company of New Jersey.[142] The government sought a "decree declaring it a combination in restraint of trade and a monopoly, and enjoining the Standard Oil Company of New Jersey from exercising any control over the defendant corporations by stock ownership or otherwise."[143] It is noteworthy that the case was filed in the United States Circuit Court for the Eastern Division of the Eastern District of Missouri at St. Louis; this was the same court that had declared the Northern Securities holding company illegal in 1903.[144]

The time between the original filing of the suit and the next report from the Bureau of Corporations was filled primarily with legal maneuvering by both the government and Standard Oil. On May 20, 1907, the Bureau of Corporations' *Report on the Petroleum Industry, Part I: Position of the Standard Oil Company in the Petroleum Industry* was published. This report concluded that Standard Oil had monopolized the U.S. petroleum industry and that it maintained its dominant position through the use of various anticompetitive tactics.[145] Standard Oil continued to deny any wrongdoing on its part saying that it had achieved its position through superior efficiency; it also denied that it had ever monopolized the industry. However, the evidence contained in the report together with the conclusions emanating from it served to further damage Standard's reputation and legal position.

Following several postponements, government prosecutors began taking testimony on September 17, 1907; this process lasted until mid 1909. "The prosecution and defense called a total of 444 witnesses to the stand and introduced

1,374 exhibits. The final record extended to 14,495 printed pages in twenty-three volumes."[146] The circuit court ruled, on November 20, 1909, that Standard Oil of New Jersey was "a combination and conspiracy in restraint of trade and its continued execution, which have been found to exist, constitute illegal means by which the conspiring defendants combined, and still combine and conspire, to monopolize a part of interstate and international commerce, and by which they have secured an unlawful monopoly of a substantial part of it, and this conspiracy constitutes as clear and complete a violation of the second as of the first section of the act."[147] The court's reasoning allowed it "to avoid ruling on the overwhelming mass of evidence in the case"; in fact, the court offered no opinion on any of the alleged illegal means.[148] The court went on to order the dissolution of the holding company known as Standard Oil of New Jersey.[149]

The government was very pleased with the outcome; however, as expected, Standard Oil appealed to the U.S. Supreme Court. Both Standard Oil as appellant and the United States as defendant filed new briefs and presented their arguments anew in January 1911.

The Supreme Court handed down its decision on May 15, 1911. Chief Justice White delivered the opinion that upheld the ruling of the circuit court. White's opinion stated that the creation of Standard Oil of New Jersey as the holding company in 1899 "necessarily involved the intent to drive others from the field and to exclude them from their right to trade, and thus accomplish the mastery which was the end in view."[150] Thus Standard Oil was found guilty of monopolization, continued attempts to monopolize, and restraint of trade. The Supreme Court, like the circuit court, refused to pass judgment on the "jungle of conflicting testimony covering a period of forty years."[151] Thus, no legal authority ever examined and ruled upon Standard's conduct during its period of dominance of the U.S. petroleum industry.

The Court also generally affirmed the decree dissolving the holding company and ordered the transfer by the New Jersey corporation back to the stockholders of the various subsidiary corporations entitled to the same of the stock which had been turned over to the New Jersey company in exchange for its stock."[152] The Court did increase the time span available to complete the dissolution from thirty days to six months and allowed all Standard companies to engage in interstate commerce while the dissolution was being carried out.

The wording of the dissolution decree meant that a small number of individuals "would hold a majority interest in all the newly independent companies."[153] The head of Standard Oil of New Jersey's legal department, referring to the decree's impact, stated that "[w]e will be able to continue business as before, except that officers of the different companies will control the business, instead of the Standard Oil Company of New Jersey."[154] Supposedly, dominance ended as Standard Oil was broken up. In reality, independent regional monopolies that tended not to compete with each other were substituted for subsidiaries of a national monopoly that did not compete with each other.

CONCLUSION

Out of the chaos that characterized the early oil industry John D. Rockefeller and his partners created Standard Oil, a firm that dominated the industry from 1870 to 1911. The creation and maintenance of Standard Oil's dominant position depended primarily on three factors: mergers, railroad rebates, and production efficiencies.

Through the extensive use of mergers, Rockefeller was able to dominate the refining industry in Cleveland. As of 1870, Standard Oil was not only the largest refiner in Cleveland, it was also the largest in the United States with 10 percent of the nation's refining capacity. Using Standard's near-monopoly position in Cleveland, Rockefeller was then able to extract large rebates from the railroads, the effect of which was to significantly lower Standard's transportation costs. These lower costs, together with technologically efficient plants, allowed Standard to extend its control beyond Cleveland.

Mergers continued to be Standard's tool of choice for growth. By 1880 Standard controlled 90 to 95 percent of the total refining capacity of the United States. As a way to diversify and protect its refining monopoly, Standard began to vertically integrate in the late 1870s. To ensure a steady supply of crude oil for its refineries, Standard bought up many of the largest pipeline companies; it also embarked on a massive pipeline construction campaign. At the same time Standard moved into the wholesale marketing of refined petroleum products, primarily through the acquisition of well-established regional firms throughout the United States. Standard's successful program of vertical integration enabled it to capture greater cost savings and further widened its advantage over its non-integrated competitors.

The formation of Standard Oil of New Jersey in 1899 found Standard with 82 percent of U.S. refining capacity. Its share of capacity continued to erode to 70 percent in 1906, the same year the antitrust case was filed against Standard by the Justice Department.[155] Prior to Standard's dissolution in 1911, Standard's share of refining capacity stood at 64 percent.[156] What caused this erosion in Standard's market share? Entry certainly played a role, but entry was slow in coming and, until the 1900s, generally on a small scale. Because of Standard's size and the number of markets in which it operated, competitors found it impossible to engage in large-scale, multi-market entry. As the dominant firm in the industry, Standard sought to limit entry whenever possible. As a result, it did not use its monopoly power to charge monopoly prices. Instead, it appears to have "pursued a sophisticated region-by-region limit-pricing strategy" geared toward limiting entry and maximizing profits over the long run.[157]

The acceleration in Standard's loss of market share was primarily due to the huge discoveries of crude oil in the early 1900s in Texas and California. New fields flush with crude oil, combined with easy access to cheap water transportation, made it possible for small firms to grow into viable competitors with Standard Oil in a relatively short period of time. Furthermore, the crude produced in both Texas and California needed little refining to serve as fuel oil, which was blossoming market segment after 1900. This combination of factors played a very significant role in Standard's loss of market share.

The government's successful prosecution of Standard Oil under the Sherman Act was also very important in whittling the firm down to size. Standard's share of refining only dropped 6 percent between 1906 and 1911, and this was a time when entrants had supposedly gained a significant foothold. Granted, Standard's refining share of 64 percent in 1911 was "low," but no other firm was remotely close to that number. When Standard's presence in wholesale marketing and pipeline transportation were factored in, it was still the dominant firm at the time of the break up.

In the case of Standard Oil, the market worked very slowly to erode its position of dominance and Standard used all the weapons available to it to maintain its position. Public policy, via the government's successful prosecution of the antitrust case against Standard Oil, created 20 firms where there had been one. The newly orphaned subsidiaries of the former Standard Oil of New Jersey were now more vulnerable to the market pressures that competition could generate and the U.S. petroleum industry would never again see the likes of Standard Oil of New Jersey.

NOTES

1. See, for example, Dominick T. Armentano, *Antitrust and Monopoly: Anatomy of a Policy Failure* (New York: John Wiley and Sons, 1982); Robert H. Bork, *The Antitrust Paradox: A Policy at War with Itself* (New York: Basic Books, 1978); Bruce Bringhurst, *Antitrust and the Oil Monopoly: The Standard Oil Cases, 1890-1911* (Westport, CT: Greenwood Press, 1979); Wayne A. Leeman, "The Limitations of Local Price Cutting as a Barrier to Entry," *Journal of Political Economy* 64 (1956): 329-334; Randall Mariger, "Predatory Price Cutting: The Standard Oil of New Jersey Case Revisited," *Explorations in Economic History* 15 (1978): 341-367; Alfred Marshall, *Industry and Trade*, 4th ed., (London: Macmillan, 1923); John S. McGee, "Predatory Price Cutting: The Standard Oil (N.J.) Case," *Journal of Law and Economics* 1 (1958): 137-169; Richard A. Posner, *Antitrust Law: An Economic Perspective* (Chicago: University of Chicago Press, 1976); and F. M. Scherer and David Ross, *Industrial Market Structure and Economic Performance*, 3 ed. (Boston: Houghton Mifflin, 1990).

2. *Standard Oil Company of New Jersey v United States*, 31 Sup. Ct. 502 (1911), p. 509.

3. 31 Sup. Ct. 504.

4. Ralph W. Hidy and Muriel E. Hidy, *Pioneering in Big Business, 1882-1911* (New York: Harper and Brothers, 1955), p. 13.

5. Ibid.

6. Ibid., pp. 14-15.

7. Harold F. Williamson and Arnold R. Daum, *The American Petroleum Industry: Volume I, The Age of Illumination, 1859–1899* (Evanston, IL.: Northwestern University Press, 1959), p. 308.

8. *United States v Standard Oil Company of New Jersey*, 173 Fed. 177. In the Circuit Court of the United States for the Eastern Division of the Eastern Judicial District of Missouri (1909), *Brief of Facts and Argument for Petitioner*, vol. 1 (Washington, D.C.: U.S. Government Printing Office, 1909), p. 3.

9. Bringhurst, *Antitrust*, p. 10.

10. H. L. Wilgus, "The Standard Oil Decision; The Rule of Reason," *Michigan Law Review* 9 (1911): 647.

11. Ida M. Tarbell, *The History of the Standard Oil Company*, vol. 1 (Gloucester, MA: Peter Smith, 1963), p. 54.

12. Allan Nevins, *John D. Rockefeller: The Heroic Age of American Enterprise*, vol. 1 (New York: Charles Scribner's Sons, 1940), p. 292.

13. Ibid., p. 296.

14. Tarbell, *History*, vol. 1, p. 49.

15. Williamson and Daum, *Petroleum Industry*, p. 306.

16. Nevins, *Heroic Age,* vol. 1, p. 309.

17. Ibid., p. 312.

18. Ibid., p. 314.

19. Ibid.

20. Ibid., pp. 321-322.

21. *United States v Standard Oil Company of New Jersey, Brief of Facts and Argument for Petitioner*, vol. 1, 1909, p. 6.

22. Nevins, *Heroic Age*, vol. 1, p. 324.

23. Gilbert Holland Montague, *The Rise and Progress of the Standard Oil Company* (New York: Harper and Brothers, 1903), p. 27.

24. Ibid., pp. 27-29.

25. Ibid., p. 27.

26. Williamson and Daum, *Petroleum Industry,* p. 355.

27. Nevins, *Heroic Age,* vol. 1, p. 367.

28. Tarbell, *History*, vol. 1, p. 67.

29. Williamson and Daum, *Petroleum Industry*, pp. 354-355.

30. Wilgus, *Standard Oil Decision*, p. 646.

31. Nevins, *Heroic Age*, vol. 1, p. 366.

32. Ibid., p. 392.

33. Tarbell, *History*, vol. 2, p. 109.

34. See Nevins, *Heroic Age*, vol. 1, chapters 17-18.

35. Williams and Daum, *Petroleum Industry*, pp. 353-367.

36. Ibid., p. 412.

37. Ibid.

38. Nevins, *Heroic Age*, vol. 1, p. 443.

39. Ibid., pp. 458-459.

40. Williamson and Daum, *Petroleum Industry*, p. 413.

41. Nevins, *Heroic Age*, vol. 1, pp. 476-477.

42. Williams and Daum, *Petroleum Industry*, p. 417.

43. Nevins, *Heroic Age*, vol. 1, pp. 483.

44. Ibid., p. 492.

45. Williamson and Daum, *Petroleum Age*, p. 419.

46. Tarbell, *History*, vol. 1, pp. 197-198.

47. Nevins, *Heroic Age*, vol. 1, p. 500.

48. Williamson and Daum, *Petroleum Industry*, pp. 282-283.

49. Nevins, *Heroic Age*, vol. 1, p. 517.

50. Ibid., p. 519.

51. For more extreme examples of Rockefeller's views on dealing with competitors, see Allan Nevins, *Study in Power: John D. Rockefeller*, vol. 2 (New York: Charles Scribner's Sons, 1953), pp. 56, 65; Nevins quotes two different letters Rockefeller wrote to associates regarding competitors. In the one on page 56, Rockefeller states that "A good sweating will be healthy for them and they ought to have it, and it is not money lost for us to have other people see them get it. Our chances for fair play in the future will be better." In the letter on page 65, Rockefeller states that "We want to watch, and when our volume of business is to be cut down by the increase of competition to 50 percent, or less, it may be a very serious question whether we had not better make an important reduction, with a view of taking substantially all the business there is."

52. Nevins, *Heroic Age*, vol. 1, p. 521.

53. Ibid., p. 529.

54. Williamson and Daum, *Petroleum Industry*, 423.

55. Nevins, *Heroic Age*, vol. 1, p. 533.

56. *United States v Standard Oil Company of New Jersey, Brief of Facts and Argument for Petitioner*, Vol. 1, 1909, p. 48.

57. Williamson and Daum, *Petroleum Industry*, p. 426.

58. Nevins, *Heroic Age*, vol. 1, p. 543.

59. Ibid., p. 554.

60. Williamson and Daum, *Petroleum Industry*, p. 432.

61. Tarbell, *History*, vol. 1, p. 239.

62. Nevins, *Heroic Age*, vol. 1, pp. 572-573.

63. Ibid., p. 573.

64. Tarbell, *History*, vol. 2, p. 4.

65. Nevins, *Heroic Age*, vol. 1, p. 579.

66. Williamson and Daum, *Petroleum Industry*, p. 447.

67. Ibid., p. 453.

68. Ibid., p. 454.

69. Tarbell, *History*, vol. 2, p. 23.

70. Nevins, *Heroic Age*, vol. 1, p. 602.

71. *United States v Standard Oil Company of New Jersey, Brief of Facts and Argument for Petitioner*, vol. 1, 1909, p. 21.

72. Ibid.

73. Ibid., p. 60.

74. Williamson and Daum, *Petroleum Industry*, p. 710.

75. Nevins, *Heroic Age*, vol. 1, p. 650.

76. Williamson and Daum, *Petroleum Industry*, p. 616.

77. Nevins, *Heroic Age*, vol. 2, p. 8.

78. Ibid., p. 10.

79. Ibid., p. 16.

80. Ibid., p. 22.

81. See Williamson and Daum, *Petroleum Industry*, chapter 24.

82. Nevins, *Heroic Age*, vol. 2, p. 35.

83. Ibid., p. 89.

84. Hidy and Hidy, *Big Business*, p. 194.

85. Ibid.

86. McGee, after an exhaustive review of the evidence presented in the case against Standard Oil, concluded that "Standard Oil did not use predatory price discrimination to drive out competing refiners, nor did its pricing practice have that effect," *Pedatory Price*

Cutting, p. 168; Posner, referring to McGee's analysis, states that "McGee's study of the record in the *Standard Oil* case might not have uncovered the extent to which Standard Oil owed its market position to predatory tactics. (Moreover, that a practice is not discovered by the lawyers for a party to a lawsuit is not always compelling evidence that the practice did not occur.) *Antitrust Law*, p. 186.

87. Hidy and Hidy, *Big Business*, p. 297.

88. Williamson and Daum, *Petroleum Industry*, pp. 626-628.

89. Nevins, *Heroic Age*, vol. 2, p. 307.

90. Ibid., p. 93.

91. Ibid., p. 144.

92. Bringhurst, *Oil Monopoly*, p. 17.

93. Ibid., p. 20.

94. Ibid., p. 21.

95. Nevins, *Heroic Age*, vol. 2, p. 311.

96. Williamson and Daum, *Petroleum Industry*, p. 572.

97. Nevins, *Heroic Age*, vol. 2, p. 316.

98. Williamson and Daum, *Petroleum Industry*, p. 575.

99. Nevins, *Heroic Age*, vol. 2, p. 317.

100. Williamson and Daum, *Petroleum Industry*, p. 574.

101. Ibid., p. 576.

102. Nevins, *Heroic Age*, vol. 2, p. 341.

103. Ibid., p. 428.

104. Bringhurst, *Oil Monopoly*, p. 25.

105. Ibid.

106. Nevins, *Heroic Age*, vol. 2, p. 355.

107. Ibid.

108. Ibid.

109. Ibid., p. 356.

110. See Table 2 on page 74 in Harold F. Williamson and Ralph L. Andreano, "Competitive Structure of the American Petroleum Industry, 1880–1911: A Reappraisal," in *Oil's First Century* (Boston: Harvard Graduate School of Business Administration, 1960), pp. 71-84.

111. Hidy and Hidy, *Big Business*, p. 417.

112. Nevins, *Heroic Age*, vol. 2, p. 431.

113. Ibid.

114. Hidy and Hidy, *Big Business*, p. 296.

115. Nevins, *Heroic Age*, vol. 2, p. 570.

116. Hidy and Hidy, *Big Business*, p. 466.

117. Ibid., p. 468.

118. Ibid., p. 469.

119. Nevins, *Heroic Age*, vol. 2, p. 428.

120. Hidy and Hidy, *Big Business*, p. 417.

121. Ibid., p. 410.

122. Hidy and Hidy, *Big Business*, p. 417; and Montague, *Rise and Progress*, p. 135.

123. Hidy and Hidy, *Big Business*, p. 417.

124. *United States v Standard Oil Company of New Jersey*, 173 Fed. 177, in the Circuit Court of the United States for the Eastern Division of the Eastern Judicial District of Missouri (1909), *Brief of the Law for Petitioner* (Washington, D.C.: U.S. Government Printing Office, 1909), pp. 33-34.

125. Hidy and Hidy, *Big Business*, p. 682.

126. Nevins, *Heroic Age*, vol. 2, p. 569.

127. Bringhurst, *Oil Monopoly*, p. 109.

128. *United States v. Standard Oil Company of New Jersey, Brief of the Law for Petitioner*, 1909, p. 33.

129. Ibid.

130. Hidy and Hidy, *Big Business*, p. 422.

131. Ibid.

132. Ibid., p. 423.

133. Ibid., p. 424.

134. Harold F. Williamson et al., *The American Petroleum Industry: Volume 2, The Age of Energy, 1900–1959* (Evanston, IL: Northwestern University Press, 1963), p. 125.

135. Hidy and Hidy, *Big Business*, p. 426.

136. Williamson et al., *Age of Energy*, p. 126.

137. Hidy and Hidy, *Big Business*, p. 426.

138. Ibid., p. 422.

139. Ibid., p. 650.

140. Bringhurst, *Oil Monopoly*, p. 130.

141. Ibid., pp. 131-132.

142. *United States v Standard Oil Company of New Jersey, Brief of Facts and Argument for Petitioner*, vol. 1, 1909, p. 1.

143. *United States v Standard Oil Company of New Jersey, Brief of the Law for Petitioner*, 1909, p. 194.

144. Bringhurst, *Oil Monopoly*, p. 133.

145. Hidy and Hidy, *Big Business*, p. 688.

146. Bringhurst, Oil Monopoly, p. 134.

147. *United States v Standard Oil Company of New Jersey*, 173 Fed. 177, in the Circuit Court of the United States for the Eastern Division of the Eastern Judicial District of Missouri (1909), p. 191.

148. Bringhurst, *Oil Monopoly*, p. 151.

149. 173 Fed. 192-193.

150. 31 Sup. Ct. 522.

151. 31 Sup. Ct. 511.

152. 31 Sup. Ct. 523.

153. Bringhurst, *Oil Monopoly*, p. 180.

154. Ibid., pp. 180-181.

155. Williamson and Andreano, *Competitive Structure*, p. 74.

156. Ibid.

157. Scherer and Ross, *Market Structure*, p. 450.

3

TOBACCO: PREDATION AND PERSISTENT MARKET POWER

Walter Adams and James W. Brock

More than eighty years ago, in 1911, the three largest cigarette producers controlled 80 percent of the U.S. market.[1] A decade and a half later, in 1925, the top four firms accounted for 91 percent of the market.[2] Four decades later, in 1949, the four largest firms accounted for 87 percent of the field.[3] Seventy years later, in 1980, the four firms continued to control 88 percent of national cigarette sales.[4] Today, the four largest firms still collectively dominate the field, accounting for approximately 98 percent of the American market.[5]

This entrenched market dominance raises a number of questions: How was such market power originally attained? How has it defended and sustained itself? How has it done so despite three major challenges under the nation's antitrust laws, including two convictions? And what public policy lessons are suggested by this persistent market power? It is to these questions that we turn.

MARKET POWER ATTAINED

In 1889, the Durham, North Carolina, firm of Washington Duke & Sons was a relatively small concern in a fiercely competitive field. In the major tobacco product lines of that earlier era, it accounted for less than 8 percent of smoking tobacco, a third of the nation's cigarette output, and produced no plug or snuff tobacco products.[6] Twenty years later, the structural milieu had radically changed. The American Tobacco Company forged by one of the Duke sons, James, was a colossus standing astride all aspects of the industry: by 1910, Duke's Tobacco Trust commanded 76 percent of smoking tobacco production, 80 percent of fine-cut tobacco, 85 percent of plug tobacco, 86 percent of cigarette output, 91 percent of little cigars, and 97 percent of snuff.[7]

What factors explain this drastic change in industry structure? The advent of mass-production techniques, including the Bonsack automated cigarette-rolling machine, played a role. So, too, did Duke's heavy emphasis on mass marketing, promotion, and advertising. Transcending these in importance, however, was the Trust's relentless, mutually reinforcing use of mergers and predation to achieve industry-wide dominance. Acquisitions enabled the Trust to establish a beachhead in a particular product market; this was followed by consolidation offers from the Trust to its rivals; and, once consolidation was achieved, the resulting monopoly profits fueled the Trust's expansion into the next target on its list.

Key to the success of this strategy was the Trust's strategic use of price wars and predatory pricing to render rivals amenable to its consolidation and/or monopolization overtures. According to a leading student of the field, "important minority interests were secured by purchase, and violent selling pressures were applied to expand the business so acquired. Policy was directed as much to harassing competitors as it was to positive promotion of the Trust's own brands, and losses were willingly assumed if business could only be increased. Competitors were given the choice of joining forces with Duke or of going under, and it was usual for these wars to end in a compromise settlement in which all parties joined in a new and greater tobacco monopoly."[8]

The cornerstone in American Tobacco's rise to all-encompassing monopolization was laid in 1890, when Duke successfully engineered a consolidation fusing together five of the nation's leading cigarette producers. The combination's objectives, as declared in its articles of incorporation, were "to cure leaf tobacco, and to buy, manufacture, and sell tobacco in all its forms, to establish factories, agencies, and depots for the sale and distribution thereof, and . . . to do all things incidental to the business of trading and manufacturing."[9] With 90 percent of the cigarette market in hand as a result of this amalgamation, the American Tobacco Company had obtained the critical mass for parlaying its cigarette monopoly throughout the rest of the tobacco industry.[10]

Thus, in plug, one of the largest and most important tobacco product markets of that day, the Trust acquired the National Tobacco Works in 1891; the J. G. Butler Company in 1895; the plug-cut business of A. H. Motley Company in 1896; the Brown Tobacco, Drummond Tobacco, and Continental Tobacco firms in 1898; the firms of Buchanan & Lyall, Wright Brothers, Liggett & Myers in 1899; Rice & Vaughan, T. L. Vaughan, Brown Brothers, and Hanes & Company in 1900; Wellman-Dwire, Venable, Addison Tinsley, Wetmore, and Wilson & McCallay in 1901; the Weissinger Tobacco Company in 1902; R. A. Patterson Tobacco, Nall & Williams Tobacco, F. R. Penn Tobacco, Martin Tobacco, Butler & Brosher, Michigan Tobacco Company, Manufacturers' Tobacco Company, T. C. Williams, Spencer, and Lipfert-Scales Company in 1903; the Bland Tobacco concern in 1904; the Rucker & Witten Tobacco Company in 1905; and the Nashville Tobacco Works in 1906.[11] Through these acquisitions the Trust raised its share of plug tobacco from less than 3 percent in 1891 to 82 percent by 1906.[12]

In the markets for snuff, smoking, and fine-cut tobacco products, the pattern was the same: the Trust acquired control of Gail & Ax, and Marburg Brothers in 1891; the H. W. Meyer Tobacco Company in 1895; American Eagle Tobacco Company in 1897; Catlin Tobacco Company, Irby Company, Banner Tobacco, Union Tobacco, Gradle & Strotz, Felgner, and Beck & Co. in 1899; Atlantic Snuff, and Helme Co. in 1900; Winfree Tobacco Company, DeVoe Snuff, and McAlpin & Co. in 1901; Stewart Snuff Co., McNamara-Laird, F. F. Adams, Spaulding & Merrick, and Independent Snuff Mills in 1902; Skinner & Co., Morris, Venable, Standard Snuff, Leidersdorf, Morris & Son, Craft, and Wells-Whitehead in 1903; Bolander, Holloway Co., and Meriwether Snuff Company in 1904; Weyman & Brothers, and Carroll Tobacco Company in 1905; and Fye & Co., Sun Tobacco, Starr & Co., and Arnd Brothers in 1906.[13] As a result of these acquisitions and consolidations, the Trust's share of the national snuff market jumped from 4 percent in 1891 to 96 percent by 1906; its share of smoking tobacco jumped from 8 percent to 71 percent; and its share of fine-cut tobacco leaped from 3 percent to 81 percent.[14]

In all, American Tobacco acquired some 250 formerly independent businesses, firms, and operations in its merger-based march to mastery of tobacco.[15]

At key points, predation played a decisive role. In plug tobacco, for example, the Trust's initial offers of consolidation following its entry into the field were spurned by rival producers. In response, American Tobacco launched the notorious "plug wars," employing, appropriately enough, the "Battle Ax" brand as its prime "fighting brand," and slashing prices by more than 70 percent.[16] Similar price wars were instigated in the snuff field, as well as in American's successful drive to monopolize the British tobacco market.[17]

The Trust targeted its price cuts (and limited its financial losses) by sharply focusing them on specific firms in specific geographic regions of the country—a strategy expertly articulated in internal correspondence among Trust officials. "[I]t was agreed," wrote one, "that I should make an active campaign in the State of Ohio, which I am now doing, and losing money in that fight. We have been in there about a month, and up to this writing have sold about 19,000 pounds, but we have six men in that field, and of course, this means a loss, but we are making some headway, and I think if the fight is kept up in that field, we will put 'Index' [a rival brand] out of business, just as we did in Indiana."[18] The Trust also took explicit account of its capacity to cross-subsidize its losses on sales in targeted territories with profits drawn from other, less competitive and more profitable regions. "In view of the fact that we practically control the plug smoking business in Maine," wrote a Trust official, "it seems to me that it would be well for you to change your deals some in New England, and try to make some money there to help defray expenses in the fighting territory, such as Michigan, Indiana and the North West."[19] "My idea," explained another, "has been to get Texas and the New England States on a good solid basis, and after this was accomplished, I could then take the profits of the two territories mentioned, and apply it to the territories where we had no trade, and where we proposed a vigorous fight."[20] Again: "I think it is a splendid suggestion you make, that you get out a brand similar to 'Gorman.' If he decides within a few days to trade with you, there can be no harm done in having this brand ready, and in the event that he does not show an inclination to trade, you can probably pound him so hard that he will be willing a little later on."[21] Massive advertising and marketing programs—including extensive distributions of free goods—increased the predatory pressure that the Trust brought to bear on its victims.

Temporarily, American's predation campaigns were financially costly, generating annual losses in plug tobacco that escalated from $215,000 in 1893 to a peak loss of nearly $1.4 million in 1896, and accumulating to some $4 million over the 1895 to 1898 period (a substantial amount compared to total company-wide profits of approximately $15 million over the same period).[22] But unlike its smaller victims, American Tobacco could offset its losses with profits drawn from other, monopolized products and regions. It also could limit its losses at each step to the specific markets and regions under attack in order to compel compliance and consolidation, without having to clumsily (and expensively) impose them nationwide and across-the-board. And each success—in plug, in snuff, and in the markets for other tobacco products—enlarged the pot of monopoly profits which American could draw from in financing each subsequent step in its drive to industry-wide domination.

In the end, American's rivals succumbed to Duke's acquisitive advances and, when additional "persuasion" was required, to his predatory practices. In fact, American's notoriety as a predator served the firm well, as subsequent rivals sold out rather than suffer the attacks they knew Duke would unleash should they refuse his consolidation offers. Often they sold out at acquisition prices substantially less than what they might otherwise have been tempted to seek.[23] Each success thus served to cumulatively solidify the Trust's market power by enhancing its reputation as an organization willing and able to resort to predation.

In this fashion, then, commanding market power was attained in tobacco. As summarized by Seager and Gulick in their classic study of the industry, "Utilization of the immense profits of the early cigarette combination in financing these methods and in buying up competitors" was crucial to the Trust's success. "These cash resources were at once the bludgeon by which a competitor was subdued and the net by which he was drawn into the combination. Without them it seems highly improbable that so large a measure of concentration would have been achieved."[24] Predation, merger, and Duke's relentless will to dominate the field thus were keys to the formation of market power in tobacco.

MARKET POWER MAINTAINED

The government filed a massive antitrust suit against the American Tobacco Company in 1907, charging it with illegal monopolization of the industry in violation of the Sherman Act. In 1911 the Supreme Court upheld the government's charges. It found the record "replete with the doing of acts which it was the obvious purpose of the statute to forbid," including ample evidence to justify the conclusion "that the intention existed to use the power of the combination as a vantage ground to further monopolize the trade in tobacco by means of trade conflicts designed to injure others, either by driving competitors out of the business or compelling them to become parties to a combination."[25] The Court declared illegal "the combination in and of itself, as well as each and all of the elements composing it, whether corporate or individual, whether considered collectively or separately." It ordered the lower court to develop a plan for "dissolving the combination and of recreating, out of the elements now composing it, a new condition which shall be honestly in harmony with and not repugnant to the law."[26]

Rather than expunging market power from the field, however, the dissolution decree that eventually issued merely reconfigured it: Although the court's order divided the American Tobacco Trust into fourteen successor firms, the four largest of these, known as the Big Four, collectively dominated the industry.[27] This was especially the case in the cigarette market, which thereafter came to account for the bulk of the nation's tobacco business: In 1911, immediately following the court-ordered "dissolution," the top four cigarette producers accounted for a combined 80 percent share of the U.S. cigarette market.[28] The court had thus substituted tight-knit oligopoly in place of monopoly—an oligopoly that proved itself as adept at retaining market power through predatory practices as the Tobacco Trust had been in utilizing these same techniques to amass its market control in the first place.

As traditional industrial organization theory predicts, the court-ordered oligopoly soon displayed the hallmarks of non-competitive oligopolistic behavior: The Big Four firms came to recognize that their individual decision making was subject to a critical degree of mutual interdependence—that any move contemplated by one of them would have an important impact on the others; that the others could be expected to react; and that these reactions would have to rationally be considered in assessing their rivalry. Price competition, in particular, vanished as the oligopolists learned that a price reduction by any one of them would trigger price cuts by the others in response, and that as a result none would gain market share and all would sacrifice the profits which otherwise could have been obtained.

Thus, a strikingly non-competitive pattern of identical, uniform, and immediately matched pricing has persisted in the industry from the 1920s down to the present day. Of the 1923 to 1931 period, for example, Nicholls writes that "price relationships among the four successor firms crystallized into a clear-cut oligopolistic pattern—characterized by price leadership, virtual list and net price identity, and increasingly non-aggressive price behavior."[29] A decade later, in 1944, the Sixth Circuit Court of Appeals found "list prices and discounts for all three appellant companies [Reynolds, Liggett, American] have been practically identical since 1923, and absolutely identical since 1928." The oligopoly's prices, the court emphasized, "have no relationship to costs of production or to economic conditions generally."[30] Fifty years later, in 1993, Supreme Court Justice Kennedy likewise observed that the "cigarette industry also has long been one of America's most profitable, in part because for many years there was no significant price competition among the rival firms. . . . List prices for cigarettes increased in lockstep, twice a year, for a number of years, irrespective of the rate of inflation, changes in the cost of production, or shifts in consumer demand."[31]

Predation and the Maintenance of Market Power

Sustaining this collective market control and protecting it from competitive encroachment has required the oligopoly to engage in major predatory campaigns on two important occasions.

1930s: Predation and Elimination of the "Ten-Cent" Brands. Intoxicated with its capacity to implement ever higher prices and reap ever greater profits, the cigarette oligopoly overreached itself in 1931 when—in the depth of the Great Depression and with tobacco production costs and consumer incomes at record lows—a substantial price hike by Reynolds was matched by its fellow oligopolists. Ostensibly implemented, according to the firm's president, "to express our own courage for the future and our own confidence in our industry," this price boost produced one of the most profitable years ever for the oligopoly.[32]

But it also triggered a flood of entry by new competitors into the market. Pricing their cigarettes at ten cents per pack, or a third less than the price charged by the oligopoly on its standard brands, these new independents became known as the economy or "ten-cent brands." Their lower prices were made possible by their razor-thin profit margins, as well as by their lower production costs. The latter stemmed in important part from their use of lower grade, less expensive tobacco leaf, which enabled them to produce cigarettes at an average cost approximately one-half that of the oligopoly.[33]

The success of the ten-cent brands was unprecedented: Prior to 1931, cigarette sales by firms other than the Big Four were negligible, amounting to a mere 0.28 percent of the market. A year later, however, in June of 1932, the ten-cent brands had captured 9 percent of the market; by November, their share reached 23 percent.[34] The competitive impact on the Big Four, of course, was equally profound, as sales of the oligopoly's standard brands plunged nearly 30 percent over the same period.[35]

To contain this outbreak of competition, the oligopoly responded with a lethal price-cost predation squeeze: On the output side, the oligopoly uniformly slashed cigarette prices in lockstep fashion, first by eighty-five cents, and then by another fifty cents. Each oligopolist uniformly pressed its distributors and retailers to maintain exactly the same three-cent differential between the price charged for the ten-cent brands, on the one hand, and the price of the oligopoly's standard brands, on the other. Each oligopolist employed the same system of rewards, threats, punishments, and financial blandishments to force the adoption of their uniform three-cent differential by wholesalers and distributors.[36] On the input side, the oligopoly simultaneously and uniformly commenced to make large purchases of the cheaper tobacco leaves used for the manufacture of such lower priced cigarettes. No explanation was offered as to how or where this tobacco was used. . . . The compositions of their respective brands of cigarettes calling for the use of more expensive tobaccos remained unchanged during this period of controversy. . . . The Government claimed that such purchases of cheaper tobacco evidenced a combination and a purpose among the [oligopolists] to deprive the manufacturers of cheaper cigarettes of the tobacco necessary for their manufacture, as well as to raise the price of such tobacco to such a point that cigarettes made therefrom could not be sold at a sufficiently low price to compete with the [oligopolists'] more highly advertised brands.[37]

That the oligopoly's price cuts were, in fact, predatory was clear. Its second price cut of February 1933 brought the oligopoly's net price after discounts and taxes to $1.85 per thousand, a price virtually identical to its estimated average production cost, with no profit whatsoever.[38] Evidence and testimony before the court of appeals further indicated that during this period "Camels and Lucky Strikes were actually being sold at a loss by Reynolds and American; and Liggett was forced to curtail all its normal business activity and cut its advertising to the bone in order to sell at this price."[39]

Temporarily, the adverse effect of the Big Four's predatory pricing on their profits was substantial. Although their combined annual sales rose by 8.5 billion cigarettes between 1932 and 1933, their combined net income plunged an average 45 percent over the same period, with individual oligopolists suffering profit declines ranging from 27 to 60 percent.[40] The impact on the independents, however, was catastrophic: from a peak market share of 23 percent, the ten-cent brands' share of the cigarette market dropped to 17 percent in January 1933 with the advent of the oligopoly's first price cut, and subsequently declining to 6 percent following the oligopoly's second price cut.[41]

Once the independents had been eliminated as a viable competitive force, the oligopoly returned to raising prices and restoring its monopoly profits: in January 1934, the oligopoly uniformly raised its net prices after taxes by 29 percent, and saw its combined profits increase by $10 million that year, eventually reaching a level $20 million higher by 1936. Initially, then, the market system worked in textbook fashion, as excessive profits attracted new firms into the field. Predation subsequently trumped the market, however, as the oligopoly was able to drive out the new entrants and re-establish its non-competitive prices and profits.

Once again the government filed suit, charging that the tobacco oligopoly had collectively restrained and monopolized the cigarette field in violation of the Sherman Act. Once again, struck by the degree of tacitly collusive cooperation displayed in this exercise of oligopolistic industry control, the courts agreed.

The identical objectives, the opportunity for communication between appellants in formulating policies for their mutual benefit, their concert of action in other matters in which they were mutually interested, their refusal to participate in buying at the markets unless all three appellant companies were present, the uniformity of list prices of their manufactured products, the identical and (for all practical purposes) simultaneous price increases and price reductions, their insistence on identical list prices, the similar rewards and punishments meted out to dealers by all the appellants in carrying out the same objectives, their policies which, in practice, resulted in their refusal to compete with each other in the field of prices, either in the purchase of leaf tobacco or in the sales of their finished products, are all circumstances—together with evidence of the use of many other methods earlier enumerated herein—from which an agreement on the part of appellants to act in concert, to the extent and in the manner outlined by the court, could be inferred by the jury beyond a reasonable doubt.[42]

Although in a landmark ruling the Supreme Court upheld the oligopoly's conviction of having collectively monopolized the cigarette business in violation of the Sherman Act,[43] the government's failure to seek a structural remedy left the oligopoly and its market power intact.

Summarizing this era, Nicholls writes that

having inherited 80 percent of the nation's cigarette business from the Trust, the four successor companies had achieved a market position of perhaps 97 percent by 1925 and controlled 98 percent as late as 1931. During the 1930s, the development of the first significant independent competition since the dissolution reduced the position of the successor companies to 74 percent, more than half of their loss being attributable to the rise of lower-priced 'economy' brands, which had taken over 15 percent of the domestic market by 1939. However, by 1950—thanks largely to the disappearance of the economy brands—the successor companies' position had recovered to 82 percent.[44]

Disciplined avoidance of price competition, heavy advertising outlays that promoted consumer loyalty while raising entry barriers,[45] and the collective willingness to predatorily drive new competitors from the field were the foundations for sustaining the oligopoly's market power.

1980s: Predation and Containment of "Generics." For the next thirty years, the oligopoly retained unchallenged control of the market. Price competition was nonexistent, and profits were immense. A financial analysis of the industry prepared in the early 1980s by Merrill Lynch praised the oligopoly's staunch suppression of competition: "The cigarette companies . . . have usually played the part of a well-managed oligopoly, pricing up aggressively. They have rarely indulged in excessive price promotions for any sustained period. Demand for cigarettes is relatively inelastic, enabling them to price up more aggressively than is the case for many other companies. They face virtually no threat of entry by a new competitor, as is often the case in many other consumer lines."[46]   Indeed, despite a secular decline in cigarette demand, as well as increases in tobacco taxes, the oligopoly quadrupled its profit margins over the 1972 to 1983 period (from $2.91 to $12.61 per thousand cigarettes in the case of one firm) through sustained, sizable, and noncompetitive price hikes.[47]

Then, when serious competition emerged in the early 1980s—for only the second time in fifty years—the oligopoly neutralized the threat as effectively as it had crushed the ten-cent brands a half century earlier.

This time competition appeared in the guise of low-priced "generic" cigarettes. Liggett & Myers (L&M), the smallest of the cigarette producers, had seen its market share dwindle to 2 percent of the market, as smokers lost interest in its L&M, Lark, and Chesterfield brands. Confronting the specter of liquidating its cigarette business altogether, Liggett's salvation suddenly seemed to arrive in 1980 in an inquiry from a wholesale grocery cooperative exploring Liggett's interest in producing for distribution a low-priced, private label, or "generic," cigarette. Liggett seized upon the offer. Pricing its generic cigarettes 30 to 40 percent below the oligopoly's full-price brands, Liggett's sales exploded and its share of the market tripled over the 1980 to 1984 period.

The oligopoly's strategy for neutralizing this competitive threat is explained in a series of internal documents prepared by Brown & Williamson (B&W), the third largest cigarette producer, and the firm that took the lead in acting on the oligopoly's behalf to snuff this outbreak of price competition.

As B&W officials assessed it, Liggett's generic cigarettes marked "the first time that a manufacturer has used pricing as a strategic marketing weapon in the United States since the depression era."[48] They observed that although cigarette sales generally had entered a state of permanent decline, "generic sales are growing rapidly. From a launch year volume of only 230 million units in 1980, generics have grown to over 17.5 billion units in 1983."[49] They feared that unless Liggett's expansion of generics was halted, Liggett would "continue aggressive segment development since it has virtually no stake in the branded, full price market."[50] In that event, Liggett could "grow to a total company share of over 15 percent by 1988, becoming the third largest company in the U.S. cigarette market," and low-priced generics could expand to account for 25 to 30 percent of the total cigarette market.[51] This kind of price competition, the B&W officials estimated, would cost the oligopoly billions in lost sales and hundreds of millions in lost profits.[52]

Failure to act quickly, B&W feared, could eventually require a replay of the costly price war waged against the ten-cent brands fifty years earlier, with individual oligopolists having to slash prices across the board "in an attempt to repeat the action of the mid 1930s." Declaring "that the industry's interests—other than L&M's—would be far better served had generics never been introduced," B&W officers castigated generics as "an immediate and growing threat to all other manufacturers," and argued that "counter-actions are essential and inevitable."[53]

Following a detailed assessment of the status and outlook of each member of the oligopoly, B&W officials concluded that their firm was best situated to assume the role of enforcer and defender of the oligopoly's market control. As they saw the choice confronting the oligopoly, "Cigarette manufacturers either stay on the sidelines and accept the losses to economy offerings and attempt to limit future price increases in order not to fuel the growth of generics—or—they will enter the new segment in an attempt to participate in order to manage prices and profitability upward. The latter appears to be the most predictable approach."[54] Thus, the oligopoly, led by B&W, would enter the generic segment—not to compete, but to corral Liggett, establish non-competitive oligopolistic price leadership/price followership, and, ultimately, raise generic prices in order to remove their competitive appeal. In B&W's words, entry into generics "provides B&W with the potential for improving profitability through opportunistic pricing, either to lead or to follow as appropriate."[55]

But waging a direct price war against Liggett at the retail level would only add further fuel to the growth of generics and, hence, the expansion of price competition. To avoid this outcome, the oligopoly elected to prey on Liggett at the wholesale level by matching Liggett's generic retail prices while offering greater financial inducements to distributors choosing to handle B&W generics rather than those produced by Liggett. By offering wholesalers more lucrative terms of trade, the oligopoly would limit Liggett's growth without further driving down the retail price of generics. It thus would eliminate competition from Liggett while, at the same time, protecting its high-priced, high-profit brands from further erosion by low-priced generics. Brown & Williamson expected to temporarily lose money on its generics campaign and anticipated that Liggett would react vigorously. But Liggett's vastly smaller size and its corresponding lack of financial resources, B&W officials concluded, would severely limit its capacity to withstand B&W's onslaught: As they saw it, "it is unlikely L&M can, in fact, be prepared to engage in a sustained battle because it does not have the financial resource of others in the industry."[56]

Thus conceived, the oligopoly's predatory assault on Liggett was launched in mid 1984, when B&W unveiled a line of black-and-white generic cigarettes virtually identical to those marketed by Liggett. As the oligopoly expected, a price war ensued at the wholesale level, with B&W and Liggett furiously raising and re-raising their rebate offers to distributors.

But as the oligopoly also correctly predicted, predatory warfare in generics was short-lived: In July 1985, a year after B&W initiated its generic campaign, and following the parallel entry into generics by the other oligopolists, Liggett signaled its surrender by raising its generic list prices—a price rise immediately matched by the oligopoly. The oligopoly slashed Liggett's share of the generic segment from 89 percent to 14 percent; it cut Liggett's share of all cigarette sales from a peak of nearly 6 percent in 1984 to 2.8 percent by 1988, with a subsequent drop to 1 percent by 1994. Acquisition of the American Tobacco Company—another declining old-line firm tempted into low-priced generics—by B&W enabled the oligopoly to further rein in generics as a source of price rivalry by disposing of what one industry analyst characterized as another "small but disruptive competitor."[57]

Control over pricing of generics thus had been wrested from an independently minded maverick, oligopolistic avoidance of price competition had been reasserted, and the foundation for price control throughout the market had been re-established. The oligopoly immediately turned to narrowing the generic/branded price differential that Liggett had introduced, and to establishing in generics the kind of tacitly collusive, non-competitive oligopolistic pricing uniformity that traditionally prevailed in the cigarette field more generally. By the summer of 1986, according to Justice Kennedy, "a pattern of twice yearly increases [in generic prices] in tandem with the full-priced branded cigarettes was established. The dollar amount of these increases was the same for generic and full-priced cigarettes, which resulted in a greater percentage price increase in the less expensive generic cigarettes and a narrowing of the percentage gap between the list price of branded and black-and-white cigarettes."[58] From January 1986 to June 1989, the oligopoly raised generic cigarette prices by 71 percent—nearly twice the rate at which it increased its branded cigarette prices over the same period.[59] In fact, by 1990 the oligopoly had succeeded in raising generic prices to a level higher than that at which its full-priced brands had been sold just six years earlier.

With price competition from generics contained, the oligopoly could return to engineering steady, substantial price hikes for branded cigarettes: branded cigarette prices were raised from $4.04 per carton in January 1982, to $9.23 per carton by June 1989, and to $13.25 per carton by July 1992.[60] The monopoly profits resulting from this exercise of market power have been immense: the oligopoly's profit margins increased from $3.80 per thousand cigarettes in 1980 to $11.55 per thousand by 1988;[61] on total industry shipments of $25 billion in 1990, the oligopoly enjoyed a gross profit markup of fully $15 billion (with costs, including advertising, accounting for the remaining $10 billion), as cigarette prices were increased at rates far in excess of costs, including taxes.[62]

The oligopoly thus achieved what the *Wall Street Journal* labeled "one of the great magic tricks of market economics: how to force prices up and increase profits in an industry in which demand falls by tens of billions of cigarettes each year."[63]

Finally, this exercise of oligopoly market power survived yet a third major assault under the antitrust laws. In a private Sherman Act suit filed by Liggett against B&W, the jury's verdict in favor of Liggett was overturned by the district court and eventually by the Supreme Court.[64] Although conceding that "[c]igarette manufacturing has long been one of America's most concentrated industries," and that the "cigarette industry also has long been one of America's most profitable, in part because for many years there was no significant price competition among the rival firms," the Supreme Court exonerated Brown & Williamson. It rested its decision on what it believed to be the "irrationality" and "general implausibility of predatory pricing"; on what it perceived as the theoretical implausibility of recouping predatory losses; and on the faith that predatory "schemes are even more improbable when they require coordinated action among several firms."[65] "Firms that seek to recoup predatory losses through the conscious parallelism of oligopoly," opined the Court, "must rely on uncertain and ambiguous signals to achieve concerted action. The signals are subject to misinterpretation and are a blunt and imprecise means of ensuring smooth cooperation. . . . This anticompetitive minuet is most difficult to compose and to perform, even for a disciplined oligopoly."[66] In so ruling, the majority prompted a rebuke from Justice Stevens, who, in his dissenting opinion, observed "that the professional performers who had danced the minuet for forty to fifty years would be better able to predict whether their favorite partners would follow them in the future than would an outsider, who might not know the difference between Haydn and Mozart."[67]

CONCLUSION

At least five salient conclusions are suggested by an analysis of the American tobacco industry:

First, market power is neither a fragile nor an inherently fleeting phenomenon. Nor is it congenitally vulnerable to competitive erosion.[68] In cigarettes, it has proven itself to be eminently durable for nearly a century—first as a monopoly at the hands of the American Tobacco Trust, and over the decades since then as a finely tuned, close-knit oligopoly dedicated to avoiding competition among the few.

Second, market power is not necessarily obtained "naturally," nor must its origin and persistence inevitably be ascribed to misguided government interference that blunts the self-corrective forces of the marketplace. In tobacco, market power was achieved via merger, trust formation, predation, and coercion, while government antitrust actions twice tried to break, rather than reinforce, the power of the dominant firms.

Third, the persistence of market power is neither necessarily "accidental," nor solely attributable to "superior skill, foresight and industry."[69] Rather, it can be retained by dominant firms that, when necessary, are capable of exercising it—either singly or in concert—in order to eliminate competition and reassert their collective control.

Fourth, predation can play a key role in attaining and sustaining market power. Predation, therefore, is neither inherently "irrational" nor the figment of "unscientific" imagination.[70] Instead, it may be a rational and effective strategy for maintaining market control over the long run. Temporary financial losses resulting from predation may be less costly than the loss of monopoly profits that dominant firms expect from an outbreak of competition. Disproportionate size enables dominant firms to inflict losses that are proportionately greater and, thus, much more devastating, to their victims than to themselves. Predatory price cuts need not be fecklessly and expensively imposed; instead, they can be finely focused, and the costs of predation contained, by confining price cuts to specific products, specific regions, specific firms, and for limited time periods. As a result, victims whose efficiency equals or exceeds that of their predators can nonetheless be driven from the market. Moreover, the gains from predation can be recouped instantaneously by stanching further erosion of prices and profits for monopolized products and brands. And, as events in the tobacco industry demonstrate, oligopoly can be as effective as single-firm monopoly in the use of a predation strategy. The reality and rationality of predation thus render it an important problem in industrial organization and an appropriate subject of public policy concern.

Finally, conviction under the nation's antitrust laws need not entail a loss of market control. The history of the cigarette industry demonstrates that antitrust actions that fail to remedy structurally rooted concentrations of private economic power are futile—a point brilliantly articulated by Justice Brandeis long ago. Criticizing the outcome of the government's original antitrust suit against the Tobacco Trust, Brandeis in 1911 characterized "the so-called 'disintegration' [a]s, in effect, a nullification, not only of the Sherman law, but of the decision of the Supreme Court." It was, he wrote, tantamount to legalizing illegal market power. As such, he concluded, it marked the discovery of a novel constitutional principle: "What man has illegally joined together, let no court put asunder."[71]

NOTES

1. *United States v American Tobacco Co.*, 191 F 371, 392 (Cir. SDNY 1911).

2. Richard B. Tennant, *The American Cigarette Industry* (New Haven, CT: Yale University Press, 1950), p. 94.

3. Ibid.

4. William B. Burnett, "Predation by a Nondominant Firm," *The Antitrust Revolution*, 2d ed., ed. John E. Kwoka and Lawrence J. White (New York: HarperCollins, 1994), p. 261.

5. Robert S. Lazich, *Market Share Reporter: 1997* (Detroit, MI: Gale Research, 1997), p. 103.

6. Derived from information presented in Henry R. Seager and Charles A. Gulick, *Trust and Corporation Problems* (New York: Harper & Bros., 1929), p. 163; and Tennant, *Cigarette Industry*, pp. 19, 25.

7. Seager & Gulick, *Trust*, p. 163.

8. Tennant, *Cigarette Industry*, p. 28.

9. Commissioner of Corporations, *Report on the Tobacco Industry*, Part 1 (Washington, D.C.: U.S. Government Printing Office, 1909), p. 65.

10. Seager & Gulick, *Trust*, p. 150.

11. *Report on the Tobacco Industry*, Part 1, pp. 181-190.

12. Ibid., p. 365.

13. Ibid., pp. 181-192.

14. Ibid., pp. 383, 399, 408.

15. Tennant, *Cigarette Industry*, p. 27.

16. Ibid., pp. 96-97; Tennant, *Cigarette Industry*, p. 28.

17. For detailed analysis, see Walter Adams and James W. Brock, "Predation, 'Rationality,' and Judicial Somnambulance," *University of Cincinnati Law Review* 64 (1996): 811.

18. Reproduced in Malcolm R. Burns, "New Evidence on Predatory Price Cutting," *Managerial and Decision Economics* 10 (1989): 328.

19. Ibid.

20. Ibid.

21. Ibid.

22. Commissioner of Corporations, *Report on the Tobacco Industry*, Part 3 (Washington, D.C.: U.S. Government Printing Office, 1915), p. 51; Seager and Gulick, *Trust*, p. 169.

23. Malcolm R. Burns, "Predatory Pricing and the Acquisition Cost of Competitors," *Journal of Political Economy* 94 (1986): 266-296.

24. Seager and Gulick, *Trust*, p. 165.

25. *United States v American Tobacco Co.*, 221 US 106, 181-82 (1911).

26. Ibid., p. 187.

27. The big four were American Tobacco, Liggett and Myers, R. J. Reynolds, and Lorillard.

28. *United States v American Tobacco Co.*, 191 F.2d 371, 392 (Cir. Ct., SDNY, 1911).

29. William H. Nicholls, *Price Policies in the Cigarette Industry* (Nashville, TN: Vanderbilt University Press, 1951), p. 78.

30. *American Tobacco Co. v United States*, 147 F2d 93, 103 (1944).

31. *Brook Group v Brown & Williamson Tobacco Co.*, 113 S. Ct. 2578, 2583 (1993).

32. *American Tobacco Co. v United States*, 328 US 781, 805-806 (1946).

33. Nicholls, *Price Policies*, p. 113.

34. *American Tobacco Co. v United States*, 328 US 781, 806 (1946); Nicholls, *Price Policies*, p. 111.

35. Nicholls, *Price Policies*, p. 112.

36. *American Tobacco Co. v United States*, 147 F2d 93, 104-106 (6th Cir. 1944).

37. *American Tobacco Co. v United States*, 328 US 781, 803-804 (1946).

38. Nicholls, *Price Policies*, pp. 113, 116.

39. *American Tobacco Co. v United States*, 147 F2d 93, 104 (1944).

40. Nicholls, *Price Policies*, pp. 91, 105, 120.

41. Ibid., p. 121.

42. *American Tobacco Co. v United States*, 147 F2d 93, 113 (1944).

43. *American Tobacco Co. v United States*, 328 US 781 (1946).

44. Nicholls, *Price Policies*, pp. 167-68.

45. The oligopoly's heavy advertising, in the assessment of the industry's leading student during this era, "serves to strengthen the power of the large producer vis-à-vis the small, and is the principal instrument by which the present structure of the industry is maintained." Tennant, *Cigarette Industry*, pp. 377-378. "The change to national advertising media has made the level of total advertising expenditure more important than ever, and heavy expenditures are supportable only by very large companies. . . . Any other efficiencies to large-scale enterprise are of minor extent and uncertain reliability and at most can have exerted subsidiary influence." Ibid., p. 268.

46. Quoted in Burnett, "Predation," p. 281.

47. *Liggett Group, Inc. v Brown & Williamson Tobacco Co.*, Plaintiff's Exhibit 12.

48. *Liggett Group, Inc. v Brown & Williamson Tobacco*, Plaintiff's Exhibit 12.

49. Ibid., Plaintiff's Exhibit 5.

50. Ibid., Plaintiff's Exhibit 12.

51. Ibid., Plaintiff's Exhibit 5.

52. Ibid., Plaintiff's Exhibit 12.

53. Ibid., Plaintiff's Exhibit 5.

54. Ibid., Plaintiff's Exhibit 12.

55. Ibid.

56. Ibid., Plaintiff's Exhibit 6.

57. "B.A.T. to Buy Rival American Brands' Unit," *Wall Street Journal*, 27 April 1994, p. A3. See also Suein L. Hwang, "B.A.T. Selects Nick Brookes to Succeed Sandefur as Brown & Williamson CEO," *Wall Street Journal*, 24 April 1995, p. B5, where an industry analyst observes of this acquisition: "They picked up a little market share and eliminated a competitor that was causing serious price problems."

58. *Brook Group v Brown & Williamson Tobacco*, 113 S. Ct. 2578, 2585.

59. Burnett, "Predation," p. 272.

60. Ibid., pp. 272, 294.

61. F. M. Scherer and David Ross, *Industrial Market Structure and Economic Performance*, 3rd ed. (Boston: Houghton Mifflin, 1990), p. 251.

62. Craig Howell, Frank Congelio, and Ralph Yatsko, "Pricing Practices for Tobacco Products, 1980-94," *Monthly Labor Review* (December 1994): 6-7.

63. Stephen J. Adler and Alix M. Freedman, "Tobacco Suit Exposes Ways Cigarette Firms Keep the Profits Fat," *Wall Street Journal*, 5 March 1990, p. 1.

64. See *Liggett Group, Inc. v Brown & Williamson Tobacco*, 748 F Supp. 344 (MDNC. 1990); *Liggett Group, Inc. v Brown & Williamson Tobacco*, 964 F2d 335 (4th Cir. 1992); *Brook Group v Brown & Williamson Tobacco*, 113 S. Ct. 2578 (1993).

65. *Brook Group v Brown & Williamson Tobacco*, 113 S. Ct. 2578, 2590 (1993).

66. Ibid.

67. Ibid., p. 2605.

68. For further development and case studies of this and related points, see Walter Adams and James W. Brock, *The Bigness Complex* (New York: Pantheon, 1986).

69. For a survey of contending economic points of view on this issue, see Walter Adams and James W. Brock, *Antitrust Economics on Trial: A Dialogue on the New Laissez-Faire* (Princeton, NJ: Princeton University Press, 1991).

70. For a theoretical exposition, see Walter Adams, James W. Brock, and Norman P. Obst, "Is Predation Rational? Is It Profitable?," *Review of Industrial Organization* 11 (1996): 753-758.

71. Louis D. Brandeis, "An Illegal Trust Legalized," *The World To-Day* (December 1911): 1440-1441.

4

ALCOA AND THE U.S. ALUMINUM INDUSTRY

Hayley Chouinard and David I. Rosenbaum

The Aluminum Company of America, often known as Alcoa, largely dominated the American aluminum industry for over five decades. The company enjoyed a brief patent-granted monopoly, followed by a long period of domestic monopoly with limited competition from foreign producers. Eventually, Alcoa faced domestic and foreign competition, but it managed to adapt and remain a leader in the industry. This is the story of the Aluminum Company of America, and its journey from monopoly and dominance to shared oligopoly.

THE BEGINNING OF ALCOA

Sir Humphery Davis, an English chemist, discovered aluminum in 1807. During his experiments, he also found the great difficulty involved in releasing aluminum from the other elements to which it bonds. Having no means for separation, aluminum enjoyed only limited and novel applications during most of the 1800s. Napoleon III greatly admired the lightweight and shiny metal, and displayed aluminum utensils and jewelry in his court. He desired to use the light metal to shield his army and for other military uses, but the lack of quantity and the relatively high price of aluminum, $17 a pound in 1859, dampened his enthusiasm. He sponsored research in hopes of discovering a means to mass produce aluminum, but to no avail. Napoleon died before any technology could yield any great quantity of aluminum.

Scientists around the world continued to search for a method to isolate and extract pure aluminum. In 1880, using electrochemistry, some success brought the price of aluminum down to $8 a pound. Then, in 1886, Charles Hall in the United States and Paul L. T. Heroult in France each independently developed a process of electrolytic reduction which could potentially lead to the mass production of aluminum. Hall filed for a U.S. patent to protect the process on July 9, 1886. This filing date secured Hall as the sole owner of the right to use his process to produce aluminum in the United States. He received the patent on April 2, 1889.

In 1887, Hall gave the Cowles brothers, who owned the Cowles Electric Smelting and Aluminum Company of Cleveland, an option to purchase his patent, if while working in their plant, he could demonstrate his process could support a commercial operation. The Cowles concentrated their business in aluminum alloys, not in producing aluminum ingot. Their research into alloy production led them to develop furnace-heating processes; however, when they believed Hall had been given sufficient time to demonstrate the capabilities of his process without success, the Cowles brothers allowed their option on his patent to lapse. Hall, angry, left the Cowles's plant to pursue his process elsewhere.

Hall had met Alfred Hunt through a connection at the Cowles's company. Hunt and a group of investors from Pittsburgh, all experts in the steel industry, listened to Hall describe his process and the potential of aluminum. Although Hall had yet to prove his process could provide commercial operations in aluminum, the investors on July 31, 1888, gave Hall $20,000 to continue his research. Within months, the process generated aluminum on a scale to allow mass production. On October 1, 1888, the group chartered the Pittsburgh Reduction Company to produce and sell aluminum ingot.

The Cowles brothers continued to pursue production of aluminum alloys and eventually started to sell aluminum. Through a series of legal proceedings during the late 1890s and early 1900s the Cowles brothers were found guilty of infringing on the Hall patent for the production of aluminum; however, the Pittsburgh Reduction Company was also found guilty of infringing on the Cowles-held patent for a heating process. Both companies, therefore, violated the others' patents. Thus, neither could legally produce aluminum. In 1903, the Cowles brothers licensed the Pittsburgh Reduction Company to use its patent for a large settlement, and the Cowles brothers stopped all production of aluminum. This agreement left the Pittsburgh Reduction Company with patent-protected production of aluminum until 1909.

THE EARLY HISTORY OF ALCOA: 1888 THROUGH 1914

An early concern of the company involved the limited number of applications for aluminum. Alcoa attempted to expand the market for aluminum by developing completely new markets that particularly suited the new, lightweight metal, and by attempting to replace other metals such as tin, zinc, lead, and iron in already established markets. The company also instituted a policy to keep the price of aluminum relatively low in order to promote high-volume sales. The Pittsburgh company pursued the cooking utensil market in 1893, which remained aluminum's largest market until 1900. By 1900, aluminum became a viable substitute for brass, zinc, tin, and iron in a number of applications. Aluminum found markets in bicycle parts, cameras, shoe eyelets, horseshoes, reflectors in locomotive headlights, flashlight powder, bathtubs, and selected auto parts. The researchers at Alcoa continued to seek out new markets. By 1908, aluminum wire use became well established with aluminum cable quickly following. By 1912, 20 percent of all aluminum ingot sold came in the form of cable. Alcoa also saw great potential to utilize aluminum in the growing automobile industry. Eighty percent of all American-built cars had aluminum crank and gear cases by 1914.

Along with pursuing new markets for aluminum, Alcoa also aggressively sought means to control the essential raw materials needed to produce aluminum. In 1897, the company stated its concern for its long-terms plans. Alcoa wanted to secure its position after the expiration of its critical patent in 1909 and if the government lifted current tariffs on aluminum. Alcoa continually purchased or leased rights for bauxite as new deposits became available. (Bauxite is smelted to produce aluminum.) Alcoa secured the Georgian reserve in 1883. During the period between 1899 and 1906 the company locked up much of the Arkansas deposits. In acquiring these bauxite reserves, Alcoa also entered into restrictive contracts with other bauxite-mining companies, requiring that they not sell bauxite to any other aluminum producer. Eventually it became clear that domestic deposits would not provide all of the necessary bauxite to continue aluminum production into the future. Thus, by 1915 Alcoa controlled a significant amount of the bauxite deposits in British and Dutch Guianas.

Alcoa also understood the integral part energy played in producing aluminum. In 1900, the company started pursuing a policy of acquiring water power and developing its own energy sources. In 1899, the company had a hydroelectric site in Quebec, Canada. Between 1899 and 1906, the company developed several sites around the Niagara area in Canada and the United States. By 1909, Alcoa turned its energy attention to the Little Tennessee River in Tennessee and built several sites on that river. In 1915, energy needs led Alcoa to build more power plants in North Carolina.

With all the newly acquired bauxite and energy, Alcoa wanted to increase its production of alumina, an intermediate product refined from bauxite and, in turn, smelted into aluminum. It built a large alumina refinery in East St. Louis. The refinery, when operating efficiently, generated much more output than a smelter could use as an input. Thus, the alumina was taken to any one of five different smelters in New York, Canada, Tennessee, and North Carolina. To enhance production, Alcoa controlled much of its own methods of transportation. For example, Alcoa owned several ships and barges to transport the bauxite to the refinery and operated some of its own railways to facilitate transportation of the alumina.

To improve the potential for the sale of the final aluminum goods, Alcoa consolidated three aluminum utensil fabricators in 1909. Alcoa became a 25 percent owner in the operation. Alcoa also organized many of the major foundries into one large operation with itself as 50 percent owner. By doing this, Alcoa could improve the capital base and credit positions of the firms that purchased ingot inputs from Alcoa. By 1915 Alcoa had vertically integrated into raw materials, refining, aluminum production, and aluminum-based final goods. Alcoa had also horizontally integrated with five smelters producing aluminum ingot.

During its early years, Alcoa had several encounters with international competitors and the Justice Department. In 1896, Alcoa entered into a cartel arrangement with a powerful Swiss producer. However, worried by the Sherman Act, Alcoa made further agreements through its Canadian subsidiary, Northern Aluminum Company. In 1901, the company forged an arrangement with the major producers in France, England, and Switzerland. Each producer faced a closed market in its own country with prices fixed at one cent per pound higher than for sales in the open market. All international transfers met with regulated quotas. Thus, Alcoa supplied the U.S. market and exported allotted quotas through the Northern Aluminum Company in Canada. Pricing disputes erupted in 1907, and the cartel disbanded in 1908.

The Justice Department filed a complaint against Alcoa in May 1911 for illegally participating in foreign cartels, making restrictive contracts for the purchase of alumina and bauxite, and for undertaking unfair competitive practices in some downstream markets. The case was settled within a year without going to trial. The terms of the consent decree in 1912 forbade Alcoa from entering into foreign cartels, exclusionary contracts, and marketing agreements with downstream producers.

There was only one serious attempt at new entry into U.S. production during this period. This was by a group of experienced French aluminum producers. The French had adequate European financial backing and access to bauxite through their own mines. They were familiar with production techniques through their facilities in France. While their selection of a dam site for electricity generation was less than optimal, they projected beginning production by 1915. The outbreak of World War I, however, curtailed foreign financing. Attempts were made to procure American financiers; however, no takers were found. The stockholders eventually sold out to Alcoa, the only potential buyer.

Summary of Dominance in the Early Years

Alcoa's monopoly in the aluminum industry began with its acquisition of the patent to produce aluminum via the electrolytic process. Several other factors, however, enabled Alcoa to maintain that monopoly and extend its dominance during the industry's infancy. One important factor was research and development, which really came into play in two ways. Research and development was crucial in the discovery of more economical methods to produce aluminum. Also important to the continuance of the industry, however, were Alcoa's persistent efforts to develop new uses for aluminum. Without a growing fabricated goods market, with aluminum as an input, production of ingot would have been uneconomical. Another factor in Alcoa's strategy to allow the market to grow was its pricing. Prices were purposely kept low and steady to encourage the substitution of aluminum into products where other metals had been used before. None of these actions would typically be construed as anticompetitive.

Alcoa's responses to competition, both actual and potential, were also instrumental in its gaining dominance. To prevent foreign competition, Alcoa entered into market segmentation agreements with foreign producers and steadily pushed for high import tariffs. It clearly discouraged potential domestic entry by tying up as much of the key raw materials—bauxite, alumina, and hydro power—as possible through vertical integration.

Integration was important in reducing costs. But it also helped solidify Alcoa's monopoly position. Integration meant that Alcoa had an ample supply of alumina for smelting into aluminum. But it also made it less likely that a market would form for the buying and selling of alumina. This would force an entrant to enter integrated as well, increasing the costs and risks of entry. In addition, Alcoa's integration meant that it had exclusive access to considerable bauxite reserves commercially suitable for the production of aluminum. With no market for the input alumina and dubious access to economically suitable raw bauxite, entry would be discouraged all the more.

Integration also meant that Alcoa had access to relatively cheap power. Market prices for electricity were above Alcoa's own cost of generation. This would put any likely entrant at a cost disadvantage relative to Alcoa. Another advantage of integration was that the longer it discouraged new entry, the more entrenched Alcoa could become. This would just make future entry that much harder.

Another factor that discouraged entry was lack of information. During its early years, Alcoa published few financial reports. This meant a potential entrant would have a hard time analyzing the potential profitability of entry. Alcoa's entrenched position and vertical integration also made it difficult for firms to enter the market slowly to gain information. Hence there were significant informational asymmetries between Alcoa and any potential entrant. Finally, Alcoa's rapid expansion and significant apparent production reserves acted to discourage entry.

It is significant to note that over the period 1909 to 1914, available estimates indicate that Alcoa averaged over a 17 percent rate of return on investment.[1] Yet there was only one serious attempt at entry. This was by a French firm with foreign backing. When the war denied the entrant that financial backing, no domestic financing was found. Evidently U.S. financiers viewed new entry as too risky, even with Alcoa's relatively high rate of return. Alcoa's actions combined with market conditions apparently precluded new entry.

WORLD WAR I THROUGH THE GREAT DEPRESSION

From 1909 until 1912, Alcoa faced increasing aluminum imports from European producers, which drove down prices. In 1913 and 1914, foreign imports of aluminum into the United States equaled 50 percent of domestic output.[2] Alcoa was vulnerable to imports because it had higher costs, even net of transportation, and because its aluminum was seen as being lower quality than European aluminum. The outbreak of the war in Europe in 1914 ended the threat of imports as each European producer supplied its own country's military. Alcoa increased its production capacity to meet the United States military's growing demand. From 1915 to 1918, production from Alcoa went from approximately 50,000 tons to 76,000 tons.[3]

The increased production brought many benefits to Alcoa. First, many new government-based markets found uses for aluminum. Explosives, helmets, gas masks, identification tags, and parts of aircraft all included aluminum. These many new and diverse markets made aluminum a much more familiar material to many engineering trades. Also, research efforts were intensified by Alcoa, the government, and research institutes to develop new alloys that could strengthen the lightweight metal and provide a material better suited to aircraft construction.

At the conclusion of the war, demand for aluminum decreased as military needs lessened. Imports again increased as European producers once more looked toward the United States as a growing market. This occurred at a time when both European producers and Alcoa had excess capacity. However, Alcoa remained aggressive. It greatly increased its research budget and formalized a separate research division within the company. Its research priorities encompassed production and fabrication process improvements, new uses, and new hard alloys. Process improvements steadily brought down costs. New fabricating techniques improved the quality of Alcoa's fabricated sheet and other products. The reductions in costs along with the improvements in quality helped to prevent any significant foreign penetration into the U.S. market.

During this period Alcoa dealt with foreign competition in two ways. First, it extended its investment abroad. Alcoa expanded its foreign bauxite reserves and energy sources. It also purchased foreign fabricating facilities, particularly in Europe. Entry into foreign markets can be viewed as a strategic threat to calm foreign penetration into domestic markets. To thwart foreign entry, Alcoa also lobbied hard for new tariffs on aluminum imports. A Republican administration increased the tariff in 1922 from two to five cents a pound on ingot and from five to nine cents a pound on sheet. As a result, imports stayed at less than 15 percent of domestic production. In the government's upcoming antitrust suit (to be discussed later in this chapter), it also charged that Alcoa and its Canadian subsidiary, Aluminum Ltd., acted in concert with other foreign oligopolists to control competition. These charges, however, were never accepted by the District Court of New York.

The Great Depression hit Alcoa hard. Demand declined at a time when Alcoa had been pursuing a policy of growth. Alcoa eventually decreased its employment and output. A union formed at the New Kensington plant in 1933 to protect the aluminum workers and soon the other plants also organized unions. However, Alcoa remained profitable through most of the depression years, with its worst year coming in 1932.

Summary of Maintaining Early Dominance

Several factors helped Alcoa maintain its monopoly in the post–World War I era. One was a continuing effort into research and development. Research and development led to continual reductions in production costs, better quality outputs, new alloys, and better fabrication techniques. All of these outcomes reduced the threat of competition, from both foreign and domestic sources. Foreign competition was reduced as research and development closed both the cost and quality gaps between domestic and foreign-produced aluminum. Alcoa's pursuit of new and better alloys and methods of fabrication also made it harder for any domestic firm to get a strong enough toehold in the industry for launching integrated entry.

During this period Alcoa also pursued a policy of capacity expansion. Capacity increased from 76,000 tons in 1915 to 125,000 tons by 1929.[4] As Alcoa grew, the resulting size of requisite domestic entry discouraged new competition. Alcoa also continued its investment in foreign bauxite and the development of hydroelectric sites in the United States and Canada. By this time, however, world bauxite markets were expanding and limited access to Canadian power would have been available to a potential entrant.

Another important factor that helped protect Alcoa from foreign competition was government intervention. The tariff increases of 1922 significantly reduced import penetration. It is interesting to note that during this period government policy helped Alcoa. This conflicts with earlier antitrust policies that stimulated foreign entry by curbing Alcoa's involvement in foreign cartels. Another factor was Alcoa's own strategic response of increasing its investments in Europe. This had to have a disciplining effect on the European aluminum oligopoly. A final and very important factor was very much beyond Alcoa's control: World War I insulated Alcoa from foreign competition at a time when it was vulnerable.

As with the earlier period, there was only one serious attempt at new entry into the U.S. market. This attempt was supported by the Duke family's desire to develop new hydroelectric sites in Canada. The Dukes eventually, however, developed this power in conjunction with Alcoa and the threat of entry subsided. This again shows the lack of desire to enter on the part of U.S. companies and financiers.

THE LATE 1930s THROUGH WORLD WAR II

In 1937, the Department of Justice brought a 140-count antitrust suit against Alcoa. The case accused Alcoa of monopolizing in sixteen markets and entering into conspiracies with foreign producers. Alcoa's horizontal integration into several production facilities and its vertical integration from raw materials, through production of aluminum, to final goods came under attack. Alcoa's influence on the secondary scrap market was questioned, and Alcoa was charged with intimidating competitors out of business. The Justice Department sought divestiture of Alcoa in order to create several competing companies from its assets. At the time, Alcoa was seen clearly as a monopoly, and Mellon—a significant and influential stockholder in Alcoa—epitomized the image of the uncaring capitalist in corporate America.

The antitrust trial itself, which began in June 1938 in the U.S. District Court for the Southern District of New York, lasted an unprecedented two years. In March 1942, the court found Alcoa not guilty of every charge.[5] The court explained that Alcoa's success came from sound business practices and reasonable competitive behavior. The court did not believe Alcoa had an intent to monopolize or had sought to exclude competition.

The government appealed, arguing that monopoly was a social evil that should not be allowed. The appeal went to the second circuit court, as four justices on the Supreme Court excused themselves for having heard cases involving Alcoa previously. In March 1945, Judge Learned Hand wrote the majority opinion, stating that Alcoa had illegally monopolized the ingot market. Hand wrote that what mattered was

whether [Alcoa] falls within the exception established in favor of those who do not seek, but cannot avoid, the control of a market. It seems to us that question scarcely survives its statement. It was not inevitable that it should always anticipate increases in demand for ingot and be prepared to supply them. Nothing compelled it to keep doubling and redoubling its capacity before others entered the field. It insists that it never excluded competitors; but we can think of no more effective exclusion than progressively to embrace every opportunity as it opened, and to face every newcomer with new capacity already geared into a great organization, having the advantage of experience, trade connections and the elite of personnel.[6]

Given the changed environment of the industry between the time of the trial and his final decision, Hand declined to break up the company. Instead, he referred the case back to the district court to apply a remedy.

While the antitrust proceedings were ongoing, a number of changes occurred in the world market. In 1937, military buildups drove aluminum consumption to an all-time high. Alcoa again expanded its production capacity. As World War II continued in 1940, aluminum-demand forecasts by the U.S. government and Alcoa suggested that Alcoa possessed adequate capacity to meet the wartime need. However, in 1941, a shortage of aluminum occurred. Beginning in 1941, the Defense Plant Corporation financed an increase in aluminum production with more than twenty new plants built by Alcoa. By 1943 Alcoa operated an additional eight smelters, eleven fabricating facilities, and four aluminum refineries. U.S. production had grown from 164,000 tons in 1939 to 920,000 tons in 1943, an increase of over 450 percent.[7] Alcoa still produced 93 percent of the country's aluminum ingot.

At the end of the war, the government set up the War Surplus Property Board to dispose of government-owned facilities. In 1945, the government canceled the leases to Alcoa for the additional wartime plants because of weak contract technicalities. As the surplus board allowed purchasing of the newly built plants, Alcoa could only buy one smelter and one small fabricating plant. Other plants were sold to the newly forming integrated producers, Kaiser and Reynolds. This action, in part, served as a remedy for the *Learned Hand* decision and spelled the beginning of true domestic competition.

Summary of the War Years

Once again, fate and government action had intertwined to shape the U.S. aluminum industry. Fate came in the form of World War II, which increased domestic demand and allowed Alcoa to significantly expand its production capacity. However, World War II increased demand so rapidly that two other firms were able to garner enough market share to begin to reach efficient production. Government policy in the form of Learned Hand's antitrust decision and the War Surplus Board strengthened the positions of these two new entrants. In part as a remedy for the *Learned Hand*'s decision, the surplus board created two new integrated domestic aluminum producers.

The rational behind the surplus board's decision is interesting. Their desire in distributing the myriad of wartime aluminum facilities was to create integrated producers as similar in size to Alcoa as possible.[8] Apparently it was felt that such a distribution would create the greatest chance for successful competition. As further showing of government support of the entrants, Kaiser paid just $43.5 million for its government plants that were constructed at a cost of $127 million and had an even greater reproduction cost. Reynolds paid $57.6 million for plants built at a cost of $174 million. Most of these purchases were financed by the government at preferential rates. The government also sold Kaiser and Reynolds surplus aluminum ingot out of its post-war surplus.[9] All of this suggests that non-government-supported entry must have been very difficult in this industry. Extensive support must have been needed to nurture an entrant into a viable competitor. This certainly runs counter to the free market view of long-run competition.

THE LATE 1940s THROUGH 1960

After World War II, Alcoa was no longer a monopolist in the U.S. aluminum market. Its pricing strategy between 1945 and 1958, however, reflected a price-leadership approach. In the recorded price changes during that period, Alcoa lead nine times, Kaiser three, and Reynolds one. The record of pricing over the period also shows that Kaiser and Reynold seldom could lead price changes without Alcoa's consent. Over this period Alcoa set prices relatively low to promote long-term aluminum consumption and to avoid creating an umbrella of high prices under which domestic or foreign firms could enter the market.

Alcoa's power to lead was fostered by several factors. It was clearly the low-cost American producer. It had significant capacity and the ability to increase its sales through import agreements with the Canadian producer. It is also clear that Alcoa preferred a relatively low price. Throughout its history Alcoa priced to stimulate long-term demand. Both Reynolds and Kaiser explicitly stated to various congressional committees and tariff commissions that they felt the market price was too low. For a number of years in the post-war period, the prices of secondary aluminum were above those for primary aluminum, something that would not likely occur if Alcoa were maximizing short-term profits.

In the late 1940s all three American producers expanded their capacities. The invasion of South Korea by Communist forces again made the military a primary buyer of aluminum. Federal policy stimulated capacity increases. The U.S. government supported construction of new capacity through accelerated depreciation plans, financing, and a guarantee to purchase all surplus ingot. Between 1950 and 1955, Alcoa increased its primary capacity from 449,000 tons to 654,000 tons, Kaiser increased from 170,000 to 408,200 tons, and Reynolds from 225,000 to 414,500 tons. Overall the industry increased its capacity by 75 percent.[10] By 1958, Alcoa's, Reynolds' and Kaiser's market shares of smelting capacity were 38, 27, and 24 percent, respectively. The other 11 percent of capacity was owned by two new entrants, Anaconda and Ormet. Both entered under the support of government programs aimed at stimulating production during the Korean War.

During this period the American market was fairly insulated from foreign competition, especially from established Western European producers and newly emerging Eastern European producers. Imports made up no more than 20 percent of domestic consumption. Most imported aluminum was from Canada and generally was sold at domestic market prices that were set by Alcoa.[11]

1960 TO THE PRESENT

By 1960 the aluminum market had largely matured, prices had softened, and margins had narrowed. Alcoa continued to increase capacity, but its market share also continued to decline. In 1963, the price of ingot stabilized, but most producers could not make profits in fabrication. This created new problems for ingot prices. Promotional pricing became a common occurrence, and price wars followed. In 1965, Alcoa attempted to restore price stability, which it managed until 1970. Then, although aluminum was still a growth business, stable prices administered by the North American oligopoly could not be sustained. The price of aluminum became mainly a function of market forces. The number of producers had increased again. The cost of energy, materials, and labor had all greatly increased. And new materials like plastics, ceramics, and composites infringed on the once-secure aluminum market.

By 1980, the number of aluminum producers had greatly increased. Competitive prices made it difficult for producers to remain profitable. Foreign governments subsidized unintegrated producers. These facilities were often poorly managed and technically inferior. In 1980, the world's aluminum capacity was in gross excess, and stable ingot prices could not be maintained by anyone. In 1982, the United States, Japan, Canada, Western Europe, Australia, and New Zealand, Asia, Africa, and Latin America each could produce over 500,000 metric tons of aluminum per year. Continued competition from American producers had changed the market Alcoa faced, but the addition of foreign producers eliminated its dominance.

In 1983, Alcoa embarked on redefining itself. Alcoa began to think of itself as a "materials company" instead of an aluminum producer. The company pursued a new strategy which de-emphasized aluminum ingot and promoted high technology flat-rolled products, such as aerospace applications. The growth of the new high technology product could then finance new growth into new businesses. This new approach focused on research into breakthrough technologies that could decrease Alcoa's dependence on metal. The expenditures on research doubled from $72.8 million in 1980 to $148.2 in 1986. The emphasis shifted from aluminum-related research to advanced materials development. Alcoa began to truly shift from an aluminum-based company to one that sought new materials and innovative applications for them.

CONCLUSION

Alcoa was created as a patent-fostered monopoly. It retained its patent-protected position for eleven years. However, Alcoa remained a monopolist for thirty-six more years and remained a market leader for at least thirteen years after that. It maintained its monopoly position via a number of actions, and with a little luck. It was only an aggressive government policy that led to the creation of two new viable domestic integrated producers.

Alcoa remained dominant for so long in part because of its own efforts to improve its competitive position. The firm continually invested in product and process research and development. This led to cheaper and better production methods, new products and alloys, and better techniques for fabricating goods out of aluminum. Alcoa also strove to become a vertically integrated producer. In securing the raw materials necessary to produce aluminum, it forged agreements with domestic and foreign owners of bauxite to ensure the continuous flow of the necessary material. Alcoa continually pursued new hydroelectric sites to provide inexpensive power. The company always carefully chose sites so their aluminum required less transportation to meet demand.

Alcoa constantly sought new markets for aluminum. The company's research department developed several new products that would utilize aluminum thereby increasing the demand for Alcoa aluminum. Alcoa also monitored demand and forecasted future needs. Then Alcoa expanded its operations to meet the anticipated increase in demand, which it could always meet until World War II. It also recognized the relationships between its integrated stages of production and chose to expand in an efficient manner. If one refinery had a much greater minimum efficient scale than a smelter, Alcoa built multiple smelters to use the output of one refinery.

These same policies made entry difficult for new firms. Alcoa's actions established an absolute cost advantage over potential entrants. Its continual expansion of capacity left little room for a new firm. In addition, the excess capacity generated by entry would surely threaten post-entry price stability. Alcoa's own vertical integration forced potential entrants to enter integrated.

Integration also denied potential entrants access to an alumina market. The requisite need for complex vertical coordination made entry even more difficult.

Alcoa's pricing policy also discouraged entry. Alcoa purposely set its price for aluminum ingot relatively low. This showed potential competitors that although the price a potential entrant may have faced if it entered the aluminum industry would not be the competitive price, it would be much lower than the monopoly price. This relatively low price would have been agreeable to Alcoa as a post-entry equilibrium price.

In dealing with foreign competition, Alcoa actively lobbied to increase the tariffs on foreign producers. Alcoa was only partially successful in this endeavor. At times the tariff fell to little or nothing, which did increase the amount of foreign aluminum sold in the United States. However, imports never counted for more than 20 percent of all aluminum sales in the United States while Alcoa dominated the market. Thus, even when tariff barriers were low, Alcoa continued to dominate.

Alcoa was consistently profitable over its period of dominance. Yet there were only two aborted attempts at entry. One was by the French with foreign financing. Another was by the Dukes as part of an attempt to utilize a large Canadian power project. Clearly Alcoa's actions were effective in thwarting entry. And while it may have been an efficient producer, it also consistently targeted and frequently earned more than a normal profit.

Entry eventually occurred through government intervention. Kaiser and Reynolds were created as two integrated producers, subsidized and supported by the U.S. government. If they had not received such government support, it is unclear whether any new domestic entry would have occurred. Alcoa's dominance may have continued for at least another twenty years, until international producers supported by their own governments may have eventually penetrated the U.S. market.

NOTES

1. See Donald H. Wallace, *Market Control in the Aluminum Industry* (Cambridge, MA: Harvard University Press 1937), p. 226.

2. Margaret B. W. Graham and Bettye H. Pruitt, *R&D for Industry: A Century of Technical Innovation at Alcoa* (Cambridge: Cambridge University Press, 1990), p. 103.

3. George D. Smith, *From Monopoly to Competition: The Transformation of Alcoa, 1888–1986* (Cambridge: Cambridge University Press, 1988), p. 126.

4. Wallace, *Market Control*, pp. 77-78, 115.

5. 44 F. Supp. 97.

6. 148 F2d, 416, 431.

7. Smith, *Monopoly*, p. 223.

8. See Merton J. Peck, *Competition in the Aluminum Industry, 1945–1958* (Cambridge, MA: Harvard University Press, 1961), pp. 12-13. For a detailed description of the Surplus Board's activities, see Harold Stein, *Public Administration and Policy Development* (New

York: Harcourt, 1952), pp. 313-362.
    9. Peck, *Competition*, pp. 18-19.
    10. Ibid., p. 152.
    11. Ibid., p. 19.

5

DOW CHEMICAL AND THE MAGNESIUM INDUSTRY

Marvin B. Lieberman

INTRODUCTION

Magnesium is the lightest metal in commercial use. The Dow Chemical Company has dominated the U.S. magnesium industry since the early twentieth century and continues to be the world's largest magnesium producer despite a decline in market share since the mid–1970s when Dow's strategy shifted markedly. (See Figure 5.1 for Dow's historical share of magnesium production in the United States and worldwide.) Few firms in the metals and chemicals industries have matched Dow's success in maintaining market dominance.

This chapter describes the evolution of the magnesium industry and the methods employed by Dow to acquire and sustain its dominant position.[1] The focus is mainly on the United States, although global competition is also addressed. The first part of the chapter describes how Dow's dominance can be attributed partly to superior manufacturing efficiency and partly to a pattern of sophisticated strategic behavior that was successful in deterring or delaying entry. The second section covers the development of the industry through the early 1960s, when serious attempts at commercial entry began to occur in the U.S. market. The third and fourth sections describe magnesium's end uses and its production technology. Dow exploited various features of magnesium demand and technology to maintain leadership and maximize returns. The fifth section describes the specific attempts at entry, and the deterrence tactics used by Dow, since the 1950s. Dow's behavior is consistent with a wide array of entry-deterring tactics proposed in the theoretical

Figure 5.1
Dow's Share of the Magnesium Market

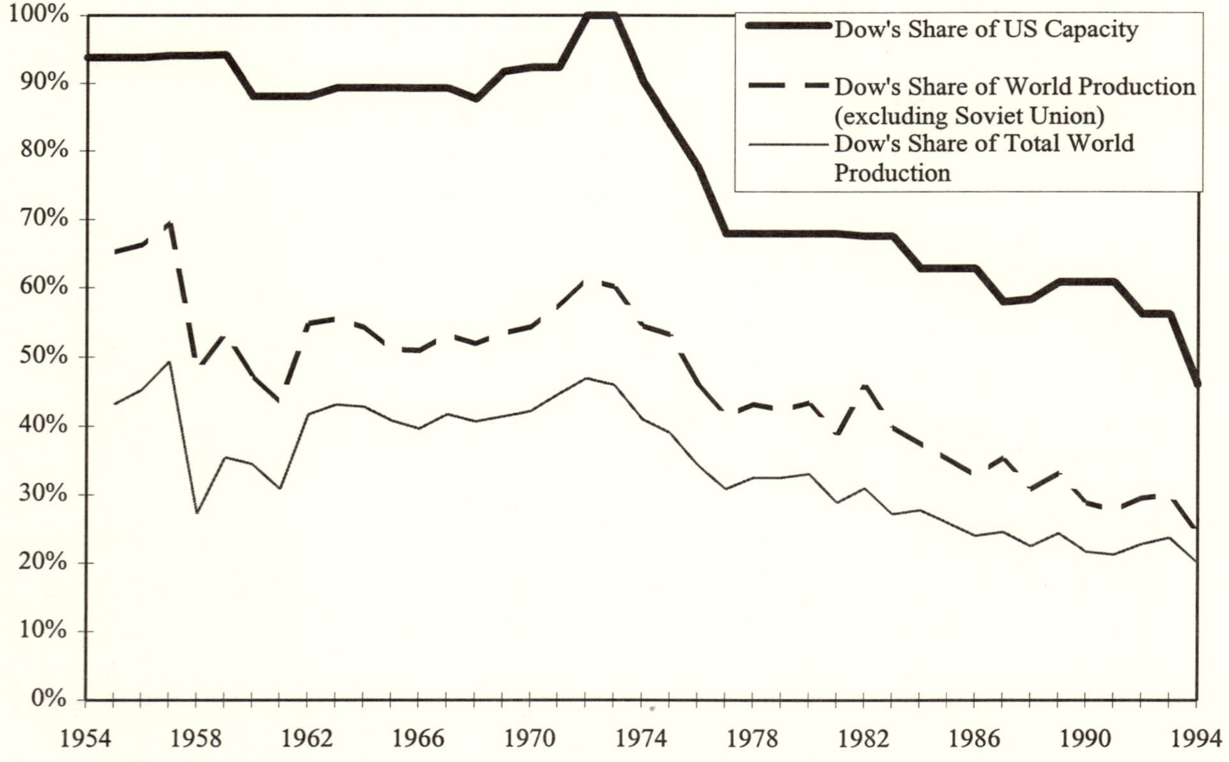

Sources: Minerals Yearbook.

economics literature, including excess capacity, inventory stockpiling, and limit pricing. Dow's implementation of these tactics shifted over time in response to changing market conditions. The final section considers Dow's behavior in the context of these entry-deterrence models.

INDUSTRY HISTORY

Early Developments

Magnesium was discovered by Sir Humphrey Davy in 1808. It was soon found that magnesium powder burned rapidly, giving off a brilliant white light. The primary early use of magnesium was as a pyrotechnic material in bombs and flares.

Magnesium was first produced commercially in the United States in the early 1860s by the American Magnesium Company of Boston, which was forced out of business in the 1880s by the availability of cheaper magnesium produced by the electrolytic process in Germany and imported to the United States. Between 1886 and 1915, German companies accounted for the world's entire magnesium production.

Dow thus became the only U.S. magnesium producer from 1928 until the outbreak of World War II. During this period, Dow worked to establish new applications for magnesium as a lightweight structural metal. During the 1920s, magnesium's principal use was in the manufacture of automotive pistons. By the mid 1920s the aircraft industry began to use magnesium, and by 1940 magnesium had found applications in a variety of machinery parts, portable tools, appliances, and instruments. Nevertheless, commercial usage of magnesium remained much less in the United States than in Europe. Dow made extensive efforts to interest the U.S. government in using magnesium for military aircraft but met with limited success.

World War II Expansion

By 1938, the eve of World War II, the four major magnesium-producing countries were Germany with 12,000 tons-per-year capacity, Britain with 5,000 tons-per-year capacity, the United States (Dow) with 3,300 tons-per-year capacity, and France with 2,500 tons-per-year capacity. During World War II, magnesium-production capacity expanded enormously throughout the world. Germany began adding capacity in 1939, and German capacity reached a peak of 34,000 tons through the expansion of existing facilities. Four magnesium plants were operating in Germany in 1944. In addition, the Germans built new plants in Austria and Norway.

Wartime expansion of magnesium production in the United States started in 1940 when Dow doubled the capacity of the Midland plant. Dow also started construction of a plant in Freeport, Texas. From 1941 to 1943, fifteen new magnesium plants were built in the United States, thirteen by the U.S. government. Dow operated only one of these government-owned plants (at Velasco, Texas) but was heavily involved as a technical consultant in a number of the other start-ups. This great wartime expansion in magnesium-production facilities resulted in a total U.S. capacity of 291,000 tons per year by 1943. Thus, the U.S. production capacity for magnesium increased by a factor of nearly one hundred during the course of the war.

In January 1941, executives of Dow, Alcoa, and I. G. Farben were indicted by the United States Justice Department and charged with monopolizing the market for magnesium. The specific charges included price-fixing and the use of patent cross-licensing agreements to monopolize magnesium production in the United States. In early 1942, the companies pleaded no contest and agreed to a consent decree which called for compulsory patent licensing and the dissolution of prior patent agreements.

Post-War Global Dominance by Dow

After the war, production of magnesium decreased drastically. U.S. production fell from a peak of 184,000 tons in 1943 to 5,300 tons in 1946. Germany was prohibited from producing magnesium; moreover, most of the German magnesium plants were located in what became the Soviet zones of Germany and Austria. After the war the Russians dismantled the plants and took them back to the Soviet Union.

As the war ended, Dow closed its original plant at Midland because of the improved economies of the Freeport, Texas, plant. Resulting from curtailment of magnesium production near the end of the war was the shutdown of five of the government-owned magnesium plants by mid 1944, and all government plants were closed by November 1945. Dow's Freeport plant remained the only plant in the United States producing magnesium in 1946. Post-war U.S. magnesium production rose very modestly from 5,300 tons in 1946 to 15,700 tons in 1950, which was significantly below the 18,000-ton capacity of the Freeport plant.

The Korean War revived magnesium production. Titanium Metal Corporation of America leased part of the government's shuttered Henderson, Nevada, plant in 1950 to produce magnesium for titanium reduction. Dow increased the capacity of its Freeport plant to 24,000 tons per year. Seven government-owned magnesium plants were reactivated and by the end of 1951 were producing at 70 percent of capacity. Overseas, Norsk Hydro Elektrisk (a private company with majority ownership by the Norwegian government) began reconstruction of the German-built plant at Heroya, Norway, at 12,000 tons-per-year capacity in 1950.

After 1953, demand for magnesium again decreased, and by June 30, 1953, all the U.S. government-owned magnesium plants were again shut down except the Velasco plant, operated by Dow, and a plant operated by Nelco Metals, which was awarded a contract to produce high-purity magnesium for the Atomic Energy Commission. In 1958 Alabama Metallurgical Corporation (Alamet) began construction of a new 6,000-ton-per-year plant at Selma, Alabama. Figure 5.2 shows the total U.S. magnesium capacity, production, imports, and exports from 1954 to 1993.

Figure 5.2
U.S. Magnesium Capacity, Production, Exports, Imports and Strategic Stockpile

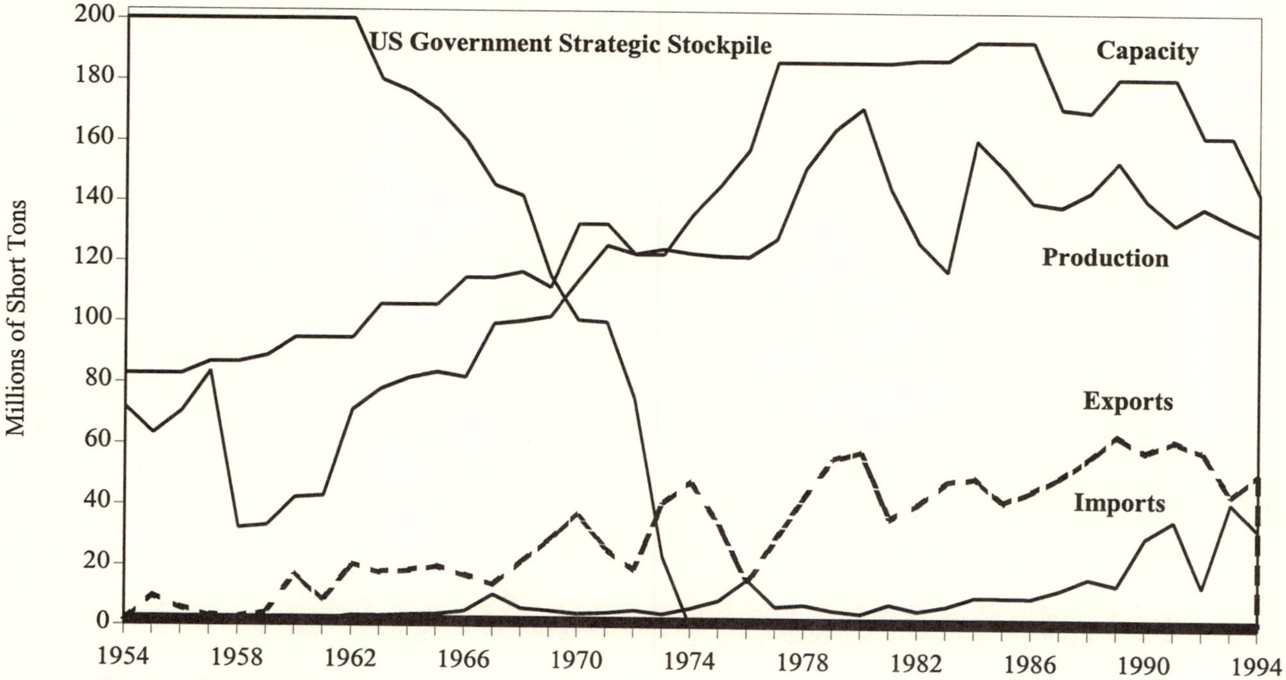

Capacity

US Government Strategic Stockpile

Production

Exports

Imports

Millions of Short Tons

1954 1958 1962 1966 1970 1974 1978 1982 1986 1990 1994

200 180 160 140 120 100 80 60 40 20 0

Source: Minerals Yearbook.

In the early 1960s, Dow Chemical was, by a considerable margin, the world's largest producer of magnesium. It had 91,750 short tons of capacity located in its two Texas plants. Dow obtained magnesium from seawater through using its proprietary electrolytic process. Alamet, the only other U.S. commercial producer of magnesium, had 6,250 tons of capacity, based on a relatively high-cost thermal-reduction process. (See Production Technology in this chapter for a discussion of manufacturing processes.) In addition to these two domestic producers, the U.S. government made periodic sales from its strategic stockpile. In early 1964 the U.S. strategic stockpile contained more than 175,000 tons of magnesium, enough to supply all domestic consumption for more than two years.

Worldwide, the second largest magnesium producer (except for the Soviet Union) was Norsk Hydro of Norway, with 27,000 tons of capacity in 1964. Like Dow, Norsk Hydro utilized an electrolytic-reduction process. Other foreign magnesium producers were significantly smaller. Most of the major industrialized countries had one, or in some cases two, small-scale domestic magnesium producers. Imported magnesium was virtually barred from the U.S. market by a 40 percent import tariff. The main rationale for this high tariff was to maintain domestic production capability in the event of war.

Attracted by magnesium's growth potential and some proposed refinements in production technology, several firms announced their intention to build magnesium plants in the United States in the mid 1960s. The section Entry Deterrence by Dow describes these potential entrants and the entry-deterrence tactics successfully used by Dow.

MAGNESIUM'S APPLICATIONS AND MARKETS

Since World War II, magnesium has been used in numerous applications with widely ranging demand characteristics. Magnesium's uses were commonly grouped into two categories: structural and non-structural. Structural uses include load-carrying applications in the form of cast or wrought products. Non-structural uses exploit magnesium's chemical properties and its use as an alloying element in aluminum and other non-ferrous alloys. Most non-structural applications have inelastic demand, whereas the elasticity of demand in structural applications varies widely. To maximize returns in this environment, Dow practiced extensive price discrimination.

Structural Markets

Magnesium is considered a premium material in applications where light weight is essential. Magnesium's density is 112 pounds per cubic foot, compared with 175 pounds for aluminum and 449 pounds for steel. In the 1960s, magnesium was being used in many aerospace applications and for consumer products such as lawn mowers, chainsaws, stepladders, luggage, and sports equipment. Structural applications accounted for about 40 percent of all magnesium consumed in the United States in the early 1960s.

Virtually all structural applications use magnesium-based alloys rather than pure magnesium. Pure magnesium is a relatively soft metal, but its hardness and other properties can be improved considerably through the addition of small amounts of alloying materials such as aluminum, zinc, and copper. A wide variety of magnesium alloys are used.

In the 1960s magnesium castings were produced by the U.S. auto companies and by a number of independent fabricators. Some observers believed that the automotive market represented a huge but essentially untapped market for magnesium castings. Automobile and truck applications of magnesium were limited by the relatively high price of magnesium and by the reluctance of U.S. automakers to have Dow as their sole supplier.

Demand for magnesium as a structural material was also heavily influenced by the historical experience of downstream fabricators. In West Germany, for example, per-capita magnesium consumption was several times higher than in the United States. This was partly attributable to substantial usage by Volkswagen and more generally was the consequence of Germany's greater experience with magnesium-fabrication techniques. With virtually no domestic supplies of aluminum raw materials and with imports cut off during the war, the Germans had developed considerable familiarity with magnesium as a structural material.

Non-Structural Markets

By far the largest non-structural usage of magnesium was as a constituent in aluminum-based alloys. (Magnesium improves the hardness and corrosion resistance of aluminum.) Continued growth was anticipated as new applications were developed. Aluminum beverage cans, containing about 2 percent magnesium, would ultimately become the largest specific application for magnesium in the United States. Aluminum-based alloys accounted for 42.5 percent of total magnesium consumption in 1963 and were growing as a percent of the total. Aluminum-based alloys were produced in the United States by the aluminum companies, principally, Alcoa, Reynolds, and Kaiser.

The second largest non-structural application of magnesium was as a reducing agent for refining beryllium, zirconium, uranium, and titanium. Magnesium of very high-purity was required for metals reduction. Alamet produced these high-purity grades, which were priced at a premium over standard ingot. High-purity magnesium was difficult to produce using the electrolytic process employed by Dow, and Dow was not a supplier to this market. The high-purity market accounted for 5 to 10 percent of total magnesium demand.

The third largest non-structural use of magnesium was for "cathodic protection," a technique for protecting metals from corrosion. Other non-structural applications of magnesium included use in zinc alloys and chemical applications of various types. Magnesium was also used as a pyrotechnic.

Pricing

Dow's policies and public statements indicated that the company favored price-inelastic applications and sought to charge a premium over substitute materials such as aluminum.[2] Dow was perceived as having reservations about pursuing automotive applications for magnesium, considered to be a huge potential market, but with concentrated, price-sensitive buyers.

Figure 5.3 gives the average U.S. list price for magnesium ingot from 1956 onward. Data on actual transaction prices were not available, but most transactions were believed to take place at, or very close to, the list price. In the early 1960s, Dow held the list price very steady at 35.25¢ per pound. This price was believed to be just marginally above Alamet's average total cost.

Magnesium alloys were priced separately from magnesium ingot. Dow practiced extensive price discrimination, selling some of these alloys below and some above the magnesium ingot price, despite only minor differences in chemical composition. Given the differences in alloying elements, it was generally impossible for buyers to convert one alloy into another.

Dow also practiced price discrimination between United States and foreign markets. The U.S. price of magnesium was significantly above the prices that prevailed in most other industrialized countries, and Dow's exports were normally priced below the U.S. domestic price. For example, sales to Volkswagen in West Germany were believed to be at a price of about 26¢ per pound in the early 1960s, as compared with the U.S. list price of 35.25¢. The 40 percent tariff on imported magnesium blocked arbitrage opportunities to resell these exports to buyers in the United States.

Substitutes

Magnesium's most outstanding property is its low density, making it the lightest metal in wide commercial use. In its structural applications, however, magnesium faced strong competition from substitute materials, especially aluminum. Magnesium is more expensive than most substitutes: for example, in 1964 magnesium cost 49 percent more per pound than aluminum (Figure 5.3).

Magnesium and aluminum are produced by similar methods. In theory, the cost of refining magnesium could be reduced to about one-half the cost of refining aluminum. Maximum theoretical efficiency had never been approached in magnesium production, however, and major technical problems remained to be solved before this would be possible. During World War II the lowest monthly cost of producing magnesium in the most efficient government-owned plant was 11.5¢ per pound, compared with 10.6¢ per pound for aluminum produced in the most efficient plant.[3] Over the two decades following World War II, aluminum production grew at a much more rapid pace than magnesium production in the United States.

Figure 5.3
Magnesium and Aluminum List Prices

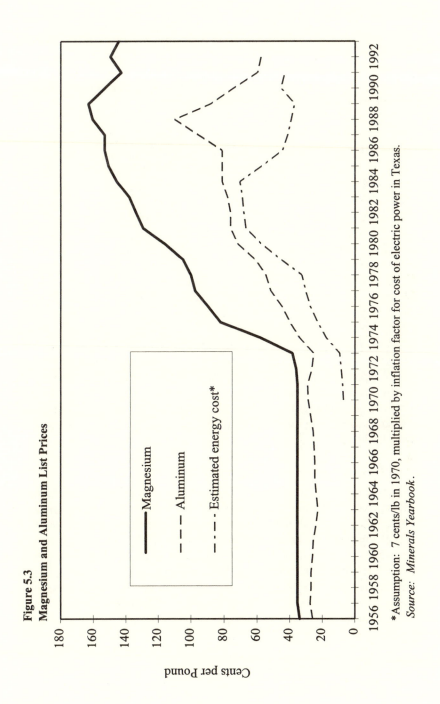

*Assumption: 7 cents/lb in 1970, multiplied by inflation factor for cost of electric power in Texas.
Source: Minerals Yearbook.

PRODUCTION TECHNOLOGY

The two principal methods used to produce magnesium are the electrolytic process and the thermic process. The electrolytic process produces magnesium by applying an electric current through magnesium chloride obtained from underground brine or seawater. The thermic process produces magnesium by heating magnesium oxide obtained from magnesium-bearing ores.

The Electrolytic Process

Dow had developed a proprietary method for magnesium production that differed slightly from the electrolytic method used by other producers. The essential difference was in the amount of water removed from the magnesium chloride before electrolysis. Dow Chemical used partially dehydrated magnesium chloride as an input into the electrolytic cells. All other electrolytic producers used completely dehydrated magnesium chloride. The Dow plants at Freeport and Velasco, Texas, obtained magnesium chloride from seawater.

Dow was known to have made steady improvements in its magnesium electrolysis process, leading to cost reductions as well as incremental expansions in plant capacity. Moreover, the Freeport and Velasco plants were both located within Dow's large integrated chemical complex along the Texas Gulf Coast. Observers noted that this gave Dow access to some low-cost process inputs, and it enabled Dow to make efficient use of production by-products.

Except for Dow, all electrolytic producers of magnesium used technology originally developed by I. G. Farben of Germany. Production costs in an efficiently run I. G. Farben–type plant were judged to be slightly higher than Dow's costs. In general, though, data collected during World War II had shown that operating costs could vary substantially from plant to plant, even for plants of the same basic type.

The Thermic Process

Alamet and most other small-scale magnesium producers utilized the thermic-reduction process. Dolomite, an abundant ore, was heated until magnesium vapor was given off. This magnesium vapor was condensed and cast into ingots.

The thermic process tended to be best suited for small-scale plants located in regions where electric power was not cheap. Compared with electrolytic plants, thermic plants had low capital costs but high operating costs. Operating costs for the thermic plant owned by Alamet were estimated by industry observers at close to 30¢ per pound in the early 1960s. Total average cost per pound for an efficiently run thermic plant was about 35¢, identical to Dow's list price for magnesium ingot.

ENTRY DETERRENCE BY DOW

Dow's post–World War II strategy can be divided into two phases. From the late 1950s through 1973, Dow used a sophisticated strategy of excess capacity and limit pricing to deter entry. Several firms attempted to enter the industry during this period but ultimately canceled their plans or failed. By 1973, the eve of the first Organization of Petroleum Exporting Countries energy price shock, Dow was again the sole magnesium producer in the United States. Dow's strategy changed abruptly during the subsequent global materials shortage, when magnesium supplies were tight and Dow's margin of excess capacity disappeared. Magnesium prices rose steadily from 38.25¢ per pound in 1973 to $1.34 in 1981, ultimately reaching a peak of $1.63 in 1989 (Figure 5.3). These dramatic price increases were motivated, in part, by a rise in the cost of energy and other inputs, but they also reflect Dow's abandonment of limit pricing in favor of a skim-pricing type of strategy. Largely as a result, Dow's market share has eroded since the mid 1970s (Figure 5.1).

The first part of this section describes Dow's entry-deterrence tactics from the 1950s through 1973. The second part describes the subsequent shift in Dow's behavior and the firm's gradual decline in market share. The next section, Dow's Behavior in the Context of Entry-Deterrence Literature, provides a more detailed discussion of this evidence in the context of the economic literature on entry deterrence.

Entry Threats and Deterrence by Dow: 1957–1973

Inventory Stockpiling as a Strategic Weapon: Auction of Velasco Plant. The Velasco, Texas, magnesium plant was built by Dow for the U.S. government in 1942. Velasco proved to be the most efficient of the twelve magnesium plants built by the government during World War II. Its lowest monthly operating cost was 11.5¢ per pound, well below that of the other government plants, which ranged from 16.3 to 57.3¢ per pound.[4] Velasco's capacity, initially 36,000 tons per year, was expanded to 45,000 tons by the mid 1950s, making it the largest economically viable magnesium facility in the world. Dow operated the plant under government lease until 1957, when it was put up for public auction.

Prior to the auction, Dow operated the Velasco facility and the company's Freeport plant at full capacity to build up a magnesium stockpile. On the eve of the auction, Dow's magnesium stockpile was estimated to exceed 60,000 tons, or about 1.5 times annual U.S. consumption. When the Velasco auction took place, Dow was the sole bidder and purchased the plant for $20.7 million, considerably less than the government's total investment cost of $56.4 million.[5] After buying the plant, Dow closed the Velasco facility for four years, choosing to meet the firm's supply commitments by drawing down the accumulated stockpile.

In addition to its own private stockpile, Dow had to consider the presence of the "strategic stockpile" of magnesium held by the U.S. government as a safeguard against future wartime requirements. The government's magnesium stockpile stood at over 206,000 tons in the late 1950s, roughly twice the authorized target level. The large government holdings put pricing pressure on Dow, because any price increases could be immediately countered by the government's release of excess inventories. This fact, and the government's view of magnesium as a strategic defense material, gave Dow impetus for stable pricing in the United States (albeit at a higher level than that prevailing abroad).

Automotive Company Efforts to Encourage Entry. Automotive applications were considered to be a huge but price-elastic potential market for magnesium.[6] Moreover, the U.S. auto companies were powerful buyers whose bargaining power was typically enhanced by the existence of multiple suppliers for vehicle components and materials. It was known that the Big-Three automakers had occasionally tried to encourage the entry of a new domestic magnesium producer. In late 1961, for example, General Motors (GM) approached Norsk Hydro of Norway, offering to purchase at least 50 percent of the output of a new U.S. magnesium plant if such a plant were built by Norsk Hydro. Norsk Hydro agreed to perform a feasibility study and selected a U.S. partner. However, GM objected to some details of the arrangement, and Norsk Hydro chose to back out of the venture.

Historically, automobile and truck applications of magnesium were limited by the metal's relatively high cost and by the problems inherent in having a sole supplier. Automobile manufacturers expressed some frustration regarding their dealings with Dow. As one executive put it, "Chrysler has maintained a periodic interest in magnesium castings. During these periods, a variety of car parts have been released as magnesium castings. Each time we were assured that adequate sources were available to produce the parts in magnesium at a satisfactory price. Each time we were led down the proverbial 'primrose path.'"

Entry Announcements by National Lead, Kaiser Aluminum, Harvey Aluminum. Given the promise of magnesium for automotive and other applications, and some new refinements in production technology suggested in the technical literature, several companies announced their intentions to enter into magnesium production in the 1960s:

- The Harvey Aluminum Company announced in November 1963 that it would build a 20,000 ton-per-year primary magnesium plant in Port Angeles, Washington, using seawater as the primary raw material.
- Standard Magnesium and Chemical Corporation, a magnesium recycler and fabricator, announced in late 1963 that it would construct an 11,500 ton-per-year primary magnesium plant in Vancouver, Washington. Magnesium chloride brine obtained as a by-product from the company's solar evaporation potash operation in Utah would be used as a raw material source. In February 1964, Standard was acquired by Kaiser Aluminum, which had previously indicated an interest in becoming a primary magnesium producer.
- The National Lead Company (NL) announced in early 1964 that it had entered into an agreement with a privately held Utah concern covering a joint development effort for the production of magnesium from the brines of the Great Salt Lake.
- Although it had not announced specific plans to re-enter the magnesium industry, Alcoa was widely considered as a possible entrant. Alcoa was the world's largest consumer of magnesium and had been an important producer prior to World War II.

Dow responded to these entry threats with a variety of tactics:

Selective price cuts. In mid 1964 Dow announced a "price-incentive program" for magnesium sales to the aluminum-alloying industry. The price of magnesium sold to qualified buyers would be reduced by 1¢ per pound in 1964, 1965, and 1966, and .5¢ per pound for the succeeding four years, reaching 30.25¢ per pound by 1970. To qualify for this discount, buyers had to use magnesium for aluminum-alloying purposes and had to purchase at least 50 percent of their total consumption from Dow. In 1967, Dow announced a similar program for AZ91B, the most popular die-casting alloy.

Announcements of excess capacity and cost reductions. In February 1965, Dow announced incremental capacity expansions obtained via improvements in electrolytic cells, raising the Velasco plant capacity from 55,000 to 60,000 tons per year and the Freeport plant capacity from 37,000 to 40,000 tons.[7] Later that year Dow unveiled additional capacity increases, obtained through further efficiency improvements, that would raise total company capacity from 100,000 to 120,000 tons per year by the end of 1966. Dow indicated that these expansions were not needed to meet immediate demand. In November 1966, Dow reported that it was reactivating one-half of the 50,000 tons of capacity at its Freeport plant that had been idle since 1957.[8] Further, Dow stated that its total capacity would equal 150,000 tons per year if all magnesium facilities were modernized and activated.[9] (Dow's excess capacity in the 1960s is shown in Figure 5.2.)

Announcement of new plants and technology. In November 1965, Dow announced that it had acquired mineral leases at the Great Salt Lake. In March 1966, Dow released information that it was considering a new plant based on magnesium brines obtained from the lake: "if the company does build, it will use new and undisclosed technology."[10] In 1967 Dow announced that this plant, with 25,000 annual tons of capacity, would be located in the Pacific Northwest. Dow completed about 15 percent of this plant by 1970 but then put construction on hold. (The plant was ultimately converted to other applications.)

These deterrence tactics by Dow (and technical problems encountered by two firms that persisted with entry plans) forestalled large-scale entry into the U.S. magnesium industry. Harvey Aluminum and Kaiser Aluminum decided not to enter, and Alcoa indicated (May 1969) that the company "hopes to go into magnesium to a greater degree someday, but has no specific plans for the present."[11] National Lead encountered a series of unforeseen problems in attempting to operate at the Great Salt Lake, which delayed the start of commercial operations until the mid 1970s.[12] An additional company, American Magnesium, opened a small magnesium plant utilizing underground brines in 1970 but soon shut down to recover from a fire and to comply with an anti-pollution order. Also, the small existing plants of Alamet and Nelco Metals closed in the late 1960s. Thus, in the early 1970s Dow again found itself as the sole producer of magnesium in the United States.

Dow's Abandonment of Limit-Pricing Strategy

Soon after Dow's return to a monopoly position in the U.S. market, the magnesium industry began to change dramatically. In 1970 magnesium was removed from the government's list of strategic materials, and the strategic stockpile was sold off. Much of the stockpile was purchased by Dow and exported from the United States. Dow ended its "magnesium price incentive program" in 1971, raising the price paid by the aluminum companies from 30.25¢ to 36.25¢ per pound. Shortly thereafter, a program of economy-wide wage and price controls was imposed by the U.S. government. At the same time the tariff on imported magnesium was reduced from 40 percent to 20 percent (and ultimately to 8 percent in the mid-1980s as the result of Tokyo Round negotiations). By 1972, steady growth in demand had eliminated Dow's excess production capacity (Figure 5.2). Dow significantly reduced its research and development (R&D) on magnesium applications by selling its magnesium research library to Battelle Laboratories and transferring key technical people to other parts of Dow. Responding to these developments, Alcoa announced in January 1973 that a new subsidiary, Northwest Alloys, would begin construction of a plant at Addy, Washington, to produce 40,000 tons per year of magnesium.

In 1974, the U.S. government lifted the general economic price freeze which could no longer be enforced in the wake of the OPEC oil price shock. Dow responded by doubling the price of magnesium ingot from 41¢ per pound in early 1974 to 82¢ by 1975. Further increases brought the U.S. price to a peak of $1.63 per pound in 1989.

As entry occurred, Dow's share declined. Alcoa opened its plant in 1976. National Lead sold its technologically troubled plant to a new owner who made the facility operational. Norsk Hydro, the world's second largest magnesium producer, built a large plant in Canada in the late 1980s. With U.S. tariffs now relatively low, the market for magnesium had essentially become global. Dow nevertheless remained the world's largest magnesium producer.

The disintegration of the Soviet Union in the early 1990s led to an intensification of competition in the world magnesium market. Magnesium plants in the former Soviet states of Russia, Ukraine, and Kazakhstan turned to exports as means of generating hard currency. This created pressure for reductions in magnesium prices. Dow responded by seeking import restrictions from the U.S. government. Meanwhile, Norsk Hydro, with large-scale magnesium plants in Canada and Norway, was approaching Dow's capacity and was believed to have attained production economies comparable to Dow's. Thus, by the 1990s, Dow's position of dominance in the world magnesium industry had eroded considerably.

DOW'S BEHAVIOR IN THE CONTEXT OF THE ENTRY-DETERRENCE LITERATURE

Dow's behavior from the late 1950s through the 1970s is consistent with the predictions of several models of entry deterrence in the economic literature. Dow's array of tactics, and their apparent effectiveness in maintaining the firm's dominance, gives insights into the ways that strategic behaviors modeled by economists may be implemented in practice. Nevertheless, comparison with other chemicals and metals industries suggests that magnesium should be viewed as an extreme case.[13]

In the 1960s, Dow executives must have recognized that potential entry posed a major threat to their magnesium business. New entry would have greatly diminished Dow's ability to practice price discrimination. Moreover, many of the announced entrants were eager to pursue price reductions to encourage the development of price-elastic applications, principally in the automotive market. Existing fringe producers such as Alamet were not a threat, but large-scale, technologically sophisticated entrants such as the aluminum companies had the potential to move down the learning curve and ultimately match Dow's costs. Dow, however, was in a strong position based on its enormous accumulated expertise in magnesium technology and, ultimately, its control of the most efficient manufacturing plant constructed during World War II.

Inventory Holding as a Strategic Weapon

Ware (1985) gives a variation on the standard excess-capacity deterrence argument (see below). In Ware's model, an inventory stockpile replaces production capacity as the mechanism by which the incumbent can credibly threaten to expand post-entry output, thereby making the entrant unprofitable. The episode of the Velasco plant auction in the late 1950s provides a compelling example of such behavior.

The evidence here is anecdotal, and hence the exact role of Dow's inventory stockpile in deterring other bidders for the Velasco plant cannot be precisely determined. Undoubtedly, potential entrants were also influenced by the fact that the Velasco magnesium plant was contiguous with other Dow facilities from which it obtained process inputs. Thus, an independent owner of the Velasco plant would have been forced to deal closely with Dow on an ongoing basis. Dow's inventory stockpile signaled not only of Dow's ability to expand output for some period following entry, but also the possibility of other forms of aggressive behavior (consistent with Dow's established reputation) that might be encountered by the entrant.

Excess Capacity as an Entry Deterrent

Many theoretical studies have presented models of excess production capacity as a deterrent to entry.[14] The basic argument is that excess capacity enables incumbents to threaten to expand output and cut prices following entry, thereby making entry unprofitable.

At first glance, the magnesium industry seems a compelling example of the use and possible effectiveness of excess capacity as a deterrent. Dow's statements regarding excess capacity feature prominently in the arsenal of tactics unleashed in response to the entry announcements of the mid-1960s. What is unusual about this case (and hence where it departs from the theoretical models) is that the capacity was not initially constructed by the incumbent. Rather, Dow exploited excess capacity built by the U.S. government during World War II. Thus, there is no evidence that Dow would have built excess capacity if forced to pay the full investment cost.[15] Indeed, once demand grew to the point where the Velasco plant was fully utilized, Dow chose not to expand any further. Dow has never built any additional plants for magnesium.

Limit Pricing

Various models of limit pricing have been proposed in the economics literature. These include the control-theoretic Gaskins (1971) formulation and more recent game-theoretic approaches (e.g., Milgrom and Roberts, 1982). The magnesium industry offers insights for both model types.

Depending on parameter values, the Gaskins model ranges between two alternative strategies for optimizing the dominant firm's profit: (1) a strategy of low but stable limit pricing, designed to sacrifice short-term profits in favor of long-term gains by minimizing the rate of entry, and (2) a skim-price strategy, where price is initially above the limit price but falls below as the fringe of entrants expands. Choice between the two depends largely on the speed of entry in response to the current market price. An interesting feature of the magnesium case is that Dow seems to have switched from the first strategy to the second as industry conditions changed. During the 1950s and 1960s, Dow kept the price of magnesium very steady at a level that was equal to or slightly below the cost of small-scale entrants. Then, when conditions shifted in the 1970s, Dow pursued dramatic price increases.

A major criticism of the Gaskins model is that it depends heavily on the assumed response of entrants to the incumbent's current price, whereas rational entrants would not be so myopic. In the case of magnesium, however, the Gaskins response function seems not too unreasonable, given the existence of the government's strategic stockpile. Price increases by Dow would likely have been met by an expansion in government sales. Moreover, some of the mothballed government plants could have been reactivated fairly quickly if price hikes were substantial enough. Thus, the likely behavior of the competitive fringe in the magnesium industry of the late 1950s and 1960s was reasonably consistent with the response function assumed in the Gaskins model.

Dow's shift in pricing strategy during the 1970s also seems to fit Gaskins' model. With the government's stockpile eliminated, the fringe supply function was diminished. Alcoa had announced its intention to enter, but construction of a plant would take several years. With Dow's capacity fully utilized amid a global capacity shortage, Dow chose to emphasize short-term profits at the expense of greater entry. The entry response proved surprisingly moderate, however, and Dow raised prices further.

The more recent game-theoretic models of limit pricing treat entrants as strategic players who recognize that the incumbent can quickly change its price.[16] Thus, the current price may differ from the post-entry price that affects the entrant's profit. The current price does, however, provide a signal about the incumbent's cost and hence its likely response to entry. Dow's steady list price for magnesium ingot may have provided such information to potential entrants. Further information may have been inferred from the "incentive program" of gradual price reductions offered to aluminum producers. One effect of this program was to selectively deter the aluminum companies by reducing their likely gains from backward integration into magnesium. The prices announced in this program also provided a signal about Dow's likely costs. Moreover, Dow made repeated announcements of incremental efficiency improvements, and it divulged the basic nature of these improvements to the trade press. Given such information, and the evidence from World War II regarding Dow's efficiency relative to other plants, most potential entrants may have concluded that the risk on the cost side was too great to justify entry.

Dow's price-incentive program was more sophisticated than the limit-price policies considered in the theoretical economics literature. The details of this unusual program were cleverly designed to deter a targeted set of entrants with minimal loss of revenue to Dow. Dow could have made the price cuts immediately but chose instead to commit to a schedule of time-phased reductions. By doing so, Dow minimized its revenue loss while still sending a credible signal on its likely production costs. Given the gestation lag of at least two years for an entrant's plant to be completed, there was no need for Dow to make the entire price cut at once. An announcement of price reductions to be implemented several years in the future would not have been credible, but Dow's public commitment to time-phased reductions was.

Dow's price-incentive program was explicit price discrimination favoring the aluminum companies, which constituted about one-third of Dow's total sales. Dow was concerned about the aluminum companies as entrants, as their high-consumption volume and substantial technical capabilities might have enabled them to emerge as efficient, large-scale producers. The 50 percent purchase requirement for participation in the program precluded the aluminum companies from obtaining the discount if they built their own magnesium plant, as the output of an efficient-scale plant exceeded 50 percent of any firm's needs. Ultimately, Alcoa chose to build its own magnesium plant but seems to have viewed this as a defensive, backward integration move, limiting the plant's capacity to cover little more than Alcoa's own alloying requirements. Alcoa utilized a proven manufacturing technology (licensed from the French) that had a low risk of failure but with a relatively high cost.

Efficiency Explanations

The evidence presented above suggests that Dow's tactics of excess capacity and limit pricing were effective in deterring entry. Yet an alternative explanation is that Dow was simply exercising its technological superiority, derived in part from its huge lead in cumulative production experience. Models of industry evolution with proprietary learning suggest that only a very small number of firms may be viable.[17] If the learning curve is steep and one firm develops a very large head start, few firms can coexist, and market shares may be highly skewed. This bears some resemblance to the market structure for magnesium.

It is impossible and probably not meaningful to gauge the amount of deterrence stemming from Dow's excess-capacity and limit-pricing policies, as opposed to the firm's cost advantage. The three factors worked together, augmenting the impact that each would have had separately. Dow's pricing strategy reinforced the perception of cost advantage inferred from the data made public following World War II. Similarly, Dow's excess capacity would have been unlikely to deter entry without recognition that this capacity could be mobilized at low cost. And Dow's cost advantage for existing output would have had little deterrent effect without Dow's ability to expand cheaply by improving and reactivating idle sections of its Texas plants. Indeed, once the excess capacity at these plants was exhausted, Dow's behavior shifted dramatically.

Concluding Caveats

The history of the magnesium industry provides rich examples of strategic behavior by a dominant firm. Nevertheless, one must be guarded about drawing generalizations, given the unusual features of the industry and the government's role. Dow's tactics seem consistent with the several deterrence models described above. But Dow's behavior would likely have been very different in the absence of excess capacity built at government expense, and the government's strategic stockpile. These structural features of the magnesium industry are unusual, and their joint influence may well be unique, despite some similarity to other defense-oriented materials (such as aluminum, discussed in Chapter 4 of this volume) during the period following World War II.

NOTES

1. For additional detail on the magnesium industry and Dow's strategic behavior, see G. B. Kenney, *An Analysis of the Energy Efficiency and Economic Viability of Expanded Magnesium Utilization* (New York: Garland, 1979), and M. B. Lieberman, "The U.S. Magnesium Industry (A), (B), and (C)," Stanford University, Graduate School of Business, Case S-BP-231 (1983).

2. In his address to the 1963 World Magnesium Congress, J. D. Hanawalt, Dow's head of magnesium operations, stated that "in practically all of its structural markets, magnesium must compete directly with aluminum. Magnesium is only used in those cases in which a careful quantitative analysis has shown that it is cheaper or is worth the premium price for the weight saved. . . . Successful growth in the magnesium industry in both the non-

structural and structural fields will depend upon more concentration on magnesium's special and unique features."

3. H. A. Klagsbrunn, "Wartime Aluminum and Magnesium Production," *Industrial and Engineering Chemistry* 37 (1945): 608-617.

4. Klagsbrunn, "Wartime."

5. Queried about possible antitrust aspects of the sale to Dow, the General Services Administration (GSA) had stated that "In connection with the sale of the Velasco plant to Dow, GSA solicited the advice of the Department of Justice and the Department of Defense. On the basis of the advice received, it was determined to be in the public interest to sell the plant."

6. See, for example, Kenney, *Magnesium Utilization.*

7. "Magnesium Use in U.S. Seen Rising 4 Percent to 77,500 Tons in 1965," *Oil, Paint and Drug Reporter*, 22 February 1965.

8. "Dow Ready to Boost Magnesium Capacity," *Oil, Paint and Drug Reporter*, 7 November 1966.

9. "Process Changes Boost Magnesium Capacity," *Chemical and Engineering News*, 14 August 1967, pp. 54-56.

10. "Major Exploitation of Great Salt Lake Chemicals Seems to Be in the Works," *Chemical Engineering*, 14 March 1966, p. 103.

11. *Chemical Week*, 17 May 1969, p. 38.

12. For example, a causeway built by the Southern Pacific Railway cut the concentration of magnesium salts in the vicinity of the plant by more than 50 percent.

13. See Lieberman, "Magnesium Industry."

14. See, for example, A. M. Spence, "Entry, Capacity, Investment and Oligopolistic Pricing," *Bell Journal of Economics* 8 (1977): 49-70; A. Dixit, "The Role of Investment in Entry-Deterrence," *Economic Journal* 90 (1980): 95-106; J. Bulow, J. Geanakoplos, and P. Klemperer, "Holding Idle Capacity to Deter Entry," *Economic Journal* 95 (1985): 178-182.

15. Empirical studies based on larger samples of industries suggest that entry rates are sensitive to the existence of excess capacity, but such capacity is seldom constructed for the purpose of deterring entry. See, for example, W. I. Kirman and R. T. Masson, "Capacity Signals and Entry Deterrence," *International Journal of Industrial Organization* 4 (1986): 25-44; and M. B. Lieberman, "Excess Capacity as a Barrier to Entry: An Empirical Appraisal," *Journal of Industrial Economics* 35 (1987): 607-627.

16. See, for example, P. Igrom and D. J. Roberts, "Predation, Reputation, and Entry Deterrence," *Journal of Economic Theory* 27(2) (1982): 280-312; and J. E. Harrington, "Limit Pricing When the Potential Entrant Is Uncertain of Its Cost Function," *Econometrica* 54(2) (1986): 429-438.

17. For such models, see A. M. Spence, "The Learning Curve and Competition," *Bell Journal of Economics* 12(1) (1981): 49-70; and M. B. Lieberman, "The Learing Curve, Diffusion, and Competitive Strategy," *Strategic Management Journal* 8 (1987): 280-312. With the exception of World War II, when Dow served as technical consultant to the government, Dow has kept its magnesium production technology highly proprietary. Dow has a reputation as the most secretive of the major U.S. chemical producers, with a general policy of refusing to grant technology licenses. See P. Spitz, *Petrochemicals: The Rise of an Industry* (New York: Wiley, 1987), p. 547.

6

EASTMAN KODAK IN THE PHOTOGRAPHIC FILM INDUSTRY: PICTURE IMPERFECT?

Vrinda Kadiyali

INTRODUCTION

Eastman Kodak, or the "Big Yellow Father," is a giant in the photographic film industry. A recent survey by Total Research Corporation found that Kodak was number 1 in its overall brand quality survey, beating icons like Disney and Mercedes-Benz, proving that consumers believe strongly in Kodak quality. However, the history of Kodak in the U.S. photographic film industry has not always been one of unparalleled success. Kodak has gone from being a near monopoly in film (and other related markets of photofinishing and cameras) until around 1978, to being besieged on various fronts by the late 1980s, and in the 1990s it seems to be undergoing serious corporate plastic surgery. How did Kodak achieve dominance in film and related industries? How did it lose this dominance? Or did it lose it at all? Is there a comeback story waiting to be told?

Any analysis of Kodak has to begin with the analysis of the amateur photography industry. This industry is one with many component industries within it. For example, the industry encompasses the cameras, film, print paper, developing chemicals, and developing machinery industries, among others. As Brock (1981) argues, the economic and technical dependencies in this industry make the functional location of the film industry very critical. "Functionally viewed, . . . film is at the heart of the industry. For in traveling through a sequence of successive stages (from raw exposed film, to exposed but unprocessed film, to finished photograph) . . . , film binds the industry's markets together. . . . A host of compatibility requirements is established as film percolates through the industry . . . affecting the design of equipment, photofinishing services, and the chemicals, paper, and equipment required to process and print film. In short, the industry is functionally organized around the manufacture, exposure, processing, and printing of film."[1]

This chapter discusses the rise of Kodak in the photographic film and related industries. Competition between Kodak and its rivals has comprised various battles, for example, price wars, advertising blitzes, compatibility requirements between film and cameras, huge research and development (R&D) budgets, legal battles, and so on. This chapter is a study of these competitive contests, starting from 1881 when George Eastman established Eastman Kodak's corporate predecessor. Next, we explore how Kodak achieved dominance, and the reasons for this dominance. This is followed by a description of Kodak's woes in the 1980s and early 1990s, and how and why it lost market power. The chapter ends with the story of Kodak's current corporate make-over strategy.

THE INDUSTRY: EARLY HISTORY

The year 1839 marked the official start of the U.S. photographic industry when the French daguerreotype was introduced. This process imprinted an image on a silver-coated copper sheet. However, this plate could be used only when it was coated with wet chemicals. The entire contraption required to do this, including a camera to take the pictures, was as big as a microwave oven! Eastman read in British magazines of a gelatin emulsion that continued to be light-sensitive even after they were dry, and could, therefore, be exposed at leisure. In 1880, after three years of photographic experiments, Eastman used a formula from one of these British journals to develop a "dry plate," where a chemical mixture was coated on a glass plate, to be exposed at a later time. This dry plate could be purchased by the photographer, who did not then have to make it on the spot just before taking a photograph. This turned out be a landmark event in the history of photography.

By 1880, Eastman had also invented and patented a machine for preparing a large number of plates. Eastman continued to experiment with the use of a lighter and more flexible support than glass. The next major event in this industry was in 1884 when the glass plate could be replaced by paper or celluloid, marking the beginning of the roll film. The roll film was small enough to fit into smaller, more portable cameras. These innovations greatly expanded the demand for photography. At this time, Eastman Dry Plate Company was renamed the Eastman Dry Plate and Film Company.

The history of the expansion of the industry from then on is closely tied to the history of the expansion of Kodak. In 1885, the Eastman American film was introduced, the first transparent film negative as we know it today. In 1888, Eastman coined the name "Kodak," and the Kodak camera was introduced, with the slogan "You press the button—we do the rest." In 1891, the first daylight-loading camera was introduced, which meant that photographers no longer needed to be in a dark room in order to reload their cameras. Following that, in 1895, the Pocket Kodak camera was introduced; in 1900, the first of the famous Brownie cameras was introduced. In 1902, the Kodak developing machine simplified the processing of roll film and made it possible to develop film without a darkroom. In 1921, Kodak made amateur motion pictures practical with the introduction of 16-millimeter reversal film, and the introduction of the color version of this in 1928 proved to be a major hit. Over the next few years, Kodak introduced several more types of film (motion and snapshot, rolls and slides, etc.), and cameras, and made several advances in photofinishing as well.

The strides made by Kodak in those decades and even later were matched by giant strides in the volume of business in the photographic film industry. The *Wolfman Report* (various issues) states the growth of the imaging industry was 38 percent from 1955 to 1960 (when gross national product [GNP] growth was 26.6 percent), 86.7 percent from 1960 to 1965 (36 percent in GNP), 68.9 percent from 1965 to 1970 (42.7 percent in GNP), and so on.[2] The growth in the imaging industry meant growth in all of Kodak's markets: film, cameras, photoprocessing chemicals and equipment, and other related businesses, such as projectors and other viewing devices, photocopiers, and so on.

KODAK: DOMINANCE IN A "MOSAIC OF CONNECTED MARKETS"

In 1979, "To millions of Americans, the name Kodak is virtually synonymous with photography. . . . It provides products and services covering every step in the creation of an enduring photographic record from an evanescent image. Snapshots may be taken with a Kodak camera on Kodak film, developed by Kodak's Color Print and Processing Laboratories, and printed on Kodak photographic paper. The firm has rivals at each stage of this process, but in many of them it stands, and has long stood, dominant."[3] "No company dominated a major consumer product market more thoroughly than Eastman Kodak."[4] Kodak's motto, "You press the button—we do the rest," summed up the reach of the company. It had market power in cameras, film, and film processing, that is, in all the three stages of the photographic film industry.

Estimates suggest that Kodak controlled 90 percent of the amateur film trade in 1904; in 1915 its share was 88 percent. In 1932, *Fortune* estimated the Kodak film market share to be 84 percent. Table 6.1 shows that through 1976 Kodak's monopoly in film was uncontested. Over the period 1958 to 1976, Kodak's market share averaged 68 percent in the snapshot market, 86 percent in the film market, and 89 percent in the color photographic paper market.[5]

Given that the industry is "a mosaic of interconnected markets," we will analyze the factors contributing to Kodak's success in each of these three markets. As the film market was at the functional center of this mosaic, we will examine that market in greater detail. This section will focus on the time period prior to 1980, that is, before the threat of Fuji became important. The strategies that we will discuss are quality control, distribution, advertising, R&D, cost strategies, systems

Table 6.1
Kodak Market Shares as Percentages of Units Sold in Market

Year	Film Rolls	Cameras	Color Paper
1955	84	67	n.a.
1956	84	71	n.a.
1957	85	66	n.a
1958	86	67	85
1959	86	69	95
1960	86	72	95
1961	83	65	97
1962	82	61	99
1963	82	65	94
1964	82	71	97
1965	85	80	95
1966	88	74	98
1967	91	71	98
1968	90	72	94
1969	89	73	91
1970	87	65	91
1971	88	70	89
1972	87	69	86
1973	87	74	85
1974	87	67	76
1975	86	63	67
1976	86	53	60

Source: *Berkey Photo Inc. v Eastman Kodak Company*   (1979). 603 F2d.

selling, planned obsolescence of products, pricing of photofinishing products to rivals, and patents used as entry barriers.

Kodak was the first film company to manufacture consistently high-quality film that amateurs could use. In the early years of the company, it faced total collapse at least once when dry plates in the hands of the dealers went bad. Eastman recalled and replaced them. He said, "Making good on those plates took our last dollar. But what we had left was more important—reputation."[6] This commitment to quality has never weakened. As Eastman said, "To make good goods requires experience and is a slow matter . . . but when we get there, we get there to stay." Kodak films and other products were (and are) produced to demanding standards, so that these products performed consistently when purchased anywhere in the world. As his young company grew because of its reputation for quality, George Eastman himself monitored quality starting from his R&D laboratories through the manufacturing process. The attention to quality proved to be highly profitable, and provided the resources to tide over the difficult decades of 1890s and 1900s when several small firms in the industry went bankrupt.

A critical component of the strategy to popularize the amateur uses of film was Kodak's distribution strategy. Rather than only sell the products in photographic supplies stores, Kodak chose to distribute its products through what were then non-traditional outlets such drug stores and department and hardware stores.[7] Here, its initial advantage over rivals was its dry plate relative to the rival wet plate technology, and later, its roll film over rival plate technology. By the time rivals caught up on Kodak's technical expertise, Kodak had already established a wide distribution network (and had lower costs, as we will soon discuss).

Eastman also recognized the importance of overseas distribution very early in the company's history. European interest in photography was strong, and early developments in photography (including the wet plate) had taken place there. Therefore, only five years after the company was established in the United States, it opened a sales office in London. In 1889, the Eastman Photographic Materials Company, Limited, was incorporated in London, England, to handle overseas distribution. Soon after that, in 1891, the first overseas plant was set up in Harrow, England, because the domestic capacity had become inadequate to service overseas demand. These two developments marked the beginning of an explosion of international production and networks for distribution.

Almost from the very beginning of Kodak's history, advertising has been a key competitive strategy. The very first Kodak products were advertised in leading papers and periodicals of the day, with ads written by Eastman himself. He coined the "You push the button—we do the rest" slogan when he introduced the Kodak camera in 1888, a phrase that was hugely popular within a year of its introduction. In an act of marketing genius, the word "Kodak" itself was coined by Eastman. He said, "The letter 'K' has always been a favorite with me—it seems a strong, incisive sort of letter. It became a question of trying out a great number of combinations of letters that made words starting and ending with 'K'. The word 'Kodak' is the result." Before long, it was a widely recognized brand name. The "Kodak Girl" was also devised, with her style of clothes and model of camera changing every year, and also became an enduring icon of the times. Kodak's distinctive yellow trade dress, also selected by Eastman, remains one of the company's more valued assets.

Eastman was the original researcher for his firm, and he was its R&D department. However, in 1886, he became one of the first American industrialists to employ a full-time research scientist. This was to aid in the commercialization of a flexible, transparent film base. Thereafter, the company employed an increasing number of scientists for R&D purposes. Eastman was a great admirer of the Massachusetts Institute of Technology; he had hired some of its best graduates, who went on to become some of his best assistants. Eastman's obsession with quality products set the tone for the company's R&D efforts. From the R&D laboratories of Kodak came a stream of the best photography products of the day—film, cameras, photofinishing products, and later, plastics and other imaging products.

In addition to outstanding in-house R&D, Eastman also undertook clever R&D partnerships. An early example was in 1889 when the first commercial transparent roll film was introduced, enabling the development of Thomas Edison's motion picture camera in 1891, and the subsequent partnership between Eastman and Edison. Another example was in 1896, one year after the discovery of X-rays, when Eastman entered into an agreement to supply plates and paper for the new process. Kodak also partnered with the U.S. government in 1917 when it developed aerial cameras during World War I. In 1933, Kodak and Western Electric jointly commercialized high-speed industrial photography with a high-speed camera synchronized with an electric timer.

The advertising and R&D endeavors of the company dovetailed with the cost strategy of the firm. In the very early years of the company, Eastman was determined to supply the tools of photography at the lowest possible price to the greatest number of people. The rapid growth of the business bolstered by advertising made large-scale production a necessity. The creation of ingenious tools and processes for manufacturing through the R&D efforts enabled the company to turn out high-quality merchandise at selling prices that the public could afford, which in turn made advertising credible. In 1896, the 100,000th Kodak camera was manufactured, and film and photographic paper were being made at the rate of about four hundred miles per month.[8] As a result, the company enjoyed economies of scale as well as learning-by-doing. In those days the pocket Kodak camera sold for $5. Over the coming few years, cost economies and R&D efforts resulted in a camera that would could be sold for $1—this was the first of the long line of popular Brownie cameras introduced in 1900. In sum, cost frontiers were constantly being pushed at the company, and this proved to be a formidable entry barrier.

The systems-selling approach was arguably one of the best marketing strategies of Kodak. This strategy was employed somewhat later in the history of the company, and greatly helped consolidate Kodak's power over the mosaic of interconnected markets. Starting with the Instamatic camera and processing to the disc camera, Kodak introduced a unique film format designed to be compatible with only Kodak cameras. Some of these systems were very successful. The Instamatic, first introduced in 1963, was one such system. These film formats were vastly superior to existing competitors' products and were protected by patents. Hence, Kodak created monopolistic new markets for its new film and made profits on the sales of the complementary camera products as well. Ostensibly to stay out of antitrust trouble, Kodak licensed out its system. That is, it shared its proprietary technology with competitors by selling it to them for a price. However, this too was beneficial to Kodak because it increased the total market for its most profitable product, that is, film.

Two relatively unsuccessful attempts at exploiting the systems-selling approach were the disc and instant cameras. The disc camera—disc film system—flopped because of the graininess of the picture. The instant camera entry was not a success because Kodak was sued by Polaroid for patent infringement and eventually lost the case at great cost. Even though Kodak lost some systems-selling approach battles, and its share in the camera market decreased over time (see Tables 6.1 and 6.2) as other competitors caught up in both the film and camera markets, it still had substantial market power.

Table 6.2
Annual Film Market Shares

Year	Kodak	Fuji
1977	80.00	N.A
1978	79.92	3.65
1979	79.92	4.12
1980	79.57	5.60
1981	77.95	5.75
1982	74.42	6.27
1983	69.25	8.38
1984	66.17	9.87
1985	63.96	11.48
1986	62.33	13.80
1987	63.57	16.36
1988	66.46	17.21
1989	65.14	17.33
1990	62.93	17.37

Source: Vrinda Kadiyali, "Entry, Its Deterrence and Its Accommodation: A Study of the U.S. Photographic Film Industry," *Rand Journal of Economics* 27 (1996): 452-478.

Given that Kodak had a near lock on the film market, it dictated the technological standards in the camera market. Only those camera formats could survive for which Kodak was willing to make compatible film. For example,

Kodak has never supplied film to fit the Minox, a small camera . . . similar to the Instamatics . . . that has been on the market since the 1930s, or similar cameras by Minolta and Mamiya that were also introduced before Kodak [Instamatic]. Merchants of these cameras . . . made numerous requests that Kodak sell film packaged in their formats, with or without the Kodak name. As an alternative, they asked Kodak to sell bulk film rolls large enough to permit the camera manufacturers economically to cut the film down to the appropriate size and spool it. Kodak denied all such appeals . . . Its policy drastically reduced the ability of manufacturers to compete by introducing new camera formats.[9]

A similar story was played out in the movie formats other than Kodak's own. This policy enabled Kodak to gain market power in the camera market, which, in turn, fed into market power in the film market. The superiority of Kodak film over rival film meant that rival camera formats for which Kodak refused to supply film could not survive.

Another strategy to hold on to market power was planned obsolescence and secrecy of product formulation. Kodak kept competitors at bay by continuously surprising them with radical design changes with almost no advance notice. The

Berkey v. Kodak case is replete with examples where Kodak deliberately did not disclose the state-of-the-art procedures to rival photofinishers, or did not give them advance notice of changes in technology so they could prepare for them. This enabled Kodak to gain a first-mover advantage each time its R&D department came up with a successful photofinishing technique. Often, these first-mover advantages endured a long time and provided a source of profits for the firm. For example, Kodacolor II, the film introduced with its 110 Instamatic camera-and-film system in early 1972, required a new photoprocessing technique (the C-41 technique instead of the C-22 technique). Independent photofinishers were not able to offer processing service for this film, and all the additional business went to Kodak's own processing division. Berkey alleges that this effect lasted till late 1973.

A 1954 decree forbade Kodak from tying processing of film to selling of film, and this led to various entrants in the photofinishing market. This decree was in response to concern that Kodak was using its market power in film to keep entrants out of the photofinishing industry by tying sales of film with photofinishing. However, Kodak's own Color Print and Process division (CP&P) controlled critical technical information on how best to photofinish Kodak film. The CP&P division could determine which photofinishers it chose to share this information with, and whether it would give them access to the best technology for photofinishing. Therefore, Kodak controlled the quality of services provided by its rivals in the photofinishing industry. This effectively kept big rivals out of the photofinishing market, thereby negating the effect of the 1954 decree in promoting competition in this market. Reduced competition in the photofinishing market was, of course, a source of profits to the company. Additionally, it also served to make the name Kodak synonymous with each step of the film industry.

In addition, Kodak exploited the other connections in the photography industry by appropriate pricing of products to rival firms. Kodak supplied key chemicals, as well as print paper, to rivals. Often, it charged these rivals "twice the price" than it did its internal CP&P division.[10] Moreover, these photofinishing rivals performed wholesaling activities for Kodak, that is, they redistributed Kodak film to retailers. Kodak did not give them any discounts for this, which meant that these photofinishers had to carry the cost of performing this function for Kodak, putting them at a cost disadvantage when competing with CP&P. Once again, this meant market power in the photofinishing market, as well as the ability to price the processing fee for rival film products in a manner to make Kodak film purchase more attractive.

Another piece of evidence in Kodak's exercise of market power was that its CP&P division would charge low prices in the relatively competitive photofinishing market, making up for lost profit by charging very high prices for film where Kodak enjoyed a near monopoly. In sum, photofinishers were in a relationship of extreme dependence on Kodak, a fact aided by the fragmented photofinishing industry that had no large, strong player.

To summarize, there is ample evidence of Kodak's market power in both the camera and photofinishing market. Much of the market power in these functionally ancillary markets came from market power in the functionally central market of film. Levin has analyzed the film market for the period 1955 through 1965 in detail. In particular, he has examined the reasons for Kodak's dominance in the film market and the entry barriers in the industry, as well as the attempted (and failed) entry by DuPont in this period. His findings demonstrate how all the strategies discussed above contribute to Kodak's market power, as well as demonstrate the links between the three markets of film, cameras, and photofinishing.

In 1955, Kodak was a near monopolist in the film market. GAF (General Aniline and Film Co.), which sold Ansco brand film, was another player in the market. Ansco had been in the film business since the beginning of the U.S. film industry and, after several changes, was under government control after World War II until 1962. Agfa of Germany was the third producer in the market, importing film from Germany. In 1957, Dynacolor (acquired by 3M in 1963) became another minor player in the market. Yet, over the period 1955 through 1965, Eastman Kodak had an average of 90.7 percent of the market.[11] From all accounts, it made huge margins, and yet this did not attract major entry.

There were several entry barriers in the industry. One was Kodak's patent policy. Jenkins (1975) says of George Eastman, "Eastman did not abandon patents as a method of gaining a 'natural monopoly' . . . instead of relying exclusively on production patents he now sought to develop a system of patents covering both product and production. This strategy, in the long run, was the key to his success."[12] George Eastman had said in the early years of the company, when it was expanding in the United Kingdom, "I believe that $25,000 would put our patents in England on a foundation that would be unassailable. We have got so many patents that if we get beaten on one, we could try another and it would take our competitors ten or fifteen years to break them all down."[13]

This patent barrier deterred entry for the current Kodak technology. Additionally, it deterred entry in new technologies, which were usually incrementally built on older technologies where Kodak held the patent. By the time rivals found ways around the current technology, Kodak was on to the next technology, which would also be protected by another patent.

Kodak's policy against licensing its film technology reinforced this incumbency advantage. As mentioned earlier, Kodak had on occasion licensed out technology for its cameras, after being a sole producer for a while. However, it never licensed out its film technology. This reinforces the argument of the centrality of film in the photographic film market nexus, and how power in this market was critical.

This entry barrier was not completely effective, as the entry of Dynachrome in 1957 indicates. However, the R&D costs associated with entry, as well as the potential patent-infringement litigation costs after entry kept other potential entrants at bay (Jenkins and Ackerman have references to this type of behavior in the earlier history of Kodak in the film market).[14] DuPont spent $15 million in

R&D costs for color film up until 1960, and even then they were several years away from having a product ready for the market.[15] In addition, DuPont had spent $10 million for plant and equipment, and it would have had to incur advertising expenditure to the tune of $4 million if had decided to enter. As mentioned earlier, Kodak had from the very beginning employed a very R&D- and advertising-intensive competitive strategies, and these two strategies, in turn, were carefully planned with its other strategies. Even for a company of DuPont's size and deep pockets matching Kodak's R&D and advertising expenses in the film market alone was too burdensome.

Additionally, it is not clear that (as the subsequent *Berkey v. Kodak* litigation revealed) any firm with presence in the film market alone or any other related market alone could sustain profit.[16] This is because Kodak had the ability and willingness to cross-subsidize entry-deterrence battles across its various markets and squeeze rivals in any one market. Therefore, capital requirements were a serious entry barrier in the industry to enter any one market, and perhaps an underestimate given the desirability of entering the "mosaic" of markets simultaneously.

Photofinishing defines another barrier to entry. An entrant would need to find distribution outlets for film sales, to collect the film for photofinishing, and to return the processed film to the consumer. As mentioned earlier, Kodak had developed a formidable mass-distribution system as part of its attempt to expand the amateur photography market. To get film to consumers, the entrant would have to match this distribution network.

In addition, after delivering film to the customer, the entrant would also need several photofinishing laboratories across the country to be able to promptly return processed film to consumers. Here also, Kodak's CP&P had a wide network. To be able to process film quickly, the entrant would either have to go with independent processors, who would be willing (at affordable costs) to process film only if it were compatible with Kodak's photofinishing process, or the entrant could devise a new type of film and a new combination of chemicals to develop the film. However, it would be difficult to persuade independent processors to adopt new developing procedures for an entrant without a guarantee of a minimum volume of business in the new line of film. Therefore, the entrant's best alternative would be to devise a new type of film that could be developed using Kodak processes, or be "Kodak-compatible." How an entrant could make Kodak-compatible film without violating Kodak's patents was indeed a conundrum.

Kodak's commitment to high quality, coupled with high advertising budgets, proved to be another barrier of entry. There was persuasive evidence that product differentiation was a successful entry barrier. Both Ansco and Dynachrome priced below comparable Kodak film (15 percent and 40 percent, as reported by Levin).[17] Despite these price differentials, Kodak successfully maintained its market share because of the (real or perceived) quality differentials, as well as the other entry barriers outline above.

In addition to these demand advantages, there was evidence that Kodak's costs of production were low because of substantial economies of scale, as well as economies of scope across its vertically integrated business units. These also constituted barriers. However, the effectiveness of these is questionable as both Ansco and Dynacolor were far less vertically integrated than Kodak and yet managed successful entries.

DuPont along with Bell and Howell formed a joint venture in 1960 (announced in 1961) with the intention to enter the photographic film market. Both companies had previous experience in related markets. For example, DuPont produced a polyester film base for use in X-ray film and other film uses, but only in black-and-white film. Together they proposed to start manufacturing and selling reversal film, that is, film that is used both for movies and slides, rather than the regular negative-positive film used for prints. DuPont and Bell and Howell had carefully thought out the product line, pricing, photofinishing, and distribution issues associated with entry.

Levin catalogs the actions Kodak took upon DuPont's announcement of its intentions to enter.[18] Soon after the agreement between the companies had been signed, Kodak introduced an improved version of its color reversal film, Kodachrome III. In 1962, Kodak introduced yet another improved version of the same film. The most important product innovation response was in 1963, when Kodak introduced the Instamatic camera and film. This new camera-and-film system made it possible for amateurs to easily change rolls of film. This resulted in an explosion of sales, and profits for Kodak. More importantly, it defined a new format for photography, one that DuPont was not in a position to imitate (patent barriers) or benefit from. Following this announcement, Kodak even introduced a new amateur movie film format in 1965, the "super 8" millimeter film. This move was especially detrimental for DuPont-Bell and Howell as the latter was a major producer in the movie equipment market. This illustrates the use of the systems approach (mentioned earlier) by Kodak, that is, the introduction of new film and new cameras, which it alone could make. Such a move would leave producers in both markets at a technical disadvantage, and in the case of DuPont-Bell and Howell, a tough response to entry.

As Levin argues, all these actions could be attributed to reasons other than active entry deterrence on part of Kodak.[19] Whatever the intention, the effect of these actions was that DuPont as well as Bell and Howell decided to scrap their entry plans. The DuPont-Bell and Howell entry episode serves as a good example of Kodak's market dominance and interconnectedness of the film, camera, and photofinishing markets. Over the period of 1965 to 1979, Kodak's near monopoly over the film market continued. Several firms had minor market shares, including Fotomat (Konoshiroko), 3M, Agfa, Fuji, and private brands. None of these small firms were able to make a serious dent in the film market power of Kodak. However, things were about to start changing.

THE ENTRY OF FUJI

Fuji was founded in 1936 and had various business interests including film, cameras, copiers, bicycles, medical equipment, and videotape. However, film was its main business, and Fuji was recognized for its expertise in the imaging industry. Fuji had pursued a growth strategy using product diversification and strong foreign sales. As we will see shortly, its experience in selling in foreign markets would prove to be invaluable in its U.S. expansion strategy.

Like Kodak, Fuji had large a R&D budget, which was responsible for several new, high-quality products. These included office and medical equipment, home computers, and semiconductors. Fuji also has a highly flexible work force, with employees able to move between different plants for different product lines.

Fuji has a long presence in the U.S. film market. Fuji Photo Film, U.S.A. is a subsidiary of Fuji Photo Film, Japan. Fuji started selling film in the United States in 1964, and from 1964 until 1972, Fuji sold private-label film in the United States. In 1972, it started selling film under its own name, but even then its competitive stance was very conciliatory—its film was sold as a promotional item given free with the purchase of Japanese cameras. However, in 1978, the photographic market in Japan was mature, leaving little room for growth. Fuji then decided to push into the U.S. market more aggressively.

The rivalry between Kodak and Fuji already went back several years. They had competed in several product categories and in several countries. In the following analysis, we will focus on the film market because we are interested in learning why Kodak lost its market power in this market. Fuji had learned to go in whatever direction Kodak went. Every so often it would beat Kodak by moving first. An early example of this was when in 1967, Fuji released the 8-millimeter home movie system before Kodak could announce its own 8-millimeter film. However, Kodak soon announced its Super 8 format, which was incompatible with Fuji's, and Fuji soon withdrew its entry. After this, Fuji seems to have realized that its optimal strategy was to follow Kodak. From then, until almost the mid 1980s, Fuji's strategy in its U.S. operation was to stay small.

In its attempt to gain market presence in the U.S. film market, Fuji knew that it faced the formidable lock that Kodak had in this and related markets. However, as said earlier, Fuji had considerable market power in the Japanese market and could subsidize its initial losses in the United States market. Moreover, Fuji had been selling film overseas, including in the United States, and had accumulated enough knowledge on what strategies might work. It decided to target a 15 percent market share in the United States, hoping that this would not attract the ire of Kodak. The announced plan was to take market share away from rivals other than Kodak, for example, 3M and Konika. Not surprisingly, the tone of statements coming out of the company were conciliatory. President Ohnishi said, "We are a piquant but small Japanese pepper. If I were Kodak, I wouldn't worry about us at all."[20] "Fuji is gun-shy; they've found that they can live happily under the Kodak umbrella," said analyst Duquesnoy.[21] "Both Fuji and Kodak make fat margins, and they're not in the business of destroying that profitability."

Fuji was well aware of the need to keep a low profile in any battle with Kodak, given the long history of Kodak's response to any threat to its market power (witness Kodak's response to the DuPont-Bell and Howell episode discussed above). Fuji itself had been at the receiving end of some of this treatment. In 1977, Kodak and Fuji got into a price war over print paper, and again in 1983, when Fuji beat Kodak in introducing a new line of high-resolution film, Kodak responded by introducing four new high-resolution films of its own. Ohnishi said that Fuji would "only enter areas where Fuji can modify and improve on product. . . . We want a small part of the large pie."[22]

What was the actual competition between Kodak and Fuji like?

THE BATTLE BETWEEN KODAK AND FUJI

Kodak had not always taken Fuji's presence in the film market seriously. It thought that Fuji's colors were unnaturally bright and oversaturated. However, it soon had a wake-up call and was forced to accommodate Fuji in several ways.

While its "puppy dog" stance attempted to keep Kodak in a competitive fog, Fuji was working on ways to get to the 15 percent market share. As a first step, to counteract Kodak's wide distribution, it also went beyond specialty store outlets to being sold in food, drug, and discount stores. It was always priced below Kodak's premium prices, but, unlike other potential entrants, Fuji did not have a problem with convincing consumers of its high quality. If anything, consumers seem to like its saturated colors very much. It also undertook major advertising campaigns about this time. So, why did Kodak not respond with even lower prices (or match Fuji's low price) and/or not increase its own advertising in response to Fuji's, or even change its film hues?

In a study of the U.S. market for film over the period 1970 to 1990, Kadiyali found that the response of Kodak to Fuji's entry, and the pattern of competition in the years after, shows how Fuji played its cards very well.[23] Evidence from the 1970 to 1980 period suggests that Kodak priced low enough and advertised high enough to keep potential entrants out of the market and existing rivals limited to small market shares.

Things changed around 1980. Fuji's market expansion plan was aided by several factors. First, there was adequate demand for its film, that is, there were no quality concerns. Second, Fuji was importing film from Japan, enabling it to avail of economies of scale, which would not have been possible if it had built a separate plant to serve the small U.S. demand. Additionally, this was a time of a strong dollar. This meant that importing film from Japan was cheap, and this gave Fuji a substantial cost advantage over Kodak. In fact, Fuji seemed to have lower manufacturing costs than Kodak. Third, Kodak's advertising benefited Fuji rather than detracted from its market share. This unusual phenomenon is quite easily explained by the relative size of Fuji. Kodak's advertising increased the demand for film as a whole, that is, its advertising was market-expanding. Fuji could ride on the coattails of Kodak advertising; therefore, it did not need as big an advertising budget of its own to generate demand.

Given these demand and cost advantages that Fuji had over Kodak, Kodak was compelled to accommodate Fuji's expansion plans for the U.S. market. In addition, Kodak's accommodation path had to be conciliatory, that is, it was not in a position to retaliate aggressively. For example, it could not aggressively cut prices because Fuji could always match these, given its lower costs. Increasing advertising budgets to keep Fuji out would not work because consumers seemed to like Fuji's colors and Kodak's advertising served to increase the demand for the entire film industry, Fuji included. The price and advertising paths for the decade of 1980 to 1990 suggest that the two firms were coexisting near peacefully in terms of Fuji playing the role of the small firm growing bigger over the decade, and Kodak left with little choice but to go along.

These two firms followed each other's moves and imitated them meticulously. One researcher at Kodak said, "It's me-too technology. We do what Fuji does. We're obsessed with Fuji."[24] When Kodak realized that consumers want Fuji's supersaturated colors, it introduced its VR-G line of films. Another example of the firms imitating each other is the near-simultaneous introduction of single-use or disposable cameras in 1987. Here, Kodak beat Fuji by scheduling its press conference to announce this new product just a day before Fuji's scheduled press conference for the same purpose.

Sometimes the competition between the two firms bordered on the ridiculous. One such episode involved Kodak copying Fuji's tactic of flying a blimp above sporting events in Japan by flying its own blimp in sight of Fuji's headquarters. Kodak also took to flying its blimps above sporting events in Japan, and in January 1987 sent New Year's cards to its Japanese customers showing Kodak's blimp flying above Mt. Fuji. Even before that, Fuji had outsmarted Kodak by being declared the official film of the 1984 Olympics in Los Angeles and flying its blimp over various events in the games. In response, Kodak bought large blocks of commercial time on television networks in an attempt to reduce the exposure of the Fuji blimp.

Another theatrical episode in the competition between these two firms involved the admission of a Fuji employee (a planner of new imaging products) to University of Rochester's business school master's program in 1987. Kodak, which had long supported University of Rochester, and the business school in particular, put pressure on the university to withdraw the admission offer and even secured admission to MIT for the same student. Perhaps Kodak feared that its new product secrets would leak. Reacting to press criticism of its response, the university readmitted the student. A few months later, Fuji fired another shot in the academic battle by instituting a scholarship at the Rochester Institute for Technology (RIT) for photography students. This institute had also benefited in the past from Kodak's largesse, and Fuji claimed that it had chosen RIT "because of its reputation, not because it was Rochester [home of Kodak]."[25]

In the decade of 1980 to 1990, when this competition was unfolding in the United States, the two firms were competing in other parts of the world, in particular, in Japan. Fuji might have been at a disadvantage in the United States, but in Japan and later in Europe, Fuji had a strong market position. Like many other Japanese companies, Fuji could subsidize its U.S. operations with its Japanese profits. Kodak had a minor presence in the Japanese market for a few years before that, but it made a major push in that market starting 1984, the same time as Fuji was the official sponsor of the Los Angeles Olympics. However, Kodak was limited in its attack by the entrenched position of Fuji that was very similar to the position that Kodak had in the years prior to 1978 in the United States. Interestingly, Kodak film prices in Japan were lower than Fuji's prices in Japan, which was the opposite situation from United States where Kodak was the premium-priced product. Certainly, it helped that after November 1985, the yen started appreciating, making it cheaper to import film into Japan.

We can speculate whether Kodak's entry into the Japanese market was in retaliation to Fuji's expansion in the United States, and further, if Kodak's entry into Japan helped achieve some measure of peace between the two firms in the United States (and Japan), given that each held the other hostage in its home country. While there is no overt evidence in the trade press to confirm this, it is true that the Japanese market was not a terribly more attractive entry option for Kodak independently. Additionally, there has been no further entry into the U.S. film market after the entry of Fuji, despite both firms making profits. This might suggest some kind of entry deterrence on part of the two firms, and, therefore, some measure of cooperation between them.

KODAK: THE BATTLES WITHIN

As the battle with Fuji was unfolding both in the United States and Japan, Kodak was also going through serious introspection and changes through the 1980s. Profits at Kodak were plummeting in the early 1980s. Given Fuji's cost competitiveness, Kodak had to do some cost trimming of its own. From 1983 to 1986, 24,000 jobs were cut at Kodak, despite Kodak's informal lifetime employment policies. Among those who left the company was Walter Fallon, the chief executive officer (CEO) who had introduced several major product lines during his tenure. At the time he left, that is, 1983, only the copier business introduced by him was doing well. Fallon's failures included the instant camera that was the subject of the expensive lawsuit by Polaroid, the disc camera which gave low-resolution pictures, and an unreliable blood analysis machine, the Ektachem 400.

Fallon's successor was Colby Chandler, who gave marketing a stronger say in what was until then a mostly technical company. He also directed Kodak's move into electronics. This was deemed essential after Kodak was unpleasantly surprised by a Sony invention in 1982 of filmless video cameras. However, some of Kodak's moves into electronics meant that it was competing in areas far removed from its technical, competitive advantage, for example, in floppy disks, where giants Hitachi and (archrival) Fuji were far superior. A critical concern in the development of electronic products was Kodak's managerial culture: glacially slow, bloated, stodgy, conservative, and lacking marketing savvy. Chandler indeed faced a daunting task.

One of Chandler's debacles was the purchase of Sterling Drugs in 1988 for $5.1 billion. Prior to the acquisition, Sterling had no proven products on the market, and the potential fit between Kodak and Sterling was questionable. Kodak increased its debt three-fold to overpay for the company. Yet another scheme that went wrong in the 1980s was Kodak setting itself up as a venture capitalist for various new technologies.[26] Kodak's bureaucracy had neither the skill to manage entrepreneurial companies, nor the wisdom to acknowledge these shortcomings. An example of such a venture gone bad was Atex, a copy-processing system for the publishing industry. Kodak bought this company in 1981. The founders of the company left a decade later, stifled by the culture at Kodak.

Worse than the sins of focusing on wrong businesses was the sin of not focusing on the right one. Chandler's successor, Kay Whitmore, has recently been blamed for much of this. Kodak's management was too hasty in concluding that the traditional print film industry was declining. The management overplayed the importance and urgency of electronic photography, which even today seems to be a few years away in this country, not to speak of the vast markets overseas where the electronic photography technology is even further away. The *Wolfman Report* shows how in the entire 1970 to 1995 period, there has been only one year where the number of photographs taken has decreased.[27] This core market is still growing at about 4 percent a year, which given the gross margins on the film, still constitutes a very lucrative market for Kodak. This market was not given adequate attention in the internal management of the company. This cash-rich division in the company seemed to be subsidizing other losing divisions, as well as other costly mistakes of Kodak. Morale in the division was particularly low as it was felt that the division was not getting the care, attention, and respect that it deserved.

THE 1990s AND WHAT LIES AHEAD

In late 1993, George Fisher was appointed CEO of Eastman Kodak. He has made several bold initiatives since taking.[28] The company has decided to focus on its competitive advantage in film. Consequently, Kodak sold Sterling after the disastrous, and relatively short, marriage. He has also undertaken several changes in the managerial organization of Kodak by stressing accountability, quality, and cycle time. The link between pay and performance has been strengthened. In addition, Fisher has brought focus to Kodak's electronic/digital photography effort by consolidating various pieces of the project that were spread across the company. Fisher has also hired marketing-oriented managers, and he himself brings much needed marketing vision to the company.

Kodak has launched or announced several new products since Fisher took charge. One of these is a much improved version of the single-use camera. Others include copyprint station which consumers use to make copies and enlargements from prints (without using negatives), the relaunch of the photo CD in 1995, and "smart" film that stores data of the photographic environment on the film as the picture is taken, enabling more precise photofinishing.

Kodak has made two successful alliances: one with Microsoft in order to send pictures faster and sharper over the Internet, and the another with archrival Fuji and two camera manufacturers.[29] This latter collaboration comprises a new "smart" film-and-camera system, that is, the camera can adjust film exposure depending on light conditions, among other things. Note that this is yet another example of the systems approach that Kodak has used before, but this time the fact that the standard was jointly developed by all competitors shows how much market power Kodak has lost over the years. The new system has been widely seen as an attempt to revitalize the slow growth of the traditional photography industry.

Kodak has also been favored by the courts in the 1990s. The 1954 decree that prevented Kodak from bundling the selling and developing of film was repealed on the grounds of there being adequate competition in both film and processing markets. Therefore, Kodak can now include the cost of photofinishing in the cost of film and specify what photofinisher must be used. This change in law should give Kodak new flexibility, as well as increased demand for its print paper and chemicals. Kodak currently owns 49 percent of Qualex, the nation's largest wholesale photofinisher which has 70 percent of the wholesale market, and about 30 percent of the entire photofinishing market.[30] It also acquired Eckerd, which was then the fourth largest outlet for film sales and fifth in processing.[31] This purchase has consolidated Kodak's strength in the photofinishing market, which it can use to gain strength in the film market (given that the court decree allows it to bundle these two services). Not to be outdone, Fuji has bought Wal Mart's photo business.[32]

The other court decision in favor of Kodak removed the 1921 decree that prevented Kodak from selling private-label film. The decree was put in place to prevent Kodak from selling its film in an unbranded, low-price version which would hurt its potential rivals. Now that the decree is no more, Kodak's strategy hereon is less clear-cut. If Kodak were to introduce a low-priced private-label brand, the move could well cannibalize Kodak's premium-product sales. Such a move could also set off an industry price war, a war that Kodak cannot yet win because its costs are still higher than Fuji's. A strategy related to selling private-label film that Kodak has adopted is selling low-end branded film, called "Funtime." It is priced about 20 percent less than other Kodak film and is an attempt to compete with lower priced competitors and private labelers. The performance of this film has been below analysts' expectations.

Kodak has also been getting tough with Fuji in the courts. First, in the United States, it filed an International Trade Commission (ITC) case against Fuji for dumping print paper. It won the case in 1994, gaining temporary relief from Fuji's low prices in this market. However, Fuji has decided to invest $100 million in a plant in South Carolina in order to get around the import restrictions, as well as to enable a quick response to retailer-demand fluctuations. In May 1995, Kodak filed yet another case with ITC against Fuji. Kodak alleges that Fuji and the Japanese government have conspired to restrict Kodak's access to distribution systems in Japan for film and photographic paper markets. Fuji has locked up the four biggest distributors that account for 70 percent of film sales in Japan.[33] Much to Kodak's disappointment, the U.S. government has taken a mild course and shifted Kodak's complaint to the World Trade Organization.[34]

Legal battle victories and responsive management notwithstanding, Kodak faces several challenges ahead. Kodak needs to target global markets, a strategy that stood rival Fuji in good stead all these years. In particular, Asian markets like China, where Fuji has a lead, need to be attacked. Industry experts believe that Kodak needs to generate joint-ventures with firms that have the relevant technological resources that Kodak lacks in order to improve its digital technology. Moreover, there is still room for cost cutting in the firm.[35] Other threats include Polaroid's proposed entry into regular and "smart" film categories and in single-use cameras. Kodak's market power in the point-and-shoot camera market has been declining over the 1980s anyway, with the entry of several models by Japanese manufacturers.

SUMMARY

In 1880, George Eastman's obsession with photography led to the forerunner of Eastman Kodak Company. Eastman's belief in mass-produced, mass-distributed quality products, supported by heavy advertising and R&D expenditures, was the foundation for the might of the company in the photographic industry. Starting from capturing the film market by producing the first dry plate in 1880, the company steadily expanded into related markets of photofinishing and cameras. It cleverly exploited the systems approach of coordinated film and cameras, invented in the famous Rochester, New York, laboratories, to gain market power in these interconnected markets. All these corporate strategies proved to be effective entry barriers, and Eastman Kodak dominated the photographic film market until the late 1970s.

However, in the late 1970s, Fuji Photo Film successfully started expanding its market presence. Fuji's cost structure favored expansion; its saturated colors appealed to consumers. Fuji also gained from Kodak's advertising campaigns that enlarged the market for film. Its corporate focus on product innovation and global sales bolstered its U.S. market entry strategy. As a result, Kodak lost its market dominance in film.

At the same time, Kodak faced serious internal problems in terms of diffused corporate focus and unresponsive management. On another front, Kodak was losing market share in cameras as cheap, ready-to-shoot cameras flooded the market. Kodak also bled when it lost the *Berkey v. Kodak* suit in the late 1970s, and then the *Polaroid v. Kodak* case in the late 1980s.

Recent events seem to indicate that Kodak may be turning around. Fuji's cost advantage has eroded with the strong yen, making Fuji establish a U.S. plant. Kodak is also attempting to gain back its market power in the photofinishing market by recently acquiring Eckerd. In the camera market, Kodak, with cooperation from some rival firms, has introduced the Advanced Photo System cameras, which are being hailed as the next big amateur camera wave. It also began using alliances with other companies to branch out into new imaging markets like Photo CD and Internet photographic uses. More importantly, Kodak is attempting to get rid of corporate fat and refocus on its core strength in the imaging market. Recent court rulings may have given Kodak ammunition to fight back for its market dominance, for example, the removal of the no-tying clause for selling film and photofinishing, and the removal of the no store-brand film sales by Kodak.

Several challenges and threats lie ahead for Kodak, including bringing the electronic technology to mass market, resuscitating the traditional photography market, and focusing on global markets, among others. Time will tell whether Kodak is up to facing these challenges and regaining its old imposing dominance in the twenty-first century.

NOTES

1. J. Brock, "Market Control in the amateur photography industry," Ph.D. dissertation, Michigan State University.

2. *Wolfman Report on the Photographic and Imaging Industry in the U.S.* (1969-96). New York: ABC Leisure magazines.

3. *Berkey Photo Inc. v Eastman Kodak Company.* (1979) 603 F2d. Henceforth, *Berkey v Kodak.*

4. *Forbes*, 1 April 1963.

5. *Berkey v Kodak.*

6. "From Glass Plates to Digital Images: The Kodak Story," Pamphlet published by Eastman Kodak Company, 1994.

7. R. Jenkins, *Images and Enterprise: Technology and the American Photographic Industry 1839 to 1925* (Baltimore: Johns Hopkins University Press, 1975).

8. *From Glass Plates to Digital Images: The Kodak Story.* Kodak document, 1994.

9. *Berkey v Kodak.*

10. *Berkey v Kodak.*

11. *Berkey v Kodak.*

12. Jenkins, *Images and Enterprise.*

13. Jenkins, *Images and Enterprise.*

14. Jenkins, *Images and Enterprise.* C. Ackerman, *George Eastman* (Boston: Houghton Mifflin, 1930).

15. *Berkey v Kodak.*

16. *Berkey v Kodak.*

17. J. Levin, "The Potential Entrant and the Decision about Entry: Two Case Studies," Ph.D. dissertation, Boston College, 1985.

18. Levin, "Potential Entrant."

19. Levin, "Potential Entrant."

20. *Fortune*, 22 August, 1983, p. 122.

21. *Forbes*, 22 November, 1982, p. 56.

22. *Business Week*, 24 October, 1983, pp. 88, 92.

23. V. Kadiyal, "Pricing and Advertising Strategies for Entry and Accommodation: The Case of the U.S. Photographic Film Industry," Ph.D. dissertation, Dept. of Economics, Northwestern University, 1994. V. Kadiyal, "Entry, Its Deterrence and Its Accommodation: A Study of the U.S. Photographic Film Industry," *Rand Journal of Economics*, 1996.

24. *Business Week*, 23 February 1987, p. 138.
25. *Wall Street Journal*, 30 December 1986, p. A1.
26. *Forbes*, 30 August 1993, p. 40-41.
27. *Wolfman Report*.
28. *Business Week,* 30 January 1995.
29. *Wall Street Journal*, 29 May 1996.
30. *Wall Street Journal,* 6 February 1996.
31. *Wall Street Journal*, 6 February 1996.
32. *Wall Street Journal*, 9 July 1996.
33. *Business Week*, 10 July 1995.
34. *Wall Street Journal*, 14 June 1996.
35. *Business Week*, 30 January 1995.

7

THE RISE AND FALL OF FORD AND GENERAL MOTORS IN THE U.S. AUTOMOBILE INDUSTRY: A TALE TWICE TOLD

Lawrence J. White

How are the mighty fallen in the midst of the battle!
— 2 Samuel 1:23

INTRODUCTION

The U.S. automobile industry's existence has now reached the century mark, with formal production of motor vehicles having started in the last decade of the nineteenth century. During these hundred years there have been two eras during which a single firm played a role as the dominant firm in the industry: The Ford Motor Company had this position from about 1913 until the mid-1920s, and the General Motors Corporation had it from the early 1930s through the late 1970s.

This industry thus provides us with two opportunities to examine the behaviors of dominant firms and of the other firms in its industry. The particular eras during which these separate episodes occurred—the first during the comparative youth of the industry, the second encompassing its considerably more mature phase—provide differing backdrops. There are interesting insights that can be gained from these experiences.

As will be clear in the discussion that follows, basic economic forces were clearly important in the shaping of the automobile industry and in the rise and fall of its dominant firms. But individuals were important as well. The right person, in the right place, at the right time, with the right ideas and skills, could make a difference. The wrong person could also make a difference. This importance of individuals for a single industry should not be a surprise. Economics is best at explaining the broad trends and tendencies of an economy and of the markets, industries, companies, and individuals within it. But economics (and economists) cannot (and should not be expected to) provide a complete explanation for all events at all times by all parties. And, as the focus of analysis moves toward single industries and even single companies, the influence of singular individuals in helping explain some of the outcomes should not be slighted.

This chapter will be organized as follows: The next section will relate the experience of the first (Ford) era; following this is a description of the second (General Motors [GM]) era. In both of these sections, we will first describe the rise of the firm to its dominant position, then its behavior (and that of its smaller rivals) during its period of dominance, the reasons for its decline, and finally an evaluation of the episode. Following the discussion of Ford and GM is a brief conclusion that summarizes the insights that can be gained from these two separate occurrences.

THE FORD ERA

The Development of the Dominant Position

The early decades of the U.S. automobile industry were ones of great fluidity and experimentation. For a while, the even basic technology of locomotion for automobiles—steam engines, electric batteries and motors, or gasoline-powered internal combustion engines—was up for grabs; as of 1898, a fleet of a hundred electric taxicabs plied the streets of New York City. But the superior features of the internal combustion engine eventually won the field.

Technological innovation was rapid, and entry was comparatively easy. The Ford Motor Company, incorporated in 1903, was capitalized at $150,000 but had only $28,000 in cash initially.[1] By one count, more than eleven hundred companies were reported to have "entered" the automobile industry between 1895 and 1926, although many of them never actually got into production.[2] Only 181 companies lasted beyond the manufacture of one or two cars, however. Table 7.1 shows the pattern of effective entry and exit in the industry during the first two decades of the twentieth century.

As of 1903, the leading manufacturer was Ransom E. Olds; the Oldsmobile held about a quarter of the market. Other familiar nameplates in the market at the time included Ford, Cadillac, Buick, Packard, Rambler, Stanley, Pierce, Locomobile, Auburn, Autocar, Franklin, and Marmon. Prices ranged from $650 and up.

Henry Ford, born in 1863, became involved in the early development of automobiles in the mid-1890s as an after-hours sideline to his job as an engineer at the Edison Illuminating Company in Detroit. In 1899 he left the company to

Table 7.1
Entry into and Exit from the U.S. Automobile Industry, 1902-1922

	Number of Entrants	Number of Exits	Number of Firms Remaining
1902	-	-	12
1903	13	1	24
1904	12	1	35
1905	5	2	38
1906	6	1	43
1907	1	0	44
1908	10	2	52
1909	18	1	69
1910	1	18	52
1911	3	2	53
1912	12	8	57
1913	20	7	70
1914	8	7	71
1915	10	6	75
1916	6	7	74
1917	8	6	76
1918	1	6	71
1919	10	4	77
1920	12	5	84
1921	5	1	88
1922	4	9	83

Source: R. C. Epstein, *The Automobile Industry: Its Economic and Commercial Development* (Chicago: A. W. Shaw, 1978, p. 176).

devote his full time to developing automobiles. After four years of false starts and financial failures, the Ford Motor Company was incorporated on June 16, 1903.

Henry Ford's vision was to develop a car that would be reliable and inexpensive, so as to reach a mass market. To achieve this goal, he needed to achieve technological gains with respect to the product and also with respect to manufacturing processes. After a few years of development and production of other car models, in 1906 the company began serious development of what would eventually be called the Model T. The car was announced and first produced in 1908. It offered major advances in basic features, such as gears, ignition, and body strength. A few years later, in 1912 to 1913, the continuously moving assembly line was perfected, first for individual parts and later for the assembly of the overall vehicle.

The concepts of mass production, standardization, division of labor, and the moving assembly line had been known in other industries. But it was Henry Ford and his associates who were able to combine them into a powerful force for achieving cost reductions in the automobile industry. Part of Ford's achievement was in realizing that parts and features of the finished product could be—indeed, needed to be—designed and engineered specifically to accommodate ease and low cost of assembly. Also, as early as 1909 Ford realized that it would be considerably less expensive to ship stacked and boxed parts and have them assembled at regional assembly plants across the country than to ship whole cars in boxcars.[3]

Table 7.2 provides prices, production, and market shares for the Model T for the 1909 to 1925 period. As can be seen, by 1913 Ford automobiles had achieved almost a 40 percent market share (with GM and Willys-Overland as runners-up, each with about 10 percent of the shares), and by the early 1920s the company's auto sales accounted for over half the market. The success of the Model T vaulted Ford from a position of simply one of the principal companies in a small (but growing) industry to the largest company in a major American industry.

Behavior

The success of the Ford Motor Company rested on a number of foundations, all of which involved the personal influence of Henry Ford. First, Henry Ford had the vision that the automobile could be a mass-market item, not just the luxury vehicle that many manufacturers envisioned; and, second, as already stated, he had the design and engineering genius to be able to translate this vision into a reality. As of 1912 (when the price of the Model T touring car had dropped to $600), the company had the inexpensive end of the car market virtually to itself, accounting for 96 percent of the vehicles selling for $600 or less. Other manufacturers instead focused on the relatively few customers who could afford higher priced cars; these manufacturers sold vehicles in price ranges extending up to $7,000. (To provide a sense of comparison, this last figure would be the equivalent of about $110,000 at 1996 price levels.) As Table 7.2 shows, Ford was able to cut the price of the Model T substantially during the following decade—despite the fact that the general price level of the United States climbed by over 80 percent between 1912 and 1925!

Table 7.2
Prices, Sales, and Market Shares for the Model T, 1909-1925

	Price of a Model T Touring Car	Total Ford Car Sales	Total Industry Car Sales	Ford as a %
1909	950	12,000	124,000	9.7%
1911	690	40,000	199,000	20.1%
1913	550	182,000	462,000	39.4%
1915	440	342,000	896,000	38.2%
1917	450	741,000	1,746,000	42.4%
1919	525	664,000	1,658,000	40.0%
1921	355	845,000	1,518,000	55.7%
1923	295	1,669,000	3,625,000	46.0%
1925	290	1,495,000	3,735,000	40.0%

Source: United States Federal Trade Commission, *Report on the Motor Vehicle Industry* (Washington, D.C.: U.S. Government Printing Office, 1939), pp. 29, 632.

Second, Ford was able to accomplish this feat of a substantial reduction in the real prices of its cars because of phenomenal technological improvements in manufacturing processes. As early as 1914, the main Ford manufacturing operations at Highland Park (a Detroit suburb) were considered a world-class marvel of efficiency, attracting management experts, corporate executives, and government officials from around the world. With the standardization of the product—during the eighteen years of production of the Model T, the motor and chassis were largely unchanged (though improvements in mechanical features and components continued)—Henry Ford and his engineers had ample opportunity to exercise their plentiful and multi-dimensional ingenuities in developing more efficient ways to manufacture and assemble the components as well as the overall vehicles.[4]

Third, Henry Ford had an excellent knack for promotion—of himself, his company, his manufacturing methods, and his vehicles. He was able to capture the imagination of the American (and world) public with his concept of a car that was affordable to "the common man," as well as with his achievements in mass-production methods that allowed costs and prices to fall to those affordable levels. In early 1914 his announcement of the "$5 day" (for an eight-hour work day) for his workers (whose wages had previously been around $2.50 for a ten-hour day) "was like the dazzling burst of a rocket in velvet skies. Headlines blazed throughout the globe."[5] His efforts the following year to lead a peace delegation to Europe to try to bring an end to "the Great War" again brought banner headlines.

Because Ford's manufacturing technology was improving so rapidly, its sharp decrease in prices did not interfere with substantial profits for the company.[6] Within the first few years of production of the Model T, the Ford Motor Company was earning profit margins of about 20 to 30 percent on sales and above 100 percent on net worth (stockholders' equity); the latter figure was substantially above prevailing levels for competitive firms then or since. Even in the early 1920s, after large investments in a new manufacturing facility at the River Rouge location (near Dearborn, another Detroit suburb) and continued price decreases, the company was earning rates of return on equity that were in the 25 to 50 percent range—still substantially above competitors' levels.[7]

What of the other automobile manufacturers? From the discussion above, it is clear that Ford had the low-cost segment of the automobile industry largely to itself, at least through the early 1920s. But other manufacturers were able to carve niches for themselves with vehicles for individuals who were looking for more than just a low-priced car. Innovations in product design and functionality were important for these manufacturers; improved transmissions, brakes, engines, and the development of the battery-powered self-starter to replace the front-end crank were among the important innovations. And, especially after 1915, other manufacturers—not Ford—were the innovators. Still, these other manufacturers were acutely aware of Ford's presence in the market and of the pressures that Ford's ever-falling prices placed on them.

Decline

The flexibility, ingenuity, and true genius that had characterized Henry Ford before 1920 seemed to dissipate after that date.

After the opening of the new decade [Henry] Ford's temper stiffened. The acceptance of the Model T by the American masses, its worldwide fame, and the huge revenues from its sale confirmed his belief in the infallibility of his handiwork. As he reached sixty, his mind became less pliant, his disposition more autocratic. Success . . . shut him off from the free relationship with a variety of men, the give-and-take of frank criticism, the necessities of change and compromise, which he had known on his way up. He began to regard the Model T as immutable. He had standardized it for cheap universal use; very well, he would keep it standardized.[8]

As the decade of the 1920s progressed, other manufacturers caught up with Ford's manufacturing methods (often with the help of engineers who were hired away from Ford) and surpassed him in the development of automotive technologies that allowed cars to become increasingly convenient to use. Other companies—especially GM—had formulated product strategies that were appropriate to the more mature automobile industry of the 1920s (as will be discussed in the next section), and they had focused engineering and product development in formal research laboratories. By contrast, the Ford Motor Company was still operated in important ways (including engineering and product development) "out of the hip pocket" of Henry Ford and was still driven by his vision of a low-cost car for the masses. The Model T was rapidly eclipsed by the technologically superior offerings of its rivals, and its low prices were unable to provide an adequate offset.[9]

As a further self-imposed handicap, Ford resisted establishing a retail finance subsidiary of the company (making it harder for his dealers and their customers to finance the purchase of their vehicles) until 1928, ten years after GM had established the General Motors Acceptance Corporation (GMAC) as its financing arm; in this case it was Ford's antipathy toward debt of all kinds, especially personal debt, that fueled this delay.[10] By the middle of the decade, the Model T's sales—in absolute numbers and as a share of the still-expanding overall auto market—were faltering.

Further, Henry Ford's attentions were diverted elsewhere. His farm upbringing had instilled in him an interest in tractors, and after 1917 Fordson tractors were an important product of the company. In the mid-1920s, the rising airplane industry (also powered by internal combustion engines) caught his interest, and the Ford Trimotor airplane became one of the leading models of the era. The company also operated a modest-sized airline and two airmail routes. Further, the sharp rises in input prices generally and especially for raw materials during the 1914 to 1918 World War I period had made Henry Ford increasingly wary of relying on suppliers and concomitantly interested in greater self-reliance of supply. These interests led him to ever greater efforts at vertical integration, which included steelmaking facilities, glassmaking facilities, iron mines, coal mines, timber forests and sawmills, a Great Lakes shipping fleet (to carry the iron ore from the mines to the River Rouge blast furnaces), a railroad, and even a rubber plantation (for tire production) in Brazil![11] His management skills had never been strong; this ever expanding boundary of vertical integration and conglomerateness stretched them even further and contributed to the eventual organizational and financial decline of the company.

Finally, in 1926 even Henry Ford became convinced that the era of the Model T was over and that a new vehicle was necessary to replace it. In May 1927 the last Model T rolled off the assembly line, and Ford shut down production until the end of the year, when production of the Model A began.[12] General Motors was the market leader that year and the next. The Model A vaulted Ford back into market leadership in 1929 and 1930. But the car still embodied Henry Ford's vision and outlook: a single model that would remain largely unchanged for a number of years.[13] Ford lost the market leadership of the automobile industry to General Motors in 1931 and never regained it.

Evaluation

There is little question that the Ford Motor Company occupied a dominant position in the U.S. automobile industry from about 1913 to about 1925. The company had the largest market share in the industry during this period, and in the early 1920s that share briefly exceeded 50 percent. The company enjoyed sizable profits during this period; and its dominance was based, at least partially, on a superior manufacturing technology and a favorable brand-name position. Further, until the early 1920s, the other manufacturers suffered from inferior production technologies and were acutely aware of Ford's dominance and the pressures of his low-priced vehicles.

During its dozen or so years of dominance, was the Ford Motor Company behaving in a way that is consistent with the standard model of a profit-maximizing firm that dominates its market?[14] More specifically, was the Ford Motor Company pursuing a profit-maximizing strategy? Was it taking account of the expected reactions of its rivals in the formulations of its own product and pricing decisions? The latter question is easier to answer. It appears that Henry Ford paid scant attention to the actions of his rivals, at least until the mid-1920s, except when they were able to achieve major technological leaps in product improvement that warranted a product-based response. He was largely driven by his vision of providing a pretty good low-priced car for the general public and of developing the mass-manufacturing technologies to support that goal. The size of the gap between his prices and those of the next lowest seller provided him with plenty of leeway for the sole pursuit of his objectives. As of 1920, the Model T touring car sold for $440; the nearest competitor was the Willys-Overland touring car, which sold for over twice as much at $895. Two years later, the price gaps for comparable cars had narrowed somewhat, as Table 7.3 indicates, but they were still substantial. In sum, with price gaps of these magnitudes, the cross-elasticities of demand between Ford's products and those of his rivals—at least as perceived by Ford—may well have been quite low. There may have been little practical need to take account of the rivals' responses, since they would have had little effect on the demands for Ford's products and, hence, on his decisions.

Table 7.3
Prices for Comparable Automobile Models, 1922

Model	Price ($)
Ford Sedan	645.00
Chevrolet	875.00
Overland 4	895.00
Chrysler (Maxwell)	1485.00
Dodge	1785.00

Source: Nevins and Hill, *Ford: Expansion and Challenge*, 1957, p. 394.

Were Ford's decisions consistent with the maximization of profits for the company, at least before the early 1920s (after which his sluggishness in introducing innovations and especially in abandoning the Model T clearly harmed the company)? It is tempting to conclude that they were not, that his low-cost vision overrode profit maximization and that Ford could have been even more profitable with higher price—especially given the gaps between his prices and those of his nearest rival. But this conclusion would miss an important point: The demand for Ford automobiles was surely driven by more than the price and quality parameters that were offered in the marketplace. Henry Ford's persona and his vision were themselves important phenomena that helped attract attention to his cars and generated demand. It was probably important for the enthusiasm (and thus the demand) generated for his cars that he be perceived as offering a pretty good car at a strikingly low price (that declined concomitantly with the mass-manufacturing achievements that he was simultaneously trumpeting). In essence, there may well have been a "bandwagon effect"[15] that required dramatic actions to generate the sizable demand that did in fact appear for his cars; higher prices might well have undercut the image, slowed the bandwagon considerably, and yielded lower profits.

This discussion falls far short of a conclusive demonstration that Ford's pre-1925 actions were profit-maximizing ones for his company. But it does provide the basis for agnosticism toward arguments that his actions were wholly inconsistent with profit maximization for the company.

In sum, the rise of the Ford Motor Company was clearly due to Henry Ford's vision and to the design and engineering ingenuity of Ford and his associates (as well as Ford's personality and penchant for promotion). Though other entrepreneurs might have combined the same vision and expertise and thereby challenged Ford on his home turf, none did (and few could have replicated his personality). But the decline too was due to Henry Ford's vision (and personality) and his sluggishness in adapting that vision to the changed circumstances of the automobile market. The lead in the automobile industry would be taken by others, who better understood these changed circumstances, as is described in the next section.

GENERAL MOTORS

The Development of the Dominant Position

The General Motors Corporation was formally launched in 1908 as the creation of a shrewd and colorful financier of the era, William Crapo Durant.[16] Over the next decade, Durant would lose control over the company, regain it, and then lose it again for good in 1920. During his reign he acquired the automobile companies and parts companies that would eventually provide the basis for GM's five major car brands (Chevrolet, Pontiac, Oldsmobile, Buick, and Cadillac) and for GM's vertical integration into metal body production (Fisher Body), electrical components (Dayton Engineering Laboratories Company [Delco]), and bearings (Hyatt Roller Bearing Company). With Delco came Charles F. Kettering, who would provide important product innovations for GM over the next decade; with Hyatt came Alfred P. Sloan Jr. whose visions of product strategies and also of organizational structure would guide the company successfully through the next fifty years.

In the early 1920s, after Durant's departure, Sloan's managerial influence became the guiding spirit of the company. Starting from the assets that he had at hand—a collection of companies and brands that were loosely connected under the GM ownership structure—Sloan laid out two complementary visions of product strategy and organizational design.

For the maturing car market of the 1920s (and after) he saw that a successful automobile company needed to have more than just one type of car. Instead, a portfolio of different types would be far better. There would always be a need for an inexpensive, basic vehicle for younger and lower-income families. But as family incomes grew, and as middle- and upper-class families considered replacing their vehicles, they were often looking to "trade up"—to purchase more luxurious cars with more features at higher prices. General Motors' different car brands would span all of those possible demands—"a car for every purse and purpose." Chevrolet would be the inexpensive, basic, bottom-of-the-line vehicle; Pontiac, Oldsmobile, and Buick would offer varying degrees of greater luxury; and Cadillac would be the top-of-the-line car for those who wanted the best. The company could try to instill brand loyalty in those customers who did not want to trade up at replacement time and corporate loyalty for those who did.

Further, to encourage replacement and trading up, GM would institute a program of annual model changes, which included a combination of modest engineering advances, convenience improvements, and modifications to interior and exterior styling; more fundamental changes in design would be less frequent and would usually accompany major changes in engines, transmissions, or other features. The annual model changes would give the company more frequent opportunities to trumpet its "new and different" claims. These would be extra inducements to bring replacement customers into GM dealers' showrooms.

In essence, GM would provide extensive product differentiation to the automobile market at a time when the market was maturing, growth was slowing, and replacement demand was becoming crucial.

To implement these product strategies, Sloan envisioned a divisional structure, with the manufacturing and sales responsibilities for the individual car brands (and for the major components as well) placed in separate divisions and with divisional managers that would have a maximum of independence and autonomy; the central management of GM would serve as overall coordinators and as financial managers.[17] General Motors thus hoped to capture most of the available economies of mass production while also retaining the flexibility and responsiveness that would come with a decentralized divisional structure.

These concepts—for both product strategy and organizational structure—were the antithesis of those of Ford. In the maturing car market of the 1920s and after, GM's structure and strategy proved to be far more successful.

At the beginning of the 1920s GM had sales volumes that were less than half of Ford's. But, as the decade progressed, Ford faltered and GM gained. General

Motors took first place in market share permanently in 1931, and from the mid 1930s through the mid 1980s consistently had sales that gave it shares of 40 percent or above; during the mid 1950s through the mid 1960s its market shares sometimes rose slightly above 50 percent. Table 7.4 provides some relevant market share data.

By the end of the 1920s entry into the automobile industry had become much more difficult, as was expansion by the smaller companies. Though product differentiation was now more important (which offered market niches that entrants and smaller firms might pursue), the maturing market also meant that brand-name reputation and loyalty were growing in importance, which favored larger incumbents. Also, the mass-production methods pioneered by Ford meant that cost advantages came with high volumes. A cruel dilemma for entrants and small-scale

Table 7.4
Market Shares in the U.S. Automobile Industry, 1933-1994[a], by Percentage

	General Motors	Ford	Chrysler	Other U.S. Manufacturers	Imports[b]
1933	41.4	20.7	25.4	12.5	-
1937	41.8	21.4	25.4	11.4	-
1946-1950	41.8	21.4	21.6	15.1	0.2
1951-1955	46.2	25.7	18.6	8.9	0.6
1956-1960	45.5	28.0	14.6	5.7	6.2
1961-1965	49.7	26.2	12.2	6.0	6.1
1966-1970	46.2	24.5	15.8	2.8	10.6
1971-1975	44.1	24.0	13.4	3.3	15.2
1976-1980	46.8	21.1	10.1	1.8	20.1
1981-1985	43.9	17.7	10.4	1.9	26.1
1986-1990[c]	36.0	23.8	13.1[d]	-	27.1
1991-1995	33.9	24.9	13.9	-	27.3

[a] Arithmetic averages are used for multi-year shares.
[b] Includes sales of vehicles manufactured in the United States by companies headquartered abroad ("transplants").
[c] Includes light trucks (mini-vans, pickup trucks, etc.).
[d] Includes American Motors for 1986.
Source: White, "The Automobile Industry," 1982, p. 147; *Ward's Automotive Yearbook* (Detroit: Ward's Reports).

producers thus arose: They could remain small, try to find product niches, and hope that they could survive as high-cost, high-price firms; or they could take the large risks of major investments in high-volume production facilities and hope that the resultant large-scale output could be sold to buyers at remunerative prices. In the mid 1920s, Walter P. Chrysler, a GM "graduate," was the last entrepreneur to achieve a significant expansion of a relatively small company and thereby gain a permanent place among the major companies of the industry. At the beginning of the decade the industry had eighty-four active firms; by 1929 it had less than half of that number, and in 1941 there were only eight firms remaining.

General Motors' success did not rest solely on Sloan's vision. From the mid 1930s through the late 1970s the company was able to execute that vision in an effective fashion. In an industry where manufacturing scale economies were significant, GM's volume gave it advantages over its rivals. General Motors' management quality was generally considered to be the best in the industry. It made few major product errors, and its use of labor and consequent labor costs were the best among its peers.[18]

Behavior

From the mid-1930s forward there was general recognition that GM was the dominant firm in the industry.[19] When the United Automobile Workers (UAW) formulated their plans to organize the industry in the mid-1930s, GM was a key target; and success at GM for the UAW eventually meant success in the industry.

In the 1930s, however, Ford's presence was still significant, and Henry Ford's persistence with his strategy of offering low-priced cars had an inhibiting effect on GM's pricing.[20] But by the 1950s the price leadership of GM was widely recognized. In a famous incident in the fall of 1956, the Ford Motor Company was the first to announce its prices for the new (1957) models. General Motors followed two weeks later with prices of comparable Chevrolets that were 3 percent higher. Ford promptly raised its prices to Chevrolet's levels; a firm that was less inclined to be a follower might have waited for GM to lower its prices. In the late 1960s Ford and Chrysler tended to announce first with higher prices and then subsequently drop their prices to GM's levels.

The question of "small cars"—cars that were smaller than the standard models produced by GM, Ford, and Chrysler (the "Big Three")—was one that occupied the industry from the mid-1950s onward.[21] There was clearly a segment of the automobile-buying public that wanted smaller cars, but the Big Three saw these vehicles as likely to cannibalize sales and profits from their larger (more profitable) vehicles.[22] Though American Motors (which accounted for only 2 percent of industry sales in the mid 1950s) was prepared to break ranks and offer a small car (the Rambler) to the market, Ford and Chrysler were not. Only at the end of the 1950s did the pressure provided by imported small cars cause the Big Three simultaneously to offer small cars ("compacts") of their own.

During the 1960s, the Big Three allowed their compacts to increase in size, luxury, and price, believing that the import surge had been effectively defeated.

They were wrong. Import volumes again grew during the 1960s, and GM and Ford brought out a new set of small cars (subcompacts) in 1969 and 1970. (Chrysler dithered on this subject and delayed bringing out a subcompact until 1978).[23] Only after the sharp increases in petroleum prices in the fall of 1973 and again in early 1979 did the Big Three come to a grudging acceptance of small cars among their product array.

From the late 1920s through the mid-1970s, GM's profits reflected its dominant-firm strengths. Though not at the heady levels of Ford's early years, they were nevertheless considerably above the levels of GM's pee s in the auto industry and in manufacturing generally, as can be seen in Table 7.5.

Table 7.5
Profit Rates as a Percentage of Stockholders' Equity, 1927-1973

	1927-1937[a]	1946-1973[a]
General Motors	35.5	19.7
Ford	-0.4	12.3
Chrysler	27.3	10.7
American Motors	18.9[b]	7.3
All Manufacturing Corporations	5.0[c]	9.2

[a] Arithmetic averages.
[b] Includes Nash only.
[c] Estimated from G. J. Stigler, *Capital and Rates of Return in Manufacturing Industries* (Princeton, NJ: Princeton University Press, 1963), p. 203.
Sources: White, "The Automobile Industry," 1982, p. 168); USFTC, *Report*, 1939, pp. 649, 657.

Decline

By the late 1970s GM's magic was fading.[24] The entire industry was under severe pressure from imports, especially from Japan. The U.S. companies were losing market shares to the imports; price cuts by the domestic producers, especially in the form of widely announced rebates off list prices, were much more common than had been true a decade or two earlier. Japanese vehicles had been designed for an environment of high gasoline prices (Japan had sizable excise taxes on gasoline), which made them ideally suited for the high-gasoline-price car market of the United States in the late 1970s and early 1980s. The Japanese companies had lower labor costs (at extant exchange rates) and superior manufacturing technologies, and the perceived quality ("fit and finish") of their vehicles was higher, as can be seen from the data compiled by *Consumer Reports* and reproduced in Table 7.6.[25] Chrysler ran losses in four of the six years encompassing 1974 through 1979; in 1979 its loss was the largest that (until then) had ever been incurred by a U.S. corporation of any kind.

Table 7.6
Repair Ratings of Automobiles Sold in the United States, 1979 and 1990

	1979		1990		
	U.S. Manufac- turers	Japan Manufac- turers	U.S. Manufac- turers	Japan Manufac- turers	Japan-U.S. Transplant Manufac- turers
Much better than average	0	94	0	43	23
Better than average	15	6	4	40	54
Average	39	0	51	17	15
Worse than average	18	0	24	0	0
Much worse than average	28	0	22	0	8

Source: *Consumer Reports*, April 1980 and April 1991, as reported in Kwoka, "Overtaking an Oligopoly," 1993, pp. 72, 78.

In 1980 all of the U.S. auto companies experienced sizable losses. Ford and Chrysler actively lobbied the federal government for import restrictions; GM, reversing a decades-long stance of favoring free trade, indicated that it would not oppose restraints. The Reagan administration responded with five years of "voluntary" export restraints (VERs) that it forced on the Japanese.

The U.S. auto companies clearly benefited from the relief that the VERs offered, but their gains were primarily short term, in terms of an enhanced ability to raise prices and earn higher profits.[26] General Motors, in particular, despite some efforts to reverse its course—it had established a joint venture with Toyota to assemble vehicles at a California assembly plant in order to learn more about the vaunted Japanese management systems,[27] and it had begun the Saturn brand and division as an opportunity to rethink production and sales methods[28]—did not fruitfully use this respite to revamp its management structure, its labor relations, and its high production costs and thereby lost the opportunity to regain some of the market share that it had ceded to the Japanese producers.[29] (And an ironic consequence of the VERs was that they actually strengthened the Japanese producers in two ways: since they were limited in the number of vehicles that they could ship to the United States, the Japanese producers refocused their efforts on larger, more luxurious models, thereby offering new challenges to a segment of the market where the U.S. producers had previously been less vulnerable; and the Japanese established U.S. manufacturing facilities, which served them well as the

Japanese yen strengthened relative to the U.S. dollar and made production in Japan relatively less economic.)

By 1986 GM's market share of cars and light trucks (including minivans and pickup trucks) had fallen below 40 percent and continued to sink. In 1992 it fell below 35 percent; in 1994 it was 33.2 percent—over ten percentage points lower than its level of fifteen years earlier.[30] Rebates and price-cutting were again a common phenomenon. For a few months in early 1992 the GM board of directors seriously contemplated the possibility of GM's declaring bankruptcy. Though still the largest producer in a very large industry, GM was no longer the dominant firm that it had been two and three decades earlier, and the U.S. auto industry was far more competitive than it had been in decades.

What had happened? In part, GM and the wider U.S. auto industry faced competition that it did not face before 1970.[31] Until then, the Japanese auto industry had simply not matured sufficiently—in managerial capability and in manufacturing capacity—to offer a serious and sustained challenge to the U.S. producers.[32] These were thus a set of entrants that had not previously challenged the U.S. industry in an economically significant way. After 1970, the U.S. producers would have found themselves competitively challenged in any event.

But the U.S. producers, and especially GM, made it worse for themselves in the ways that they did and did not respond to the Japanese challenge. Their responses combined assumptions that the problems were temporary and would recede on their own after U.S. car buyers "came to their senses" and resumed their traditional preferences for American-made vehicles, that the fit-and-finish problems were more a creation of *Consumer Reports* and its anti-Detroit bias than anything of substance, that massive mechanization and applications of new technology would create lower manufacturing costs and repel the invaders, and ultimately that the federal government should provide the U.S. producers with more protection from the "unfair" competition of the Japanese producers. None of their responses addressed the true problems that the challenge by a new set of efficient entrants posed for the U.S. manufacturers.

Especially for GM, its management had ossified.[33] The company's management had simply become accustomed to its dominance and to the notion that its methods and products were the best and always would be. It became substantially more centralized than Sloan had envisioned, and with the erosion of divisional autonomy came a loss in flexibility and nimbleness;[34] "plodding giant" was an accurate characterization.[35] The company allowed its labor relations and labor costs to get out of control. For example, between 1970 and 1981, hourly compensation in the auto industry generally rose 5.3 percent per year, even though productivity rose by only 1.9 percent annually; wages in the industry were 31.5 percent above the all-manufacturing average in the first year and had risen to 53.9 percent above in the second year.[36] General Motors' labor costs had increased so much that, from the position of low-cost domestic producer in the 1950s and 1960s, it had become the high-cost producer in the 1990s.[37] By early 1996 its labor costs (including very generous fringe benefits and restrictive work rules) were so high that specialized parts producers in the United States, employing largely non-union labor, could produce some components with labor costs that were less than half of those of GM.[38] Ironically, GM's extensive vertical integration—which had been seen as one of its sources of efficiencies in the 1950s and 1960s—was now an expensive liability.[39] It was not surprising that GM was trying—with only modest success—to induce the UAW to allow the company to "outsource" more of its component production.

Further, much of its efforts at greater mechanization and automation were a waste, and efforts to centralize production of components production made it more vulnerable to UAW strikes—as a costly two-and-a-half week strike at a brake plant in early 1996, which shut down virtually all of GM's operations, indicated.

In sum, GM and the other U.S. manufacturers would have faced challenges after the early 1970s in any event. Perhaps better management and better labor relations might have softened the impact of the import challenges and even have allowed GM to retain its dominant market share, although greater levels of actual and potential competition would inevitably have meant reduced profit margins. The companies' actual responses, however—and especially GM's—only made things worse for themselves.

Evaluation

There is little doubt that General Motors was the dominant firm in the U.S. automobile industry from the early 1930s through the late 1970s. Its market share was always over 40 percent and generally about twice the size of the second-place company (the Chrysler Corporation in the 1930s and 1940s; the Ford Motor Company in the 1950s and after). Its profits were, by far, the healthiest in the industry and above competitive levels. Again, as was true of Ford's dominance earlier, the smaller companies in the industry recognized and understood that GM was the dominant company.

Earlier in this chapter we asked whether Ford's behavior during its period of dominance was consistent with the workings of the dominant-firm model. A similar question can be asked about GM. In this latter case, an alternative model would be that of oligopolistic coordination among the Big Three, with GM as the leading firm among the three but the other companies as more powerful than mere passive fringe firms.[40]

Ford and Chrysler did suffer production-cost disadvantages vis-à-vis GM, which is consistent with the dominant-firm model. And the pricing and small car behavior examples discussed above are instances of Ford and Chrysler reacting somewhat passively with respect to General Motors' actions and thus have the flavor of the dominant-firm model. But these examples could also be consistent with the broader oligopoly model. Further, the Ford division of the Ford Motor Company was always a weighty presence as a rival to Chevrolet—not just a passive fringe responder—and similarly the Dodge division of the Chrysler Corporation was a significant rival to Pontiac. (The other brands of Ford and Chrysler were lesser presences in their respective market segments.) Also, in sales to fleet customers (e.g., rental car companies; large corporations; and local, state, and federal governments) vehicle prices have often been substantially lower than those in normal retail channels;[41] these lower prices are easier to reconcile with a collapse of oligopolistic coordination in this part of the market (triggered by the ability of these sizable customers to shop around and to present tempting targets for surreptitious price cuts by sellers eager quickly to grab a sizable chunk of sales[42]) than with the dominant-firm model somehow breaking down.[43]

Finally, in discussions and descriptions of GM's behavior, rarely has there been a sense that GM's decision makers treated its rivals merely as passive fringe firms. Instead, GM's executives were concerned about meeting sales volume targets and about the likely pricing and promotion responses of Ford and Chrysler. This is the stuff of oligopolistic coordination, not of a dominant-firm model.

In sum, General Motors' rise to dominance in the automobile industry in the late 1920s was the result of a number of factors: partly, Durant's helter-skelter aggregation of fledgling automobile and parts brands and facilities provided the basis (after some pruning) for Sloan's strategy; partly, Sloan (whose arrival at GM was a fortuitous result of Durant's acquisitions) had a vision of strategy and structure for the company that fit well with the maturing car market of the 1920s; and, partly, Henry Ford's inflexibility and faulty vision for the maturing market gave GM the opportunity to vault ahead.

By the 1920s entry and survival in the U.S. automobile industry was far more difficult than it had been a decade earlier, so only an extensive set of mergers among the lesser manufacturers of the era, combined with a Sloan-like vision, might have allowed a rival to have replicated GM's efforts. In principle, it was possible; in practice, none really tried. Chrysler came the closest.

GM's decline was more lengthy. New entrants (primarily from Japan) in the 1960s and 1970s meant new market pressures in any event. But GM's senior managers allowed a challenge to become a semi-rout. They were over-confident and over-bearing. They allowed a serious erosion in labor relations and in collective bargaining outcomes to occur; and they made disastrous choices in pursuing ill-conceived automation. Much, though not all, of this decline occurred during Roger Smith's decade of the 1980s. As of 1996, GM's decline may not yet be completed.

CONCLUSION

The U.S. automobile industry has experienced two periods during which a single firm dominated the industry: the Ford Motor Company for the years 1913 until the mid-1920s, and the General Motors Corporation for the considerably longer period of the early 1930s through the late 1970s. In each instance the firm's market share was above 40 percent and for a few years briefly above 50 percent; its profit rates were substantially above those of its rivals and above those earned in competitive industries; and it was generally recognized to be the dominant firm in the industry.

The ascents of both firms were strongly related to key individuals—Henry Ford, Alfred Sloan, and, to a lesser extent, William Durant—who were able to formulate and implement visions for their companies that were the right ones for their specific eras in the development of the auto industry. Ford's vision was the right one for the nascent industry of 1913, but it was a disaster for the maturing one of 1925. Sloan's vision was far more appropriate to the maturing state of the industry and carried GM to dominance for over forty years.

Perhaps more interesting are the declines of both firms and the endings of their periods of dominance. In both instances the declines were characterized by managerial arrogance, hubris, and inflexibility, and by challenges by upstarts with superior management systems and better approaches to the marketplace. In the 1920s the challenger was GM, and its product strategy and organizational strategy were instrumental in toppling Ford; in the 1970s the challengers were the Japanese auto manufacturers, with lower costs of production and superior attention to detail and quality.

It appears that market dominance may well bring with it, sooner or later, managerial arrogance and inflexibility; if there are upstart rivals waiting in the wings, the firm's dominant position will erode. In the latter half of the twentieth century this has been true of IBM, Xerox, U.S. Steel, and American Can, as well as GM. This recounting should provide some reassurance to students of industrial organization (and to consumers), as well as a cautionary warning to the managements of some currently dominant firms (e.g., Coca-Cola, Microsoft, Intel, AT&T) that market-dominant positions—unlike diamonds—may not be forever.

NOTES

1. The definitive history of Ford—the company and the man—is provided by A. Nevins, *Ford: The Times, the Man, the Company* (New York: Charles Scribner's Sons, 1954); A. Nevins and F. E. Hill, *Ford: Expansion and Challenge, 1915-1932* (New York: Charles Scribner's Sons, 1957); A. Nevins and F. E. Hill, *Ford: Decline and Rebirth, 1933-1962* (New York: Charles Scribner's Sons, 1963); see also B. Herndon, *Ford: An Unconventional Biography of the Men and Their Times* (New York: Weybright and Talley, 1969); and C. Gelderman, *Henry Ford: The Wayward Capitalist* (New York: Dial, 1981).

2. See R. G. Cleveland and S. T. Williamson, *The Road Is Yours* (New York: Hawthorn, 1951), pp. 270-291.

3. Only in the 1960s, with the development of bilevel and trilevel rack (drive-on-drive-off) railroad cars, which allowed the economical shipment of whole (assembled) cars, was the economic advantage of the regional assembly plants substantially reduced.

4. These improvements would today be described as "sliding down the learning curve."

5. Nevins, *Times, Man, Company*, p. 534.

6. Profit data can be found in Nevins, *Times, Man, Company* (1954), and L. H. Seltzer, *A Financial History of the American Automobile Industry* (Boston: Houghton Mifflin, 1928).

7. Many industrial organization analysts have questioned the use of accounting profit data in determinations of whether a firm is earning excess profits, arguing that the accounting data frequently do not reveal the crucial economic concepts that are necessary for such determinations. See, for example, Franklin Fisher and John McGowan, "On the

Misuse of Accounting Rates of Return to Infer Monopoly Profits," *American Economic Review* 13 (1983): 82-97. In the case of the Ford Motor Company, however, the profit rates were so high that there can be little doubt that they were substantially above a competitive rate of return.

8. Nevins and Hill, *Expansion and Challenge*, p. 388.

9. In modern terms, the Model T was nearing the end of a product life cycle. For an updated application to the automobile industry, see J. E. Kwoka Jr., "Altering the Product Life Cycle of Consumer Durables: The Case of Minivans," *Managerial and Decision Economics* 17 (1996): 17-25.

10. And the financing subsidiary was sold in 1933 and would not be re-established until 1959.

11. Ford also acquired a lead mine, explored for oil, took steps to produce adhesives, and bought dolomite lands so as to produce magnesium.

12. The hardship that this lengthy shutdown caused for Ford's workers and dealers (and the consequences for the morale and goodwill of these two important groups) apparently was of little concern to Henry Ford.

13. The Ford Motor Company never did produce tires commercially, and the rubber plantations were eventually sold. In addition to the activities mentioned in the text, Ford operated, as is explained in the next section (General Motors), this vision was no longer appropriate for a company that hoped to remain as the dominant firm in a market that had reached the level of maturity of the automobile market of the late 1920s.

14. The origins of this model are to be found in George Stigler, "Monopoly and Oligopoly by Merger," *American Economic Review* 40 (1950): 23-34, and George Stigler, "The Dominant Firm and the Inverted Price Umbrella," *Journal of Law and Economics* 8 (1965): 167-172; a compact presentation of the model is provided by Dennis W. Carlton and Jeffrey M. Perloff, *Modern Industrial Organization* (New York: HarperCollins, 1994): 157-174.

15. See H. Leibenstein, "Bandwagon, Snob, and Veblen Effects in the Theory of Consumers' Demand," *Quarterly Journal of Economics* 64 (1950): 183-207.

16. The rise of GM and its overtaking of Ford is discussed by A. J. Kuhn, *GM Passes Ford, 1918-1938: Designing the General Motors Performance-Control System* (University Park: Pennsylvania State University Press, 1986).

17. This managerial and organizational structure was quite innovative at the time and has since formed the bases for many other corporate organizations. It has come to be known as the "M-form" structure; see O. E. Williamson, *Markets and Hierarchies—Analysis and Antitrust Implications: A Study in the Economics of Internal Organization* (New York: Free Press, 1975). Also, as was noted above, GM had formal research laboratories that were largely under the direction of the central management.

18. See R. M. MacDonald, *Collective Bargaining in the Automobile Industry* (New Haven, CT: Yale University Press, 1963).

19. The behavior of GM and the automobile industry more generally during the heyday of GM's dominance—the 1950s and 1960s—can be found in L. J. White, *The Automobile Industry in the Postwar Period* (Cambridge, MA: Harvard University Press, 1971); L. J. White, "The Automobile Industry," in W. Adams, ed., *The Structure of American Industry*, 5th ed. (New York: Macmillan, 1977a), pp. 165-220; L. J. White, "The Automobile Industry," in W. Adams, ed., *The Structure of American Industry*, 6th ed. (New York: Macmillan, 1982), pp. 136-190.

20. In 1932, after GM had attained its leadership in the industry, a GM vice president was quoted as saying, "Mr. Ford, who won't play, is pretty much the price setter in this industry. I'll bet if Mr. Ford's cars were $50 higher, ours would be $50 higher. We care about Ford. We have been struggling with him for years," United States Federal Trade Commission, *Report on the Motor Vehicle Industry* (Washington, D.C.: U.S. Government Printing Office, 1939), p. 33.

21. See White, *Postwar Period*, 1971; and L. J. White, "The American Automobile Industry and the Small Car, 1945-1970," *Journal of Industrial Economics* 20 (1972): 179-192.

22. Models that can explain this reluctance are found in L. J. White, "Market Structure and Product Varieties," *American Economic Review* 67 (1977b): 179-182; M. Mussa and S. Rosen, "Monopoly and Product Quality," *Journal of Economic Theory* 18 (August 1978): 301-317, and S. Donnenfeld and L. J. White, "Product Variety and the Inefficiency of Monopoly," *Economica* 55 (1988): 393-401.

23. This was just one of many errors that Chrysler's management made during the 1960s and 1970s; by the end of the 1970s the company hovered near bankruptcy, and the federal government proceeded to bail out the company at the end of 1979 with a program of $1.5 billion in loan guarantees. Also, Chrysler benefited from the program of "voluntary export restraints" that the Reagan administration forced on the Japanese government from 1981 until 1986.

24. General Motors' decline, and that of the U.S. auto industry more generally, is documented by M. Keller, *Rude Awakening* (New York: William Morrow, 1989); J. E. Kwoka Jr., "Automobiles: Overtaking an Oligopoly," in L. L. Duetsch, ed., *Industry Studies* (Englewood Cliffs, NJ: Prentice Hall, 1993), pp. 63-84; see also J. P. Wright, *On a Clear Day You Can See General Motors: John Z. De Lorean's Look Inside the Automotive Giant* (Grosse Pointe, MI: Wright Enterprises, 1979); and B. Yates, *The Decline and Fall of the American Automobile Industry* (New York: Vintage, 1983); also note that Kuhn, "GM Passes Ford," places the beginning of the decline a decade earlier.

25. Many of these advantages of the Japanese industry are documented in J. Womack, D. Jones, and D. Roos, *The Machine That Changed the World* (New York: Macmillan, 1990); and Kwoka, "Overtaking an Oligopoly."

26. Discussions of the VER experience can be found in R. Crandall, "Import Quotas and the Automobile Industry: The Costs of Protectionism," *Brookings Review* 2 (1984): 8-16; R. C. Feenstra, "Automobile Prices and Protection: The U.S.-Japan Trade Restraint," *Journal of Political Modeling* 7 (March 1985): 49-68; United States International Trade Commission, "A Review of Recent Developments in the U.S. Automobile Industry, Including an Assessment of the Japanese Voluntary Restraint Agreements," Publication No. 1648 (February 1985); and L. J. White, "The United States Automobile Industry: A Case Study of a De Facto Industrial Policy," in H. Muto, S. Sekiguchi, K. Suzumura, and I. Yamazawa, eds., *Industrial Policies for Pacific Economic Growth* (Boston: Allen & Unwin, 1986), pp. 196-210.

27. See J. E. Kwoka Jr., "International Joint Venture: General Motors and Toyota (1983)," in J. E. Kwoka Jr., and L. J. White, eds., *The Antitrust Revolution: The Role of Economics* (New York: HarperCollins, 1994), pp. 46-75.

28. See M. Darling, "Saturn: GM's $5 Billion Blunder?," *Stern Business* 1 (1995): 26-31.

29. And neither the joint venture with Toyota nor the Saturn experiment turned out to have the long-run beneficial consequences that had been promised. Whatever lessons there were to be learned did not seem to be easily transferred and propagated more widely within the GM management structure. See Keller, *Rude Awakening*; Kwoka, "Overtaking an

Oligopoly"; and Darling, "Saturn."

30. As of mid-1996, GM's market share had fallen below 32 percent; See K. Bradsher, "What's New at GM? Cars, for a Change" *New York Times* (8 September, 1996): 3-1.

31. As an historical footnote, it is interesting to speculate about what might have occurred in the U.S. automobile market decades earlier if World War II had not occurred and eventually yielded the total destruction of the manufacturing facilities of Japan and Germany. The import challenges from Germany in the late 1950s and from Japan in the early 1970s might well have otherwise occurred as early as the 1940s.

32. At about the same time the Japanese companies began substantial shipments to European markets.

33. Though many of GM's mistakes of the 1970s preceded his managerial reign, Roger Smith—who was GM's CEO from the early 1980s until the early 1990s—presided over many of the automation and investment mistakes of the 1980s and continued GM's newly acquired tradition of mishandling its labor relations. See Keller, *Rude Awakening*.

34. In fairness, the substantially tightened pollutant emissions control, fuel economy, and safety regulations of the 1970s and after required substantially more planning, engineering, and lead times; but the same regulatory structure applied to Ford, Chrysler, and the Japanese companies, who seemed to be able to respond more nimbly. See Womack, Jones, and Roos, *The Machine*.

35. See Bradsher, "What's New?"

36. Kwoka, "Overtaking an Oligopoly," p. 68.

37. Ford had become the low-cost producer. See Womack, Jones, and Roos, *The Machine*.

38. See N. M. Christian and A. Sharpe, "A Rich Benefits Plan Gives GM Competitors Cost Edge," *Wall Street Journal* (21 March 1996): B1.

39. One estimate, as of mid-1996, placed GM's disadvantage as the result of its greater vertical integration at $440 and $600 per vehicle vis-à-vis Ford and Chrysler, respectively.

40. T. F. Bresnahan, "Competition and Collusion in the American Automobile Industry: The 1955 Price War," *Journal of Industrial Economics* 35 (June 1987): 457-482; for example, provides econometric tests that are consistent with oligopolistic behavior for the industry in 1954 and 1956 (but not 1955, which he argues was much more competitive and an anomaly). But he does not explicitly test for a dominant-firm model as an alternative.

41. See L. J. White, "A Legal Attack on Oligopoly Pricing: The Automobile Fleet Sales Case," *Journal of Economic* Issues 9 (June 1975).

42. This exactly what the general oligopoly model of G. J. Stigler, "A Theory of Oligopoly," *Journal of Political Economy* 72 (February 1964): 55-69, would predict.

43. An attempt to integrate the fleet sales experience with the dominant-firm model, however, would run as follows: in the normal retail channels, GM's lower manufacturing costs and greater brand-name reputation provided the basis for its dominant position and for its rivals' limited abilities to expand at GM's expense; in the fleet sales area, GM's brand-name reputation was much less important, so its rivals could more readily attempt to steal customers on the basis of price cuts.

8

THE RISE AND FALL OF IBM

Don E. Waldman

> The toughest thing about success is that you've got
> to keep on being a success.
> — Irving Berlin

INTRODUCTION

Few firms have gone from the top of an industry to the middle of the pack more
quickly than International Business Machines, known as IBM. For decades IBM
was the firm that stood for high technology and computers, yet today it is clinging
to its slight market share lead in the computer industry. Worse yet for the
company's management, its potential to dominate the industry has been lost to
Microsoft and Intel. What happened in such a short time to a true industrial giant
of the twentieth century? Is IBM's reign over, or will it bounce back and re-
emerge as the industry leader? These issues will be addressed in this chapter. The
major hypothesis advanced is that IBM fell victim to two major problems: the fear
of antitrust prosecution and an inbred, outdated, and complacent managerial
structure. These two factors combined to ultimately destroy the company's
dominant position.

A decade ago IBM produced over 60 percent of the mainframe computers sold
in the world; its annual gross revenues consistently exceeded $50 billion, peaking
at $68.9 billion in 1990, and it employed over 400,000 people around the world.[1]
Furthermore, as Table 8.1 shows, its net earnings in 1984 were a staggering $6.5
billion. By 1993, IBM's total world employment had declined by 36.8 percent to
256,000 and IBM sustained an $8.1 billion loss. How did this turn of events
happen?

Table 8.1
IBM Revenues, Net Earnings, and Worldwide Employment

Year	Gross Income ($ millions)	Net Earnings ($ millions)	Employment
1945	138	11	18,257
1946	116	19	22,492
1947	139	24	22,591
1948	156	28	24,940
1949	183	33	27,236
1950	266	37	30,261
1951	355	32	35,124
1952	412	34	41,458
1953	497	39	46,170
1954	570	59	50,225
1955	696	73	56,297
1956	892	87	72,504
1957	1,203	110	83,588
1958	1,418	152	86,736
1959	1,613	176	94,912
1960	1,817	205	104,241
1961	2,202	254	116,276
1962	2,591	305	127,468
1963	2,863	364	137,612
1964	3,239	431	149,834
1965	3,573	477	172,445
1966	4,248	526	198,186
1967	5,345	651	221,866
1968	6,889	871	241,974
1969	7,197	934	258,662
1970	7,504	1,018	269,291
1971	8,274	1,079	265,493
1972	9,533	1,279	262,152
1973	10,993	1,575	274,108
1974	12,675	1,838	292,350
1975	14,437	1,990	288,647
1976	16,304	2,398	291,977
1977	18,133	2,719	310,155

Continued

1978	21,076	3,111	325,517
1979	22,863	3,011	337,119
1980	26,213	3,397	341,279
1981	29,070	3,610	354,936
1982	34,364	4,409	364,196
1983	40,180	5,485	369,545
1984	46,309	6,582	394,930
1985	50,718	6,555	405,535
1986	52,160	4,789	403,508
1987	55,256	5,258	389,348
1988	59,598	5,741	387,112
1989	62,654	3,722	383,220
1990	68,931	5,967	373,289
1991	64,766	(-2,861)	344,396
1992	64,523	(-4,965)	301,542
1993	62,716	(-8,101)	256,207
1994	64,052	2,965	215,000[a]

[a] estimate

Sources: Emerson W. Pugh, *Building IBM: Shaping an Industry and Its Technology* (Cambridge, MA: MIT Press, 1995), pp. 323-324; "IBM Posts First Annual Profit Since 1990," *New York Times*, 24 January 1995, D-1; and "Lessons in Rebounds From GM and IBM," *New York Times*, 24 October 1994, D-1.

The chapter begins with a review of IBM's historical rise to power and then moves to an analysis of how IBM maintained dominance in the computer industry. The following sections explore IBM's loss of market power. It is argued that antitrust policy combined with the firm's managerial structure resulted in a hierarchy that was inefficient in a rapidly developing high technology industry. Finally, some conclusions are presented.

IBM'S RISE TO DOMINANCE

Thomas J. Watson Sr. built IBM by emphasizing to its salesmen an understanding of and commitment to its customers' needs and a dedication to quality and to on-time delivery.[2] Watson Sr. was a salesman, not a technological genius, and IBM's chief executive officers (CEOs) for decades to come followed in his footsteps. Watson Sr. had taken a small firm, the Computing Tabulating Recording Company, changed to IBM in 1924, specializing in scales and measuring devices, and by focusing its attention on how to provide solutions to the accounting problems of large corporations had built up a highly profitable business. Watson Sr. trained his sales representatives to have one overriding objective—to solve each individual customer's problems with an individual solution. He was convinced that as long as IBM's machines helped its customers' businesses operate more efficiently, IBM would remain the industry's dominant force.[3]

IBM did not start out as the leader in the computer industry. The world's first important commercial computer, the UNIVAC, was produced by Remington Rand. The UNIVAC revolutionized the speed at which electronic calculations could be completed. While Rand was producing the UNIVAC in the late 1940s, IBM was concentrating on producing large electronic business calculators that operated on vacuum tubes and could complete payroll functions ten times faster than IBM's punch-card machines.[4] By 1952 IBM had succeeded in introducing the IBM 702, an electronic calculator designed to replace its punch-card machines. When Thomas Watson Jr. took control of the company from his father, he decided to push IBM into the computer age. Under Thomas Watson Jr.'s leadership IBM spent over 50 percent of its net income on research and development (R&D) in the 1960s and 1970s. This represented a huge increase over the 15 percent Watson Sr. spent during the 1940s.[5] Spurred on by Thomas Watson Jr., IBM moved quickly to gain the lead in transistor technology, and by 1957 its sales had reached $1 billion. This was a remarkable achievement considering that in 1946 its sales were a mere $116 million.[6]

One recurring theme in IBM's rise to dominance was the firm's emphasis on sales and service. In many markets, IBM has managed to dominate without being the technological leader. Early in the history of the computer industry buyers were uninformed about the technical capabilities of these new machines. Watson Sr. followed his old practice of training the IBM sales force to handle any possible problems quickly and efficiently. The sales force was trained extensively in how to operate the computers, how to work with software applications, and perhaps most importantly, how to hold a new buyer's hand during the adjustment period.[7]

Thomas Watson Sr. realized far more quickly than his rivals that the typical business firm, as distinguished from scientific computer users, lacked any sophisticated knowledge of computer usage. IBM was determined to fill this knowledge void with its own sales force. Furthermore, IBM committed to making computers available to educational institutions at huge discounts in an effort to tie students to IBM products after graduation. This strategy worked extremely well. In the 1960s an entire first generation of computer users was trained in college on IBM machines. Upon graduation, these former students thought first to purchase IBM products.

Once business firms purchased an IBM computer, they quickly became dependent on IBM's software. This phenomenon came to be known as "software lock-in."[8] Up until the point of purchase of a computer system, buyers had a choice regarding what brand to install. After the purchase of an IBM computer, however, the buyer became completely dependent on IBM's software and programming, and the cost of switching to another manufacturer often became prohibitively high. Once a large corporation had paid IBM thousands or millions of dollars to install and organize its data base, there was little chance it would switch to a new system to save a mere 10 or 15 percent in monthly leasing charges.

In the early years of its growing dominance, IBM benefited from "learning-by-doing." Certain production processes result in lower costs as output increases because experience gained through the actual production process results in lower direct labor costs.[9] When learning-by-doing is important, early entrants are able to maintain a large market share and increase their present value of profits by strategically producing significantly larger outputs early on than would be justified by short-run profit-maximizing behavior. By producing large quantities in early time periods, the first firms into the market are able to significantly reduce their costs in later time periods. A new firm attempting to enter the market in later periods faces a significant cost disadvantage because it has not moved down its learning curve. In markets characterized by significant learning-by-doing, entry is likely to be difficult.

Learning-by-doing can be viewed as an investment in cost reduction. The early entrant is willing to invest in large current outputs in order to reduce its future costs, even if this investment significantly reduces current profits. There is evidence that learning-by-doing was important in the early years of the computer industry. Brock suggests that long-run average costs for IBM's 370/168 central processing unit decreased dramatically as total accumulated output increased from 300 units to 700 units.[10]

Once IBM established a large customer base, it may also have taken advantage of economies of scale associated with R&D. According to the Federal Trade Commission, the computer industry was second only to the pharmaceuticals industry in intensity of R&D efforts between 1974 and 1977.[11] During those four years, the industry spent an average of 8.9 percent of sales on research and development.[12] Because of its large volume, IBM was able to spread the overhead costs of R&D over more units, and this may have resulted in a cost advantage vis-à-vis competitors.

In addition to the advantages of a superior sales force, software lock-ins, learning-by-doing, and economies of scale in research and development, IBM benefited from a superior service operation. Early computers were constantly breaking down because they were dependent upon vacuum tubes rather than semiconductors. A system "crash" created complete havoc in a company trying to process its monthly payroll. To avoid this havoc, companies were willing to pay premium prices to IBM to gain access to the company's national service network.[13] IBM covered the nation with service centers to take care of problems, while smaller competitors had far fewer service providers nationwide. This extensive service network meant that customers came to rely on IBM to provide fast low-cost service.

To further reinforce its service advantage, IBM adopted a pricing policy of tying (or bundling) service with its sale or lease price, so that the marginal cost of an additional service call was zero. The tying of service to IBM's sale and lease prices prevented the development of an independent service industry to service all brands of computers. The development of a national independent service market, like the one that currently exists for personal computers, would have made entry into the computer industry easier by providing efficient, quick service for all brands anywhere in the country.

IBM's early ride to dominance was primarily the result of Thomas Watson Sr.'s recognition of the company's continued need to emphasize a highly trained professional sales force, combined with its taking advantage of learning-by-doing and the tying of free service to the sale or lease of its computers.

THE MAINTENANCE OF POWER

By the early 1960s IBM was firmly established as the computer industry's dominant firm. In 1964 IBM held an 80 percent market share of the "value of installed and on-order data processing equipment."[14] As shown in Table 8.2, its profit in 1964 was 19.1 percent of stockholders' equity, making IBM one of the nation's most profitable companies. The maintenance of its dominance in the 1960s and 1970s was built upon the development of the System/360 series of mainframe computers. At the time of the System/360's development, IBM's market share was being reduced by the inroads of such corporate giants as General Electric (GE), RCA, Rand, and Control Data. The objective of the System/360 series was to replace all existing computers, including IBM's existing machines.

Under Thomas Watson Jr., the company was willing to produce a new model that would replace its entire line of leased computers, including IBM's then leading mainframe model, the 1401. In the words of Vic Learson, the System/360 project leader, "[c]orporate policy . . . is that by 1967 the 1401 will be dead as a Dodo."[15] We will show shortly that this aggressive managerial approach disappeared completely in the 1970s and 1980s.

The idea behind the System/360 was that all of IBM's computers would be compatible because they would all run the same software. Machines that leased for $2,500 per month would run on the same software as machines leased for over $100,000 per month. Furthermore, the 360 could run all the programs that ran on the 1401, and, therefore, the 1401's customer could easily transfer their programs directly to the 360. As a customer's needs expanded, IBM would simply add new devices, such as a faster processor or more memory. The development of the System/360 line was an extremely risky gamble. Failure to successfully develop the System/360 could have destroyed IBM, but Thomas Watson Jr. took the huge gamble associated with development. He hired 60,000 new employees, invested $750 million into engineering development, and opened five new manufacturing facilities at a cost of $4.5 billion.[16] Every component of IBM's product line had to be redesigned to assure compatibility. The success of the System/360 established IBM's dominance for twenty years.

As the time for the introduction of the System/360 approached, IBM was concerned that several competitors would introduce technically superior machines before IBM's official introduction of the System/360 models. One solution to this problem was for IBM to "preannounce" all five main System/360 models well in advance of when most of these computers would be ready for delivery. In fact in

Table 8.2
Profit Rate as a Percentage of Stockholders' Equity: IBM, Top 47 Manufacturers, and All Manufacturers, 1960-1975

Year	IBM (%)	Top 47 Manufacturers (%)	All Manufacturers (%)
1960	17.3	—	9.2
1961	17.5	—	8.9
1962	17.5	12.1	9.8
1963	18.2	12.3	10.3
1964	19.1	13.5	11.6
1965	18.5	14.3	13.0
1966	15.8	14.1	13.4
1967	17.0	12.6	11.7
1968	19.1	12.3	12.1
1969	17.7	10.3	11.5
1970	17.1	7.8	9.3
1971	16.2	8.6	9.7
1972	16.9	11.0	10.6
1973	17.9	13.4	12.8
1974	18.2	15.5	14.9
1975	17.4	12.7	11.6

Source: Richard T. DeLamarter, *Big Blue: IBM's Use and Abuse of Power* (New York: Dodd, Mead, 1986), p. 101.

April 1964, IBM announced the forthcoming availability of five System/360 models, even though several of these models were not fully developed, and many technical problems remained to be dealt with before delivery would be possible.

In the words of Thomas Watson Jr.:

By the spring of '64 our hand was forced and we had to, with our eyes wide open, announce a complete line–some of the machines twenty-four months early, and the total line an average of twelve months early. I guess all of us who were thinking about the matter realized that we should have problems when we did this, but I don't think any of us anticipated that the problems would reach the serious proportions that they now have. . . .

[W]e were so up against the wall saleswise that had we waited another nine months to announce the line we would have lost positions that we could ill afford to lose.[17]

The decision to preannounce the introduction of the System/360 line proved to be a brilliant business strategy. Despite the fact that the first machines were not delivered until April 1965 and that some of the promised models were never developed, the mere announcement of IBM's coming new line prevented buyers from committing to competitors' new machines, some of which were technically superior to the System/360 computers. Ironically, by the time buyers became disgusted by the long IBM delays, many of IBM's competitors, including industrial giants RCA and General Electric, had left the market. When the dust settled in the early 1970s, IBM had a firmly established market share of approximately 75 percent, and the remaining firms, such as Sperry Rand, Burroughs, Honeywell, NCR, and Control Data, were left to fill relatively small niches in the market.

In addition to preannouncement, IBM used other strategies to maintain its market leadership. One of the most important strategies was the selective use of price discrimination. Generally IBM charged much higher list prices than its competitors for individual pieces of equipment. IBM, however, bundled entire systems together by charging one price for the central processing unit (CPU), related software, and maintenance, rather than charging different prices for each individual piece of a system. By bundling systems together IBM was able to discriminate effectively between different users because the price a user paid for an individual piece of equipment was unknown. Once a customer made a decision to buy from IBM, it received an entire computer system, and there was no possibility of competition for any components from competitors.

The bundling system worked extremely well for IBM until customers were ready to upgrade their systems in the late 1960s. As noted above, IBM's list prices for individual pieces of equipment were priced very high compared to IBM's competitors. The high prices for replacement equipment were necessitated by IBM's need to cover the costs of providing free service to all customers and free systems to educational institutions. In November 1967 the first of many small firms began to market individual pieces of "plug-compatible IBM equipment," such as tape and disk drives, at much lower prices than IBM's prices.

The market for plug-compatible computer equipment grew rapidly in the late 1960s. In 1966 there were only three manufacturers of plug-compatible equipment, whereas by 1972 there were approximately a hundred manufacturers. Of these hundred, twelve firms were primarily manufacturers of only IBM-plug-compatible equipment. In the late 1960s, these firms were offering IBM-plug-compatible equipment at prices well below IBM's prices. As a result, IBM lost a significant share of the market.

The erosion in IBM's share of the IBM peripheral equipment market continued well into 1970, at which time IBM decided to respond to these inroads with a series of actions. In September and December 1970, IBM selectively and dramatically reduced the price of peripheral equipment. IBM also redesigned certain components so that they could be connected to the IBM CPU only through an integrated file adapter, rather than through the traditional external disk control unit. This change made the use of non-IBM equipment much less attractive to users. In May 1971 IBM announced a fixed-term leasing plan, which provided for an 8 percent price reduction for users signing a one-year lease on peripheral equipment and a 16 percent price reduction for signers of a two-year lease. Finally, at the same time that IBM announced large price reductions on peripheral equipment, it announced large price increases on its central processing units to recoup lost revenues.

As a result of IBM's actions, the manufacturers of peripheral equipment were forced to cut prices drastically. These actions resulted in a series of private antitrust actions by the manufacturers of peripheral equipment.[18]

One of the unanticipated effects of IBM's new pricing strategy was to set the price of IBM's CPUs high enough to encourage entry. The first major entrant was Amdahl Corporation, which was founded by Gene Amdahl after he left IBM. Amdahl had been deeply involved in the development of the System/360. In 1975, he introduced the Amdahl 470 computer, which was fully compatible with IBM's best System/370 computer (which was the technologically advanced successor to the System/360), but was much faster and priced much lower.[19] By 1978 several other firms were producing CPUs to challenge IBM's machines.[20]

Threatened with a significant decrease in its CPU market share, IBM once again responded with a series of aggressive actions. In March 1977 it introduced a more powerful computer, the 3033. Later in 1977 IBM reduced prices on its System/370 computers by between 20 and 35 percent.[21] Observing IBM's pricing policy in response to entry in the 1970s, Scherer concluded, "it seems reasonable to infer that, having learned that each segment of its computer business would induce competitive entry if prices were set too high, it adopted something closer to an across-the-board limit pricing policy."[22]

We have seen that IBM maintained its power in the 1960s and 1970s by taking the huge risks associated with developing and introducing a new computer model, the System/360, which made its own established base of installed computers obsolete. Thomas Watson Jr. was willing to gamble the company on the risky strategy of preannouncement of products before development was completed. Furthermore, IBM bundled equipment into full systems to facilitate price discrimination and responded aggressively to the entry of new firms by cutting prices and changing IBM's system configurations. Were all of these actions legal for a firm with a dominant market share? The Justice Department concluded that they were not, and in 1969 filed an antitrust suit against IBM. With the filing of the 1969 Justice Department antitrust suit the seeds were sown for the beginning of the end of IBM's dominance.

THE LOSS OF POWER

We have observed how IBM was able to build and maintain dominance in the 1950s, 1960s, and early 1970s. Sometime in the mid-1970s, however, IBM began to lose its stranglehold over the industry. Two factors were primarily responsible for this relative decline: the filing of the 1969 antitrust case and the failure of IBM's management to respond to the changing nature of the computer industry as it moved rapidly from a world of large mainframe computers to a world of small personal computers.

The 1969 Government Antitrust Case

On the last day of the Johnson administration, the Justice Department charged IBM with attempting to monopolize the general-purpose electronic digital computer market.[23] The Justice Department measured IBM's market share at approximately 75 percent, based on the lease value of the installed base of electronic data processing equipment. IBM contended that its market share was only 33 percent of the correct relevant market, which it defined as all data processing equipment, including computers, programmable handheld calculators, message-switching equipment, and just about any other piece of equipment imaginable.

Specifically, the government charged IBM with a series of aggressive actions. The complaint alleged that IBM bundled systems together by charging a single price for the central processor, related software, and maintenance, rather than charging different prices for each individual piece of equipment. Such a bundling policy made it possible for IBM to discriminate effectively between different users, because the price a user paid for an individual piece of equipment was unknown. IBM was also accused of introducing new computer lines (particularly the System/360) in ways that were aimed at destroying the sales of machines recently introduced by competitors. In particular, the government complained about IBM's practice of announcing the introduction of a new line well in advance of its actual introduction. Furthermore, according to the government, there were instances when IBM announced a machine would be forthcoming even though no such machine existed or was even planned.

The filing and prosecution of the antitrust case affected IBM's business behavior for the next twenty years. For example, when Frank Cary became chairman of the board in 1973 he realized that personal computers were the wave of the future and was prepared to break an old IBM corporate taboo and use non-IBM technology to produce personal computers. Cary quickly discovered, however, that the IBM legal defense team would step in to thwart any effort to obtain technology from competitors. According to Paul Carroll:

Cary had to spend much of his time fighting [the] federal government antitrust suit that lasted from 1969 to 1982 and that limited the sorts of things IBM management could discuss. The government collected more than 760 million documents from IBM during that stretch. The case had everyone working so hard that one lawyer from IBM billed twenty-seven hours in a single day (by taking a flight from New York to the West Coast and picking up three hours because of the time change). IBM's top executives were afraid to put anything down on paper for fear the government would subpoena the document. Lawyers, who were developing a stranglehold on the business, decided what could be said at meetings. No one could talk about IBM's market share, or if they did, they'd talk in meaningless terms, describing the market for word processors as though it included everything from the supercomputer on down to paper and pencils. Executives couldn't do any competitive analysis. Developers weren't allowed to buy a competitor's machine; they were just supposed to know what was in it.[24]

Perhaps the greatest negative impact on IBM of the antitrust case was the company's hesitance to accept Bill Gates's 1986 offer to sell IBM a 10 percent interest in Microsoft. That interest would have cost IBM $100 million in 1986 and would have been worth $3 billion in 1993.[25] To put this mistake in perspective, IBM could have earned far more on a 10 percent stock interest in Microsoft than it has earned in its entire history in the personal computer (PC) business. Despite the 1982 Justice Department decision to drop the antitrust suit, in 1986 IBM decided against purchasing an interest in Microsoft because it was afraid to be seen as "throwing [its] weight around too much by gaining control over Microsoft."[26]

The antitrust suit even affected IBM's research and development program in direct ways.[27] Remarkably, after the government suit was filed in 1969, lawyers gained control over even the most technical elements of IBM's business. The lawyers made the researchers' jobs much more difficult by setting up elaborate procedures before R&D programs could go forward. If a research team wanted to enter into a contract with an outside company, the team had to first get approval from IBM's antitrust lawyers, then from the corporate lawyers at IBM's research headquarters in Yorktown Heights, and finally from the lawyers at Armonk. The process could take up to two years.[28]

Of course IBM's legal defense was nothing if not aggressive. It was estimated that the firm spent over $1 billion on its defense.[29] Frank Cary is said to have once told his legal team to spend whatever was necessary, "and they still went over budget."[30] Massachusetts Institute of Technology economist Franklin Fisher named his new yacht the *Section 3* to show who paid for the boat—IBM.[31] The opportunity costs of spending $1 billion on an antitrust defense are astounding. If IBM had invested that $1 billion in developing an operating system for its PC, Microsoft might still be a small consulting firm rather than the most important force in the global computer industry.

It has been suggested that IBM might have fared better if it had agreed to settle the antitrust case by breaking itself up into several different companies.[32] For instance, according to Scherer if IBM had voluntarily dismantled, "[i]t is arguable that at least one of the survivors would have entered the personal computer field earlier than the parent did and, by moving quickly and aggressively, established an operating system standard over which it could maintain control."[33]

It would be inaccurate, however, to blame the antitrust case for all or even most of IBM's demise. For undoubtedly the primary cause of IBM's downfall was its reliance on a 1950's management structure and philosophy when trying to compete in the high technology world of the 1980s and 1990s.

The Failures of IBM Management

Economists have recognized for many years that a loss of hierarchical control can result in grave problems for a corporation, and IBM's recent history is a textbook example of such problems. As early as 1959 Edith Penrose emphasized the potential negative impact of a managerial talent constraint on a firm's growth.[34] According to Penrose the act of continuously hiring new managers is subject to diminishing returns.[35] Furthermore, the hiring of a large number of new managers limits the growth of the firm because existing managers are required to spend valuable time training new managers instead of providing managerial services related directly to the growth of production.

Scherer explained the issue of diminishing returns to managerial inputs in a somewhat different way.[36] In any large corporation there is only one chief executive officer, who may be viewed as the firm's entrepreneur. This is the person who ultimately assumes responsibility for decision making. According to Scherer:

[A]s enterprises increase in size, their chief executives are confronted with more and more decisions, and they are removed farther and farther from the reality of front-line production and marketing operations. Their ability to make sound decisions is attenuated, with a consequent rise in costs and/or fall in revenues. The problem is aggravated when the firm operates in a complex or rapidly changing environment, for it is the non-routine decisions associated with change that press most heavily upon top managers capacities.[37]

Scherer's argument is related to Williamson's position that large corporations are burdened by a loss of hierarchical control.[38] In the typical corporate pyramid, such as the one that existed for decades at IBM, the CEO sits atop a complex structure of high-level, middle-level and low-level managers. As the size of the firm expands (recall that IBM had a workforce of over 400,000), it requires an army of managers to run the operation. This throng of managers eventually overwhelms a firm's ability to run a cost-efficient operation capable of making rapid decisions. At the top of the IBM management structure was the Management Committee in Armonk, New York, that consisted of from three to six members and which historically decided all matters, even trivial ones. Until 1989, for example, the Management Committee sat in judgment on everything from what a product looked like to whether a salesperson could grant a reduced price to keep a customer.[39] IBM's managerial system was slow and cumbersome and simply not suited to the fast-paced computer industry of the 1980s. Furthermore, the decision makers typically had only limited technical insight into the computer industry, since the CEOs and other top managers were generally drawn from the ranks of the sales department, not from technical areas.

Many of IBM's recent problems have resulted from management's failure to recognize that the personal computer would one day be something more than a home toy. To IBM's senior management in the 1970s and early 1980s the future was still in mainframes and minicomputers for commercial use. According to one member of the Management Committee, "[t]he general attitude was that you don't have big problems in small markets, and we thought the personal computer was a very small market."[40] In 1985, for example, Don Estridge, the original mastermind of the IBM PC operation, wanted to produce a new line of PCs based on Intel's fast 80386 microprocessor. Estridge theorized that the way to fight the PC clones was to destroy them by producing much faster and better PCs. The Management Committee, fearing that faster PCs would threaten IBM's mainframe business, which still was the basis for most of IBM's revenues, refused to approve Estridge's plan. Contrast this decision with Thomas Watson Jr.'s willingness to destroy the IBM 1401 line and risk the entire company to produce the System/360. By the 1980s, the Management Committee had become so conservative that it refused to take even moderate risks of damaging or making obsolete some of IBM's product lines. According to Carroll,

The senior executives, all ex-salesmen, preferred the less disruptive approach that was more conventional around IBM and that had helped it wring such extraordinary profits out of the mainframe business. The executives wanted to milk the existing product line as long as possible. After all, all the expensive work that goes into designing PCs had already been paid for. So why not just sit back and keep producing PCs that cost IBM about half what customers would pay? Only when IBM couldn't delay any longer would it pay to design and bring out products using new technology.[41]

By 1980, IBM had suffered a series of personal computer disasters. First there was the IBM SCAMP, then the 5110, then the Datamaster. All three were commercial failures, and one of the biggest problems with each product was IBM's inability to develop an effective operating system.[42] With the development of the IBM-PC project in 1980, the PC group leaders decided to break with company precedent and use outside help to develop the operating system.

The IBM team first approached Bill Gates regarding an operating system, but Gates referred them to Gary Kildall the president of Digital Research Intergalactic (DRI) and the creator of the Control Program/Monitor (CP/M) operating system, which was then the most widely used operating system for personal computers. Gates set up a meeting between Kildall and IBM. Kildall then committed a faux pas of epic proportions in business history.[43] When the IBM team showed up as scheduled at his home, Kildall was off flying his airplane. Maybe Kildall's plane got off the ground, but his relationship with IBM never did, so IBM turned back to Gates to develop an operating system.

Gates had little experience writing operating systems, and he had little time to develop one, so he turned to a small local firm, Seattle Computing, for help. For $75,000, Microsoft purchased an operating system called quick and dirty operating system (QDOS) from Seattle Computing.[44] In concert with a large group of IBM programmers, Microsoft went to work around the clock to modify QDOS. The result was arguably the most significant commercial product of the later half of the century—MS-DOS. IBM management immediately made the first of three large tactical blunders in dealing with Bill Gates and Microsoft.

Blunder 1. IBM never secured the rights to the source code for DOS. Without access to the source code, IBM could not modify DOS (disk repeating system) and was completely dependent on Microsoft for any improvements. Since IBM and Microsoft were working jointly on developing the operating system, the standard industry practice would have been for IBM to obtain the rights to the source code.[45] According to Ferguson and Morris, the pending antitrust case again foiled IBM:

Failure to secure the rights to the DOS source code was clearly an error, but it was certainly an understandable one. It was made during the extraordinary rush to get the first PC out of the door, before the Justice Department's antitrust suit had been settled, at a time when IBM was extremely sensitive to even the appearance of having an unfair advantage over a small supplier—the kind of mistake, perhaps, that anyone could make.[46]

Blunder 2. IBM had another opportunity to establish its own operating system independent from Microsoft. A group of IBM researchers wrote an operating system called CP/X86 for the PC-AT.[47] Later they expanded the project to include a pictorial program that worked much like Windows. By 1984 the IBM group had developed a product that was clearly superior to DOS. When IBM management had to decide what operating system would succeed DOS, they had the following four options:

1. Develop an entirely new operating system, OS/2, in partnership with Microsoft.
2. Use CP/X86 as the new standard for IBM machines and fight it out with Microsoft to see whether CP/X86 or DOS would become the long-run industry standard.
3. License CP/X86 to Microsoft and work together on a new operating system.
4. Move to a new operating system, such as UNIX, that was not controlled by Microsoft.[48]

The final decision was made by a group of senior executives, who narrowed the choices down to one of the first two, and then chose number 1—to develop the OS/2 operating system with Microsoft. Apparently a major reason for their decision was Gates's threat that if IBM developed an operating system without Microsoft, Gates would never release the source code for DOS to IBM.[49] This would mean that IBM would be on its own with CP/X86 in direct competition with DOS. IBM feared that given the large base of established DOS users it would be difficult to establish CP/X86 as the industry standard. This may have been a major error. In 1984 IBM was the dominant firm in the PC market, and since CP/X86 was a superior product to DOS and could be modified to run DOS programs, IBM likely would have won any operating system war with Microsoft and established CP/X86 as the industry standard. The relative ease with which Windows replaced DOS as the number one operating system suggests that users are open to operating system improvements. The more recent success of Windows 95 suggests the same thing.

This episode suggests how conservative IBM's management had become by the mid-1980s. While Bill Gates played hardball, the IBM executives backed down. Would Thomas Watson Jr. have backed down under similar circumstances? One can only speculate that the man who took on GE and RCA and risked his father's firm to develop the System/360 in the 1960s would not have hesitated to challenge Microsoft for leadership of the software industry.

The OS/2 partnership between IBM and Microsoft was a disaster from the beginning in large part because OS/2 was tied to a weak 286 microprocessor.[50] By the time the project began, Gates knew that the future was tied to Intel's 386 microprocessor chip, but IBM's management was committed to the 286 chip. Gates thought the 286 chip was "brain dead," but went along with IBM's decision.[51] It has been suggested that Gates went along with the 286 decision in order to sabotage the OS/2 project so that OS/2 would not threaten Microsoft's Windows when it was introduced. In any event, OS/2 was a dinosaur when it was introduced along with the Personal System 2 (PS/2) in 1987.[52]

Blunder 3. Although IBM failed to secure the source code to DOS, because IBM and Microsoft had jointly developed DOS, IBM was in a position to negotiate with Microsoft over how to split the royalties on DOS sales and the royalties on any future operating systems (e.g., OS/2) that the two firms might develop jointly. In 1985, IBM had one final opportunity to prevent Microsoft from taking control of the personal computer operating system industry. At that time, IBM had 80 percent of the PC business, its mainframe revenues were doing extremely well, it had earned $6.582 billion in 1984 and would earn $6.555 billion in 1985. IBM's management was convinced that the old adage, "nobody was ever fired for buying from IBM," would continue to keep IBM firmly established as the industry leader regardless of future competitive threats.

IBM's management had one objective in its negotiations with Microsoft over a royalty split: to pay as low a price for the rights to DOS on IBM machines as possible.[53] Since all other PC producers combined controlled only a 20 percent market share, IBM cared little about royalties on these non-IBM machines. Gates then pulled off a master negotiating stroke, by offering to give DOS to IBM essentially free of charge. All Microsoft wanted in return was the right to collect the royalties on DOS from clone manufacturers. IBM, figuring it had pulled off quite a coup by getting the rights to DOS for its machines at essentially no cost, quickly agreed and a contract was signed in June 1985. Following this third blunder there would be no opportunity for IBM to regain control of the computer industry. Its fall from dominance became inevitable.

Without control over either the operating system or the microprocessor for the IBM-PC, IBM was unable to prevent a flood of low-priced clones from capturing a growing share of the personal computer market. Once consumers became aware that the quality of the PC clones was at least equal to the quality of the IBM-PC, buyers bought the cheaper clones in droves. Within a decade, IBM was relegated to being one of the pack in the personal computer market.

According to *Datamation*, by 1993 IBM's share of the personal computer market had declined to just 17.2 percent, while Apple's market share was 12.1 percent.[54] Even more ominously, IBM's share of the U.S. PC market for 1995 was only 8.3 percent, placing it in fourth place behind Compaq, Packard Bell, and Apple.[55] This meant that Microsoft collected royalties on over 70 percent of the personal computers sold. Furthermore, as Table 8.3 indicates, by 1993 computer hardware accounted for only 48.9 percent of computer industry revenues, and mainframes accounted for only 49.1 percent of computer hardware revenues.

Table 8.3
1993 Revenues in the World Computer Industry by Segment (in Billions of Dollars)

Total Revenues	233
Computer Hardware	114

Mainframes and Minicomputers	56
Personal Computers	46
Workstations	10
Supercomputers	2

Computer Services	84
Computer Software	35

Source: U.S. International Trade Commission, *Global Competitiveness of U.S. Advanced Technology Industries*, Investigation 332-339, ITC Publication 2705, December 1993, p. 22.

As late as the mid-1980s, IBM's management had completely missed the coming industry revolution. Gates, on the other hand, had seen the future a full decade earlier. In a 1995 interview Gates noted that

[in the mid-1970s m]icroprocessors were instantly attractive to [Paul Allen and me] because you could build something for a fraction of the cost of conventional electronics. . . . . I remember, from the very beginning, we wondered, "What would it mean for DEC [Digital Equipment Corporation] once microcomputers were powerful and cheap enough? What would it mean for IBM?" To us it seemed that they were screwed tomorrow. We were saying, "God, how come these guys aren't stunned? How come they're not just amazed and scared?" . . . [T]he notion was fairly clear to us that computers were going to be a big, big personal tool.[56]

Other Managerial Problems

A Lack of Entrepreneurship. The corporate bureaucracy at IBM made it difficult to encourage true entrepreneurship among managers or workers. During the complacent 1970s and early 1980s, a successful manager was rewarded with a large staff, access to corporate perks, and a title. Workers in other areas were rewarded with IBM's promise of job security. As Carroll notes, "Neither security nor the desire for importance translated well into greed."[57]

John Akers, who became chairman in June 1986, attempted to add some greed to the corporate culture. The top workers at Microsoft and other small computer software companies had always been rewarded with huge payoffs in the form of stock ownership. Akers, however, could only bring himself to offer small bonuses for excellent work. The IBM corporate culture simply did not permit him to create the potential for large windfall gains to some workers. Ultimately Akers offered bonuses up to 3 percent to workers in units that did well.[58] Such small bonus payments could hardly be expected to result in a sudden burst of entrepreneurship.

The Slow Rate of Decentralization. Akers took other actions to stem the IBM slide. He restructured the firm into thirteen autonomous divisions, and these divisions could buy and sell in the open market. IBM had attempted to decentralize its operations as early as the 1970s, but these early attempts had failed. During these attempts, responsibility for decisions technically moved down to the division level, but the top managers remained in place to oversee the "process" of decentralization. According to Ferguson and Morris,

[I]nstead of driving a strategy, the managers began to administer process. Coordinative, consultative, and deliberative machinery proliferated, and a slow process of politicization crept over the company. The newer fast-track executives were good at presentations, quick to sniff out majority sentiment, skilled at stitching together consensus. Armonk became dead weight, spinners of grand but harmless visions, rule-makers and administrators, not leaders. Fearful of challenging entrenched marketing baronies, they piled political and bureaucratic baggage on promising new technologies, muffling their impact, blunting their effectiveness.[59]

IBM's problem was never a failure to recognize the need to decentralize. Quite to the contrary, the firm set up one task force after another to look into the issue. Despite these efforts, however, the problem was never solved. Decentralization continued to plague IBM because of the state of technology and the perceived need to be integrated worldwide.

The Transformation from a Leasing to a Sales Business. John Opel, who succeeded Frank Cary as chairman in 1980, changed IBM's pricing policy from one that encouraged leasing to one that encouraged buying. Opel feared that a competitor would develop a technologically advanced mainframe that would cause IBM's customers to cancel their leases in droves.[60] The short-run impact of Opel's decision on cash flow and profits was extremely positive. Instead of receiving a small amount of rental income each year, IBM collected the entire price for its machines up front. A shift to selling combined with the introduction of the PC in

1981 sent revenues through the ceiling. Revenues increased from $29 billion in 1981 to $46 billion in 1984, a 58.6 percent increase. During the same period, profits almost doubled from $3.6 billion to $6.6 billion. Given this excellent financial news, a sense of myopia crept into IBM as management failed to realize the extent to which the shift from leasing to selling caused these results. One member of the Management Committee during this period noted later that "[t]here were lots of analyses about what would happen if the growth rates didn't last, but no one believed them."[61]

The shift from leasing to selling also created a principal-agent problem. Under a leasing system, sales representatives earned most of their commissions by making sure existing customers remained happy with existing equipment. As long as customers kept leasing the same machines, the sales representatives kept receiving commissions. Under a selling policy, sales representatives had less of an incentive to keep customers happy with their existing equipment. Instead, there was an incentive to push new equipment. It took several years for IBM to recognize this shift in incentives, and the company is still working to overcome the damage to customer relations.[62]

A Failure of the Capital-Allocation Process. IBM's capital-allocation process paid little attention to traditional financial analysis. Instead resources flowed to the strongest political powers within IBM. Furthermore, since the accounting system was completely centralized, there were no separate financial statements by business units, and the Management Committee had remarkably little knowledge about the relative performance of different units. While each unit fought to prevent superior in-house technology from encroaching on its market share and political power, top management did not even have the financial facts to make educated decisions concerning the relative payoffs from different projects. Time and again the bureaucracy killed promising technologies and elected to maintain the status quo.

The Future at IBM

Toward the middle of his term as chairman, Akers took several important steps to halt the bleeding. As noted above, he restructured the firm into thirteen autonomous divisions. Furthermore, IBM began to sell components to original equipment manufacturers. Previously all IBM components had to be used internally.[63] Several new R&D joint ventures were also begun, including ventures with Apple, to (1) design a new microprocessor, to be called the Power PC, to challenge Intel, and (2) develop an operating system, tentatively named Taligent, to challenge Microsoft's Windows.

Despite these changes, in April 1993, IBM replaced Akers with Louis V. Gerstner Jr. This appointment marked the first time IBM had gone outside the company to bring in a CEO. Gerstner had previous experience as the CEO at both American Express and RJR Nabisco, but he had no direct experience in the computer industry. Gerstner's selection showed how strongly IBM's board of directors believed a complete overhaul of the company was necessary.[64] The new CEO immediately began bringing other outsiders into IBM's top management.[65]

Within a few months, Gerstner announced that IBM would eliminate 60,000 jobs, close down factories, and sell off equipment in a bold attempt to cut costs.[66] These efforts paid off, and the company managed to earn a $1.2 billion profit in 1994 compared to an $8.1 billion loss in 1993.[67] By the end of 1994 it was estimated that IBM's employment was down to 215,000 worldwide, representing a reduction of almost 50 percent of its workforce in less than a decade.[68]

Despite Gerstner's cost-cutting success, some problems have persisted for IBM. Its R&D effort with Apple to create the Power PC microprocessor and Taligent operating system have both faltered. In 1994 both companies admitted "off the record" that it may be a long time before the Power PC and Taligent could challenge Intel and Microsoft respectively.[69] IBM also continued to have difficulty predicting demand for its various products. It produced far too many Value Point personal computers and found itself stuck with $700 million in unsold inventories in 1994.[70] Simultaneously it failed to keep up with demand for its new multimedia personal computer, the Aptiva.[71]

CONCLUSIONS

IBM's early rise to dominance was primarily the result of Thomas Watson Sr.'s organizational genius and his recognition of the company's need to emphasize a highly trained professional sales force. In the 1960s and 1970s IBM maintained power by taking the huge research risks associated with the development and introduction of a new computer model, the System/360. Thomas Watson Jr., like his father, was willing to take risky gambles to maintain dominance.

By boldly undertaking risks, Thomas Watson Jr., who died in January 1994, had built IBM into one of the most profitable corporations in history. He recognized long before others that high technology electronics would rule the end of the twentieth century. Much like Bill Gates after him, Thomas Watson Jr. saw the future and moved to gain control of it. Thirty years later, IBM's management had become ossified and was unable to stay ahead of its smaller, quicker-reacting competitors. This ossification combined with the detrimental effects of the government's 1969 antitrust case on the firm's desire and ability to respond aggressively to competitive threats ultimately resulted in IBM's loss of dominance.

IBM's recent history supports the theory that unconstrained growth, which results in an ever expanding management structure, eventually results in a slowdown in a firm's growth rate. As the ratio of new managers to old managers grew at IBM, managerial resources were drained away from productive activities and into training activities instead. Consistent with Scherer's theory, as IBM's CEOs confronted more and more complex issues in a high technology industry, they were unable to make the rapid changes that were necessary to keep up with the competition. IBM's overgrown managerial structure eventually sank the firm into a high-cost environment that was simply incapable of competing in a rapidly changing environment. Perhaps such outcomes are inevitable whenever a large dominant firm competes in a rapidly changing high technology industry. The challenge for Microsoft and Intel is to avoid these same problems in the long run.

The challenge for IBM is to continue to adjust to the new economic realities.

Finally, it is worth speculating that this entire story would have played out much differently in the absence of the 1969 Justice Department case. Without that case, IBM may have stayed farther ahead of its small rivals in the 1970s and may have been more up-to-date on the technologies developed by its competitors. One cannot be sure that history would have played out differently in the absence of the 1969 case, but there are strong reasons to believe that it would have.

NOTES

1. Emerson W. Pugh, *Building IBM: Shaping an Industry and Its Technology* (Cambridge, MA: MIT Press, 1995), p. 324.

2. For more on the life of Thomas Watson Sr., see Thomas G. Belden and Marva R. Belden, *The Lengthening Shadow: The Life of Thomas J. Watson* (Boston: Little, Brown and Company, 1962); Pugh, *Building IBM*, pp. 29-36; and Robert Sobel, *IBM vs. Japan: The Struggle for the Future* (New York: Stein and Day, 1986), pp. 28-34.

3. Charles H. Ferguson and Charles R. Morris, *Computer Wars* (New York: Random House, 1993), pp. 3-4.

4. Ibid., p. 4.

5. Ibid., p. 5.

6. Pugh, *Building IBM*, pp. 323-324.

7. Richard T. DeLamarter, *Big Blue: IBM's Use and Abuse of Power* (New York: Dodd, Mead, 1986), p. 29.

8. Ibid., pp. 43-45.

9. For explanations of the theory see Jack Hirshleifer, "The Firm's Cost Function: A Successful Reconstruction?" *Journal of Business* 35 (July 1962): 235-255; Kenneth J. Arrow, "The Economic Implications of Learning by Doing," *Review of Economic Studies* 29 (April 1962): 155-173; L. E. Preston and E. C. Keachie, "Cost Functions and Progress Functions: An Integration," *American Economic Review* 54 (March 1964): 100-106; Sherwin Rosen, "Learning by Experience as Joint Production," *Quarterly Journal of Economics* 87 (August 1972): 366-382; Karl F. Habermeier, "The Learning Curve and Competition: A Stochastic Model of Duopolistic Rivalry," *International Journal of Industrial Organization* 10 (September 1992): 369-392; and Clement G. Krouse, "Market Rivalry and Learning-by-Doing," *International Journal of Industrial Organization* 12 (December 1994): 437-456.

10. Gerald Brock, *The U.S. Computer Industry: A Study of Market Power* (Cambridge, MA: Ballinger, 1975), p. 29.

11. Federal Trade Commission, *Statistical Report: Annual Line of Business Report,* (Washington, D.C.: U.S. Government Printing Office), 1974-1977 editions.

12. Ibid.

13. Brock, *Market Power*, pp. 33-37.

14. DeLamarter, *Big Blue*, p. 57.

15. Ferguson and Morris, *Computer Wars*, p. 7.

16. Ibid., p. 8.

17. DeLamarter, *Big Blue*, p. 57.

18. See for examples, *Telex Corporation v International Business Machines*, 510 F2d 894 (1975); *ILC Peripherals Leasing Company v International Business Machines,* 458 FSupp. 423 (1978); and *Memorex Corporation v International Business Machines*, 636 F2d 1188 (1980).

19. "A Tyro Challenges IBM in Big Computers," *Business Week*, 12 May 1975, pp. 65-67.

20. "New Wave of Change Challenging IBM," *Business Week*, 29 May 1978, pp. 92-99.

21. "IBM Foresees Benefits from Price Cuts," *New York Times*, 26 April 1977, p. A51; and "More Tumult for the Computer Industry," *Business Week*, 30 May 1977, pp. 58-66.

22. F. M. Scherer, *Industry Structure, Strategy, and Public Policy* (New York: HarperCollins, 1996), p. 261.

23. For two dramatically different views of the case see Richard T. DeLamarter, *Big Blue*; and Franklin M. Fisher, John J. McGowan, and Joen E. Greenwood, *Folded, Spindled, and Mutilated: Economic Analysis and U.S. v. IBM* (Cambridge, MA: MIT Press, 1983).

24. Paul Carroll, *Big Blues: The Unmaking of IBM* (New York: Crown, 1993), p. 57.

25. Ibid., p. 119. For a detailed study of how Microsoft came to be the dominant firm in the computer software industry, see Daniel Ichbiah and Susan L. Knepper, *The Making of Microsoft* (Rocklin, CA: Prima, 1993), pp. 73- 74.

26. Carroll, *Unmaking of IBM*, p. 118.

27. Ibid., p. 341.

28. Ibid., p. 243.

29. Neil B. Niman and Manley R. Irwin, "Computers," in Walter Adams and James Brock, *The Structure of American Industry* (Englewood Cliffs, NJ: Prentice Hall, 1995), p. 157.

30. Ferguson and Morris, *Computer Wars*, p. 11.

31. Ibid. p. 11.

32. F. M. Scherer, *Industry Structure, Strategy, and Public Policy* (New York: HarperCollins, 1996), p. 275; Allan Sloan, "Why Jumbo Has to Take Dance Lessons," *Boston Globe*, 9 December 1991, p. 98; "Breaking Up IBM," *Fortune*, 27 July 1992, p. 51; and "Too Big Blue," *The Economist*, 22 May 1993, p. 17.

33. F. M. Scherer, *Industry Structure*, p. 275.

34. Edith Penrose, *The Theory of Growth of the Firm* (Oxford: Oxford University Press, 1959). For a simple theoretical model based on Penrose's arguments, see Donald A. Hay and Derek J. Morris, *Industrial Economics and Organization* (Oxford: Oxford University Press, 1991), pp. 347-351.

35. Penrose argued that diminishing returns exist for several reasons. First, faster growth requires exploiting more opportunities, which implies that at the margin, profitable opportunities are certain to face more competition, be more difficult to undertake, and be more uncertain. For the rapidly growing firm, therefore, exploiting marginal opportunities requires more managerial inputs per unit of increased output. Second, Penrose assumed that the marginal product of newly hired managers decreased the faster the rate of growth of the firm, because rapid growth leaves fewer hours for established managers to train new managers, and thereby reduces the rate of integration of new managers into the managerial workforce. These arguments suggest a positive relationship between the growth of the firm and the number of managers.

36. F. M. Scherer, *Industrial Market Structure and Economic Performance* (Boston: Houghton Mifflin, 1990), pp. 104-105.

37. Ibid., p. 104.

38. Oliver E. Williamson, "Hierarchical Control and Optimum Firm Size," *Journal of Political Economy* 70 (1967): 123-138.

39. Carroll, *Unmaking of IBM*, p. 20.

40. Ibid., p. 23.

41. Ibid., p. 123.

42. Ibid., pp. 22-23.

43. Ichbiah and Knepper, *Making of Microsoft*, pp. 73-74.

44. The $75,000 figure is taken from Ferguson and Morris, *Computer Wars*, pp. 66-67. Ichbiah and Knepper claim that Microsoft "acquired QDOS for less than $100,000," see Ichbiah and Knepper, *Making of Microsoft*, p. 76.

45. Ferguson and Morris, *Computer Wars*, p. 71.

46. Ibid., p. 71.

47. Ibid., p. 72.

48. Ibid., p. 74.

49. Ibid., p. 74.

50. Ibid., p. 76.

51. Ibid.

52. Ibid., pp. 80-81.

53. Carroll, *Unmaking of IBM*, p. 89.

54. *Datamation*, 15 June 1993.

55. "Compaq Increases PC Sales Lead," *Syracuse Post-Standard*, 30 January 1996, p. D-7.

56. "Bill Gates & Paul Allen Talk," *Fortune*, 2 October 1995, p. 70.

57. Carroll, *Unmaking of IBM*, p. 299.

58. Ibid., p. 299.

59. Ferguson and Morris, *Computer Wars*, p. 36.

60. Carroll, *Unmaking of IBM*, p. 59.

61. Ibid., p. 60.

62. Ibid., p. 63.

63. Niman and Irwin, "Computers," p. 165.

64. "RJR Leader in IBM Spotlight," *New York Times*, 22 March 1993, D-1.

65. "Another Outsider Is Appointed at IBM," *New York Times*, 6 May 1993, D-4.

66. "IBM Chief Making Drastic New Cuts," *New York Times*, 28 July 1993, A-1.

67. "IBM Posts First Annual Profit Since 1990," *New York Times*, 24 January 1995, D-1.

68. "Lessons in Rebounds from G.M. and IBM," *New York Times*, 24 October 1994, D-1.

69. "Computing's Bold Alliance Falters," *New York Times*, 14 September 1994, D-1.

70. "Lessons in Rebounds from G.M. and IBM," *New York Times*, 24 October 1994, D-1.

71. Ibid.

9

MICROSOFT

Rochelle Ruffer and Don E. Waldman

INTRODUCTION

In July 1975, Bill Gates and Paul Allen started a company, known as Micro-Soft (the hyphen was later removed). The market for personal computers was in its infancy but Gates and Allen believed personal computers would play a great role in the future. This ability to forecast the future has been a continuing theme in Microsoft's growth. There were many key moments in Microsoft's history when Bill Gates anticipated the future and took the path towards innovation and success. Only time will tell whether Microsoft will remain a dominant firm, but certainly if the first twenty years are any indication, Microsoft will be a dominant player in the operating systems and software markets and many newly emerging markets for some time to come.

This chapter begins with a brief introduction to Bill Gates's life and how his early experience with computers helped to make him a successful entrepreneur. We then examine the issues behind Microsoft's rise to power, and in particular the emergence of the MS-DOS and Windows operating systems. We will see that a vision for the future, luck, hard work, the use of various marketing and business strategies, and network externalities all played a role in Microsoft's rise to power. Microsoft's maintenance of power is then analyzed. Microsoft's continued success can be attributed to its aggressive management style and various strategic behaviors in the announcement, licensing, and pricing of products. Finally, the outcome of the government antitrust action against Microsoft is considered and assessed.

GAINING POWER

Gates's Early Experience

William Henry Gates III was born on October 28, 1955. Gates was first introduced to computers in the spring of 1968, when he was a seventh-grade student at Lakeside. That year, Lakeside, an all-boys prepatory school, purchased a teletype machine. Users could type commands on the teletype and communicate via telephone with a program data processor minicomputer in downtown Seattle. Gates, Paul Allen, and Kent Evans played with the computer so diligently that their parents were later asked by the school to help with the electric bill.[1] Gates wrote programs in BASIC including a tic-tac-toe game.

Many people believe the success of Bill Gates is partially attributable to his early experiences with business. In fact Kent Evans's father is quoted as saying, "[i]f anybody wants to know why Bill Gates is where he is today, in my judgment it's because of this early experience cutting deals."[2] Gates, Allen, Evans, and Richard Weiland received their first job from Computer Center Corporation (CCC). After being persuaded by Gates and Allen of their programming skills, CCC signed an agreement with the newly established Lakeside Programming Group where, in exchange for lists of bugs in the software, the boys received free computer time. They spent their evenings and weekends on the computer, carefully documenting each bug. This experience gave Gates a chance to deepen his knowledge of how the minicomputer's hardware and software operated.

Gates and Allen received many other experiences early in their careers. They were hired by Lakeside to work on a computer scheduling program.[3] After Allen graduated from Lakeside High School in 1971, Allen and Gates formed Traf-O-Data, a company that programmed a computer to analyze the traffic counter tapes that were produced by cities and counties. During the 1972–1973 school year, Traf-O-Data earned $20,000 from clients.[4] In the spring of 1973, however, the federal government decided to offer states a similar service at no charge, and Traf-O-Data went out of business.

Vision of the Future

Before Microsoft was formed, Bill Gates had experience negotiating contracts, meeting tight deadlines, writing countless computer programs, and debugging computers. Gates's experience and intellectual capability are two of the major driving forces as to why Microsoft has been so successful, but his vision of the future and willingness to take risks is what ultimately enabled Microsoft to become an industry leader.

Gates entered Harvard in the fall of 1973. During the summer of 1974, Allen and Gates worked at Honeywell. It was Paul Allen, however, who pushed Gates to see the vision described by the following scenario:

Gates and Allen were convinced the computer industry was about to reach critical mass, and when it exploded it would usher in a technological revolution of astounding magnitude. They were on the threshold of one of those moments when history held its breath . . . and jumped, as it had done with the development of the car and airplane. Computer power was about to come to the masses. Their vision of a computer in every home was no longer a wild dream. "It's going to happen," Allen kept telling his friend. And they could either lead the revolution or be swept along with it. Allen was much more eager to start a company than Gates, who was worried about the reaction from his family if he dropped out of school.[5]

The cover of the January 1975 issue of *Popular Mechanics* showed the Altair 8080 accompanied by the headline "World's First Microcomputer Kit to Rival Commercial Models" on its cover. The article was about Ed Roberts of Micro Instrumentation and Telemetry Systems (MITS) who coined the term "personal computer." Gates and Allen had promised Roberts that a version of BASIC existed for the Altair and worked solidly for eight weeks to provide the promised, but non-existent, version of BASIC. They did not have an Altair computer so Allen worked on making the PDP-10 computer to mimic the Altair's 8080 chip. Gates worked on the difficult task of writing the code to fit in the Altair's 4 kilobytes (4K) of memory knowing that he would need extra memory to run the programs. Allen and Gates then recorded Gates's 8,000 lines of machine language code onto punched paper tape because there were no plans for a keyboard for the Altair. After two months of hard work, Allen took the program to Roberts in Albuquerque, New Mexico. On the plane, Allen wrote the instruction program for loading BASIC on the Altair. The BASIC program worked and thus was born Microsoft.

Early on, Microsoft worked on FORTRAN (released in July 1977), COBOL, and PASCAL for chips other than the 8080. These languages were more advanced than BASIC, and Microsoft chose to write them to run with the then-advanced Control Program for Microcomputer (CP/M) operating system. For Microsoft's languages to be widely successful, CP/M, created by Gary Kildall, needed to become the standard for microcomputer operating systems. After a refinement making CP/M easily adaptable to many different kinds of computers, many firms leaped on the CP/M bandwagon in the late 1970s. Apple, Tandy, and Commodore continued to use their own operating systems, but CP/M was becoming the industry standard. The foresight (or luck) of Gates and Allen to latch onto the emerging standard is what enabled them to follow the next path to success. Once again, anticipation of the market was key to Microsoft's success. In another feat of foresightedness, Gates got a jump on the competition by launching into foreign markets. In 1978, Bill Gates and Kazuhkio Nishi, who developed ASCII, signed a one-page contract for Nishi to become the Microsoft representative for the Far East. Immediately upon his return to Japan, Nishi contacted a NEC Corporation executive and convinced him to meet Gates. As a result of this meeting, NEC decided to produce the first Japanese microcomputer and enlist the help of Microsoft in designing it. Microsoft's involvement in foreign markets from its inception is one of the keys to its later success. From 1986 to 1995, a minimum of 65 percent of Microsoft's annual sales have been in international markets.[6]

Microsoft's first significant industry-wide success began with the release of the 8086 chip by Intel in April 1978. Many believed the 8086 chip would never become the industry standard. Microsoft, however, saw an opportunity to position

itself as an industry pioneer and agreed to write BASIC for the 8086. Gates said
it would take three weeks and it ended up taking six months. As we will see, this
was not the last time that Microsoft severely underanticipated the length of time to
complete a project.

Luck and Hard Work

While development of BASIC established Microsoft in the computer industry,
it was Microsoft's development of MS-DOS that put them on the path to becoming
the dominant firm in the operating systems market. This part of Microsoft's history
owes a great deal to luck. Gates was initially approached by IBM in 1980 to write
a version of BASIC for the permanent memory of an 8-bit computer. IBM went
to Microsoft in part because Gates and Allen had a good reputation for delivering
BASIC.[7] Gates suggested to IBM using Intel's 8086 chip and a 16-bit microprocessor. Gates also suggested that IBM meet with Gary Kildall of Digital Research
to acquire CP/M as IBM's operating system.

Here is where Microsoft's stroke of luck came into play. Having been
unimpressed with potential clients sent by Microsoft in the past, Kildall was off
flying his new plane when IBM arrived for the meeting.[8] IBM representatives
asked Kildall's wife, a lawyer, to sign a document agreeing to keep anything
revealed in the meeting confidential and stipulating that Digital Research would
never be able to sue IBM. IBM had asked Gates to sign the same agreement, but
Kildall's wife felt unsure about signing the document, and the IBM team left
without holding the meeting with Digital Research. After Kildall returned from his
plane trip, he was involved with negotiations with Hewlett-Packard for a job that
seemed potentially more lucrative than any possible job with IBM. In addition,
Kildall doubted that CPM/86 could be ready in time to meet IBM's April deadline.[9]
Kildall and his wife then went on a week-long cruise, prolonging a decision on the
IBM job until after they returned from vacation.

IBM did not appreciate being put off by Kildall and returned to Gates. Once
again Gates tried to get Digital Research to commit to IBM, but eventually Gates
realized Kildall was not interested. Had Kildall decided to sign an agreement with
IBM, it is unclear what path Microsoft's history would have taken.

At this point Gates and Allen thought about providing the operating system
themselves, but they knew they did not have sufficient time to develop a system.
Instead, they bought a newly developed operating system from Seattle Computer
Products. Tim Patterson developed Quick and Dirty Operating System (QDOS) in
order to sell a computer he had built for Seattle Computer Products. Patterson
wrote QDOS so that software written for the Digital Research system could easily
be ported to QDOS.[10] Allen contacted Patterson in October 1980 for the right to
buy QDOS. He said Microsoft already had an interested customer, but did not say
the customer was IBM. Microsoft paid Seattle Computer Products $75,000 for the
right to sell QDOS.[11] The agreement provided for additional payments each time
the license was granted to another manufacturer.

Microsoft and IBM signed a contract on November 6, 1980. This new contract prohibited IBM from licensing DOS, but placed no restrictions on Microsoft. Standard industry practice would have been for IBM to maintain the source code.[12] The stipulation in the contract that enabled Microsoft to license MS-DOS, but not IBM, is what enabled Microsoft to push MS-DOS as the industry standard by licensing it to clone manufacturers. Although many hours of hard work were put into revising QDOS into MS-DOS, it is remarkable that Microsoft got started in the operating systems market by using a product they bought from another company. When IBM announced the introduction of its first personal computer on August 12, 1981, it included Microsoft's MS-DOS operating system. By December 1984, it was clear that MS-DOS was the operating system industry leader. By June of 1986, income from the sale of Microsoft's operating system accounted for half its annual revenues of $60.9 million.[13]

Marketing Strategies

Battle with CP/M. For almost two years after the release of the IBM PC, it was unclear whether MS-DOS or CP/M would dominate the market. Microsoft repeatedly marketed MS-DOS by promising easy adaptation of CP/M programs.[14] Other key strategic maneuvers from Microsoft helped to make MS-DOS and later Windows the dominant operating systems. Digital Research's CP/M-86 reportedly had many advantages over MS-DOS, but Microsoft was the leading producer of computer languages and thus had control over what operating systems would work well with its languages. Microsoft was slow to deliver versions of its languages compatible with CP/M-86, and when it did, they were priced 50 percent higher than the versions compatible with MS-DOS. In addition, BASIC for CP/M-86 was stripped of graphics. As a result, applications developers found it difficult to develop software for any operating system except MS-DOS, and MS-DOS became the market leader.[15]

Product Improvements. Microsoft is commonly criticized for its inability to release a problem-free product with the first version.[16] Microsoft, however, continually makes incremental changes to improve its products. During Microsoft's first summer of existence, Gates continued to work on improving BASIC for Altair before it was officially released for sale. Gates's persistence in providing as reliable a product as possible has continued over the years and is one of the reasons Microsoft has such a good reputation for quality. Since 1981, MS-DOS has gone through six different versions. MS-DOS 5.0, introduced in 1991, made it possible for more than one application to be loaded, although it was still impossible to run applications simultaneously. This upgrade was a good launching platform for Windows, which has sold tens of millions of copies.[17] In fact, it is estimated that by 1993 Microsoft had sold 100 million copies of MS-DOS and 25 million copies of Windows.[18]

Battle with IBM. Microsoft's biggest challenge in the development of Windows was the question of how to break off Microsoft's working relationship with IBM and move from joint development of operating systems to Microsoft's internal development of Windows. By the mid-1980s, both IBM and Microsoft recognized the need to move beyond the technical limitations of MS-DOS into a new graphical user interface operating system (GUI, pronounced "gooey"). MS-DOS is limited because it is a character-based operating system that requires users to type in commands. GUIs rely on using a mouse to select menu commands or icons. Apple was far ahead of Microsoft and IBM in terms of GUI technology when it introduced the Macintosh computer.

For Microsoft, the Windows project began in September 1981 and was officially announced on November 10, 1983. It was not until November of 1985, however, that Windows 1.03 was officially released despite an earlier promised release date. Initially the public did not take well to Windows. There were no application programs to run with it, and it was very slow. It appeared that software manufacturers had tired of waiting for the delayed introduction of Windows and lost interest in writing applications programs.[19] Despite Microsoft's claims that Windows was a success, most of the copies were sold by bundling Windows with MS-DOS, and only an estimated 20 percent of users actually installed Windows on their machines.[20]

Throughout the mid and late 1980s, Gates followed a risky strategy of simultaneously working on the development of the OS/2 operating system with IBM and independent development of Windows. This often caused great tensions between IBM and Microsoft, which culminated in a meeting between the IBM–Microsoft team and leading software developers in Las Vegas in 1989.[21] At that meeting IBM wanted Bill Gates to inform the software developers that Microsoft was firmly committed to OS/2 as the next major operating system. Gates refused. Instead he tried to finesse the issue, but the software developers left the Las Vegas meeting convinced that Windows, not OS/2, would come to dominate the market for operating systems.

Gates had pulled off a remarkable ploy. Microsoft had successfully sabotaged the development of OS/2 by continuing to invest resources in a partnership with IBM on the OS/2 development project while knowing full well that Microsoft was really committed to Windows as the operating system of the future. As noted in Chapter 8, IBM probably had the ability to call Microsoft's bluff by developing a new operating system on its own and attempting to displace MS-DOS as the dominant technology, but IBM was extremely hesitant to do so. Microsoft had played "chicken" with one of the most powerful corporations in the world, and won.

As a result of the 1989 Las Vegas meeting, software developers believed Windows would become the dominant operating system in the future. At this point, the software developers jumped on the Windows bandwagon by developing their software programs to be compatible with Windows. In 1990, Windows version 3.0 sold in the millions, selling nearly four hundred thousand copies in the first five weeks on the market.[22] The success of Windows is partly attributable to the software developers' commitment to Windows because customers are more likely to buy an operating system that has adequate applications software compatibility with the operating system. In March 1992, Microsoft introduced an enhanced version of Windows, version 3.1, which sold in the tens of millions and became the new market standard.[23]

Network Externalities

It has been argued that Microsoft took advantage of "network externalities" to gain a monopoly over operating systems.[24] According to Katz and Shapiro, network externalities exist if "the utility that a user derives from consumption of the good increases with the number of other agents consuming the good."[25] For example, the utility that a consumer derives from a telephone is clearly related to the number of other users on the telephone network.

Consider a customer contemplating the purchase of a computer and operating system at a moment in time. If customers as a group make their purchasing decisions at different times, then, with network externalities, the customer's utility will be affected by the number of users already using a given model of computer and operating system, and the number of users expected to use the system in the future. The more customers currently using or expected to use the same computer and operating system, the greater will be the availability of software applications for that computer and operating system, and the greater will be the consumer's expected utility. In addition, the greater the number of current users of a particular computer and operating system, the easier it will be to obtain post-purchase service and technical support. The current demand for a given computer and operating system, therefore, is a function of the current installed-base and expected future demand for the computer and operating system.

If computers and operating systems are produced by non-integrated manufacturers under classic U-shaped average costs, the perfectly competitive first-best equilibrium results. More realistically, however, if computers and/or operating systems are produced under conditions of economies of scale or significant learning-by-doing, then the equilibrium outcome will diverge from the competitive result. In such cases, the first firm to gain a large installed-base will have significantly lower costs and can charge significantly lower prices. A relatively large market share and low price, combined with network externalities, may induce more and more customers to buy a product. It may also induce more and more firms to supply ancillary goods (like software) compatible with the product. As a result, the market may become tipped to the first well-established product. This may, in turn, allow the firm eventually to dominate the market. Economists have suggested the following examples of tipped markets: the dominance of VHS-formatted videocassettes over Beta-formatted videocassettes, the dominance of IBM-compatible PCs over Apple, and the dominance of MS-DOS over competitive operating systems.

Microsoft adopted several strategies that may have helped tip the operating system market to its favor. First, Microsoft initially priced MS-DOS at a level low enough to gain a large installed-base of MS-DOS users. The strategy of pushing volume sales by charging low prices has been one of Microsoft's favorite strategies. It is Microsoft's philosophy that high volume ensures that Microsoft will remain the industry standard. Gates recognized early on that the real profits to be made were in licensing MS-DOS to PC clones, not to IBM. By licensing to the clone manufacturers at low fees Microsoft was able to capture the market before others entered it.[26] Second, Microsoft worked with independent software developers to build up a large variety of complementary software applications. Third, Microsoft preannounced new versions of MS-DOS to discourage buyers from purchasing competitive operating systems, which might become obsolete. Finally, Microsoft committed itself to low prices on marginal units of MS-DOS by charging computer manufacturers a fixed fee to install MS-DOS on all their machines rather than charging a per computer installed fee. This effectively set the marginal cost of installing MS-DOS on additional computers equal to zero.

There has been considerable disagreement whether network externalities result in natural monopoly and the ability of inferior products to block the introduction of technologically superior products. If network externalities are widespread in computer operating systems, however, then the operating system market may be a natural monopoly, and Microsoft's control may have been inevitable once it gained the contract to write an operating system for the IBM PC. According to this theory, once the operating system market was tipped in Microsoft's favor, its dominance became certain.

MAINTAINING POWER

We have observed that one of the most influential reasons why Microsoft has been so successful is Gates himself. Gates's philosophy for attacking the future can be seen as early as 1975 when he entered the industry. His willingness to take risks helped to place Microsoft on top in the market. Microsoft, and Bill Gates in particular, used a number of strategies and key events to help it gain market power. For example, Microsoft entered foreign markets before the first PC even existed. The company's motto has been to "attack the future" and not sit still in the face of rapidly changing technology. At times, Gates was in the right place at the right time, but most of the time, he was in that place because of his reputation for good work and a good product. Gates' ability to maintain complete control of MS-DOS in the licensing contract with IBM was a key component to the firm's success. An emphasis on large sales volume also contributed to Microsoft's success, and this strategy may have enabled Microsoft to take advantage of network externalities. All of these factors helped Microsoft gain the power it has today. The next section will analyze how Microsoft has managed to maintain the power it worked so hard to create.

An Aggressive Management

No factor has been more important to Microsoft's maintenance of market power over computer operating systems and its successful expansion into new areas than its aggressive management style. Microsoft has consistently been willing to destroy its own product base by introducing new products. Rather than watch competitors chip away at its dominant market share in operating systems, Microsoft has done the chipping away by making its flagship product, MS-DOS, obsolete by introducing Windows 95.

The importance of continuous technological change is firmly established in Microsoft's corporate culture. Chris Peters, Microsoft's vice president of the Office products unit, put it this way: "Bill [Gates] always understood and internalized that you [must]. . . radically change things and really have big plans. . . . A classic example is, DOS was doing great. [We could have said,] 'Let's just come out with new versions of DOS. Why make Windows?"[27]

Microsoft's management has also recognized the importance of moving beyond operating systems into new areas in the computing industry. After establishing dominance over operating systems, Microsoft moved into applications software by challenging the two industry leaders in that market, WordPerfect in word processing and Lotus in spreadsheets. In both markets, Microsoft's initial products were inferior to the dominant firms' products, but using its ability to invest liberally in research and development, Microsoft was able to continually improve the quality of its products until it wrestled leadership away from both WordPerfect and Lotus.

Microsoft's development of new products has been in no small measure due to its investment of hundreds of millions of dollars into research and developoment (R&D) each year. As Table 9.1 shows, since 1986, when Microsoft went public and the data started to be recorded, Microsoft has put a minimum of 11 percent of its revenues into R&D, and some years that figure has been as high as 15 percent. In 1995, Microsoft spent $830 million on R&D.[28] This aggressive R&D expenditure plan has been one of the major reasons why Microsoft has been able to develop new products and change existing products in order to maintain power.

Consider the pattern in both the word processor and spreadsheet markets. WordPerfect was introduced in 1979 by a new company, WordPerfect Corporation, and rapidly gained a dominant market share based on its high-powered features and excellent support services. Microsoft introduced its major word processor, Microsoft Word, in 1983, but the first version was clearly inferior to WordPerfect. Microsoft initially gained only a 10 percent market share, compared to a 30 percent share for WordPerfect.[29] This was in spite of Microsoft's introduction of Word with a marketing blitz that included giving away 450,000 demonstration disks.[30] WordPerfect clearly was the market leader and in early 1989, it was estimated that in the past twelve months, 937,000 copies of WordPerfect had been sold compared to 650,000 copies of Microsoft Word.[31] Microsoft went through several more unsuccessful versions of Word until it finally came out with a greatly improved version of Word for Windows in 1990. Shortly thereafter Word passed WordPerfect to become the leading word processing program.

Similarly, in spreadsheets, Lotus 1-2-3 became the standard for the IBM PC. Lotus 1-2-3 was introduced in 1983 after Microsoft had introduced a competitive product, Multiplan, in 1982. Lotus 1-2-3, however, was so superior to Multiplan

Table 9.1
Microsoft Company Data, 1975-1995

Year	Revenues ($1,000)	Growth Rate (%)	Employees	Operating Profit (%)	R&D/ Revenues (%)
1975	16	–	3	na	na
1976	22	38	7	na	na
1977	382	636	9	na	na
1978	1,356	256	13	na	na
1979	2,390	663	28	na	na
1980	8,000	235	38	na	na
1981	16,000	100	130	na	na
1982	24,486	53	220	na	na
1983	50,065	104	476	na	na
1984	97,479	95	778	na	na
1985	140,417	44	1,001	na	na
1986	197,514	41	1,442	31	11
1987	345,890	75	2,258	37	11
1988	590,827	71	2,793	32	12
1989	803,530	36	4,037	30	14
1990	1,183,000	47	5,635	33	15
1991	1,843,000	56	8,226	35	13
1992	2,759,000	50	11,542	36	13
1993	3,753,000	36	14,430	35	13
1994	4,649,000	24	15,257	37	13
1995	5,937,000	28	17,800	36	14

Source: Michael A. Cusumano and Richard W. Selby, *Microsoft Secrets* (New York: Free Press, 1995), p. 3.

that it rapidly gained a dominant market share in the spreadsheet market, a share that reached 80 percent.[32] In this case, Microsoft failed to see the future and was tailoring its product to the low end when machines with more memory were becoming more popular. Microsoft attempted many strategies to compete with Lotus 1-2-3, but over the years, the gap widened. In 1986, sales of Lotus 1-2-3 were three times as high as Multiplan sales (750,000 vs. 250,000), and by the end of the 1980s, Lotus 1-2-3 had sold 5 million copies.[33]

In response to the success of Lotus 1-2-3, Microsoft decided to scrap the Multiplan framework entirely and start development o′ a new spreadsheet. Eventually a new product, Excel, evolved. Once again, however, the first version of Excel was viewed as significantly inferior to Lotus 1-2-3, and it took until 1988, with the introduction of Excel version 2.0, for Microsoft to surpass Lotus. Early on, Microsoft learned the lesson of having to continually upgrade its products, even if the upgrades were small incremental changes. Furthermore, Microsoft had an advantage in terms of upgrading its applications software because it had advanced knowledge of impending changes in its operating system. Microsoft, therefore, could incorporate upcoming changes in its operating system into changes in its software more quickly than its competitors. Excel 5.0 is now the best selling Windows and Macintosh spreadsheet.

More recently Microsoft has placed its sites on the Internet. The dominant software for browsing the Internet is Netscape's Navigator. Microsoft has gone directly after Netscape's Navigator by including a connection to its network software program, Microsoft Network, with Windows. So far Netscape's Navigator has remained dominant, but if history repeats itself, Microsoft may eventually perfect Microsoft Network and gain a large market share.

MICROSOFT'S STRATEGIC BEHAVIOR

In June 1990, the Federal Trade Commission (FTC) initiated an inquiry into Microsoft's business practices. Initially the investigation was aimed at the relationship between Microsoft and IBM and their plans to develop jointly the OS/2 operating system. The FTC's investigation, however, turned quickly to Microsoft's marketing practices for MS-DOS and Windows. According to the FTC staff, once Microsoft's basic control over operating systems was established, it continued to maintain power through a variety of practices including the preannouncement of products, exclusionary per processor licenses for MS-DOS and Windows, unreasonably long-term licensing agreements, and restrictive non-disclosure agreements. It is useful to consider the effects of each of these practices in more detail.

The Preannouncement of Products

In April 1990 Digital Research Incorporated (DRI) introduced a new operating system DR-DOS 5.0 to critical industry acclaim. Most experts considered DR-DOS to be superior to MS-DOS.[34] DR-DOS began to make significant inroads into

MS-DOS's market share, and by the end of 1990, DRI had captured a 10 percent market share of new DOS-based operating system shipments.[35] By comparison, as shown in Table 9.2, IBM's operating systems held an 18 percent market share, and Microsoft's MS-DOS held a 70 percent share of new DOS-based operating system shipments.

Table 9.2
New Shipments of Personal Computer Operating Systems, 1990-1992

		1990		1991		1992	
Company	Operating System	1,000	Total Ship-ments (%)	1,000	Total Ship-ments (%)	1,000	Total Ship-ments (%)
Micro-soft	MS-DOS	11,648	49.7	13,178	51.3	18,525	59.6
IBM	PC-DOS	3,031	12.9	3,003	11.7	2,315	7.4
DRI/ Novell	DR-DOS	1,737	7.4	1,819	7.1	1,617	5.2
Other	Other DOS	187	0.8	288	1.1	390	1.3
	DOS Subtotal	16,603	70.8	18,288	71.2	22,847	73.5
Apple	Macin-tosh	1,411	6.0	2,204	8.6	2,570	8.3
UNIX	UNIX	357	1.5	582	2.3	797	2.6
IBM	OS/2	0	0	0	0	409	1.3
Other		5,079	21.7	4,628	18.0	4,458	14.3
Totals		23,450	100.0	25,702	100.0	31,080	100.0

Source: Kenneth C. Baseman, Frederick R. Warren-Boulton, and Glenn A. Woroch, "Microsoft Plays Hardball: The Use of Exclusionary Pricing and Technical Incompatibility to Maintain Monopoly Power in Markets for Operating System Software," *Antitrust Bulletin* (summer 1995): 273.

Within one month of the introduction of DR-DOS, Microsoft announced the "forthcoming" new version of MS-DOS, MS-DOS 5.0. Microsoft's announcement made the introduction of MS-DOS 5.0 appear imminent, but it took Microsoft over a year to market MS-DOS 5.0, which was finally introduced in July 1991. The FTC staff argued that in the summer of 1990 the new version of MS-DOS 5.0 was nothing more than "vaporware," meaning that Microsoft was not even close to having a marketable product. To make matters worse for DRI, during the year between June 1990 and June 1991, Microsoft continuously announced that its introduction of MS-DOS 5.0 was "imminent."

The "vaporware strategy" worked, and the growth of DR-DOS was stopped. As Table 9.2 indicates, by 1992, Microsoft's share of DOS-based operating systems had increased to 81 percent and DRI's (by now DRI had been acquired by Novell) share had shrunk to just 7 percent.

Exclusionary Licenses

Typically a patent license is based on the number of units of the product used by the licensee. Beginning as early as 1983, however, Microsoft negotiated many, but not all, licenses based on the total number of computer processors (CPU) shipped by an original equipment manufacturer (OEM). Furthermore, every Microsoft license was individually negotiated and an official list price for MS-DOS never existed. The effect of this system was to ensure that Microsoft received a royalty on every computer shipped by an OEM regardless of whether or not the computer had a copy of MS-DOS installed. Licenses based on the total number of computers shipped came to be known as "CPU licenses." CPU licenses gained an increasing share of Microsoft's licensing activity over time, increasing from 20 percent of licenses in 1989 to 22 percent in 1990, 27 percent in 1991 to 50 percent by 1992.[36]

Microsoft's CPU licenses required OEMs to agree to pay for a minimum number of licenses, and this minimum number was typically greater than or equal to the anticipated computer shipments of the OEM. If, for example, an OEM expected to ship 100,000 computers in a year, it would agree to pay a license fee, f, on a minimum of 100,000 units. If it shipped machines with a non-Microsoft operating system, say PC-DOS or DR-DOS, it paid a royalty to Microsoft anyway. If it shipped less than 100,000 units it still paid Microsoft for 100,000 licenses. If it shipped more than 100,000 units the licensee agreed to pay an additional royalty of f per unit shipped. Again the licensee paid the fee regardless of whether or not the units shipped included MS-DOS. The CPU licenses set the marginal cost of installing additional units of MS-DOS equal to zero up to the minimum number of units agreed to in the license, and then the marginal cost per license jumped to f for each CPU shipped beyond the minimum number.

By effectively setting marginal cost equal to zero, the CPU licenses created a system whereby an OEM had to pay double to install a non-Microsoft operating system on a computer. Under such a pricing system, buyers would pay for a second system only if the system was technologically superior to MS-DOS.

Furthermore, the technological advantage had to be worth the full cost of the second operating system. This is a far more difficult hurdle to overcome for a competitive operating system, such as PC-DOS or DR-DOS, than a simple choice of which operating system to purchase for a given price.

The CPU licenses typically ran for two years. Furthermore, Microsoft usually tried to negotiate licenses that set a higher minimum number of units than expected shipments by offering a lower per-unit-shipped fee. At the end of a year the licensee typically had a credit for unused licenses, but Microsoft would only permit the licensee to carry the credit forward into the next year. This created an incentive for OEMs to install MS-DOS–based operating systems on next year's machines.

In addition to the implicit penalties associated with the use of a competitor's operating system, Microsoft utilized direct penalties for the installation of non–MS-DOS operating systems. An OEM using large numbers of non–MS-DOS–based systems might be prohibited from carrying forward unused credits from previous years, or it might be required to agree to a higher minimum number of licenses in future years. In addition, technical support services might be withheld from firms installing non-Microsoft operating systems, making it difficult to manufacture hardware configurations that worked efficiently with MS-DOS. Finally, Microsoft was known to increase the price of Windows for firms installing non–MS-DOS operating systems on their computers.

Creating Technical Incompatibilities

It is critical for the developers of alternative operating systems, such as DR-DOS and PC-DOS, and the developers of software to have access to the application programming interfaces (APIs) for Windows. Without the APIs, coordination between Windows and either the operating system or applications software becomes very difficult to achieve. Microsoft left some of the important APIs undocumented, thus giving its version of MS-DOS a distinct advantage for programmers over competitive versions of DOS, and giving Microsoft's application software, such as Microsoft's word processing software Word and spreadsheet Excel, an advantage over competitive software such as WordPerfect and Lotus. Furthermore, even if competitors discovered the necessary APIs, Microsoft could subsequently change any undocumented interfaces at a later time to sabotage compatability.

Generally, it is in Microsoft's interests for application developers to manufacture a large variety of applications software for Microsoft's operating systems, so Microsoft has made advanced copies of its new or updated operating systems available to software programmers. The software developers then test the compatibility of their software with the new or updated operating system. The compatibility-testing procedure is referred to as "beta testing."

To create compatibility problems for DR-DOS, Microsoft denied access for beta testing to DRI when it introduced Microsoft Windows 3.1 and Microsoft Windows for Workgroups products. In addition, Microsoft's version of Windows for beta testing was programmed to check to see if the program developers were using DR-DOS. If they were, an error message appeared on the screen asking the programmer to contact Microsoft for a version of MS-DOS or else risk incompatibility with DR-DOS. In reality there were no incompatibility problems between Windows and DR-DOS, and if the programmer ignored the error message and continued working, everything would run fine. The error message, however, was aimed at creating uncertainty in the minds of the programmers that running Windows with a non-Microsoft operating system would result in serious problems.

The CPU Licenses: Exclusionary or Optimal Price Discrimination

Functionally, Microsoft's CPU licenses served as an effective method of price discrimination. The licenses were individually negotiated and set marginal cost equal to zero to install MS-DOS on a CPU up to the minimum number of CPUs agreed to in the contract. Microsoft was practicing a form of first-degree price discrimination whereby each buyer agreed to pay a different fixed fee for the right to install MS-DOS. Under many circumstances the use of first-degree price discrimination improves economic welfare. There is, however, one exception to this rule: when the input is used in fixed proportions in relation to the output.

Ordover and Panzar first noted this important, and in Microsoft's case highly relevant, exception to the general welfare rule.[37] Suppose an upstream monopolist (Microsoft's MS-DOS) sells to downstream firms (OEMs) that compete in a perfectly competitive market. The downstream firms are identical and face U-shaped average cost curves. The upstream monopolist uses a two-part tariff that combines a per unit price, r, for the input with a fixed entry fee of e. Ordover and Panzar have shown that an increase in the entry fee, e, relative to the per unit price, r, will affect the number of firms in the downstream market. Specifically, it can be shown that an increase in the entry fee results in a decrease in the equilibrium number of firms in the downstream competitive market.[38]

Ordover and Panzar describe the intuition behind the above results in the following terms:

An increase in the fixed charges affects the average but not the marginal cost curve of the firm, and results in increased optimal firm output. But because $\partial p/\partial e > 0$ [where p represents the price of the final product], the market demand for the final product declines. This smaller demand will be produced by a smaller number of firms each producing a larger output.[39]

The result that the number of firms declines with an increase in the size of the entry fee, e, has great relevance in the case where the input, MS-DOS, is used in fixed proportions to the output, computers. In the case of fixed proportions, Ordover and Panzar show that the upstream monopolist must set $e=0$ in order to maximize profits.[40] The intuition is as follows: Under conditions of fixed proportions with an upstream monopolist and downstream competitive firms, the upstream monopolist can always set the input price, r, at a level that extracts all the profits an integrated uniform pricing monopolist could earn. Since downstream competition ensures a uniform price for the final good, there is nothing the upstream monopolist could gain by using a uniform entry fee, e, combined with a reduced input price, r. As noted above, however, if the upstream monopolist sets $e>0$, it causes a decrease in the total number of firms in the industry combined with an increase in the output per firm. In the words of Ordover and Panzar, "[t]otal (upstream and downstream) costs are not minimized and a portion of this deadweight burden falls on the monopolist."[41] The implication is simple: the use of an entry fee $e>0$ results in too few firms and each produces too much output, the upstream monopolist's profits must decline.

The case of Microsoft comes close to the case of fixed proportions between the input, MS-DOS, and the output, personal computers. The implication of Ordover and Panzar's finding is that Microsoft could have extracted more profit by charging a higher price per installed unit of MS-DOS combined with $e=0$. Since Microsoft effectively set a high entry fee, that is, $e>0$, and a zero marginal cost on additional units of MS-DOS installed up to the contracted minimum number of units, Microsoft's policy probably resulted in Ordover and Panzar's result: fewer but larger computer manufacturers and lower profits for Microsoft. If Microsoft could have earned larger profits but purposely choose not to, it provides evidence that its CPU licensing policy was a strategic attempt to prevent other manufacturers of operating systems from gaining a larger market share.

Bundling of Products

In the applications software market, Microsoft typically competes against companies that produce one major product, for example, WordPerfect in word processing, Lotus in spreadsheets, and Intuit in home financial management. Beginning in 1990 Microsoft began to bundle several pieces of applications software together and sell them as an application "suite."

Today the dominant application suite is Microsoft Office. In 1993 Bill Gates noted,

For the first time, we're positioning our primary application as being Office as opposed to the individual applications. . . . Now, this is not to say that the individual applications are not important. They are. But already today we sell over half the units of Excel and Word as part of our Office package. And so we've turned Office into far more than simply a way of marketing a group of applications at a discount and rather into an individual product.[42]

As Gates noted, the price of the bundled pieces of software in Office has been greatly discounted. Buyers can purchase the standard version of Office, including Word, Excel, PowerPoint, and Access, for approximately $250 retail. This represents a huge discount compared to the retail list price of approximately $300 per application. Office has not only resulted in a greatly increased market share for Word and Excel but has established PowerPoint as a major factor in a market where Microsoft had previously played only a minor role. Microsoft has also been bundling its Internet browsing software, Microsoft Network, with Windows and Windows 95.

There is a great deal of disagreement among economists and judges concerning whether market power in one market can be leveraged into market power in another market. Since the *Berkey Photo* decision, the courts have been less than sympathetic to arguments that power in one market can be illegally extended to another market.[43] In *Berkey Photo*, the court ruled that despite Kodak's film monopoly, Kodak was under no legal obligation to pre-disclose new technology to competitors in the camera and film processing markets. In its recent antitrust settlement with Microsoft, the Justice Department ignored the issues associated with economic leveraging of market power from operating systems into applications software.

Despite the legal trend, Blair and Esquibel have argued that it may be possible for a monopolist in one market to gain market share in a second market through the use of unfair competitive advantages, and this increased market share in the second market may result in a reduction in economic welfare.[44] Blair and Esquibel note that "[i]f the facts and the admissible evidence support a monopoly leveraging charge [against Microsoft,] . . . this is a serious indictment of the Department of Justice's enforcement efforts."[45]

While Microsoft may well have used bundling of software applications to gain market share for its applications software programs, it is unclear that the net effects on welfare were negative. For one thing, there is little doubt that the net impact of bundling was to lower the price of many Microsoft applications programs. Furthermore, Microsoft has been unable to gain a large market share in markets where its applications software is significantly inferior. The best example of this inferiority is the continuing dominance of Intuit's Quicken in the home financial management market. In this market Microsoft Money has failed to gain a large share.

There is also little evidence that Microsoft has been able to leverage its market dominance over operating systems into power over most of its software applications. The only exception may be Microsoft's tying of Microsoft Network to Windows. It is interesting to note that rather than challenge Intuit's Quicken by developing a better version of Money, in 1995 Microsoft attempted to acquire Intuit. However, the Justice Department challenged the merger, and Microsoft withdrew its offer. If Microsoft could easily leverage its market power into applications software, why did it fail to succeed with Money? It may, in fact, be true that Microsoft ultimately succeeded with Word and Excel because the most recent versions were of very high quality.

THE OUTCOME OF THE GOVERNMENT ANTITRUST ACTIONS

The antitrust action against Microsoft was started by the Federal Trade Commission (FTC) but concluded by the Department of Justice. This is highly unusual. There are other unusual aspects of the legal proceeding against Microsoft. Recall that the FTC staff argued that once Microsoft's basic control over operating systems was established, it continued to maintain power through a variety of practices including the preannouncement of products, exclusionary per-processor licenses for MS-DOS and Windows, unreasonably long-term licensing agreements, and restrictive non-disclosure agreements.

The FTC staff presented its case to the full FTC and in February 1993 the Commission deadlocked two to two over whether or not to issue a preliminary injunction against several Microsoft practices. Six months later the FTC met again and deadlocked for a second time two to two on the Microsoft case. This marked the end of the FTC case, but in an unprecedented action the Department of Justice decided to pursue the FTC case against Microsoft. The Justice Department expanded the investigation and on July 15, 1994, proposed a consent decree.[46] The case then took yet another bizarre twist—in February 1995 Federal Judge Sporkin rejected the Justice Department's consent decree. After analyzing the arguments presented by Microsoft's competitors, Judge Sporkin feared that the decree would not protect the public from Microsoft's monopoly power. The Justice Department and Microsoft jointly appealed Judge Sporkin's ruling. On appeal the Court found for the Justice Department and Microsoft, and the consent decree was finalized.

The major points in the consent decree were

1. Microsoft agreed to stop offering large discounts for CPU licenses based on the total number of CPUs shipped instead of the number of copies of MS-DOS shipped. This changed about 60 percent of Microsoft's licensing agreements.

2. Microsoft agreed to end its use of long-term contracts that committed OEMs to purchasing large volumes of software in the future.

3. Microsoft agreed to end its policy of requiring non-disclosure by software developers. This ended Microsoft's practice of requiring beta testers not to disclose details of Microsoft's operating systems for three years after the systems came to market. The non-disclosure requirement had restricted the ability of programmers to move from one company to another, unless the programmer moved from another company *to* Microsoft.

The consent decree is likely to have only limited impact on the market. Because of network externalities, virtually all OEMs continue to load MS-DOS and Windows on their computers, even if they also load another operating system, such as OS/2. It has, however, had some impact on the European market. Europe's largest PC vendor, Vobis Microcomputer, now ships its computers with OS/2 and Windows, but not MS-DOS. This has greatly increased the share of European computers with OS/2 installed at the time of manufacture.[47] In the final analysis, however, the Justice Department's action to prevent Microsoft from acquiring Intuit probably will have a greater market impact than the consent decree.

CONCLUSION

Although there are many factors that have contributed to Microsoft's rise to and maintenance of power, the most prominent factor is probably Bill Gates. There were many times in Microsoft's history that the future would have taken a far different turn if it had not been for Gates's ambition, hard work, and intellect. The ability to create dominant products is partly due to Gates's insights into the future. Microsoft's languages became dominant because Gates anticipated that CP/M would become the dominant operating system in the 1970s. More importantly, MS-DOS became dominant because Gates negotiated a contract that allowed Microsoft to license MS-DOS to clone manufacturers. Fortunately for Gates, at the time, IBM believed that the clone market would never be significant. Finally, Gates's willingness to stand up to IBM in the battle between Windows and OS/2 gave Windows the edge in that market as well.

Once Microsoft dominated the market, there were many factors that allowed it to maintain power. Microsoft's strategic behavior of preannouncing MS-DOS 5.0 and fabricating technical incompatibilities for DR-DOS with Windows 3.1 enabled Microsoft to ward off competition from the superior DR-DOS product. Microsoft's battles with Lotus 1-2-3 and WordPerfect were won by continually upgrading its products and, in the case of Multiplan, replacing an inferior product with the new and improved Excel. Microsoft's aggressive R&D strategy has enabled it to continue to improve its products and replace its obsolete products. Many companies would have ridden on their success with MS-DOS as long as possible, but Microsoft developed a new product, Windows 95, that basically made MS-DOS obsolete. Finally, Microsoft's unique and aggressive pricing strategies have given original equipment manufacturers no choice but to install MS-DOS on their computers. This aggressive management style has enabled Microsoft to maintain its power in the operating systems market and to gain power in the software market.

Recently, however, Microsoft seemed to change strategies. Instead of attempting to produce a superior home financial management product, Microsoft's answer to gaining dominance over Quicken was to buy the company. Such a strategy is completely contrary to the aggressive stand Microsoft took in its fight for dominance over Lotus 1-2-3 and WordPerfect. The fact that Microsoft has not attempted to compete with Quicken in the same manner creates questions about the future direction of the company.

Given the reliance of Microsoft on Gates himself, however, one has to wonder what will happen to Microsoft when Gates relinquishes control. One of the major assets of Microsoft, Bill Gates, will one day reduce his active participation in the company. Even as large as Microsoft has become, Gates still plays the leading role in Microsoft's strategic decisions as well as its product strategy.[48] Gates is expected to head Microsoft for the next ten years and then assume a smaller role in the company.[49] This raises uncertainty about Microsoft's future. Consider, for example, if we had done a synopsis of IBM after its first twenty years of computer dominance, we would not have predicted that IBM would sustain an $8.1 billion loss in 1993. IBM had a similarly aggressive management style under the reigns of Thomas J. Watson Sr. and Thomas J. Watson Jr. Just as it would have been impossible to predict the future of IBM in 1975, it is impossible to predict what the future will hold for Microsoft.

NOTES

1. James Wallace and Jim Erickson, *Hard Drive: Bill Gates and the Making of the Microsoft Empire* (New York: John Wiley & Sons, 1992), p. 23. See this book for more information on Gates's early experiences.

2. Ibid., p. 44.

3. There seem to be some contradictions in the recording of the next two events. Wallace and Erickson, *Hard Drive*, p. 46, say that Gates and Evans were asked to work on the school's computerized class schedule in May of 1972 and that Evans was killed on May 28. Gates then asked Allen to help him over the summer of 1972 with the program after Allen returned from college. In Daniel Ichbiah and Susan L. Knepper, *The Making of Microsoft: How Bill Gates and His Team Created the World's Most Successful Software Company* (Rocklin, CA: Prima, 1993), pp. 9-10, the authors state that the scheduling program was written in the summer of 1971, right after Allen graduated. They also report the death of Kent Evans as occurring in 1971.

4. Ichbiah and Knepper, *Making of Microsoft*, p. 12.

5. Wallace and Erickson, *Hard Drive*, p. 60.

6. Michael A. Cusumano and Richard W. Selby, *Microsoft Secrets* (New York: Free Press, 1995), p. 5.

7. Ibid., p. 137.

8. Paul Carroll, *Big Blues: The Unmaking of IBM* (New York: Crown Trade Paperbacks, 1993), p. 18.

9. Ichbiah and Knepper, *Making of Microsoft*, p. 74.

10. Ibid., p. 76.

11. The $75,000 figure is stated in both Cusumano and Selby, *Secrets*, p. 137, and in Charles H. Ferguson and Charles R. Morris, *Computer Wars* (New York: Random House, 1993), pp. 66-67. Ichbiah and Knepper, *Making of Microsoft*, p. 76, state "the exact amount is not clear, but indications are that Microsoft paid less than $100,000 for QDOS."

12. It is suggested by Ferguson and Morris, *Wars*, p. 71, that the reason for IBM not insisting on the rights to the source code was due to the rush of getting the IBM PC out the door and the pending antitrust suit which made IBM weary of appearing to take unfair advantage of a small supplier. Also, see Chapter 8 on IBM in this book for more discussion on this topic.

13. Ichbiah and Knepper, *Making of Microsoft*, p. 93.

14. Ibid., p. 92.

15. Cusumano and Selby, *Secrets*, pp. 159-160.

16. Ibid., p. 147.

17. Ibid., p. 148.

18. F. M. Scherer, *Industry Structure, Strategy, and Public Policy* (New York: HarperCollins, 1996), p. 276.

19. Ichbiah and Knepper, *Making of Microsoft*, p. 190.

20. Cusumano and Selby, *Secrets*, p. 161.

21. Carroll, *Big Blues*, pp. 191-196.

22. Cusumano and Selby, *Secrets*, p. 152.

23. Ibid., p. 142.

24. Important articles in the area of network externalities include Michael L. Katz and Carl Shapiro, "Network Externalities, Competition, and Compatibility," *American Economic Review* 75 (June 1985): 424-440; Joseph Farrell and Garth Saloner, "Installed Base and Compatibility: Innovation, Product Preannouncements, and Predation," *American Economic Review* 76 (December 1986): 940-955; Michael L. Katz and Carl Shapiro, "Technical Adoption in the Presence of Network Externalities," *Journal of Political Economy* 94 (September 1986): 822-841; Michael L. Katz and Carl Shapiro, "Product Introduction with Network Externalities," *Journal of Industrial Economics* 40 (March 1992): 55-84; Michael L. Katz and Carl Shapiro, "Systems Competition and Network Effects," *Journal of Economic Perspectives* 8 (Spring 1994): 93-115; Stanley M. Besen and Joseph Farrell, "Choosing How to Compete Strategies and Tactics in Standardization," *Journal of Economic Perspectives* 8 (Spring 1994): 117-131; and S. J. Liebowitz and Stephen E. Margolis, "Network Externality: An Uncommon Tragedy," *Journal of Economic Perspectives* 8 (Spring 1994):133-150.

25. Michael L. Katz and Carl Shapiro, "Network Externalities, Competition, and Compatibility," *American Economic Review* 75 (June 1985): 424.

26. Cusumano and Selby, *Secrets*, p. 159.

27. Cusumano and Selby, *Secrets*, p. 146.

28. Ibid., p. 158.

29. Ibid., pp. 149-150.

30. Ibid., pp. 139-140.

31. Ichbiah and Knepper, *Making of Microsoft*, p. 136.

32. Cusumano and Selby, *Secrets,* p. 139.

33. Ichbiah and Knepper, *Making of Microsoft*, p. 113.

34. Kenneth C. Baseman, Frederick R. Warren-Boulton, and Glenn A. Woroch, "Microsoft Plays Hardball: The Use of Exclusionary Pricing and Technical Incompatibility to Maintain Monopoly Power in Markets for Operating System Software," *Antitrust Bulletin* (summer 1995): 272.

35. Ibid., p. 272.

36. *United States v Microsoft*, No. 94-1564 (DDC filed July 15, 1995).

37. Janusz A. Ordover and John C. Panzar, "On the Nonlinear Pricing of Inputs," *International Economic Review* 23 (1982): 659-675.

38. Ibid., p. 662.

39. Ibid., p. 666.

40. Ibid., p. 666.

41. Ibid., p. 667.

42. Cusumano and Selby, *Secrets*, p. 141.

43. *Berkey Photo v Eastman Kodak Co.*, 603 F2d 263 (1979).

44. Roger D. Blair and Amanda K. Esquibel, "Some Remarks on Monopoly Leveraging," *The Antitrust Bulletin* (summer 1995): 371-396.

45. Ibid., p. 395.

46. *United States v Microsoft Corp.*, No. 94-1564 (DDC filed July 15, 1994). Amended versions filed with the court on July 27, 1994.

47. Cusumano and Selby, *Secrets*, p. 165.

48. Cusumano and Selby, *Secrets*, p. 418.

49. Ibid., p. 419.

10

BLUE CROSS: HEALTH INSURANCE

Erwin A. Blackstone and Joseph P. Fuhr

INTRODUCTION

Blue Cross began in the depths of the Great Depression as a device to try to maintain the financial solvency of the nation's voluntary hospitals. It rapidly rose to dominance in the provision of hospital insurance. Blue Cross maintained that position for many years. Eventually a number of factors led to its loss of dominance. However, Blue Cross still remains a major provider of health insurance.

BACKGROUND

In the 1920s, the period immediately before the Great Depression, hospital capacity increased as a result of philanthropic giving. For example, between 1921 and 1931 hospital capacity as measured by beds grew by 55 percent.[1] The rise in capacity created a concomitant rise in operating costs which had to be covered by patient charges or charitable contributions. The higher charges resulted in a decline in occupancy by the end of the 1920s. For example, occupancy rates at New York City voluntary (non-profit but not public) hospitals declined to 50 percent in 1928.

The Great Depression hit hospitals hard. Occupancy declined from an average rate of 71 percent in 1929 to 64 percent in 1930.[2] Over the same period revenues per patient declined from $236.12 to $59.26. Even before the Great Depression, Americans faced great difficulty in paying for anything but a very short hospital stay. There was essentially no hospital insurance. The president of the American Hospital Association (AHA) stated that the organization's basic goal was to provide "hospitalization for the great bulk of people of moderate means . . .

confronted with the necessity of amassing a debt or the alternative of casting aside all pride and accepting the provisions that are intended for the poor."[3]

The person widely credited with creating hospital insurance was John Kimball who had developed a plan called the Sick Benefit Fund for Dallas public school teachers. The teachers contributed $1 per month for the right to draw $6 per day if ill. Kimball had witnessed many teachers who lost all their income as a result of the influenza outbreak of 1918 through 1919. In 1929 while at Baylor University he found that many teachers covered by the Sick Benefit Fund could not pay their hospital bills to the University hospital. He extended the concept of prepayment to cover some hospital expenses. For fifty cents per month a subscriber would receive twenty-one days of hospital care and a one-third discount on the next 344 days (except in periods of epidemics).[4] The plan covered some private hospitalization at Baylor University Hospital.[5] This concept became the precursor of the Blue Cross (hereafter referred to as "BC") plan.

Dr. Kimball initially calculated that on the average teachers spent fifteen cents per month for hospital services. He thought that fifty cents per month per teacher would cover any hospital expenses, reasoning that the teachers probably used twice as much as they paid for. However, the plan, with 1,500 subscribers, lost $900 in its first year of operation. Utilization was stimulated by the absence of prices emanating from pre-payment.

About the same time as the Baylor experiment, Dr. Roren, an accounting professor and expert on hospital accounting, was advocating the use of pre-payments to protect consumers against the rising cost and uncertainty of the need for hospital care and to ensure public confidence in hospitals. Dr. Roren arranged to have the Baylor plan discussed at the 1931 convention of the AHA.

Another step in the development of hospital insurance occurred in Essex County, New Jersey, in 1932 when Frank Van Dyke, the executive secretary of the county's Hospital Council, extended the concept he had learned about in the 1931 AHA meetings to encompass pre-payment for all the seventeen hospitals in the county. Subscribers could choose any hospital and, accordingly, would be less likely to have to change physicians. Soon regional plans were developed in other parts of the country and BC was underway.

CORPORATE ENTITY

The BC and Blue Shield (BS) organization is a network of sixty-seven independent, locally operated companies called plans.[6] These plans can be not-for-profit corporations or for-profit companies. All the plans are related through their membership in the BC and BS Association, which licenses the plans to use the BC and BS names and symbols. The Association not only licenses the plans, but also serves as a trade association and as a contractor to the federal government. Together, the independent BC and BS plans provide health-care financing for almost 65.2 million people.

Originally BC plans were formed to cover the costs of hospital care while BS plans were established to cover physicians' services. Now, both plans represent the full spectrum of health-care coverage. In nearly every state BC and BS plans have evolved into joint corporations or closely cooperate with each other. In a few locations, they remain separate operations.

In 1939 the BC symbol was officially adopted by a commission of the AHA as the national emblem for plans that met certain guidelines. In 1960, the commission was replaced by the BC Association (BCA), which was independent of AHA. All formal ties to the AHA were severed in 1972. The BC and BS Association, created in 1982, is the result of a merger of the BCA and the National Association of BS Plans. In 1996 BC plans were beginning to compete with each other; some new plans were also merging.[7]

BLUE CROSS MARKET SHARE

Blue Cross was originally the dominant provider of hospital insurance (and has maintained that dominance in some states). Tables 10.1 and 10.2 illustrate the dominance and the decline in market share. Table 10.1 shows the decline in BC's market share compared to commercial companies, self-insurance plans, health maintenance organizations (HMOs), and third-party administered plans. It is far less marked, evidently because self-insurance by business existed from the beginnings of BC. The tables also show that BC lost market share to the commercials until 1969 but since then has maintained its relative position. BC has continued to lose market share to self-insurance policies.

Another illustration of the decline in BC market share comes from the experience of individual states. In Kansas, in 1980 for example, BC insured 46 percent of the population and by 1985 the figure declined to 37 percent.[8] In the Philadelphia, Pennsylvania, area, BC of Philadelphia annually lost more than 1 percent of its enrollment between the early 1970s and 1986. A large number of the defectors chose HMO coverage.[9] For example, U.S. Healthcare, which began in the early 1970s and by 1986 had almost 600,000 members, was the largest HMO in the Philadelphia area. In Texas, BC had 29 percent of the hospital insurance market in 1978, but in 1996 its share was estimated to be about 12 percent.[10] Another indication of the loss of market share is that in the mid-1970s, BC had only 33 percent of the hospital insurance market in Maryland.[11]

THE BLUE CROSS RELATIONSHIP WITH HOSPITALS

BC has had a long-lasting relationship with the voluntary hospitals. For example, in 1960 the AHA operated its Council on BC prepayment and financing to approve new BC plans and license use of BC symbol, among other activities.[12] One-half of the council members were BC personnel. The BCA was composed of representatives of the individual BC plans and formulated such policies for the group as subscriber transfer between BC plans. Three AHA representatives served on its board, and two BCA representatives served on the AHA board. In 1972 the interlocking directorate at the national level was ended and ownership of the BC symbol was transferred to the BCA.

Table 10.1
Market Share of BC Compared to Commercial, Self-Insured, HMOs, and Third-Party Administered (United States as a Whole)

	Blue Cross	All Others
1940	50	50
1950	48	52
1960	44	56
1970	43	57
1980	38	62
1989	30	70

Source: Calculated from *Source Book of Health Insurance Data 1991*, Health Insurance Association of America, 1991, p. 24.

Table 10.2
Market Share of BC Compared to Commercial Insurance Companies (United States as a Whole)

	Blue Cross	Commercial Insurance Companies
1938	93	7
1945	65	35
1951	53	47

Source: Calculated from Sylvia A. Law, *Blue Cross: What Went Wrong?* (New Haven, CT: Yale University Press, 1976), p. 11, and *Source Book of Health Insurance Data 1991*, Health Insurance Assocociation of America, 1991, p. 24.

CURRENT INDUSTRY STRUCTURE

The hospital insurance industry has evolved into one with many firms supplying various forms of insurance. The clear demarcation has eroded between the BC plans, which originally provided insurance for hospital services, and the BS plans, which insured physician services, in regional territories immune from competition from other BC and BS plans.

Specifically, BC and BS nationally faced substantial competition from other private insurance carriers and lost 12 percent of their subscribers between 1989 and 1992. Blue Cross and BS originally provided indemnity coverage, which in this case involved paying to provide the services. However, indemnity coverage, which is expensive because few constraints are placed on subscribers, declined from 73 percent of the market in 1988 to less than 33 percent in 1995.[13] Managed care, which involves more constraints on subscribers' use of services, increased from 50 to 63 percent of the market in 1994 alone. Further, in 1995 more than 30 percent of BC enrollees were in managed care versus 10 percent just a few years ago.[14] Managed care comprises HMOs, which provide for a fixed monthly fee all necessary medical and hospital services but with the requirement that the primary-care physician approve all services provided; preferred provider organizations (PPOs), which involve physicians and hospitals that agree to provide services to subscribers at discounted prices; and point of service (POS) plans, which involve discounts for using participating providers coordinated by a primary-care physician. Subscribers who go outside the plan pay higher prices. The bulk of subscribers are in managed care plans. For example, in 1994 50 million were in HMO plans compared to only 9 million in 1980. PPOs had 85 million enrollees in 1991 compared to 28 million in 1987. Finally, in 1996 self-insurance by major employers was quite common. Self-insured firms avoided some of the regulations imposed on insurance companies. Often these firms use insurance companies to administer their plans, and these firms sometimes obtain outside coverage to provide for extremely expensive cases.

The expenses per employee for indemnity, PPOs, and HMOs in 1992 were, respectively, $4,080; $3,708; and $3,566.[15] Not surprisingly, the more restricted choice plans contain costs but at the expense of less consumer choice.

In 1996 BC competed with many other providers. Competition was also beginning to occur between BC plans. For example, BC and BS of New Jersey planned to acquire BC of Delaware and together continue their challenge to the dominance of Independence BC and U.S. Healthcare in the Philadelphia region. BC of New Jersey was already competing in the Philadelphia region (the Pennsylvania portion) with an HMO offering. Independence BC was competing in New Jersey and Delaware with a wholly owned subsidiary, AmeriHealth, which had garnered 100,000 enrollees in less than one year.[16]

The industry also witnessed many mergers including mergers of BC plans. For example, BC of Texas and BC of Illinois were in the process of merging in 1996. Another major structural development was the eroding of the separation between hospital and medical service insurance. The growth of managed care, in particular HMOs, has eroded the previous distinctions. For example, BC of New Jersey's HMO provides insurance for both physician and hospital services.

REASONS FOR DOMINANCE

Blue Cross was initially able to dominate the market because it was the first mover and it had the image and responsibilities of a firm with a public interest and service motivation. As Herbert B. Cohen, then majority leader of the Pennsylvania House of Representatives, stated in commenting on passage of the Pennsylvania Nonprofit Hospital Plan Act of 1937,

The Legislature of Pennsylvania in approving this law was attempting to meet a severe need of providing citizens of Pennsylvania with hospital care at a cost within their means and also of providing hospitals with a source of financial support which would place them in a more stable financial position and therefore less dependent upon state and local tax funds. The Legislature therefore was attempting to fill a gap created by commercial insurance companies' underwriting policies which left the mass of Pennsylvania citizens unprotected from hospitalization expenses and hospital bills in many instances unpaid. It proceeded to close this gap by authorizing the creation of non-profit hospital plans, now known as BC plans, which through contracts with hospitals would provide hospital services for subscribers and guarantee the payment of their hospital care.[17]

The plans were subject to state regulation of their rates, payments to hospitals, reserves, solicitation expenses incurred for obtaining subscribers, and all other aspects of their operation. In the case of Pennsylvania the Insurance Department was the regulator. In exchange for state regulation and a commitment to public service, the BC plans were exempt from taxation and other insurance laws. Such advantages as not having to pay tax on premium income could be substantial. Premium taxes amount to 4 percent of premium income, which translates to about 33 to 40 percent of the cost of insurance companies since administrative costs comprise about 10 to 12 percent of premiums.[18] Part of BC's dominance thus derived from its status as a regulated monopoly providing non-profit hospital insurance.

As mentioned previously, BC was closely connected to the hospitals that created it. Hospitals benefited from prompt BC payment. One hospital administrator testified: "You must understand that for the most part inasmuch as hospitals created BC in the first place, that we look on BC as the partnership of the hospitals."[19] The hospitals especially desired an insurance company whose goals would be similar to theirs. Blue Cross' non-profit status meant that it wanted expanded coverage and use of hospital services similar to the desires of the hospitals. Not surprisingly BC received discounts from the hospitals that helped it obtain its dominant position. As recently as the late 1970s the BC discount in New York state compared to other hospital payers was as much as 30 percent.[20] Under BC's standard hospital contract in western Pennsylvania, BC did not pay hospitals for their construction expenses, for care for indigents, or for those who could but did not pay. BC would also only pay audited costs up to a maximum that depended on the category of hospital (there were nine categories).

The BC discount in western Pennsylvania in the 1960s and early 1970s averaged 14 to 15 percent.[21] Further, commercial insurance companies recognized that they needed the cooperation of hospitals and physicians and hence they "could be expected to be temperate in their rivalry with the providers' chosen instruments—BC and BS."[22] The commercials also recognized that BC played an important role in staving off even more intrusive government involvement in health insurance. Hospitals strongly supported BC; for example, they accepted subscribers' BC insurance without demanding cash deposits that were sometimes required in the case of subscribers of commercial insurance companies. The first-mover advantages combined with regulatory and tax advantages and an accommodating hospital industry permitted BC to become dominant in most regions.

The regulatory advantages, however, had a price—BC was expected to expand insurance coverage by offering policies for individuals or small groups. Blue Cross employed community rating, which involved charging the same rates for all who had a particular policy. The hospital discounts and the other tax and regulatory advantages initially were sufficient to permit BC to follow a community rating policy, which did help expand insurance coverage. Blue Cross initially did not differentiate based on the expected health status of the individual. Its losses from community rating were substantial. For example, BC was found to have subsidized poor-risk subscribers in western Pennsylvania by a total amount of $27 million in the years 1960 through 1970.[23] Blue Cross' dominance and pricing policy led to expanded insurance and use of hospital and medical services.

MAINTENANCE

Blue Cross was able to maintain its dominance and control most of the indemnity[24] market through the 1990s. This was in part due to its competitive advantage over the commercials as a result of favorable public policy. Blue Cross, as a non-profit with a social mission, was exempt from all state and federal income taxes, as well as local property taxes. Also, many states put a tax on health insurance premiums and, as mentioned, BC was exempt from this tax. Thus BC had lower costs as a result of these public policies. Also, BC received hospital discounts as a result of its large market share and the interests of the hospitals in promoting BC insurance.

For many years it was thought that learned professions including the health-care providers were exempt from antitrust statutes. It was not until the *Goldfarb*[25] case that this perceived exemption was shown to be false. However, before this case the American Medical Association (AMA) and AHA controlled the health-care market and any attempt to promote competition was resisted by the AMA. For example, in almost any other industry the agreement of firms not to compete with each other in the same geographic market would be looked upon almost as a per se violation of antitrust. However, BC was able to achieve these agreements and thus create geographic segmentation of the Blues' market.[26]

Another example of anticompetitive activity involved organized medicine's role in preventing formation of HMOs by banishing from the local medical society doctors who attempted to form HMOs and PPOs, which meant that the banned doctors lost hospital privileges. Groups of physicians have also attempted unsuccessfully to boycott insurance companies that attempted cost containment.

Blue Cross was also helped by the reluctance of the commercials to be too aggressive. The commercials and BC both benefited from the great growth in demand for health insurance during the 1940s and early 1950s, and there was little reason for the commercials to mount a frontal assault on BC, the chosen instrument of the hospital industry. For example, between 1940 and 1950, BC/BS enrollment grew from 6 to 38.8 million while commercial enrollment grew from 3.7 to 37 million.

In some areas of the country, BC has maintained its dominance. For example, in the seventeen county area in New York State in and around New York City and Albany, Empire BC (EBC) in the 1990s insured 9 million out of a total population of 11 million, a market share of about 80 percent.[27] In fact, BC increased its market share of hospital insurance from 72.4 percent in 1976 to 80.1 percent in 1980 as its enrollment grew from 8.9 million to 9.5 million.[28] The large hospital discount (in 1978 it was 25 percent but it was reduced in 1979 to 12 percent) and the strong support of unions (New York in particular and the Northeast and Midwest in general) also helped EBC maintain its dominance. Unions tended to favor BC coverage over commercial insurance.[29]

A similar pattern of dominance occurred in the case of BC of western Pennsylvania (BCWP). In the twenty-nine county area of western Pennsylvania, BCWP subscribers accounted for 62 percent of all hospital days during 1965 through 1969.[30] Its large hospital discount of 14 percent contributed to its maintaining dominance. For example, BCWP extensively promoted and featured its subscribers' ability to obtain hospital services at lower rates than subscribers of other companies. Blue Cross of western Pennsylvania also paid hospitals that did not agree to its contractual terms on a per diem basis, which was much less than its normal payment rates. Hospitals thus had a strong incentive to contract with BCWP and provide the discount. The discount thus helped maintain the BC share, but the share also helped BC obtain the discounts. Incidentally, BCWP's market share in the early 1990s had increased to approximately 75 percent.[31]

REASONS FOR DECLINE

There are many reasons for the decline in market share of BC from once having a virtual monopoly to now in some states controlling less than 15 percent of the market. Many of these reasons are interrelated and also take on a continuum. During the 1950s and 1960s BC experienced gains in enrollment but began losing market share to the commercial insurance firms. For example, between 1950 and 1970 BC/BS enrollment grew from 39 to 75 million but commercial enrollment grew from 37 to 90 million.[32] Blue Cross seemed to be following a policy of pricing high and offering insurance with few deductibles or co-payments and tolerating loss of market share. By the mid 1970s there were 322 commercial companies offering health insurance in the United States.[33] Market shares were low and entry and exit were easy.[34] In effect, BC facilitated entry by a competitive fringe of firms which then expanded its share.

The absence of a single company, structure became a problem for BC. Large national firms often found it easier to transact business with a single commercial insurance company. The alliance of separate regional BC plans inhibited the ability of BC to compete. One commentator noted, "Attempts to provide Blue Cross and Blue Shield with the appropriate national management systems were delayed and then limited by a persistent preference for autonomy among some plans, especially the smaller ones."[35]

The alliance with hospitals also began to become a liability. Insurance commissioners, as well as other public officials, began to question whether BC was acting in the interest of its subscribers or in the interest of the hospitals. Blue Cross practiced a cost-plus system for reimbursing hospitals and a pricing plan for consumers that had few deductibles or co-payments. The coverage was very comprehensive for expensive hospital care but was generally less comprehensive for preventive care. This lack of concern with restraining usage had a twofold effect on inflation. The cost-plus system gave the hospitals no incentive to control cost and thus as cost increased, prices increased. At the same time the benefit plan led to an effective price of close to zero to the consumer, thus increasing demand for hospital service which, in turn, increased prices.

Moreover BC in general paid for services only if they were provided in hospitals. As a result, patients needing diagnostic studies were admitted to hospitals for services that could have been provided on an outpatient basis at much lower cost.[36] Whether BC followed such a policy because of its connection to hospitals is unclear, but at the least BC's policy did not encourage provision of care in the least-cost manner and contributed to unnecessary hospital bed expansion.

Further, BC did not encourage price-conscious behavior on the part of consumers since the benefits were in the form of services. Most commercial insurers, even in the early 1970s, provided benefits up to a certain dollar ceiling. BC coverage was initially attractive because it absorbed the risk of extensive and costly treatment. In the 1970s the commercial insurers began to offer complete coverage for large group plans, but only BC did so for individuals or small groups.[37] In addition, BC did permit a wide choice of hospitals, which is of value. It also provided insurance to those who otherwise could not obtain insurance.

BC did not use its power over hospitals to obtain low prices, although it did receive a discount off the list prices. Given the monopoly and consequent monopsony position in health insurance and in purchasing hospital services, the explanation for BC's not exploiting its position lies with its non-profit status and its connection with hospitals. Low deductibles and co-payments encourage hospital use, and thereby benefit hospitals. They also stimulate demand for health insurance, benefiting BC and consumers who want few restraints on usage. Further, the non-profit status reduces the concern for profits and the related concern with costs and efficiency.

INFLATION AND COST CONTAINMENT

Medical care inflation has generally occurred at a higher rate than the overall consumer price index. Inflation is not a new phenomenon. In the late 1950s BC's response to cost containment brought about by rapid inflation involved state regulation of hospital entry and service offerings, such as the Certificate of Need program (CON). However, CON did not contain cost; if anything it probably increased costs.

Instead of raising co-payments and/or deductibles that would have worked to the detriment of the hospitals and, at that time, also of BC, BC pushed for planning.

In effect, planning through the CON program was essentially a cartel device to allocate beds and restrict entry. Planning would not reduce cost, which might reduce the need and hence demand for health insurance, including the demand for BC.

CON was viewed by BC and hospitals as a way of convincing the public that the rising costs were both justified and that the hospitals were trying to restrain them. It would also stave off more significant government regulation. A leader in the CON program stated, "If there is to be regulation of the voluntary hospital system, state franchising offers the best means of accomplishing the ends sought and does the least damage to the values of the voluntary system. It is a means for the public to control itself by controlling the manner in which it builds and uses its hospitals."[38]

That BC, an instrumentality of the hospitals, had a weak record in terms of cost containment is not surprising. BC was forced by the late 1950s to seek annual and large increases in its premiums because of rising hospital charges.[39] In spite of such cost increases, BC did not engage in hard bargaining to restrain hospital price increases. As in the case of CON it may have believed that cost containment would have reduced quality.

The primary problem was the method BC used to reimburse hospitals. The cost-plus retrospective reimbursement system fostered by the Blues' relationship with hospitals has led to high medical inflation. BC reimbursed hospitals retrospectively on a full-cost basis. For example, BC of Kansas reimbursed hospitals on the basis of 104 percent of their allowable costs until the mid-to-late 1970s.[40]

BC possessed the right to verify hospital costs and approve budgets and rate structures. BC was obligated to pay all reasonable costs based upon its approved rate structures. The system of retrospective reimbursement resulted in marked differences in hospital charges and payments for the same diagnosis within a geographic area.[41] Consumers had very little incentive to seek out low-cost hospitals because of both the low deductibles and co-payments. This system of retrospective cost-plus reimbursement enabled the elite hospitals to prosper without having to concern themselves with competition from smaller and less expensive suburban or community hospitals. The system resulted in substantial price increases, prompting some legislators to threaten to use their control over BC to restrain hospital rate increases.

Finally, high inflation was accompanied by higher premiums and more calls for cost containment, which led to increased competition. Since health care is generally a benefit to an employee, this rapid escalation of health-care premiums hurt corporate profits. Similar to electric rates before the 1970s, few really cared about efficiency or other factors when inflation was low, but given the high inflation in health care, firms began to recognize this as a significant cost and one which they had little control over so long as they were insured by BC. As the payout for medical insurance increased, firms had considerable incentive to control health-care cost because of the greater effect on their bottom line. For example, the proportion of compensation costs going towards health benefits increased from 1.6 percent of wages and salaries in 1965 to 5.3 percent in 1985[42] and to 6.7 percent in 1993.[43] Large corporations started to look toward sources other than the Blues for health insurance. A movement towards self-insurance where corporations had more direct control over costs began.

Some corporations tried to get control of their health-care costs by starting self-funded plans.[44] By 1985 the Health Care Finance Administration estimated that over 50 percent of covered employees were in self-insured plans.[45] Tables 10.1 and 10.2 illustrate that BC lost substantial market share to self-funded plans.

Other corporations began to look toward deductibles and co-payments not only to decrease the direct cost to the firm but also to decrease the demand for medical service which, in turn, would decrease the cost to the firm even more. As patients begin to pay out of pocket for a portion of their medical bills, they will be more cost conscious and question the need for certain medical services.

In the first case BC lost customers because the internal market was more cost effective. In the latter, BC's policies allowed others to exploit market niches created because of its product voids. For example the BC product line was limited to benefit structures that involved only minimal cost sharing. Many BC plans did not sell policies that required deductibles or cost sharing so commercials did not have to compete with BC in this market segment.[46]

With increased competition, BC was at a competitive disadvantage because of community rating,[47] which involved charging all subscribers the same (community rates) and led to cross-subsidization of those who use a considerable amount of health care by those who use very little. This public policy was put into place to ensure that people who were in relatively poorer health (high risk) than others could receive affordable health care. Such public policy will work only when there is little or no competition. However, if competitors, such as commercials, can experience rate then they can give lower rates to the lower-risk customers. BC would and did lose the low-risk subscribers who were subsidizing the high-risk ones. Thus, BC costs increased. Community rating can only exist in a market that is regulated or one in which a firm has considerable monopoly power.

ADMINISTRATIVE COST

Given BC's lack of competition in many areas, its relationship with hospitals, and its competitive advantages, the administration of BC in many instances had become lax. This has led to both dynamic inefficiencies and X-inefficiency and in some cases to allegations of outright fraud.[48]

In the 1960s and early 1970s many believed that national health insurance was the wave of the future and BC would play a major role in its administration. Many BC plans responded by initiating extensive construction projects:

[Many BCs] launched extensive construction projects in the late 1960s and early 1970s in anticipation of this role, and to help meet their responsibilities under Medicare and, frequently, Medicaid. These new headquarters cost more than $330 million and were completed, inconveniently enough, in the early and mid-1970s, the very time that the Blues were seeking widely publicized rate increases to keep pace with increasing expenses. The buildings were perceived by the public as another instance of wasteful, selfish spending by BC, the non-profit health insurance company which enjoyed special legal privileges because of its record of "public service." Insurance commissioners held press conferences in front of the large, frequently lavish new BC quarters to announce that they were rejecting yet another rate increase request.[49]

There has been increasing federal and state scrutiny of the spending habits of the Blue plans. In 1990 the West Virginia plan was the first plan to become insolvent. A Senate investigatory hearing alleged that political corruption, mismanagement, fraud, and lax regulation all played a role in the insolvency. The officers and directors of West Virginia BC established an extensive network of for-profit subsidiaries that led to substantial losses. While Capital BC was having financial difficulty, three plan executives billed the plan and its subsidiaries for more than $1 million in travel expenses. According to a U.S. Senate investigatory panel, the District of Columbia plan created some forty-five subsidiaries that entered into numerous ventures for which plan executives had no expertise.[50] These subsidiaries drained more than $180 million from the plan and caused premiums to rise over the past decade.[51] This has led to a decrease in the public confidence in BC as well as problems with state insurance commissioners.

Further, the competitive advantages that BC enjoyed were partially or fully offset by the higher average administrative expenses per dollars of claims processed. Frech has shown that these administrative expenses were 15 percent higher in nonprofit (BC largely) medical insurers than in for-profit plans.[52] Frech states that BC plans "spent" their advantage on administrative slack, which is often inevitable when a company has a long-standing competitive advantage.[53] Also an audit commissioned by the Colorado legislature performed by the accounting firm of Arthur Young and Company criticized the state BC plan's administrative costs.[54]

Lax management becomes especially vulnerable to competitive pressures in the new insurance market environment. Many plans were slow to adapt, which led to the erosion of the BC market share in certain geographical areas.

Thus, a combination of various factors has led to the erosion of the BC market share. However, many BC plans have adapted by employing managed care plans. Blue Cross continues to be a prime competitor, especially in markets where it has adapted quickly.

CHANGING MEDICAL INSURANCE ENVIRONMENT

In the 1980s insurance companies began to compete on the basis of controlling costs. Co-payments and utilization control became major factors as well as the movement to managed care. Also, most large firms went to self-insurance to better control costs.

Managed care can reduce the competitive advantages of BC because competitors are able to negotiate discounts by guaranteeing a certain number of patients. They also can restrain usage by requiring primary care referrals. The HMOs increased their national market share from 2.5 percent in 1977 to 11.5 percent in 1987.[55]

Large numbers of employers switched to self-insurance. Self-insurance is attractive because of improved cash management (employers pay claims directly rather than paying premiums in advance), exemption from state insurance regulation (both premium taxes and restrictions on benefit structures), and increased control over the parameters of the health benefits plan.[56]

Tax advantages of Blues have been eroding. Some BC plans have concluded that the cost of public service activities exceeds benefits and have sought to reincorporate as mutual insurers.[57]

Blue Cross previously had been striving for a consensus, not innovation.[58] As new innovative firms entered the market, BC was forced to change its policy and respond to this competition.

RESPONSE TO COMPETITION

Under competitive pressure, BC has moved to offer services that people want, such as HMO/preferred provider option (PPO) plans and deductibles.[59] Blue Cross has also engaged in some cost control programs. For example, it supported New York State's prospective payment system, which was adopted in 1969. Blue Cross in New York State also had numerous lawsuits with hospitals that were contesting its allowances.[60]

Response to competition can take other forms. One response could involve "punishing" hospitals that affiliate with rival insurers, especially HMOs, by withdrawing normal BC contracting status. Blue Cross/Blue Shield, which had about 60 percent of the insurance market throughout Kansas, canceled its contract with Wesley Hospital in Wichita, after the hospital's parent, Hospital Corporation of American (HCA), acquired Health Care Plus, an HMO with about 10 percent of the insurance market in the county around Wichita. Wesley had a capitation agreement with Health Care Plus under which it received a certain amount per subscriber for providing all required hospital care. Reducing the use of hospital services, which is the usual result of capitation, could presumably lower the cost and improve the competitive position of Health Care Plus.

The president of BC/BS stated in a letter to all Kansas hospitals that its contract cancellation occurred because

we no longer fit into their [Wesley's] long range plans. Thus, our decision to cease contracting with HCA and the Wesley Medical Center. We cannot stand idly by and watch insurance-hospital corporations, such as HCA, monopolize the delivery and financing of care by seeking to enroll BC and BS subscribers in their insurance program. [If] hospitals decide to compete with BC and BS in the manner that HCA is competing, BC and BS must make a decision about its future relationship with those entities. Hospitals that do not seek to enroll subscribers in other programs will experience no change in the historical relationship that has historically served Kansas well.[61]

The change in contracting status meant that BC patients who use Wesley would have to submit their bills to BC instead of Wesley doing most of the work on behalf of the subscribers. Further, because Wesley is a tertiary care hospital, care might be high quality but highly costly, and BC could be in a position to reimburse patients for only a portion of their charges at Wesley. In fact, Wesley was one of the lowest-cost hospitals in Wichita.[62]

In any case, non-participating status imposes substantial costs upon a hospital. The hospital has to submit its claims on paper instead of tape, which means higher costs and more time. Further, benefits are paid only to the subscriber, leaving the hospital more susceptible to collection and bad debt problems. Subscribers risk personal financial liability for charges in excess of the maximum that BC Kansas (BCK) will pay for a service or procedure.[63]

Blue Cross Kansas also incurs higher costs and it becomes less attractive to consumers. Consumers would lose the ability to use Wesley on the same terms as other hospitals, and Wesley had 43 percent of all inpatient admissions in Wichita in 1984. Blue Cross Kansas itself would incur higher costs through having to process paper bills rather than ones on tape.

In deposition testimony BCK's then vice president of Subscriber Services stated that there was concern that HCA, through ownership of both Health Care Plus and Wesley, would control supply and demand and could direct its subscribers to certain hospitals.[64] There was concern among BCK officials that HCA's vertical integration would lead to its dominance in the Wichita market.

Response to competition also took the form of imitating rivals' policies. For example, Health Care Plus entered the Wichita market in 1981, offering an HMO choice for employers. Within three years Health Care Plus gained 40,000 subscribers, at least some of whom came from BCK. Health Care Plus capitated its physicians, which meant that primary-care physicians provided all necessary primary-care services for a certain monthly payment per subscriber. A portion was withheld and was used to cover specialist and hospital services.

In 1984 BCK established its own HMO. Like Health Care Plus, the BCK HMO (HMOK) used independent physician practices. Under one plan, HMOK capitated primary-care physicians but did not require them to be at risk for specialist and hospital services that were paid on a fee-for-service basis. In addition, HMOK had a full capitation plan under which primary-care physicians were at risk for all specialist and hospital fees for their subscribers. Interestingly, physicians participating in Health Care Plus had no choice but to accept the greater risk of the full capitation plan because HMOK required that a physician had to accept the same level of risk with HMOK as with any other HMO, like Health Care Plus with which the physician was affiliated. In Wichita, HMOK did not attract sufficient subscribers, and in 1985 it ceased operation there.[65]

Another of BCK's policies was to obtain a "most favored nations" clause in its hospital contracts, which requires a participating provider to "fully and promptly inform" BCK about the lower rates and then to charge BCK the same rates it was charging any other insurance company. In 1984 BCK then had the advantage over other insurance companies that no other buyer was receiving lower prices and obtaining a competitive advantage. The firm had such a clause in its contracts with all Kansas hospitals. In 1984 BCK was the only hospital insurance firm in Kansas with a most-favored nations clause.[66] Such contracts may well discourage price-cutting behavior because lower prices given to any buyer must be extended to BCK. As BCK had such a large market share, a hospital would find it unprofitable to give a price cut to a small insurer. New entrants may well have to offer lower prices to attract subscribers, and the most favored nations clause restricts the ability of new companies to obtain discounts from hospitals.

Blue Cross Kansas used the termination of Wesley to signal its intention to punish hospitals that cooperated with the competition, in effect competing with BCK. A senior BCK official stated that "[we] 'll have to align ourselves with hospitals that are not directly competing with us. We feel we have to align with these hospitals to get a very favorable contract."[67] The same BCK official acknowledged in responding to an HCA official that hospitals would be excluded from participation status based on their degree of competition with BCK. In responding to an HCA official, he stated that he would not reconsider the termination of Wesley: "I don't hear you say that you are not going to compete with BC. . . ."[68]

A most-favored nation type clause was also an issue in Pennsylvania. Blue Cross of Western Pennsylvania (BCWP) in the early 1990s had approximately a 75 percent share of the market, and it wanted a "Fair Payment Rate Limitation" in its hospital contracts. The U.S. Justice Department submitted a statement to the Pennsylvania Insurance Department on September 7, 1993, arguing that the BCWP proposed clause was essentially a most-favored nation clause and "implementation of the [most-favored nation provision] likely would result in higher hospital prices to [BC] competitors."[69] The Justice Department claimed that BCWP's large market share meant that hospitals would not grant lower prices to another insurance company because the lower price would have to be extended to BCWP, and hence the BCWP payment would become the "price floor." Interestingly, BCWP developed its most-favored nation plan when it learned that its competitors were paying less for hospital services.[70]

Another example of response to competition occurred in Philadelphia. Blue Cross of Greater Philadelphia (BCGP) responded after some delay to the inroads made by HMOs and in particular by U.S. Healthcare. Initially BCGP had dismissed the notion of HMOs. In the mid 1970s a senior BCGP official stated: "It will never work. Blue Cross will never have an HMO."[71] The HMOs were attractive in part because they offered greater coverage for preventive care than did traditional insurance. Blue Cross of Greater Philadelphia waited about 10 years after U.S. Healthcare entered the market to introduce in 1985 its own managed care product called Personal Choice. In 1996 BCGP, now known as Independence BC (IBC), operated several HMOs and BC/BS was the largest provider of HMO services with 8.633 million enrollees as of mid 1995.[72] In the Philadelphia area IBC had 33 percent of the managed care subscribers, second to U.S. Healthcare's

43 percent. Moreover, IBC in 1996 had more than 50 percent of its subscribers in its managed care plans.[73] The dominance of BC permitted it to be slow to respond to competition. In fact, BCGP's holding company acquired another HMO (Delaware Valley HMO) at the end of 1986 as part of its strategy of responding to HMOs.[74]

Personal Choice was essentially a preferred provider organization, which meant that subscriber services were covered if obtained within the network of hospitals and physicians, but coverage was much more limited for services obtained in non-network facilities. Generally, the insurer, by restricting access to certain institutions, can obtain substantial discounts.

To introduce its product, BCGP initiated "an aggressive and provocative" advertising campaign, which involved about $2.175 million over a six-month period in 1986.[75] One BCGP commercial depicts a grief-stricken woman saying, "The hospital my HMO sent me to just wasn't enough. It's my fault."[76]

U.S. Healthcare responded to the advertising campaign by instituting legal action for, among other things, commercial disparagement and defamation. It also began its own advertising that involved expenditures of $1.255 million and continued through late February 1987. One of its advertisements was U.S. Healthcare's own attempt to play upon the fears of the consuming public. As solemn music plays, the narrator lists the shortcomings of Personal Choice while the camera pans from a Personal Choice brochure resting on the pillow of a hospital bed to distraught family members standing at bedside. The advertisement closes with a pair of hands pulling a sheet over the Personal Choice brochure.[77]

CONCLUSION

Blue Cross originally innovated the provision of health insurance and was the dominant firm. Given its monopoly power and non-profit status, it is perhaps not surprising that it was slow to respond to competition. However, BC was to some extent hampered by regulation and the requirement to act as the "insurer of last resort." Also, its association with hospitals contributed to its pricing and reimbursement policies, which created an opportunity for competitors to enter. When BC finally competed, it became a formidable opponent. In 1994 BC had 28 million subscribers in its managed care products, 43 percent of its total subscribers. (BC plans were even competing against other BC plans.) In 1996 BC was an important player in the market but certainly no longer dominant. Through "creative destructionism," once-dominant firms are displaced by newer firms offering new products.[78]

NOTES

1. Sallyanne Payton and Rhoda M. Powsner, "Regulation Through the Looking Glass: Hospitals' Blue Cross and Certificate of Need," *Michigan Law Review* (December 1980): 215.

2. Statistics in this paragraph come from Sylvia A. Law, *Blue Cross: What Went Wrong?* (New Haven, CT: Yale University Press, 1976), p. 6.

3. Quoted in ibid.

4. This discussion comes from Payton and Powsner, "Regulation," p. 216.

5. Law, *Blue Cross*, p. 7.

6. Most of the information in this section comes from Blue Cross and Blue Shield Association, *Fact Book* (no date).

7. See, for example, Marian Uhlman, "Blue Cross Plans in N.J., Del. to Merge," *Philadelphia Inquirer*, 22 May 1996, pp. C1, C2.

8. Calculated from HIAA, *Source Book Health Insurance Data 1991*, p. 24; and *Reazin v Blue Cross and Blue Shield of Kansas*, 635 FSupp. 1287, 1296 (1986).

9. *U.S. Healthcare v Blue Cross of Greater Philadelphia*, 898 F2d, 914 (3d Cir. 1990), 917.

10. See Lawrence G. Goldberg and Warren Greenberg, "The Dominant Firm in Health Insurance," *Social Science and Medicine* 20, no. 9 (1985): 720; and "Illinois, Texas Blues Pursue Merger," *Modern Healthcare* (5 February 1996): 6.

11. *Blue Cross of Maryland, Inc. v. Franklin Square Hospital*, 352 F2d 708, 802 (1976).

12. See Payton and Powsner, "Regulation," pp. 225, 226.

13. Jack W. Plunkett and Michelle LeGate Plunkett, *Plunkett's Health Care Industry Almanac* (Dallas, TX: Corporate Jobs Outlook, 1995), p. 8.

14. Paulette Roberts, *The Hospital Industry and Its Environment* (New York: Dun and Bradstreet, 1995), p. 30.

15. These data came from a survey of 2,448 companies conducted by Foster Higgins and Co. See "Health Insurance," *Standard and Poor's Industry Surveys* (2 March 1995): I 44.

16. "Blue Cross Plans in N.J., Del. to Merge," *Philadelphia Inquirer*, 22 May 1996, p. C2.

17. Quoted in *Travelers Insurance Co. v Blue Cross of Western Pennsylvania*, 361 FSupp. 774, 776-777 (1972).

18. See H. E. Frech, III, "Health Insurance," in Larry Deutsch, *Industry Studies* (Englewood Cliffs, NJ: Prentice Hall, 1993), p. 311.

19. *Travelers Insurance Co. v Blue Cross of Western Pennsylvania*, 361 FSupp. 774, 779 (1972).

20. Robert A. Padgug, "Looking Backward: Empire Blue Cross and Blue Shield as an Object of Historical Analysis," *Journal of Health Politics, Policy, and Law* 16, no. 4 (winter 1991): 801.

21. *Travelers Insurance Co. v Blue Cross of Western Pennsylvania*, 481 F2d 80, 82 (1973).

22. Harvey M. Sapolsky, "Empire and the Business of Health Insurance," *Journal of Health Politics, Policy and Law* (winter 1991): 751.

23. Ibid.

24. Indemnity health insurance involves an insurer's paying a predetermined amount for a covered illness. In the case of BC, the predetermined amount was the charge for the service.

25. *Goldfarb v. Virginia State Bar*, 421 US 773 (1975).

26. This assessment assumes that BC was a creation of the individual plans.

27. Erwin A. Blackstone and Joseph P. Fuhr Jr., "Monopsony Power, Bunding, and Cost Containment," *Widener Law Symposium Journal* 1, no. 1 (spring 1996): 384.

28. Theodore Marmor, "A New York's Blue Cross and Blue Shield, 1934-1990: The Complicated Politics of Nonprofit Regulation," *Journal of Health Politics, Policy and Law* (winter 1991): 786, 787.

29. Sapolsky, "Empire," p. 752.

30. *Travelers Insurance Co. v Blue Cross of Western Pennsylvania*, 361 FSupp. 774, 776 (1972).

31. Anthony J. Dennis, "Most Favored Nation Contract Clauses Under the Antitrust Laws," *The University of Dayton Law Review* 20, no. 3 (1995): 846.

32. *Source Book of Health Insurance Data 1991*, p. 24.

33. *Blue Cross of Maryland, Inc. v Franklin Square Hospital*, 352 F2d 798, 802 (1976).

34. See Frech, "Health Insurance," p. 308.

35. Sapolsky, "Empire," p. 753.

36. John J. Haynes, "Rural Hospitals: In Critical Condition," *Texas Hospitals* (January 1988): p. 18.

37. *Travelers Ins. Co. v Blue Cross of Western Pennsylvania*, 481 F2d 80, 85 (1973).

38. Payton and Powsner, "Regulation," p. 248.

39. Ibid., pp. 207, 208.

40. *Reazin v Blue Cross and Blue Shield of Kansas*, Inc., 663 FSupp. 1360, 1373.

41. *Reazin v Blue Cross and Blue Shield of Kansas,* Inc., 635 FSupp. 1287, 1288.

42. Data are from U.S. Chamber of Commerce, *Employee Benefits 1985* (Washington, D.C.: U.S. Chamber Research Center, 1986).

43. U.S. Department of Labor, Bureau of Labor Statistics, *Employer Costs for Employee Compensation* (Washington, D.C.: U.S. Government Printing Office, 1994), p. 9.

44. Robert Teitelman and Ralph King Jr., "Insurance Blues," *Forbes*, 10 February 1986, 58.

45. Patricia McDonell, Abbie Guttenberg, Leonard Greenberg, and Ross H. Arnett III, "Self-Insured Health Plans," *Health Care Financing Review* 8, no. 2 (winter 1986): 1-16.

46. Ibid.

47. Community rates involve charging everyone the same rate regardless of age, sex, or health status, whereas experience rating takes account of an individual's health status. See also our discussion above in the Reasons for Dominance section.

48. It should be noted that not all BC plans are characterized by such activities as we will relate here. However, there are enough examples of such conduct that it is an overall problem for the Blues and in cases of alleged fraud there may be guilt by association. Thus, one BC plan may be working in the interest of its subscribers, but if another plan has problems of alleged fraud then the public image of the Blues as a whole and of each plan suffers.

49. Michael Schonbrun, "The Future of Blue Cross," *Journal of Health Politics, Policy and Law* 2, no. 3 (fall 1977): 326.

50. Steven Bostoff, "D.C. Blues Slammed in U.S. Senate," *National Underwriter* 8 (February 1993): 3, 7.

51. Mark A. Hofmann, "Washington BC/BS Plan Targeted by Senate Panel," *Business Insurance* (1 February 1993): 2, 4.

52. H. E. Frech III, "The Property Rights Theory of the Firm: Empirical Results from a Natural Experiment," *Journal of Political Economy* (February 1976): 149.

53. H. E. Frech III and Paul Ginsburg, "Competition Among Health Insurers, Revisited," *Journal of Health Politics, Policy and Law* (Summer 1988): 280.

54. Ibid.

55. Ibid., p. 283.

56. Paul B. Ginsburg and Jonathan Sunshine, *Cost Management in Employee Health Plans: A Handbook* (Santa Monica, CA: Rand Corporation, 1987).

57. Frech and Ginsburg, p. 285

58. Frech and Ginsburg, p. 285.

59. PPOs are a managed care product without as extensive referral requirements as most HMOs.

60. See John L. Shurleff, "Review of Blue Cross; What Went Wrong?," *Hofstra Law Review* 3 (1975): 215-218.

61. *Reazin v Blue Cross and Blue Shield of Kansas*, Inc., 663 FSupp. 1360, 1388 (1987).

62. *Reazin v Blue Cross and Blue Shield of Kansas*, Inc., 635 FSupp. 1287, 1295 (1986).

63. Ibid at 1296.

64. Ibid at 1299.

65. The difficulties of HMOK resulted in part from its paying capitation rates below those of Health Care Plus.

66. *Reazin v Blue Cross and Blue Shield of Kansas, Inc.,* 663 FSupp. 1360, 1377 (1987).

67. *Reazin v Kansas Blue Cross and Blue Shield*, 663 FSupp. 1360, 1386 (1987).

68. Ibid, p. 1387.

69. Dennis, p. 855.

70. Joseph Kattan, "Beyond Facilitating Practices: Price Signaling and Price Protection Clauses in the New Antitrust Environment," *Antitrust Law Journal* 63, no. 1 (Fall 1994): 149.

71. Gilbert M. Gaul, "U.S. Healthcare's Abramson: Dedicated, Perhaps Ruthless," *Philadelphia Inquirer* (April 2, 1996): A5.

72. Marian Uhlman and Andrea Knox, "Aetna, U.S. Healthcare Plan Merger," *Philadelphia Inquirer* (April 2, 1996): A5.

73. Marian Uhlman, "When Health Care Firms Marry Who Benefits?" *Philadelphia Inquirer* (April 3, 1996): C8.

74. *U.S. Healthcare v Blue Cross of Greater Philadelphia*, 898 F2d 914 (3rd Cir. 1990) at 918.

75. Ibid. Blue Cross of Greater Philadephia itself used such terms in describing its campaign.

76. Ibid at 919.

77. Ibid at 920.

78. Frech and Ginsberg, p. 289.

11

AT&T'S GRAND DESIGN FOR DOMINANCE IN THE GLOBAL INFORMATION AGE

Harry M. Trebing and Maurice Estabrooks

INTRODUCTION—THE ISSUE

For over a century, American Telephone and Telegraph Co. (AT&T) enjoyed a position of overwhelming dominance in the U.S. telecommunications industry as a result of a corporate strategy that it crafted, executed, and maintained with the aid of government from the late nineteenth to the first half of the twentieth century. AT&T's dominance was threatened on a number of occasions during this period by the entry of new competitors. It was also threatened periodically by federal regulatory and antitrust actions. But the company was able to successfully fend off these challenges to its dominance in all cases, with one exception. That exception was the 1982 Consent Decree between AT&T and the Department of Justice, which forced the company to divest itself of its local Bell Operating Companies. AT&T has once again set out to re-assert its dominance over telecommunications as well as the whole spectrum of other service markets as it enters the global information age. The question is whether AT&T can reclaim its traditional position of dominance in the face of three new challenges:

1. Vast technological changes that have transformed telecommunications and are in the process of creating an information highway capable of carrying voice, record, video, and data services, which, in turn, permit the delivery of an almost unlimited variety of

information, entertainment, education, and electronic commerce services to all
businesses and homes.
2. Rapid growth of demand in both business and residential markets that has complemented
   these technological changes and is creating both new national and global markets and
   opportunities for new entry.
3. The 1984 AT&T divestiture and the public policy provisions contained in the Telecommunications Act of 1996 promoting the development of a universally accessible
   information highway and competition throughout the industry.

The challenges facing AT&T are indeed formidable. The direction that the
company has established for itself can be summarized by the following statement
contained in the company's 1995 Annual Report: "Our future is a long distance
from long distance. We're moving to a full menu of communications and
information services including local and wireless calling, credit cards, online
services, consulting and electronic commerce."

The new telecommunications and information-based economy that is emerging
and the directions that AT&T has set for itself raise a number of important
questions: What do the many changes in technology, markets, and public policies
mean for AT&T and its ability to dominate the new marketplace? How has AT&T
sought to accommodate to these changes? What new kinds of strategies is it
pursuing? How successful has it been to date? Who are the new generation of
competitors? What threat do they constitute to AT&T's ability to dominate the
industry? How realistic is the new objective of public policy enunciated in the
Telecommunications Act of 1996 to exhaust all of the opportunities and economies
inherent in the network of networks under conditions of competition? How will
this be impacted by AT&T's strategies? Those of its rivals? What kind of industry
structure is likely to evolve under various conditions? Competition? Oligopoly?
Monopoly? How adequate are the existing antitrust and anti-monopoly policies at
the state, national, and international levels? This chapter addresses these issues and
problems.

1879–1960—BRIEF HISTORY OF U.S. TELECOMMUNICATIONS AND AT&T'S STRATEGY

AT&T's dominance of the U.S. telecommunications industry goes back to the
latter part of the eighteenth century, soon after the telephone was invented and
patented by Alexander Graham Bell in 1876. Bell formed the Bell Telephone
Company and began setting up local telephone franchises in the major urban
centers across the United States. Western Union, the dominant supplier of telegraph
or record communications services, also entered the market to supply telephone
service. In 1878, Bell formed National Bell to concentrate on providing long-
distance service, and it hired Theodore Vail, a former executive of the U.S. Postal
Service, as its general manager. Vail made a series of bold moves, considering the
size of the young company he was managing. He decided to meet the competitive
threat from the much larger and well-established Western Union head on by

threatening to enter the telegraph business. The threat was successful. In 1879, the two companies came to an agreement whereby Western Union agreed to withdraw from the telephone services market for seventeen years and to sell its telephone offices to Bell. Bell agreed to stay out of telegraph business. This agreement gave Vail the opportunity to embark on a bold strategy to completely dominate the telephone industry. He began expanding more aggressively in local markets and entered the telephone business (as well as manufacturing) in a number of other countries, including Canada (1880).[1] In 1884, Vail formed AT&T to concentrate on providing national long-distance services. He also strengthened the hold of the Bell Company on vertical markets through its manufacturing arm, Western Electric, which Bell purchased from Western Union. Bell's control was also exercised through horizontal market strategies including franchise licensing and through its control over the dozens of patents that the company had on the telephone. During this period, Bell launched over 600 patent-infringement suits to block new entry. The Bell Company was very profitable during this period.

In 1894, the basic Bell patents expired. New entrants came into the market and gained market share from the Bell Company. By 1907, the new entrants controlled 49 percent of the local phone markets. New equipment manufacturers, Automatic Electric and Stromberg Carlson, also appeared. Competition forced telephone prices down, reducing AT&T's profit. The situation facing AT&T was so grave that Theodore Vail was asked to come out of retirement at the age of sixty-two to become AT&T's new president. One of the first things Vail did was change AT&T into the parent company that owned the Bell patents and the stock of the local companies. He also used AT&T's control over long-distance markets to foreclose the growth of the independent companies by refusing to interconnect with them to provide local and long-distance service. Under Vail's leadership, AT&T also purchased Western Union.

The U.S. Department of Justice was never far behind AT&T's efforts to dominate the telephone and other industries in the United States (and abroad) during this period. In 1913, it forced AT&T to sell Western Union as part of an antitrust settlement. AT&T retained its private lines business but had to spin off its public message telegraph service to Western Union. In 1925, it forced AT&T to sell its interests in foreign telephone companies, except those in Canada. The 1920s was also a period when new technology opened up new opportunities for growth for AT&T. One of these was the vacuum tube, the forerunner of the transistor, which gave birth to radio broadcasting. AT&T, GTE, and RCA signed cross-licensing agreements to control the threat of new technology. AT&T also began building radio stations and entering the radio broadcasting business. In 1930, the U.S. government challenged the agreement between AT&T, GTE, and RCA. In 1932, AT&T and the government reached an out-of-court settlement whereby AT&T agreed to get out of the radio business. AT&T subsequently reasserted its dominance over the local and long-distance telephone business. In 1933, federal regulation was established with the creation of the Federal Communications Commission (FCC). The FCC sought to constrain AT&T dominance through establishing a market shares policy. AT&T was given control over voice telephone service. Western Union was given control over record service. This division applied to both domestic and overseas services and continued through the 1940s and 1950s. The 1964 trans-Atlantic cable Decision (TAT-4) reaffirmed the FCC's policy based on market shares in the overseas market.

The application of AT&T's corporate strategy during this period in combination with federal public policies and regulations based on market allocation and associated pricing principles had the effect of making AT&T and the Bell System an instrument of public policy. This relationship effectively constituted a contract between AT&T and America (i.e., the U.S. government) and it lasted until the 1960s when the FCC adopted a policy of selective competition. One of the results of this contract was the creation of what was essentially a single supplier (AT&T and the Bell System), which dominated the manufacture and supply of telephone switching and transmission systems as well as customer-premises equipment and provided end-to-end telephone services to over 80 percent of business and residential subscribers in the United States. All customers were serviced by a single company without exception. Each customer received a single bill for a completely bundled package of local and long-distance services with no options.

The architect of AT&T's contract with America was Theodore Vail who is still revered in the industry, even by his critics.[2] Through this contract, AT&T was able to control the rate of technological change and the introduction of new technology as well as meet the growth in demand for telephone service in all markets while maintaining a position of dominance in each of the basic voice telephone markets. The contract worked well for at least a quarter century after the passage of the Communications Act of 1934 in the sense that it provided significant social and economic benefits to all of the parties to the agreement, that is, to business and residential telephone customers as well as to AT&T and the Bell System. For this reason, it was not seriously challenged during this period. The principal elements of this contract were as follows:

1. Rate averaging, that is, the rates charged residential and business customers over short- and long-distances and in urban and rural communities were average rates and, therefore, bore no relationship to their costs so considerable cross-subsidies were built into the system.
2. Value-of-service pricing, that is, the rates that local business and residential customers paid for services were based on their perceived value to customer classes with the result that businesses paid very high rates and residential customers paid low rates relative to the cost of service.
3. Universal service, that is, the rate for basic local telephone service was kept very low as a matter of policy to encourage households to subscribe to the service.
4. End-to-end service, that is, the telephone companies provided local and long-distance services and leased terminal equipment.
5. Obligation to serve, that is, telephone companies were obliged to provide telephone service to all businesses and households requesting the service and willing to pay the going rate.

6. Division of revenues, that is, telephone companies shared revenues for jointly provided services through a system of separations and settlement transactions.
7. Cost-plus rate making to provide incentives for the telephone company to invest in network facilities and equipment and the expansion of the infrastructure.
8. Economics of vertical integration to provide incentives within the Bell System for research and development with the associated economic benefits flowing to all users.

Evaluating the Performance of AT&T's Contract with America

AT&T's contract with America worked exceptionally well from a public policy perspective during this period. In the absence of a government-mandated standards and interconnections policy that we take for granted today (that was probably inconceivable at that time), the only alternative was a policy of enforced competition that would have meant the complete duplication of the telephone network. Such duplication would have been highly inefficient and wasteful of economic resources (in addition to being unworkable since subscribers on separate networks would not have been able to communicate with one another). Fundamentally, it would not have succeeded in achieving the objective of universal telephone service which was and still is a key foundation of public policy in the telecommunications industry in almost every country in the world. Achieving this objective was the responsibility of the telephone companies under the terms of the contract. The elaborate system of cross-subsidies within the telephone industry ensured a continuous flow of economic benefits to the body of residential subscribers. The system also ensured a stable and predictable environment for technological innovation in new telephone systems and equipment and the source of capital investment needed to expand the telephone infrastructure into rural and remote communities throughout the country. The result was that by the 1960s the public policy objective of universal telephone service was more or less achieved in the United States. This is one case, one can conclude, where a government-mandated monopoly could achieve the very valuable public policy goal of universal service given conditions prevailing at that time.

1960–1984: TECHNOLOGICAL CHANGES PRECIPITATE REGULATORY AND ANTITRUST ACTION AND THE BREAKUP OF AT&T

Federal telecommunications policies and AT&T's dominance of the telecommunications industry came under growing pressure in the post–World War II period as a result of a number of key technological innovations. They included the transistor, the computer, and the satellite, for example, which precipitated what came to be known as the telecommunications and information technology revolutions of the 1960s and are still working their way through the economy today. These innovations were so fundamentally important that they changed the course of telecommunications history in the United States and around the world. Many of the key inventions and discoveries were made within the Bell System by

Bell Telephone Laboratories, but more and more of them have been developed elsewhere.

One of the most significant innovations was the digital computer that was developed by universities and private laboratories, including those of International Business Machines (IBM) and Bell Laboratories, in the 1940s and 1950s. This computer created new growth markets for companies like IBM and Western Electric. The computer revolution would not have occurred without the invention of the transistor, which was developed at Bell Laboratories in 1947. It played a profound role in the development of the mainframe computer industry in the 1950s and 1960s until it was subsequently replaced by the integrated circuit which precipitated the minicomputer and personal computer revolutions in the 1970s and 1980s. Another technology developed by Bell Laboratories was microwave radio communications, which made it possible to transmit hundreds of telephone calls over a very long distance without the need for wires. Microwave radio eventually provided the means by which a new entrant, Microwave Communications Inc. (MCI) was able to design a potentially more efficient and, therefore, competitive alternative to AT&T's private long-distance network and eventually its public long-distance voice network. Another key technology developed by Bell Laboratories was satellite communications, which presented yet another alternative to AT&T's long-distance and international wireline network. Technological changes were also creating markets for new kinds of equipment that could be attached to the telephone network to provide new and specialized kinds of services. These included new kinds of telephone sets, private branch exchanges, and computer terminals. Another technology, known as digital data communications, was also developed to meet the growing demand for digital communications links to access mainframe computers and serve the needs of users of distributed computing. This resulted in the blurring of the boundaries between traditional telecommunications services, which were regulated, and computing services, which were competitive. This, in turn, posed serious problems for federal regulatory and antitrust authorities.

AT&T's Response to Technological Change and Competition

AT&T responded to each of these technological and market developments very aggressively. It refused to allow business and residential telephone customers to interconnect terminal equipment produced by non-Bell manufacturers. It also refused to allow new long-distance carriers including MCI and new digital data communications carriers, such as Datran, Tymnet, and Telenet, to interconnect their networks at its local exchange switches to access customers. AT&T also employed very aggressive predatory pricing tactics on services to drive out the competition where it was greatest. It discounted its Telpak rates for private leased circuits as much as 80 percent, for example, to fend off competition from MCI. AT&T also engaged in tactics to manipulate the regulatory process to prevent, delay, or forestall entry into its markets. When these did not succeed in stemming the tide of growing competition, AT&T turned to the political arena. Among its most notable tactics was its sponsorship in 1978 of a bill in Congress, called the

Consumer Communications Reform Act, that was designed to force the FCC to return to the golden age when AT&T and the Bell System had a monopoly on telecommunications services.

The Federal Response

The impact of technological change on the FCC was immediate and significant. Beginning in the late 1950s and accelerating throughout the 1960s and 1970s, it received applications from a growing number of companies requesting approval to enter the new telecommunications markets. I.. almost all cases, the FCC determined that such entry was in the public interest. In its Above 890 Decision (1959), it allocated frequency bands for the introduction of point-to-point microwave systems and introduced rules allowing individual companies to set up private microwave communications systems for their own use. In 1969, it granted a license to MCI to begin offering private leased line facilities between Chicago and St. Louis. In 1968, it issued its Carterfone Decision which opened the terminal equipment market to competition. In its 1971 Specialized Common Carrier Decision, the FCC found that the computer revolution had created a demand for specialized common carrier facilities and services that was not being met by the traditional common carriers. Meeting the needs of specialized computer and other users, in the opinion of the FCC, was crucial to social and economic development. It, therefore, created a new class of specialized common carriers services that would be open to competition. This decision became the basis upon which the FCC made a series of related decisions opening up other specialized segments of the telecommunications services business to competition. They included the Domestic Satellite Services Decision (1972), the Value-Added Networks Decision (1973) and the Resale and Sharing Decision (1976). In 1974, the FCC ordered the Bell Operating Companies to provide specialized common carriers with access to the local exchange switches as a necessary prerequisite to the development of competition.

The FCC's policy of selective competition fell apart as a result of at least two significant developments in the late 1970s. One of these occurred in 1976 when MCI introduced a new telephone service called Execunet, which was essentially a substitute for toll telephone services and, therefore, not subject to the FCC's competition rules. The FCC tried to shut the service down, but MCI launched a legal appeal to the ruling. In 1977, the court of appeals for the D.C. Circuit ruled that the FCC could not exclude MCI from providing the service and maintain AT&T as a monopoly without showing that this was in the public interest. It was too late, however, for the FCC to roll back the rising tide of competition. On a related front, the FCC acknowledged that its framework for distinguishing between unregulated computer services and regulated telecommunications services in its First Computer Inquiry had been made obsolete by the development of distributed processing. It, therefore, launched a second inquiry to investigate the consequences for telecommunications policy, regulation, and competition. In its 1980 Computer II Decision, the FCC acknowledged the futility of making any distinction between computers and communications and decided to allow telecommunications carriers to provide computer services under conditions of structurally separate subsidiaries. The decision to allow AT&T into competitive services, however, was in violation of the Consent Decree of 1956. With the U.S. Department of Justice now in the picture, the future of telecommunications policy (and AT&T) lay with the negotiations between it and AT&T. Finally, in 1982, AT&T and the Department of Justice came to their historic settlement, referred to as the Modified Final Judgment (MFJ), otherwise known as divestiture. Divestiture became effective on January 1, 1984. It brought an end to the hegemony of AT&T and the Bell System and it created a new AT&T. It also reorganized the former Bell Operating Companies into regional entities that are known as the Regional Bell Holding Companies (RBHCs).

Implications of the MFJ and Divestiture for AT&T

To some, the MFJ was a catastrophic event for AT&T because it severed the relationship with the local Bell Operating Companies thus depriving the company of its end-to-end service mandate. AT&T also lost its ability to exclude new entry at the local level and to impose licensing contract fees on the local exchange carriers. It also lost the ability to impose purchasing practices on the local carriers. And it set the stage whereby the RBHCs would eventually and inevitably become competitors to AT&T in the future. But the MFJ also had certain benefits for AT&T. Most importantly, it preserved its vertically integrated structure. AT&T was thus still free to pursue strategies to capture important synergies and economic benefits arising through the coordination of its network services operations and Western Electric and Bell Laboratories. It also gave AT&T the freedom to enter new competitive markets, although this could be subject to challenge by the Department of Justice under certain conditions.

Assessment of the Performance of Public Policy

It is difficult to identify any viable alternative to most of the public policy actions during the transition period leading up to the MFJ and AT&T divestiture. Technological innovation was speeding up across an increasingly broad front and providing more efficient ways of delivering communications services. Business customers in particular were demanding access to these new technologies to cut costs and provide innovative and more efficient ways of delivering services. Furthermore, the FCC determined in several of its various inquiries that AT&T was not meeting these demands. On the other hand, new entrants, armed with the new technology, were lining up to deliver these benefits. AT&T fought the new entrants using every means (fair and unfair) at its disposal. Clearly, the FCC's policy of selective entry was justified. Although the FCC tried unsuccessfully to prevent entry into the long-distance voice market, such entry in retrospect did not jeopardize the policy of universal service which has been more or less achieved by then. One can argue that the real innovation during this period was in public policy, in particular, in the adoption of standards and enforced network interconnection policies which have since become central to competition policy not only in telecommunications but throughout the utilities sector in general.

There continues to be a great deal of debate as to whether the breakup of AT&T was really necessary. It has been argued that the breakup was not necessary and that it was inefficient in the sense that it almost destroyed one of the most powerful technological and innovation engines in the world, that is, Bell Laboratories. It has also been argued that the FCC had the means to successfully manage the transition to competition in a less disruptive manner while preventing AT&T from unfairly using its vast monopoly power. It is notable that no other country has found it necessary to resort to divestiture to enforce its policy of competition. One can argue, however, that AT&T and the Bell System were inefficient and too big to be regulated by the small staff at the FCC. In this sense, the breakup of AT&T was good for both AT&T and the public. In another sense, the breakup was perhaps inevitable since the company voluntarily agreed to restructure itself in 1995.

1984–1990—AT&T'S PHASE I STRATEGY: RESPONDING TO DIVESTITURE AND COMPETITION

The period 1984 to 1990 can be viewed as one of transition for AT&T for it took the company at least five years to develop strategies to cope with the aftereffects of divestiture and gain some confidence before embarking on longer term strategies to enter new markets in the period 1989 to 1994. Divested of its local operating monopoly companies and facing growing competition in its prime market for long-distance services, the company was forced to make a complete break from the past and to anticipate competition in its entirety in all markets. It undertook a number of measures to improve its internal efficiency, including taking several multi-billion dollar write-downs on obsolete facilities and equipment on at least two successive occasions. It also introduced major cost-cutting programs. One of these was an extremely aggressive program of downsizing, possibly one of the most aggressive of any company in the United States. Between 1984 and 1989, AT&T reduced its workforce from 372,716 to 273,731, or 27 percent. Further cuts were announced in 1990, 1993, and 1995.

Freeing AT&T from Regulation

A key element of AT&T's strategy in the post-divestiture period was to diversify into the new high-growth telecommunications, computer, and wireless markets to gain economies of scale and scope and take advantage of synergies among its various operations. However, the company was still subject to certain regulatory constraints and prohibitions imposed by the MFJ and the FCC. It was prohibited, for example, from entering the local telephone and information services markets by the provisions of the MFJ. The FCC also continued to regulate AT&T according to rate-base, rate-of-return rules. AT&T must have realized that as long as it continued to be the dominant player in the long-distance market, it was unlikely that the FCC or the Department of Justice would look permissively on its entry into these new markets. If AT&T had held its share of the long-distance market to its divestiture level of 85 percent, it is unlikely that federal authorities would have given it permission to enter these new markets—which they subsequently did.

The argument could thus be made that AT&T deliberately set out as a matter of strategy to reduce its market share to a level below which it would be perceived to be a non-dominant carrier in order to dispel any threat of re-regulation or antitrust action.[3] AT&T's share of the long-distance market declined for five years after divestiture until it stabilized at a level of about 63 percent in 1989. In 1989, the FCC imposed price caps on AT&T. In 1991, the United States District Court for the District of Columbia lifted the restriction barring AT&T from entering the information services business. In 1993, AT&T applied to the FCC to be classified as a non-dominant carrier, and, in 1995, the FCC agreed to re-classify it as non-dominant carrier.[4]

Leveraging on AT&T's Core Competencies in Networks and Services

Another important element of AT&T's competitive strategy in the late 1980s was to leverage on its core competencies in communications services by maximizing the efficiencies of its network infrastructure. AT&T recognized quite rightly that its greatest asset was its national and international network of telecommunications facilities, which was second to none, and it crafted a number of strategies to capitalize on these assets. Its long-distance services were its most profitable, constituting as much as 65 percent of its total revenues and 85 percent of its total profits. One of the most successful strategies it pursued was segmenting the residential and business markets and developing a package of cut-rate services for each. AT&T also pursued aggressive pricing tactics to attract big-volume business and residential customers. In general, it engaged in price leadership for tariffed services with both MCI and Sprint responding with matching changes. It also engaged in massive advertising and other forms of non-price rivalry. By 1993, for example, it was spending as much as $1 billion on advertising.

Roll-Out of New Technology Platforms

AT&T also took advantage of its combined strengths in the research, development, and manufacturing of advanced state-of-the-art systems and equipment as well as buildings and managing a state-of-the-art communications network. It rolled out several new and innovative technologies to gain competitive advantages in the domestic and international business markets which were by far its most profitable markets. These, in general, were based on its own intelligent digital technology platforms. One of these was its software-defined network service offerings. This very efficient shared (or public) network platform used software in the network to enable its big-business customers to use the network as if it were a private network. The sharing of network facilities in this way offered big savings to both AT&T and its business customers. AT&T introduced deep discounts to encourage big users to switch over to this new platform. It also introduced a series of so-called custom-tariff offerings (Tariffs 12, 15, and 16) which were designed to attract big-business customers needing very special (i.e., customized) networks, for example, to integrate their voice and data communications traffic on one network. These service offerings were among AT&T's biggest successes in the late 1980s.

AT&T's First Attempts at Diversification

Another key strategy that AT&T pursued in the late 1980s was of diversifying into new markets to provide a full range of communications services. These included voice, data, video, and computer, as well as multimedia communications markets. It entered the computer industry, for example, with a full line of AT&T designed and manufactured minicomputers and small desktop (personal computer-based) computers, as well as network-based computers. By the end of the decade, it had also entered into agreements with foreign companies, including Olivetti in Europe, for example, to manufacture computer and telecommunications equipment. AT&T also formed a new subsidiary, AT&T Capital, to finance the leasing and purchasing of equipment. In 1989, it launched the AT&T Universal Card. In 1990, it acquired EasyLink, a successful electronic mail business, from Western Union.

AT&T's attempts to diversify were not successful in all cases. Its attempts to enter foreign markets, for example, were frustrated by the fact that most of these markets were still closed for all intents and purposes. AT&T's computer strategy was also acknowledged by some to have been a disaster, and the company came under growing pressure to make major adjustments. At the same time, the entire telecom landscape was radically changing and AT&T found itself having to move more quickly and aggressively to strategically position itself for growth in the future. In hindsight, it appears that the period 1984 to 1990 was a time to try things out and gain some valuable experience and prepare itself for future competition.

1990–1995—AT&T'S PHASE II STRATEGY: GEARING UP TO MEET CHALLENGES OF THE GLOBAL INFORMATION AGE

The early 1990s witnessed dramatic changes in the telecommunications industry both in the United States and worldwide as a result of the ongoing microchip, computer, and telecommunications revolutions and the growing interdependence, integration, or convergence of technologies, markets, and industries.[5] Developments in information technology, particularly the rapid spread of personal computers throughout businesses and into homes and schools, promised to usher in the long-awaited information age and with it many new opportunities for growth and profit. The computer revolution also stimulated the rapid growth of new markets for a wide variety of networking products and services to connect the exploding numbers of personal computers and workstations in businesses into local area, wide area, and enterprise networks. One of the most promising information technology applications was multimedia which involves the integration of computer-generated images, graphics, sound and voice, and even video to create entertainment and educational and other programs. It could have dramatic implications for telecommunications in the future in the form of multimedia teleconferencing, for example.

By the early 1990s as well, the economics of fiber-optic technology had improved to a point where it was becoming attractive to deploy it in the local loop. Telephone and cable television companies across the nation became caught up in a race to test these systems in field trials. AT&T became a partner in many of these trials. These new transmission systems were significant because of their potential for carrying voice telephony, sounds, video, and a variety of multimedia information services, including entertainment and education services on demand as well as home banking, electronic commerce, retailing, and many other services. And a new switching technology, known as asynchronous transfer mode (ATM), promised to make it economically attractive to switch voice, data, and video simultaneously over the same network instead of separate networks. This offered potentially significant advantages to local and long-distance carriers in the form of economies of scale and scope. Taking advantage of the many opportunities that these technologies presented involved massive amounts of capital investment and strengths in multiple technologies and skills to develop the necessary transmission and switching products and services and terminal devices.

The years 1992 and 1993 were also those in which the Clinton–Gore administration promoted with great fanfare its vision of a national information infrastructure (NII) comprising an interconnected and modernized network of telephone, cable television, and satellite and wireless telecommunications systems, as well as computers, that would reach into every home and business of the nation. According to its promoters, the NII would launch America into the information age and stimulate economic growth and competitiveness. In December 1992, President Clinton held a national economic summit in Little Rock, Arkansas, in which all of the players in the U.S. telecommunications, cable television, and broadcasting industries endorsed the need to adopt the goal of building a national information infrastructure or information highway. The convergence of technologies, in turn, signaled the convergence of telephone, cable television, and computer industries as well as publishing, broadcasting, and entertainment. At the same time, another product of the computer revolution, known as the Internet, began to gain widespread popularity in the early 1990s. It, too, had the potential to evolve into an information highway and open up many economic opportunities but few players recognized this until 1995. Two of the exceptions were IBM and MCI, which were chosen by the National Science Foundation in 1993 to build a high-speed digital backbone network to interconnect all of the nation's supercomputers.

Developments were rapidly taking place in other parts of the telecommunications industry in the late 1980s and early 1990s as well. The cellular telephone business continued to record impressive growth rates, and a new generation of wireless, personal communications systems (PCS) showed significant promise of becoming a less expensive alternative to cellular telephone and the wireline telephone system. It was also completely digital and had greater capacities than cellular. Rapid developments were also taking place in satellite communications technologies. A new generation of geosynchronous and non-geosynchronous satellites promised to provide the entire world with voice, data, and multimedia video services on demand. Opportunities were also opening up in the global telecommunications and information services marketplace as country after country in the developing world embarked on a national goal of building a modern telecommunications infrastructure to stimulate economic growth.

These developments posed enormous opportunities as well as threats for AT&T. In almost all cases, however, AT&T was not in a position to dominate these new and emerging markets, although it was strategically positioned to benefit from many of them directly to the extent that many of them would generate communications traffic. It was in response to these forces that AT&T's new management set about devising a series of strategies to enter these new markets. One of the key elements of AT&T's new strategies was the recognition that AT&T could no longer control the introduction of new technology in America or worldwide. Wherever it could, it would have to use the technology developed by others. This meant gaining access to it either through outright acquisition, through merger, or through strategic alliances or partnerships. AT&T pursued all of these strategies. By suitably selecting strong leaders in each of a number of strategically important sectors, AT&T set about first to benefit through direct acquisition and second to take advantage of synergies between its new acquisitions and its existing operations. Suitably executed, all of its operations could benefit significantly from these acquisitions.

1991—AT&T Moves into the Computer Industry with the Acquisition of NCR

It is widely recognized that telecommunications is only one of the essential strengths that every aspiring world-class player must have to successfully execute a strategy of dominating the information and communications markets of the future. Another is computer technology and computer services. AT&T recognized this long ago, but it was barred from the business until 1984 by the Consent Decree of 1956. It was unable to build a viable, profitable computer business on its own. After years of searching, AT&T settled on NCR to lead its entry into the computer business. On September 19, 1991, the two companies announced that they had agreed to a merger. NCR brought many important strengths to AT&T, in particular its considerable computer expertise, while AT&T provided NCR with enormous networking expertise and access to the technology resources of Bell Laboratories. NCR was also a leader worldwide in point-of-sale and automated teller machines, with a very strong presence in financial and retail markets which complemented AT&T Universal Card ambitions. NCR was also a leader in building a whole range of computer systems based on open systems standards and the latest generation of Intel microchips, and this too made it very strong. One of its newly acquired strengths (through the acquisition of Teradata Corp. in 1992) was the use of these hundreds of Intel chips to design what is called massively parallel computers. These are used for processing-intensive applications in the retail and financial services markets in which NCR was very strong and had promising applications in information services and multimedia and Internet environments. NCR helped AT&T expand into the local area network/wide area network (LAN/WAN) business. Both AT&T and NCR also enjoyed a strong presence in global markets, and each anticipated reaping synergies and economic benefits from the other.

One of the objectives of the AT&T-NCR merger was to take advantage of the potential synergies between the two companies to develop a whole line of new multimedia products and services led by NCR. To this end, NCR formed two new units to meld the expertise of the two organizations together. One of these is its Multimedia Products Business Unit. Another, called Telecommunications Solutions and Integration, is intended to develop products and services derived from the merger and convergence of computers and telecommunications. One of the products of their cooperative efforts has been the development of a personal video system, announced on March 29, 1993, which was designed to facilitate the collaboration of groups of workers over telecommunications networks using video, pictures, and images. Another result of the collaboration has been the development of a (UniverCell) family of broadband (ATM) switches by NCR (announced in 1993), which targets the emerging markets for interactive, multimedia, voice, and video applications.

1993—AT&T Moves into the Cellular Communications Business with the Acquisition of McCaw Cellular Communications, Inc.

Another key market that AT&T set its sights on in the early 1990s was the cellular telephone service business, which had achieved growth rates of 40 percent and more per year in the late 1980s and early 1990s. After months of negotiation and speculation, AT&T and McCaw Cellular Communications announced a $12.6 billion merger of the two companies on August 16, 1993. One of the objectives of the merger was to build an intelligent seamless network and develop a wide variety of wireless applications for "anytime, anywhere" communications service. Achieving this objective could only be accomplished by combining and coordinating the strengths of the two companies and by taking advantage of the enormous potential synergies of the two organizations.

Cellular telephone and the McCaw Cellular merger were central to AT&T's strategy for a number of reasons. First, cellular was a natural complement to AT&T's long-distance wireline telephone service as well as its satellite services. Each long-distance call made by a cellular user generated revenue for AT&T's long-distance domestic and international telephone or satellite operations. Second the merger put AT&T in a position to offer local telephone service in competition with the Bell Operating Companies. Third, one of the strengths of Bell Laboratories was in cellular technologies. It holds the patents to some of the most important inventions in cellular technology. AT&T Network Systems also manufactured cellular switches and digital cellular systems. The merger, therefore, put AT&T in a position to offer both cellular equipment and services. The early 1990s also coincided with the opening up of a potentially huge international market for wireless cellular systems and services. Developing countries in particular were looking to cellular technology as the focal point of their infrastructure development strategy because it was faster and simpler and less expensive to deploy than wireline transmission systems. AT&T brought other strengths to the merger, including its systems integration expertise, which was central to the development of a seamless network. The merger also complemented AT&T's multimedia strategy, that is, of transmitting voice, video, and graphics over its wireline, wireless, and satellite networks. For all of these reasons, the acquisition was critical to AT&T's strategy of offering one-stop shopping domestically and globally.

AT&T's Enterprise Strategy

One of AT&T's most profitable service segments has traditionally been the business market for telecommunications systems, facilities, and services, particular those that it supplies to its biggest corporate customers in the world. This market has exploded in recent years with the convergence of computers and communications and the globalization of economic activity. Indeed, globalization and competition are forcing all corporations to increasingly rely on their national and international computer and telecommunications networks as a source of strategic competitive advantage. They rely on these networks and systems not only for communications, coordination, and control purposes, but for the design, production, marketing, and delivery of products and services around the world. The real challenge for them is to build and manage complex enterprise networks comprising systems of personal computers, minicomputers, and mainframe computers, local area and wide area networks, and private branch exchanges, as well as a variety of telephone, data and video communications equipment and services. The dilemma they face is that they must overcome serious problems relating to the interconnection and interworking of incompatible systems, equipment, and software programs.

For many businesses, the challenge of these complexities is so great that they are forced to turn to outside experts to build and/or manage their enterprise networks and systems. This has created a rapidly growing market for consulting services as well as systems integration and outsourcing services for companies, such as IBM, EDS, Andersen Consulting, and Computer Sciences Corp., for example. According to AT&T, this market constitutes a $50 billion industry and is growing at double-digit rates. AT&T has formed a new subsidiary, AT&T Solutions, to lead its entry into the consulting, systems integration, and outsourcing marketplace. One of its big competitors is MCI, which upstaged AT&T in 1995 with the $1.4 billion acquisition of Systemhouse Limited (SHL). SHL is now the core of MCI's wholly owned systems integration and outsourcing group.

AT&T has formulated what it has called its "OneVision" strategy to meet the needs of its global business customers, in AT&T's own words, as "computing and communications converge to create a networked business world linking diverse functions, data bases, users and technologies." According to AT&T, OneVision brings together many of its business units to jointly support integrated management solutions through the combined efforts of AT&T Global Information Solutions, Global Business Communications Systems, Business Communications Services, AT&T Solutions, Network Systems, and Bell Laboratories. Its objective, as stated on page 9 of its 1995 Annual Report is to offer businesses "a complete management solution . . . so they have both the technology and the ability to get the most out of it." AT&T has chosen Hewlett-Packard's OpenView management framework as its technology platform. OpenView is the de facto industry standard for enterprise management. AT&T has also been leveraging on the leadership of Novell Corp. in the network operating systems market by developing a national office communications network to interconnect the offices of business clients in the United States and throughout the world.

AT&T Plays Catchup in the Internet Services Industry

The spectacular growth of the Internet services market caught most of the big players in the telecommunications, computer, and information services industries by surprise. AT&T was no exception. Until 1995, AT&T was not represented as an Internet services provider. The biggest suppliers in 1995 included IBM and long-distance carriers MCI (Internet MCI) and Sprint (Sprint IP Services). In June 1995, AT&T made its move into the Internet services business by entering into a strategic relationship with BBN Planet, owned by BBN Corporation, a pioneer in the development of ARPANET, the predecessor of the Internet. Under the terms of the agreement, BBN Planet is the exclusive supplier of dedicated Internet access and related network management services to AT&T for resale to customers of AT&T's Business Communications Services Division in the United States for a period of three years.

AT&T officially entered the dial-up consumer market on February 27, 1996, when it announced with great fanfare that it was offering five free hours per month of Internet access for a year to its long-distance customers or unlimited access for a flat monthly rate of $19.95. Three months later, on May 22, 1996, it announced that it had become the second largest pure Internet access provider in the United States, signing up 150,000 subscribers after Netcom with 400,000 subscribers. In February 1996, AT&T formed AT&T WorldNet to manage its Internet services. The company resells access to BBN Planet as a consumer and business dial-up service in the United States and worldwide. AT&T's plan is to capture economic synergies among its various service offerings. It is planning to offer a wide variety of Internet access and other services to all of its business and residential customers in the United States and abroad through all of its local, long-distance, cellular, and satellite facilities. Its strategy involves cross-selling its Internet services offerings in all of its other markets, most importantly, the telephone market. By bundling its Internet services with its telephone, electronic mail, messaging, facsimile, and other service offerings, it hopes to achieve its objective of providing one-stop shopping to all of its business and residential subscribers.

AT&T also wants to develop a capability to provide a wide variety of Internet and information highway service offerings, including multimedia information, education, and entertainment services. On October 31, 1995, it entered the Internet education services market with the announcement that it was pledging $150 million to link schools to the information highway by the year 2000. Then, on May 31, 1996, it pledged $300 million in wireless services to schools. On June 12, 1996, it announced that it had set up the Learning Network Academy to help teachers, administrators, and libraries learn about the Internet.

AT&T's Push into Financial Services and Electronic Commerce

Another potentially huge market created by the Internet is electronic commerce, which involves the provision of a wide variety of information processing, transactions, and communications services to facilitate the buying and selling of goods and services. This includes advertising, retailing, distribution, and invoicing and payment, as well as online banking and investment services. This is another market that AT&T has targeted for its future growth. The company is already strategically positioned in this market through NCR, which is a world leader in developing and marketing of a complete line of systems and equipment for the banking and financial services community worldwide. AT&T is also well positioned here as a result of the success of its Universal Credit Card operation, which ranked as the second most popular credit card in the United States with over 22 million cardholders in 1995. This is yet another example of AT&T's strategy of cross-selling its services in all of its many markets, of bundling many of its various services, and its one-stop-shopping strategy.

AT&T's International Market Strategy

One of AT&T's core competencies and one of the markets that A&T has targeted for future growth is international services. The company advertises itself as the world's largest carrier of international telecommunications services. In 1995, it offered its customers access to its network and billing systems in 100 countries. Its most profitable international services, however, are those designed to meet the needs of its international business clients, including its video and virtual telecommunications services. In 1992, it formed two new business units, Global Business Video Services and Global Business Systems, to develop the market for dial-up international videoconferencing services. AT&T has been the leader in the formation of an alliance of global telecommunications suppliers in Asia, South America and Europe, called WorldPartners, which offered global corporations seamless communications services in twenty-seven countries in 1995.

AT&T has refocused its efforts on becoming the dominant player in the global marketplace because it expects this market to explode in the next decade. In 1995, it obtained a license to offer international services to business customers in the United Kingdom. In the same year, it signed a joint venture agreement with the

Chinese government to help China modernize its telecommunications infrastructure. AT&T has also entered into an agreement with key African governments to
build a state-of-the-art fiber-optic ring (Africa One) around the continent of Africa
by the year 2000. The network is expected to provide African nations with the
most advanced information age telecommunications capabilities and services in the
world in the next century. On January 7, 1993, AT&T announced an agreement
to acquire 20 percent of Canada's Unitel Communications, the maximum allowed
under the federal government's foreign ownership regulations. In 1996, AT&T
acquired one-third of Unitel and changed its name to AT&T Canada Long Distance
Services Co., now the second largest supplier of long-distance services in Canada.

According to AT&T's 1995 Annual Report, the global market for wireless
communications services is about $40 billion and is expected to reach $125 billion
in the next decade. The company has set out to conquer this market as well. In
1995, it won licenses for PCS franchises in twenty-one cities in the United States,
extending its potential reach to more than 80 percent of the population. It has also
won several contracts to build national wireless infrastructures, including one in
Argentina. Another market that AT&T has targeted is the information services
market outside the United States. AT&T expects this to double to $2 trillion over
the next ten years, and it has set an objective of deriving as much as 50 percent of
its revenues from this market by the year 2000.

Assessment of AT&T's Global Diversification Strategy

AT&T has set extremely ambitious goals and objectives for itself. Fortunately
for the company, many of the markets it has targeted are already huge and are
viewed by most industry watchers as having considerable future growth potential.
But there are enormous technological and market risks associated with these new
directions. The question is what can AT&T bring to these markets that other
players cannot? Does the world really need an AT&T—whether dominant or non-
dominant—any longer to provide leadership and expertise in building and
operating the information infrastructure and bringing information-age services to
the world? The answers in part will depend on its ability to achieve dynamic
efficiencies and economies of scale and scope across its diverse operations. Its
record to date has not been good. Its NCR acquisition is a case in point. The past
quarter century is littered with unsuccessful attempts by many companies to cross
what appears to be a great industrial divide separating computers and telecommunications. Leaders in both industries—including IBM, Northern Telecom, and
AT&T itself—have tried on several occasions to bring the necessary technological
and managerial expertise in both computers and telecommunications under a single
corporate entity for the purpose of realizing what they perceived were the
tremendous synergies of convergence and systems integration. But all have failed.
And it is unlikely that AT&T will succeed in doing so with its NCR acquisition.[6]
It appears that this integration and the synergies and other economic benefits
arising from them, if they do indeed exist, are best achieved through other means,
in particular, by smaller and more innovative companies.

But even in those markets where AT&T has taken only a partial equity interest in much smaller and more innovative companies, its diversification strategy has not been successful. It has withdrawn from a number of ventures that have not been successful, including several in the multimedia market, such as those with GO Corporation, EO, and with Sega. AT&T has also written off its investment in an online services company called Interchange, which it acquired from Ziff-Davis Publications in 1995, and has abandoned a plan to launch a nationwide workgroup network based on Lotus Notes. The success of the Internet made these two ventures obsolete. There is some indication that the Internet will also make AT&T's Novell network service obsolete in the coming months. Clearly, AT&T has yet to demonstrate that it can manage the huge technological and market risks associated with its new direction, and this is an important lesson for all of the players as well as for public policy.

1995–PRESENT—AT&T'S PHASE III STRATEGY: REDEFINING GOALS AND MISSIONS TO FEND OFF THE NEW INFORMATION HIGHWAY COMPETITORS

The years 1994 and 1995 witnessed accelerated developments in information technology and telecommunications as well as in policies and regulations as the realities of convergence and information highway developments entered a new phase.[7] These were the years in which the information highway and the Internet became the focus of national and international attention, and leaders around the world convened in February 1995 under the auspices of the Organization for Economic Cooperation and Development to give their support for the creation of a global information infrastructure. In the United States, the national debate over whether the federal government or industry would build and operate the national information highway came to an end. There was little or no support in industry for the federal government to take the initiative. In fact, there was widespread concern and outright opposition to government intervention of any kind. The responsibility for building the information highway would be left up to the private sector. It was industry's view, however, that this would require a new set of rules. More specifically, it would require the drafting of a new telecommunications reform bill. All parties, therefore, became involved in drafting a new telecommunications reform act. Versions of the new bill were passed by the House of Representatives and the Senate in early 1995.

Congress eventually passed the new telecommunications bill in December 1995, but it was not until February 1996 that President Clinton signed it into law. The Telecommunications Act of 1996, which has been decades in the making, represents a fundamental shift in telecommunications policy from a single supplier to pluralism, that is, competition, across the entire information and communications front. Under it, the RBHCs are now free to provide long-distance service outside their current service regions as well as inside once they take steps to remove existing barriers to competition. The RBHCs are also free to manufacture telecommunications and customer-premises equipment but through arm's-length affiliates. The Act also repealed the cross-ownership restrictions between the telephone and cable television companies.

Redefinition of AT&T's Goals, Missions, and Strategies

The shift in policy incorporated in the new Telecommunications Act had immediate and dramatic consequences for all companies in the information highway marketplace for it redefined the competitive landscape for local and long-distance telephone companies, cable television, and broadcasting companies, as well as online and computer services companies. The Act also created new threats and opportunities as well as opened new possibilities for growth. For AT&T, the good news was that it opened the road directly to millions of end users across the nation, although it would take some time to take advantage of this. One of the consequences was that a head-on confrontation between AT&T and its former subsidiaries, the Bell Operating Companies, was not only possible but inevitable.

AT&T's Push to Re-Enter the Local Telephone Market

AT&T's response to the Telecommunications Act was immediate. Indeed, the company planned and executed a response well before the bill was passed by Congress in 1995. The key element of its response was a strategy to pre-empt the entry of the RBHCs into the long-distance market, that is, to re-establish end-to-end service by entering the local wireline markets by pursuing open access strategies to reach end customers before the RBHCs had a chance to enter the long-distance market. This opportunity was presented by obligation under the new rules to demonstrate open entry in the local exchange as a pre-condition to their entry into long distance.[8] According to its 1995 Annual Report, AT&T had 15 percent of the local services market by the end of 1995. Also in its Annual Report was the statement that AT&T intends to offer local telephone service "contingent upon the course of legislation and the economics of individual markets, either by reselling network capacity" purchased from local providers or by building its own infrastructures. It made a major step in this direction in May 1996 when it announced that it was offering three months of unlimited local and short-haul toll calling up to fifteen miles free over Ameritech's local facilities.

1995–Reinventing AT&T: The Voluntary Breakup/Restructuring of AT&T

The Telecommunications Act opened up other opportunities for AT&T and the company was quick to take advantage of these as well. In particular, the Act offered potentially enormous opportunities for its subsidiaries, Bell Laboratories, Network Systems, NCR, and others to supply the RBHC with a wide range of telecommunications equipment, facilities, and services. AT&T was also quick to respond on this front as well. On September 20, 1995, its chairman and CEO, Robert Allen, made what he called one of the most important announcements in AT&T's history. He announced that the company was reinventing itself by breaking itself up into three separate companies. The new AT&T, now called AT&T Communications, would become a comprehensive services company with 1995 revenues of $51 billion. The second company, called Lucent Technologies, with 1995 revenues of $21 billion, would engage in the research, development, and manufacturing of telecommunications switching and transmission equipment and facilities. It included the former Bell Laboratories and AT&T Network Systems. The third company, with revenues of $8 billion in 1995, is called Global Information Services (GIS). It comprises the former NCR. The spin-off of Lucent and GIS was designed to enhance their acceptability as suppliers to RBHCs.

Refocusing on Core Competencies—All-in-One, End-to-End Services Strategy

The result of AT&T's voluntary breakup or reinvention is that the company is now free to focus on its core competencies of supplying communications services of every kind. According to its 1995 Annual Report, selling the tools to give consumers and businesses easy access to the information, entertainment, and electronic commerce markets of the world is expected to grow into a $13 billion industry by the year 2000. The company wants to provide these services to its 90 million customers in the United States. It also expects the Internet to spawn an online shopping market worth $57 billion by the year 2000, and it is positioning itself to be a big player in this market as well. It has already set out to supply the complete range of online information and entertainment and electronic commerce services and to bundle all of these into one bill. Its goal is to substitute the current $25-per-month average bill with a $100-per-month bill, paid by customers using the AT&T Universal Card. In launching both its new local telephone service and its new residential Internet service, AT&T allowed subscribers to bundle these charges into their total subscription base, thereby making these new rates automatically subject to the same discounts as other charges on the bill.

AT&T's 1995 reorganization also represented an opportunity to undertake a series of other measures to improve its competitive position. One of these was the announcement of another massive layoff of 40,000 employees, or 13 percent of its workforce. This action was taken in spite of the threat that this could destroy what employee loyalty and morale it had left after at least three previous rounds of major downsizing. The reinvention of AT&T also offered an opportunity for the company to reassess its diversification strategy and better focus on its core competencies. It decided to withdraw from those markets where its diversification strategy was a failure or where its presence no longer made sense. In addition to its Lotus Notes initiatives with Lotus, GO Corporation, and others, it announced its decision (June 1996) to sell AT&T Capital because the subsidiary no longer met its long-term goals.

COMPETITORS FOR AT&T COMMUNICATIONS (NETWORK) SERVICES

The Telecommunications Act of 1996 has indeed opened up a vast new landscape of opportunities for all of the players in the U.S. communications and information sectors to explore and exploit. It has also raised the stakes for every player in terms of the threats it poses to their established positions in monopoly and oligopoly markets. Most players have become engaged in a variety of pre-emption, emulation, and cooperation strategies to enter new markets while aligning themselves to fend off competition in their home markets. The biggest have devised or are devising strategies not unlike those of AT&T, that is, to enter complementary service markets to enable them to provide a relatively complete range of end-to-end voice, video, information and entertainment, and other information age services by wireline telephone, wireless, cable television, and satellite networks. At least five classes of competitors can be identified. They are the RBHC, other interexchange carriers, wireless communications service companies, and media, entertainment conglomerates as well as online/Internet service providers.

The RBHCs have begun to execute their own strategies. Within weeks of the passage of the Telecommunications Act, four of them became two when Bell Atlantic announced a merger with NYNEX and Pacific Telesis with SBC Communications. Regional Holding Companies are also moving aggressively into high-growth markets, especially long-distance and online/Internet services markets. Both Ameritech and Bell Atlantic began offering limited long-distance packages soon after the Telecommunications Act was signed into law. Several have formed buying alliances to negotiate with interexchange carriers. One of these alliances consists of BellSouth, PacTel, and Southwestern Bell. Another, comprising NYNEX and Bell Atlantic has already negotiated with Sprint to resell services in their out-of-region markets. The effective result of these incursions is bilateral oligopoly between the interexchange carriers and the RBHCs to extend service beyond their service territory.

AT&T's competitors in the interexchange market have also developed strategies for the new information highway age. Both Sprint and MCI have designed strategies to provide end-to-end service in competition with AT&T and the RBHCs. MCI has formed MCImetro to enter the local telephone market. MCI is also a big player in the Internet services industry, and it has initiated plans to launch a series of direct broadcast satellites to offer new services via satellite. Another alliance, comprising Sprint, Cox Cable, TCI, and Comcast, has been formed to enter the local telephone market. Interexchange carriers also have the option of acquiring or aligning themselves with competitive access providers (CAPs) who already offer local services in the major metropolitan areas. AT&T had already done so by September 1996. But other companies, attracted by the opportunities, are making even more aggressive moves. One of these was WorldCom Inc., which announced in August 1996 the $14.4 billion acquisition of fast-growing MFS Communications, which itself had announced only a few months previously (February 1996) that it was acquiring UUNET, one of the largest Internet access suppliers in the United States. The acquisition created what the *Wall Street Journal* called a "powerhouse" in long-distance, local phone, and Internet services with $5.4 billion in annual revenues.[9] WorldCom provides communications links throughout the United States and to more than two hundred countries. It also sells satellite transmission services through another recent acquisition, IDB Communications Group. WorldCom appears to be emulating AT&T. Perhaps the biggest threat to AT&T's global position is the planned acquisition of MCI by British Telecom (BT) for $22.9 billion. (BT already owns 20 percent of MCI.) France Telecom and German Telekom had previously acquired 20 percent of Sprint.

The third group of contenders in the new and expanding communications marketplace consists of those companies that are endeavoring to provide a complete range of voice, data, and multimedia services through the use of the new generation of wireless PCS technologies. A number of companies have invested heavily in the FCC's great sell-off of PCS licenses in an attempt to enter this new market and pre-empt others. One consortium led by Sprint (with Comcast, TCI, and Cox Cable) has bid $2.1 billion for PCS licences. Another consortium, PCS Primeco, consisting of NYNEX, Bell Atlantic, Air Touch, and U.S. West bid $1.1 billion for PCS licenses. In total, less than half a dozen key players spent $7.7 billion on buying up PCS licenses in 1995. They include AT&T ($1.7 billion), Pacific Telesis ($700 million), and Ameritech ($158 million).

A fourth class of competitors comprises the cable television, communications media, and entertainment giants, which have set out to meet the challenges of convergence between telephone and cable television by endeavoring to deliver a wide range of futuristic services to American homes, such as interactive television and video-on-demand services. One of the leading consortia, called Americast, consists of Ameritech Corp., BellSouth Corp., GTE Corp., and SBC Communications Inc., along with entertainment giant Walt Disney Co. Another consortium announced in 1994, Tele-TV, comprises Bell Atlantic, NYNEX, and Pacific Telesis. All of these strategies, however, are undergoing changes as a result of the rapid pace of Internet developments.

The fifth and final group of potential competitors for AT&T in the future are the value-added service suppliers, which includes the online and Internet access service providers. The fortunes of the online service companies, America Online, CompuServe, and Prodigy, for example, have languished in recent years primarily because their services are based on proprietary networks. The companies to watch are the Internet services access providers whose networks are based on open systems standards. This new class of competitors could be very important in the future since the Internet could become the infrastructure for delivering a wide range of information highway services, from long-distance telephone and e-mail to information, multimedia entertainment, and education and electronic commerce services. It is unlikely, however, that many of these companies will be able to survive on their own the intense competition that is already underway. The industry has been hit with wave after wave of consolidations. It is more likely that the Internet service providers will become the targets of acquisition by the other big players in the league, including the RBHCs and interexchange carriers as they continue to pursue their end-to-end services and one-stop-shopping strategies. MCI has already upgraded its Internet backbone to 620 megabits per second and is planning to upgrade this again to speeds of 2.2 gigabits per second in the coming years. Another big potential competitive threat in this market is IBM. Unlike most other players, IBM is already a global player and has committed itself to providing an entire set of network-centric solutions for both businesses and households worldwide.

One possibility is that the focal point of competition in telecommunications in the remainder of this decade will continue to shift to the Internet especially as the roll-out of new a Internet platform unfolds. The reason for this is that the Internet could become the means by which all of the key players will be able to provide a whole range of interactive, multimedia communications, entertainment, and electronic commerce services. If this turns out to be the case, the Internet service providers will become increasingly attractive candidates for acquisition by the major players. Telephone companies could look on them as their ticket to enter the information, entertainment, and electronic commerce marketplace. Non-telephone companies could use them to enter the telephone business. In both cases, telephone and Internet services could be bundled together. In other words, the timing of the opening of the local markets to competition, and the entry of the Regional Bell Holding Companies into competitive services, including Internet services, and the entry of other companies into the local markets could be critical to the future. In retrospect, the Telecommunications Act of 1996 represents the starting pistol that set off this race.

RELATIONSHIPS BETWEEN AT&T AND COMPETITORS—TOWARD A NEW THEORY OF OLIGOPOLY

The new telecommunication's industry and the evolving information highway of which it is an integral part already constitute a huge complex in interdependent interests in multiple geographical and multiple services markets with strong, indeed dominant, players in each market. All of the players in the U.S. marketplace are now free or will soon be free to bargain with one another under the 1996 Telecommunications Act. There is limited and declining regulatory oversight at all levels of this new marketplace. All of the key players are endeavoring to leverage on their dominant positions in their home market to enter and dominate wherever possible the most lucrative new markets and to provide a variety of complementary services on an all-in-one, bundled basis. This does not mean that there will not be a role for small players, but it probably means that they will have to be content with playing niche market roles until they too become absorbed by the bigger players. The infrastructures on which these events are being played out already constitute a network of networks in the sense that most of them are already interconnected, albeit not seamlessly. But the situation will likely become much more complex in the future as the various players pursue their corporate ambitions. The question is what will the future of this network of networks look like? What are the options for industry structure and strategy? Can any one player or combination of them come to dominate the new marketplace? If so, which one? Under what conditions? What are the prospects for AT&T?

What Kind of Behavior Can We Expect?

Certain possibilities should be ruled out at the outset. We are unlikely to witness a go-it-alone approach, for example. It is also unlikely that a single player will attempt an early knock-out strategy. The risks associated with these two strategies are simply too great.[10] There are too many technological and market uncertainties. It is not at all clear that residential customers want or are willing to pay for many of the new information highway services. The industry has already been disappointed with the field trials that were set up to test the market for interactive television and video-on-demand services in the early 1990s. This being the case, any company embarking on such a strategy could be significantly hurt and would probably be taken over by another. This means that we will likely witness the continued use of pre-emption, emulation, and coordination strategies as well as market structure strategies incorporating alliances, joint ventures, mergers, and acquisitions. An alliance of some kind or a merger between one of more RBHCs and MCI or Sprint, for example, is a definite possibility. Both MCI and Sprint have, after all, pursued this same strategy at the international level in their dealings with European posts, telephone, and telegraph companies. We will also likely witness the continued use of bilateral oligopoly dealing with a view to profit maximization with or without collusion. Above all, each player can be expected to seek to protect its profitability and its return on investment in the new environment. This will rule out an all-out price war. The result is that the various players will likely pursue intensive sales promotion strategies as well as strategies to rebundle and package a complete range of service offerings with discounts. We will also probably continue to see the exercise of strong price leadership and conscious parallelism. All of this will be strengthened if there is little or no regulatory oversight to these dealings.

What Kind of Industry Structure?

Another outcome that we are likely to witness is greater aggregate concentration on a national and global services level. This does not mean that there will not be a role for new entrants or niche players. There will probably continue to be an important role for them as the technology continues to open up new opportunities. Although each player will be aggressively bargaining for power, their overall desire will be for stability. Tight oligopoly will, therefore, reinforce the conduct described above.[11] One option is that the three big long-distance players—AT&T, Sprint, and MCI—will lead each of three grand alliances comprising local, long-distance, and international carriers. Various players in the RBHCs, the cable television, and entertainment-media businesses could also be members of these alliances. Each alliance will also likely have strong representation in the local wireline and wireless telephone and Internet and online services marketplace. This would make each alliance capable of offering a relatively complete range of telephone and Internet-based information, entertainment, and electronic commerce services. Each would endeavor to market these services throughout the world.

A second option is that AT&T will succeed in its efforts to realize the enormous economic synergies it is seeking across its various operating units and in its one-stop-shopping strategy of bundling local, long-distance, and Internet services into a single-service offering. But the prospects for reasserting the dominance it once enjoyed over U.S. telecommunications appears to be fading.[12] The company has been seriously hurt by a tide of management defections (as of the fall of 1996), including Alex Mandl, one of the company's chief architects, and it still has a serious morale problem. Competitors have been quick to take advantage of any mistakes it has made. As described above, many of its ventures into new and unchartered territory have been failures and it has had to withdraw from them. In yet another sign of its changing fortunes, AT&T announced the sale in September 1996 of its Skynet satellite systems to Loral Space and Communications Ltd., a former big defense contractor, now looking for new growth opportunities. AT&T is even having some trouble keeping up with the competition in its core business of long-distance services. The result is that AT&T's financial performance (in mid-1996) was disappointing. But time is not on AT&T's side. It may turn out that the period 1996 through 1998 will prove to be the make-or-break period for AT&T. These years may prove to be AT&T's one great last chance to re-establish itself as the dominant supplier of information and communications services certainly nationally and possibly internationally as well.

IMPLICATIONS FOR PUBLIC POLICY

The question of what type of industry structure will emerge in telecommunications is central to the current debate over the adequacy of deregulation and privatization programs, the attainment of public policy goals, and the future of AT&T. If the cumulative strategy of the major players culminates in a tight oligopoly (defined as four leading firms supplying 60 to 100 percent of the market with significant barriers to entry) for both network systems and final service markets, then there must be a new set of regulatory policies designed to come to grips with anticipated structural and behavioral patterns. On the other hand, if the pressure of new technology combined with procompetitive government policies is successful in achieving a transition to workable competition (defined as five or six firms of comparable size, elastic demand functions, and no significant barriers to entry), then a transitional regulatory program will be sufficient.

Both options require a preface setting forth the common public goals of telecommunications policy as a frame of reference. Public goals include (1) development of a network of networks in which wireline, wireless, and satellite networks are interconnected into a seamless local, national, and international infrastructure network, (2) assurance that each class of user will be free to select that form and mix of telecommunications services best suited to its needs while being assured that all inherent network economies and efficiencies will be available on a non-discriminatory basis, and (3) development of universal service principles that assure that each class of user is able to gain access to the entire range of information highway services at affordable rates.

Reed Hundt, FCC chairman, has outlined a comprehensive program for achieving these goals through a simple procompetitive policy designed to neutralize the market power of the incumbent firm and create new options for supply. If this program is carried out, Hundt argues, then the provision of telecommunications will be no different than the production of "soap or shoes or software."[13] Furthermore, there would be no need for government to fix prices for retail services and, indeed, Hundt would virtually eliminate government as a regulatory force.

Hundt's definition of competition is unique in that it rejects any criterion that calls for rivalry between two or more duplicative wireline networks as the test for the existence of competition. He believes that waiting for parallel rival wirelines to emerge, whether cable versus telephone or telephone versus telephone, could be a painfully slow process. Instead, he advocates positive steps to encourage the emergence of new wireless networks and the introduction of mandatory unbundling of the incumbent's network to permit both new entrants and incumbents to compete on a number of fronts. Entry into wireless communications depends on a successful auctioning process for the frequency spectrum. To make auctioning effective, Hundt argues that there should be no constraints placed on bidders. This means no rules and no restrictions on licenses, and the successful bidder should have total flexibility in determining what markets should be served and what technology should be employed. He dismisses the fear that auctioning will penalize new entrants, since both the new entrant and the incumbent would base their decisions on the incremental cost of expanding service. Sunk costs would be dismissed as irrelevant to decision making for the future. Unbundling and interconnection become pivotal because the new entrant must be able to add to or modify his supply capabilities by purchasing unbundled network components from the incumbent carrier. Access or interconnection prices must be set in a fashion that does not impede competition. He believes that the price of components must reflect a discount from retail prices so that the entrant can compete in terms of the final price paid by consumers.

Insofar as the public policy goal of universal service is concerned, Hundt believes that competition will effectively address the problem. Arguing that government cannot subsidize properly, he says that intervention will only serve to impede the competitive provision of universal service. Some prices will be set at artificially high levels while others will be set at artificially low levels. The latter will foreclose competitive entry and, therefore, serve to aggravate and prolong the problem. Where some form of direct subsidy is needed, Hundt appears to favor a plan whereby the proceeds from a universal assessment charge would go to a fund that, in turn, would be auctioned off to the successful bidder who could best demonstrate how it would be used to provide service in rural markets.

What Hundt does is to place full faith in a simplistic Schumpetarian model in which technological progress, profit incentives, and removal of economic regulation of retail prices will stimulate hoped-for sweeping changes. In effect, he is arguing for the transference to all nations, both industrialized and developing, of a set of policies based on a highly idealized interpretation of the performance history of the United States telecommunications industry in the years since 1984. Hundt emphasizes that foreign implementation of his program requires that governments negate the anticompetitive political and economic power of incumbent telephone monopolies. This requires that they forgo championing the cause of incumbent carriers and promote the removal of restrictions on foreign investment in the telecommunications infrastructure. He also states that privatization of public monopolies alone is not sufficient and that a procompetitive program must be implemented by an independent agency.

There are six significant flaws that severely circumscribe the prospects for success of the Reed Hundt program. First, it treats telecommunications as little more than a manufacturing industry (soap, shoes, and software) once interconnection and spectrum auctioning are put in place. This ignores the fact that Hundt's program would lead to high concentration which, in turn, creates a potential for exercising market and political power that can negate the effects of selective entry through open access. This is especially important when coupled with vertical integration into downstream markets and common ownership of wireline and wireless plants.

Second, unbundling network components for new entrants will not overcome the obstacles confronting such entrants when dealing with an incumbent network providing widespread rebundled retail services. An overlooked dimension of network economies is the ability to achieve a high load and diversity factors through multiple offerings for which the incremental costs can be extremely low. If the new entrant cannot match the wide range of offerings by the incumbent, then it will be confined to niche markets. Niche market rivalry is not a surrogate for workable competition, perfect contestability, or cost-based universal service. Nor is niche market competition a sufficient constraint on the profits or pricing practices of the incumbent. Where the new entrant is large and has substantial market power, as in the case of a consortium of Bell Operating Companies seeking to get long-distance capacity outside of its combined service territory, there will be a strong incentive for the interexchange carrier and the entrant to engage in bilateral oligopoly negotiations that will jeopardize neither the profits nor the discretionary behavior of either player.

Third, the scope and capital intensity of comprehensive networks create a strong pressure to assure a stream of revenues sufficient to support a capital structure that is heavily weighted by debt capital. This financial burden creates incentives for market differentiation, price leadership, and interdependent behavior whenever possible which then become further inducements for oligopoly behavior.

Fourth, the prospects for developing a set of generally accepted guidelines for access pricing that will be competitively neutral while minimizing distortions in income distribution and social welfare appear to be remote. Incumbents want high access charges covering profits forgone from not serving retail markets, a contribution to overhead costs, and the incremental cost of interconnection. Entrants want low access charges covering little more than bare-bones incremental costs. The outlook for a swift and straightforward reconciliation by the FCC is far from promising. When Hundt's agency issued its guidelines for access pricing Dockets CC96-98 and 95-185 (August 8, 1996), it is ironic to note that the order, together with supporting discussion, was almost nine hundred pages in length. Nor does it appear that the theoretical consensus on access pricing is at hand if papers presented at the First Annual Conference on Network Competition, October 13-14, 1995, are representative.[14]

Fifth, the option of rationing the spectrum is not new. In fact, it was endorsed by economists almost thirty years ago. But the process is dependent on the market structure in which auctioning takes place. In a tight oligopoly, the firm has an incentive to buy and withhold the spectrum in anticipation of high prices and profits at a later date. Similarly, oligopolistic bidders are quite happy to buy the spectrum in order to secure a place in a market where future prices and profits are dependent on being a major full-service provider capable of offering bundled wireline and wireless services. With Hundt-mandated no restrictions, the oligopolists would be free to exploit such strategies to maximum advantage. In addition, public policy goals must also be considered. Auctioning of licenses is premised on the belief that the best use of the spectrum is identical with use by those who are willing to pay the highest price. While this may be consistent with static consumer surplus analysis, questions can be raised whether this is the best way to allocate a public resource. The problem is that this involves a comparison of social values and private market values, and at the present time the latter is apt to be the clear winner.

Sixth, the Hundt approach relies on unbridled technological change implemented by interconnection access. Conspicuously absent are guidelines for evaluating interdependent oligopolistic behavior of firms. Alliances, joint ventures, mergers, and acquisitions may be motivated in part by a desire to realize network economies and reduce duplicative costs, but they also reflect a desire to establish positions of market dominance or to coexist in a tight oligopolistic industry. Yet Hundt barely touches on criteria for evaluating such collaborative efforts or the data needed to monitor market power. The only test that the FCC appears to accept is the ability of a single firm to raise and sustain a price increase on a unilateral basis.[15] But this criterion is largely irrelevant in a world of oligopoly and conscious parallelism, where a group of interdependent producers control the provision of wireline and wireless capacity while offering consumers bundled service packages as part of one-stop-shopping programs. Monitoring not only involves measures of concentration such as the Landes-Posner Index, but also oversight of strategies designed to foreclose entry—a principal example of which is the establishment of standards for assuring compatibility between different players.[16] In passing, the benefits from collaborative efforts of interdependent entities appear to be drawing increased attention in the literature. Recent books by Adam Brandenberger and Barry Nalebuff,[17] as well as James Moore,[18] may be noted as example.

On December 23, 1996, the *New York Times* quoted Reed Hundt as follows: "We can hope for competition all we want, but that doesn't mean it's going to happen."[19] Whether this is attributable to Hundt's recognition that industry structures are, in fact, not emerging as competitive, or whether it is attributable to his disenchantment with progress being made because of state commission resistance or delays because of judicial review cannot be determined. But if it is the former, public policy should be brought into line with the need to deal with an emerging industry structure in which AT&T and a small number of firms will be major players.

CONCLUSION

The dynamics described in this chapter point toward the emergence of a broadly defined telecommunications and information sector that includes traditional communications services, online and Internet services, broadcasting, entertainment services, and the incorporation of telecommunications/information transfer into banking, finance, manufacturing, and retail marketing. Powerful combinations and coalitions will have substantial control over certain markets but will vie for control in others. The challenge for public policy will be to ensure that no single company or coalition is able to dominate this new landscape, and that access to this sector, like the traditional commons, remains available to everyone. The time is probably past for imaginative solutions such as structural separations of the network from the competitive marketing of services in telecommunications. But there still remains the major task of defining what guidelines are appropriate to monitor the performance of this sector. If our interpretation of emerging oligopoly is correct, then so-called light regulations consisting of interim price caps, supposedly neutral interconnection prices, and incentive allowances will be woefully inadequate. Rather, new concepts of regulation targeted at industry structure and performance appear to be called for.

What of AT&T's role in this new sector? Clearly, it can no longer control the rate of technological change, nor is it free to specify what direction demand will take. Instead, AT&T's success will depend on how skillfully it plays the role of a giant firm in the emerging oligopoly structure. If our analysis correct, this will largely depend upon the successful employment of its network as a centerpiece while developing alliances, joint ventures, and agreements with other participants to reach domestic and international customers.

NOTES

1. AT&T was forced to divest itself of its telephone operations in other countries, except Canada, by a U.S. Department of Justice antitrust consent decree in 1925.

2. It was Theodore Vail as well as the inventor of the telephone, Alexander Graham Bell, who gave America the vision that it still has today of how the telephone (and the Bell System) should serve the nation. For Vail, this vision is best captured in a statement contained in AT&T's 1910 Annual Report which reads as follows: "The Bell system was founded on broad lines of 'One System,' 'One Policy,' 'Universal Service,' . . . One system with a common policy, common purpose and common action; comprehensive, universal, interdependent, interconnecting like the highway system of the country, extending from every door to every other door, affording electrical communications of every kind from every one at every place to every one at every other place." It is not surprising that Vail came from the U.S. Postal Service. He simply imported the public policy concepts on which the postal service was founded into the telephone industry.

3. According to the 1993 Huber Report, the long-distance market effectively constitutes a natural monopoly and AT&T has always had sufficient market power to drive both MCI and Sprint out of the market, but has not done so. See Peter W. Huber, *Geodesic Network II: 1993 Report on Competition in the Telephone Industry* (Washington, D.C.: Geodesic Co., 1992), pp. 1.42-1.44.

4. Federal Communications Commission, *Commission Declares AT&T Nondominant*, Report No. 95-60, Common Carrier Action (Washington, D.C.: Federal Communications Commission, 1995).

5. See Maurice Estabrooks, *Electronic Technology, Corporate Strategy and World Transformation* (New York: Quorum Books, 1995).

6. According to *Business Week*, for example, NCR has lost almost all of its top managers since it was taken over by AT&T. See John W. Verity, "AT&T and Computers: Any Signs of Synergy?" *Business Week*, 5 June, 1996, p. 114.

7. See "The Coming Telescramble: Deregulation Is Launching a $1 Trillion Digital Free-for-All," *Business Week*, 8 April, 1996.

8. See *The First Report and Order in the Matter of Implementation of the Local Competition Provisions in the Telecommunications Act of 1996: Interconnection Between Local Exchange Carriers and Commercial Mobile Radio Service Providers*, FCC 96-325, Adopted August 1, 1996.

9. Steven Lipin and Leslie Cauley, "WorldCom Reaches Pact with MFS in $14.4 Billion Stock Deal," *Wall Street Journal*, 26 August, 1996, p. A3.

10. The recent acquisition of MFS Communications by WorldCom is an example of the enormous risks that some of the players appear to be willing to take. WorldCom's 1995 revenues were $5.4 billion, but the total liabilities that it has taken on to acquire MFS and other companies is $22 billion.

11. For an analysis of the principles and significance of tight oligopoly, see H. M. Trebing, "Achieving Coordination in Public Utility Industries: A Critique of Troublesome Options," *Journal of Economic Issues* 30, no 2 (June 1996): pp. 561-570.

12. For an analysis of the challenges facing AT&T, see John J. Keller, "Telecommunications: The 'New' AT&T Faces Daunting Challenges," *Wall Street Journal*, 19 September 1996. Also see "AT&T: Will the Bad News Ever End?," *Business Week*, 7 October 1996, pp. 122-130.

13. "Seven Habits of Hopefully Highly Successful Deregulatory Communications Policy People." Speech by Reed Hundt, chairman, Federal Communications Commission, before Royal Institute of International Affairs, London, 4 September 1996, p. 3.

14. First Annual Conference, PURC-IDEI-CIRANO, "The Transition Towards Competition in Network Industries," 13-14 October 1995, Montreal, Canada.

15. See note 4.

16. See Robin Mansell, *The New Telecommunications—A Political Economy of Network Evolution* (London: Sage, 1993), chapters 1, 2, 9, 10.

17. See Adam M. Brandenberger and Barry J. Nalebuff, *Co-opetition* (New York: Doubleday, 1996).

18. See James F. Moore, *The Death of Competition Leadership Strategy in the Age of Business Econsystems* (New York: Harper Business, 1996).

19. See Mark Landler, "A Year of Law but Scant Competition," *New York Times*, 23 December 1996, C1 and C9, at C1.

12

CONCLUSION

David I. Rosenbaum

The conclusion begins with a review of how firms in these ten industries gained dominance. A number of commonalties arise across the studies. All but one of the firms rose to dominance either as a first mover or early in the industry's life. Several were propelled by the vision of a key individual. Most developed cost advantages over their rivals. Typically this was done through research and development, learning-by-doing and economies of scale. Most worked to stimulate demand by process and product development, differentiation, and advertising, and through the use of specialized sales forces. In a number of industries, large market shares created externalities that supported further growth toward dominance. Many maintained low prices. However, episodes of focused predation and other anticompetitive behaviors were not uncommon.

The focus then turns to the maintenance of dominance. Dominance was maintained when firms were able to maintain advantages over their rivals. The sources of the advantages varied. Some were derived through efficiency-based actions such as cost advantages or investments in creating better technologies. In a number of these industries, however, an advantage was fostered through vertical integration or tying. Integration and tying slowed the development of secondary markets and retarded entry into primary markets. In this sense, they prevented competition when it may have developed if either integration or tying were absent. Vertical and horizontal integration also supported limit pricing, price discrimination, episodes of limited predation, and key acquisitions that thwarted a concerted effort to enter. The economic efficiency of many of these actions is dubious. Strategies such as preannouncement and holding excess capacity were also used. Neither of these is rational absent their anticompetitive effects.

The demise of dominance is examined next. In two of the industries, tobacco and computer operating systems, dominance has persevered through today. The other eight industries witnessed the fall of a dominant firm. In some cases, the loss of dominance was probably inevitable given evolving markets. In others, firms made the wrong decisions or became either inefficient or cumbersome in their management. In one industry, the dominant firm chose to pursue a different strategy and allow entry. In a few cases, firms were driven from dominance, in part, by antitrust action. Finally, the analysis turns to the consequences of dominance. Did dominant firms act efficiently? Did the market system work to break up dominance? These questions are answered and some policy recommendations are made.

ACQUIRING DOMINANCE

Alcoa, Dow, Kodak, and Blue Cross initially were dominant because they were the first movers into their industries. Focusing on Alcoa and Dow, the aluminum and magnesium industries have similar histories. Both are markets for homogeneous raw intermediate goods and differentiated fabricated products. Both have technologies that exhibit significant scale economies. In their early years, both industries were fairly stable world oligopolies.

Alcoa and Dow acquired their initial monopoly positions through patents. They each pursued many of the strategies that an efficiency explanation of dominance would suggest. Both invested heavily in process improvements to drive down their own production costs. They also invested to improve product quality. Alcoa and Dow engaged in vertical integration, Alcoa to control inputs and both to acquire influence in selected output markets. Both worked to expand demand by developing new applications for their products. Both companies helped customers solve engineering problems that arose in applications. Alcoa and Dow kept prices for raw forms of their outputs low, in part to stimulate demand.

Similar factors allowed Kodak to gain dominance in its markets. While Kodak started with dominance in three markets, cameras, film, and photofinishing, its core market was film. Kodak was guided in its early years by a strong leader, George Eastman. He created Kodak's initial monopoly positions with patents. Kodak invested heavily in process development to reduce its film production costs and create higher quality films, cameras, and photofinishing techniques. Kodak also worked to increase demand by moving the point of sale from specialty photographic stores to wider distribution in a variety of retail outlets and by keeping prices in its early years as low as possible. Under Eastman's guidance, Kodak expanded distribution into European markets. Eastman's company invested heavily in product differentiation through advertising and unique packaging. It gained dominance in the camera and photographic supply markets, in part, by tying those products to its film.

Blue Cross was the nation's first hospital insurance company. Its markets and history, however, are very different from Alcoa, Dow, and Kodak. Blue Cross held no patents. It manufactured no products, and, in that sense, it could not invest to drive its costs down. Yet some of its power did arise from cost advantages that its non-profit status gave it over other indemnity insurers. Its non-profit status, for example, exempted Blue Cross from state and federal income taxes and from other state taxes on premium income. This created a significant advantage over rivals. Blue Cross initially had a reputation of meeting the public interest and as wanting to provide service for the insured. This reputation gave it special status in the regulatory environment, which worked toward its advantage in gaining power. Blue Cross was also able to build its dominant position through its close relationships with hospitals. These relationships gave hospitals and medical groups an incentive to protect Blue Cross. This meant limiting competition from, and occasionally excluding, other insurance plans in early years. Many hospitals discounted their prices to Blue Cross in an effort to help Blue Cross retain its position as a dominant health insurance provider.

Standard Oil, the tobacco companies, Ford, Microsoft, IBM, and AT&T were not the first movers into their markets, yet they were all present during the infancies of their respective industries. All were able to build dominant positions as their industries developed.

Standard Oil is a classic example of a rise to power through acquisition. John D. Rockefeller controlled Standard Oil and had been in the Eastern oil business since its inception. Chronic excess refining capacity and failure of early pool agreements demonstrated to Rockefeller that the only way stability could be brought to the industry was through monopolization. He began acquiring competing oil refiners and, because of Standard's growing size, reducing costs through better use of capacity and through discriminatory contracts with rail shippers. Standard's cost advantage allowed further growth at the expense of smaller refiners. As his company grew, Rockefeller vertically integrated Standard Oil into pipelines and distribution. Its vertical integration reinforced Standard's power, which was used to varying degrees in acquiring smaller rivals. At times, Standard was argued to use predation, price squeezes, boycotts, and input foreclosures to discipline and acquire competitors. By 1882 the Trust was formed and held a dominant position.

Two factors led to cost advantages that supported Standard's power. Its assortment of facilities allowed Standard to refine efficiently and limit excess-capacity problems. More importantly, however, its sheer volume of production allowed it to gain valuable price rebates from the railroads. These rebates were on its own shipments and those of rival refiners. Whether the rebates were cost justified or discriminatory is unclear. However, they did create a cost advantage for Standard.

The Tobacco Trust under the leadership of James Duke pursued some of the same strategies used by Kodak, Dow, and Alcoa. Mass production and automated machinery drove down manufacturing costs. Mass marketing, extensive promotion, and advertising increased demand. Yet the Trust rose to power mainly through the strategic use of price wars and predation to facilitate acquisition. Early in the Trust's life, episodes of predatory pricing helped facilitate over 250 acquisitions, which ultimately allowed it to control more than 80 percent of several tobacco-related markets. In this sense its rise was like that of Standard Oil. The initial consolidation of a select group of leading firms brought enough power to foster the eventual consolidation of most of the industry. As the Tobacco Trust grew, it could use focused price wars either to crush smaller competitors or to force their acquisition. Each price war enhanced the Trust's reputation and made future acquisitions that much easier.

Henry Ford pulled the Ford Motor Company to dominance out of the montage of car makers in the industry's early life. In essence, his overall strategy was similar to that of Alcoa, Dow, and Kodak. He worked to reduce costs, improve product, and stimulate demand. In Ford's case, production costs were reduced through better design, mass production, standardization, and division of labor. Product improvements included gears, ignition, and body strength. He stimulated demand by positioning the Model T as a car for the common working person and by setting affordable prices. These prices were made possible given Ford's relatively low production costs. As with Kodak, Ford heavily promoted his product.

IBM's rise was led by Thomas Watson Sr. and then by his son, Thomas Watson Jr. Their main emphases were on quality, service, and customer support. IBM provided customers with solutions in the early years of computers when users were relatively uninformed about computers' capabilities. IBM's computers were not always on the cutting edge of technology. However, its extensive sales force was able to sell a package of equipment and after-sale support that inexperienced consumers needed at that time in the industry's evolution. By acquiring a relatively large consumer base through its emphasis on customer support, IBM was able to generate other advantages for itself. These included production-cost reductions through learning-by-doing, and economies of scale in research and development. This was especially important in such a research-intensive industry. Having numerous customers also allowed the economical continuance of a large customer support network. IBM also influenced future demand by selling computers to schools at significant discounts. In this way, the next generation of computer users was trained on an IBM system.

Microsoft rose to power under the leadership of Bill Gates and Paul Allen. Microsoft was not the first mover into the operating system market. However, it entered very early in the industry's history. Through a combination of luck and foresight, Gates and Allen were able to write and retain control of the operating system MS-DOS for IBM's new personal computer, the IBM PC. Since the IBM PC had a large market share in the early personal computer market, Microsoft necessarily had a large market share in the operating system market. Microsoft's licensing of MS-DOS to PC clones increased its market share as well. Microsoft also controlled many software titles. Consequently, Microsoft quickly introduced new software to run on MS-DOS and more slowly introduced versions to run on the competing operating system. This made consumers hesitant to buy other operating systems.

As Microsoft increased its market share in the operating system market, other software producers made sure their versions of software ran on MS-DOS. Consumers that were concerned about the availability of software then tended to choose MS-DOS operating systems. This just reinforced Microsoft's position in the market. As network externalities reinforced market share, large sales volumes drove down the average production cost per copy of the operating system. It also drove down the average cost of new product research and development. This, in turn, allowed Microsoft to lower the price of MS-DOS to customers. Lower prices, in turn, reinforced Microsoft's dominant position. As with Alcoa, Dow, Ford, Kodak, and others, Microsoft engaged in significant research and development to improve products. This was true of its operating systems and software applications.

Under Theodore Vail, AT&T rose to dominate telephone service. Vail pursued a number of strategies in achieving this goal. Early in the industry's life he used the threat of retaliatory competition to work out a market-sharing agreement with Western Union. He led AT&T to enter local and foreign markets and to create a national long-distance system. Under Vail, AT&T became both vertically and horizontally integrated. It used pre-emptive patenting and patent protection on its equipment to preclude entry. Network externalities arising from its long-distance network and denying network access to other local operating companies helped AT&T acquire dominance in local markets. Like Standard Oil and the Tobacco Trust, AT&T used selective predation to foreclose to competitors from local markets.

General Motors rose to a leading market share in the automobile industry fairly late in the industry's evolution. Henry Ford had already dominated the industry for over a decade. However, changing conditions allowed GM to consolidate a number of manufacturers and key suppliers to displace Ford as the market share leader. GM's drive to leadership exhibited some of the basic strategies exhibited in the other industries in this book. GM produced products people wanted, sought out methods to reduce production costs, and engaged in significant marketing and product differentiation. It was competently managed by Alfred Sloan who created a divisional structure that allowed GM to be flexible yet still benefit from scale economies. GM's integration into many car models and its strategy of differentiation by improving existing models each year allowed GM to keep its customers as their tastes changed and to attract new customers. In essence, it stimulated the demand for GM cars.

Common Factors

Looking across all of these studies certain factors become apparent. Most of the firms rose to dominance relatively early in their respective industry's life. They were either first movers or were the first to consolidate a fledgling industry. The only exception is GM, and even GM rose to power when there were still several other firms vying against Ford. A second common factor is that several were controlled by a strong leader. Kodak rose under George Eastman, IBM under the Watsons, the Tobacco Trust under James Duke, Microsoft under Bill Gates, Ford under Henry Ford, GM under Alfred Sloan, Standard Oil under John D. Rockefeller, and AT&T under Theodore Vail.

A third factor is that many of these companies were able to acquire some type of advantage over their rivals. Many developed cost advantages. They came about a number of ways. Some companies invested heavily in process improvements to produce more efficiently and at a lower cost. Almost all were able to lower their costs as they grew and benefitted from learning-by-doing and economies of scale. Several used vertical integration to reduce their costs. Blue Cross derived its cost advantage through regulatory and tax policy. Other ways they developed advantages were through product differentiation and network externalities.

A fourth factor leading to dominance is that many of these companies actively worked to stimulate demand. They did so with new product development, design improvement and innovation, expansion of retail outlets, customer support, and product promotion, and by generally meeting their consumers' needs. Another integral part of stimulating demand was pricing. Many, but not all, kept prices low in their early years to help acquire sales and market share.

A fifth factor is that they used technology to their advantage. They used technology to cut costs. They used it to make better products. They used it with a first-mover advantage to stay one generation ahead of competitors. Many rose to power via the protection patents provided new technologies. They used patents and technology to pre-empt new entry.

A sixth factor is that as these firms grew, their size—in either relative or absolute measure—created advantages that made the acquisition of dominance all the more likely. For companies like Alcoa, Dow, Standard Oil, Ford, and General Motors, size brought significant scale economies. For others, size brought the power to successfully vanquish smaller competitors in restricted regional or product markets. This included AT&T, Standard Oil, and the Tobacco Trust's selective and successful use of price discrimination and predation against smaller rivals. Many became integrated producers. Integration further increased their flexibility in strategy choices and their power. Size also created important network externalities for IBM, AT&T, and Microsoft. Network externalities, in turn, reinforced the move toward dominance.

These factors certainly are not sufficient for any firm to rise to dominance. Lots of other industries and firms exhibit these characteristics. In the cases of these ten industries, however, they seemed to be common factors that facilitated a rise to dominance. The above factors also suggest that efficiency and dominance are related. Visionary leaders gained dominance early in an industry's life by working with technology to reduce costs and meet customers needs. But the histories of some of these firms tell a corollary. AT&T, Standard Oil, the tobacco companies, and probably some of the other companies engaged in episodes of anticompetitive, predatory acts to gain market control. Clearly, efficiency was not the only route to dominance.

In some cases, government policy was intertwined with the move toward dominance. Patent policy supported the rise to dominance for Alcoa, Dow, Kodak, and AT&T. Non-profit status exempted Blue Cross from many federal, state, and local taxes, giving it a cost advantage over rivals. In attempting to block dominance, AT&T had several of its actions annulled under agreements with federal authorities. State law enforcement in Ohio unsuccessfully tried to break up the Standard Oil Trust. Government antitrust policy evolved in part out of the desire to block the dominance shown by Standard Oil and the Tobacco Trust. In neither case, however, were the government's efforts successful. Standard Oil reorganized at least twice under court decree, yet still kept power among a small group of investors. While the Tobacco Trust was dissolved, power was shared among a tight oligopoly.

MAINTAINING DOMINANCE

All of the firms in the preceding chapters were dominant for some period of time. In that sense, they were all able to maintain dominance. Some remained dominant for little more than a decade. Others have been dominant for nearly a century. This section examines the factors that affected these firms over the lives of their dominant positions. There were a number of efficiency-related reasons these firms maintained their dominance. Investing to reduce costs was one. Kodak created a research and development division to work, in part, on reducing costs. Alcoa and Dow had a long history of cost-reducing process improvements. Henry Ford continually pushed for cost savings through improvements in production and design. Standard Oil continually invested in new refining technologies that significantly increased its minimum efficient scale and reduced average costs.

Most of these firms were able to reduce their costs through the benefits of scale economies. Alcoa and Dow experienced significant scale economies at several production stages. Companies like Dow could push their costs down by producing in integrated facilities where by-products from the production of one good could be used in the production of another good. Ford was the first car company to use automated assembly lines. This brought it enormous cost savings through scale economies. GM had relatively low costs as a result of the scale economies it attained from its huge sales volume. Its five car divisions brought multi-plant economies as well. Kodak's volume of film and camera sales allowed it significant scale economies and learning-by-doing in both markets. IBM's computer sales allowed it to benefit from economics of scale in production as well as in research and development. Microsoft benefitted from similar effects. The tobacco companies achieved scale economies in their automated rolling of cigarettes. Standard Oil's volume allowed it to build efficiently sized refineries and to limit excess capacity problems by coordinating the use of various plants.

Product development was another efficiency-related strategy that helped maintain dominance. Alcoa and Dow were continually working on new applications for their raw materials. They also worked to improve alloys and create better fabrication techniques. IBM invested in the new 360 line. It brought out the IBM PC and tried to create OS/2 as an operating system in competition with Microsoft's Windows. Kodak brought out a number of new film and camera technologies. It also made several advances in photo- finishing. Microsoft spent heavily on research and development. It introduced several updates on its operating system and forced its own MS-DOS into obsolescence with the introduction of its Windows operating system. Continual upgrading of its other software made Microsoft Word and Excel market leaders. AT&T was always working to improve telephone equipment and create new technologies for transmitting voice and data. Standard Oil invested so that it could economically remove excess sulfur from its Ohio crude oil reserves. Ford and GM introduced product improvements in automobiles. GM set up formal research labs. Not all of GM's new product introductions, however, were clear product improvements. Model year changes were frequently geared to selling more cars rather than introducing new and better technologies.

Another factor that allowed these firms to maintain their dominance was good management. Their managers made good decisions. They were progressive leaders, able to respond to changing market conditions. They led the evolution of their industries. They were willing to take calculated risks and to pursue active strategies to maintain their dominance and to stop their rivals from gaining market share.

Other strategies were less clearly efficiency related, yet they helped to maintain dominance. Vertical integration had a mixed impact on dominance. Integration seemed to nurture dominance when it led to lower costs. Dow and Alcoa, for example, were integrated producers. In Alcoa's case, its integration in early years assured access to raw materials and, therefore, of low energy costs. Ford and GM had less success with vertical integration. Initially integration made GM a low-cost producer. In later years, however, integration helped contribute to GM's relatively high cost per car. The Ford Motor Company under Henry Ford seemed unable to effectively manage its integrated system.

Integration also helped firms maintain dominance through other less obviously efficient tactics. Alcoa was integrated from raw materials, through primary goods production, and on to fabricated goods. Dow was integrated into final output markets. Alcoa's backward integration stalled the development of input markets. This meant that a firm considering entry into the aluminum ingot stage of production would have to enter further upstream as well. Forward integration allowed both firms to limit prices in primary output markets and recover profits by discriminating in downstream fabrication markets. Again, this would make entry at the ingot stage alone more difficult. In some markets, they squeezed other fabricators by keeping prices for fabricated goods relatively near the prices they charged for primary inputs.

Standard Oil was integrated from oil reserves to pipelines and crude oil storage facilities to refineries and some distribution capacity. Its extensive integration allowed it to coordinate production and reduce costs. However, integration also allowed Standard to rebuke competitors. Its ability to bring competing refineries into its integrated system foreclosed at least one major competing pipeline. Standard's ability to transport and store crude oil allowed it to curtail partially crude overproduction while simultaneously benefiting its refining operations by creating excessively low crude prices. Its control over crude in the ground and the pipeline transportation of crude denied inputs to competing refiners. Its integrated status also allowed Standard to buy up competitors in specific product and geographic markets to preserve or extend its monopoly. This included buying the refineries of companies that had the financial resources to significantly compete against Standard.

In some cases Standard paid a premium to acquire key resources to prevent the loss of its monopoly. This was particularly true when it was dealing with owners that had the financial resources to compete vigorously with Standard if they chose to. In other cases, however, Standard would use some combination of predation, price wars, and price squeezes to weaken smaller competitors. It would then acquire enough of these precarious firms to end any type of consolidated threat to its monopoly position. Standard's integration allowed it to weather periods of unprofitable pricing in isolated markets. AT&T pursued a similar strategy when it squeezed local operating companies out of selected markets.

General Motors was an "integrated" producer in that it sold several lines of automobiles, each largely designed for people in different phases of their lives. Chevrolet was its introductory line. Pontiacs, Buicks, and Oldsmobiles were designed to be cars that consumers graduated into as family income grew. For those who eventually reached upper ends of the income spectrum, there was the trade up to Cadillac. In this sense, consumers were offered cars to meet their automotive needs throughout their lives, and their purchases were still kept within the General Motors Corporation.

Kodak used a meld of integration and tying to maintain dominance in several markets. It sold cameras, film, photofinishing supplies, and photofinishing. Its systems-selling approach allowed it to introduce a new film in a new camera format. This put other camera makers at a disadvantage in that they were always second movers to Kodak's new format introductions. Since people typically bought one camera and held it for a while, being second meant a more limited market. This would discourage entry. Camera producers also were limited in their ability to introduce new formats on their own in that any new camera had to be compatible with existing Kodak film. Otherwise, a producer would have to enter camera and film production simultaneously. This would have been more difficult than entry into just the camera market.

Kodak's systems approach effectively tied new films to a specific chemical process for finishing. A new system typically meant a new chemical developing process. By not giving advance information on the new chemical process, a new system gave Kodak a first-mover advantage in the film-developing market. An antitrust decree forced Kodak to license new photofinishing technologies. However, Kodak could selectively control the dissemination of this information as a mechanism for excluding or disciplining competing photofinishers.

Kodak tied its film to processing by charging one price for both products. Since Kodak had a monopoly in film, it effectively created a monopoly in film finishing as well. This practice was eventually stopped under an antitrust decree. However, the nature of the chemical process involved in film developing meant that most photofinishers invested in equipment that processed Kodak film. Any firm that wanted to produce film and access the existing photofinishing network would have to make a film that could be developed via the same chemical process as Kodak's film. Otherwise, an entrant would have to create a new photofinishing network to go with its new film. Kodak's use of pre-emptive patenting, however, hampered competitors' attempts to create competing finish-compatible films.

Kodak's vertical integration meant that in addition to being a photofinisher, it also sold finishing chemicals and film for resale to other photofinishers. Kodak squeezed these competitors by creating a low margin between supply prices and finished-picture prices. This created low capital accumulation expectations among competing photofinishers and limited incentives for new entry into that market.

IBM used a combination of tying and integration to its benefit. IBM was integrated in that it sold computers and it sold after-purchase service. Its tying of the two goods into one price depressed the development of an independent service market. The lack of a competitive service market put potential computer manufacturers at a disadvantage as customers considered the availability of rapid service important when making a computer purchase decision. This deterred entry into computers by forcing integrated entry. It would also put an entrant at a potentially significant cost disadvantage until it built enough market share to economically support an extensive service network.

IBM's bundling of CPUs, software, and maintenance allowed it to engage in price discrimination. Price discrimination allowed it more freedom in pricing to customers prone to competition. It also meant that customers could not observe real prices for peripheral equipment. This delayed the development of a peripheral market. However, the market began to emerge as improving technology made users want to upgrade parts of IBM systems with new, more advanced peripherals. IBM's response to the development of a peripheral market was interesting. IBM reduced its prices to compete with some peripherals. However, IBM also integrated some peripheral equipment onto its CPUs by reconfiguring peripheral adapters. In essence, IBM physically tied the equipment together. To upgrade, users would have to either buy a whole new non-IBM machine, or replace peripheral parts with new, more advanced IBM peripheral parts. This severely reduced the emerging peripheral market.

In the operating system market Microsoft used a strategy similar to tying. Its CPU license effectively tied Microsoft's operating system to a producer's computer. Under the CPU license arrangement, a producer paid a fixed fee for the potential use of Microsoft's operating system. If a manufacturer wanted to make another operating system available to consumers, it would increase the manufacturer's costs. These cost increases would have to be passed on to final customers. Most customers would rather not pay the extra fee for another operating system when they could have a machine with Microsoft's operating system at a lower price. Microsoft's strategies of carrying credits forward, varying prices based on installations of non-Microsoft operating systems, and retaliatory withholding of technical support only reinforced manufacturers' incentives to offer only MS-DOS. This made entry of new operating systems difficult.

A type of software operating system network externality developed in the computer operating system industry. As more and more people used a Microsoft operating system, more and more software developers put their primary efforts into writing versions of software that would run on that operating system. But then new computer purchasers wanted computers with that operating system to ensure they had access to the latest versions of software. This provided current and future users with network externalities. Microsoft also worked with independent software developers to build a number of DOS-based and later Windows-based applications. This reinforced its network externalities in that the more people who used a Microsoft operating system, the more likely the newest versions of software would be available for a Microsoft operating system, the greater the network externality. Microsoft's success in software just strengthened its success in operating systems because Microsoft would be inclined to support most extensively software running on its own operating system. Furthermore, as the Internet grew, users wanted to make sure they had software and operating systems that were compatible across the Internet.

Another factor that helped firms stay dominant was consumer "lock-in." Lock-in occurs when a customer makes an investment into capital that will only perform in conjunction with specific equipment. As long as the two are used together, the initial capital has value. If new non-compatible equipment is purchased in the future, the initial capital is sunk and lost. This imposes a potentially significant cost on firms in switching from one type of equipment to another.

IBM was a beneficiary of lock-in. Especially in the early years, a customer that purchased IBM-compatible software could only run it on an IBM platform. Customers typically also had to make significant investments in capital to support computing on that platform. This capital included software, data bases, and human capital. The customer would face a potentially enormous cost in converting the sunk cost to another platform. Hence, customers became tied to IBM, which made IBM's preannouncement of the 360 line all the more significant. It gave the locked-in customers an incentive to wait for new IBM technology rather than switch. As with earlier generations of computers, the 360 was not necessarily the most technologically advanced computer on the market. However, lock-in, combined with IBM's reputation for support, convinced many consumers to stay with IBM. Notice that IBM designed the 360 to be compatible with all of its previous systems and software. In that way customers would not have to lose any of their sunk costs in capital that supported IBM-based computing.

Microsoft was in the same position with respect to its operating system. Once firms were committed to software, and so forth that ran on computers using a Microsoft operating system, they were extremely hesitant to switch to another platform requiring a different operating system. Interestingly, in Apple Computer's recent quest to regain market share, it redesigned its system so that Microsoft-compatible software could run on an Apple platform. This reduced non-Apple users' disincentives to switch to Apple.

Chemical processes locked photofinishers into processing either Kodak film or films that used a similar process. Kodak's pre-emptive patenting policy, however, partially prevented the creation of many alternative films. These factors hampered the development of a non-Kodak finishing network and forced any would-be entrants to enter integrated with both film and a photofinishing network. In a sense, product differentiation acted like lock-in. Once consumers were locked into a brand like Kodak or a GM car, they had psychic capital invested. This reinforced the dominant firm's position and made entry more difficult. Kodak's differentiation advantage was evidenced by the deep price discounts rivals set for their films and their resulting small market shares.

Alcoa and Dow also benefited from a form of consumer lock-in. Once a final goods producer invested in capital to produce finished products out of aluminum or magnesium, there were potentially significant sunk costs that would be lost if the finished goods producer switched to another input. This did not necessarily prevent the entry of other aluminum or magnesium producers. It did, however, reinforce the industries in their earlier days against competing metal inputs. It also meant sales to support scale economies and an advantage over would-be entrants. Notice that to avoid lock-in with magnesium, the automobile producers would not switch to using magnesium as an input until a market with at least two sellers developed. An expensive conversion would lock them into Dow as the sole supplier.

A number of these firms used tactics that colored potential entrant's expectations of future market conditions in a way that would deter entry. Entry is a forward-looking process in that the decision to enter is based on a potential entrant's estimate of the profitability of a market in the future, once existing competition has adjusted to its entry. Two particular strategies were used by these dominant firms to indicate to potential entrants that expected market conditions, once their entry occurred, would leave little chance for profits. The first was the strategic use of excess capacity by both Dow and Alcoa. Alcoa consistently built before demand. Dow bought a surplus magnesium plant that it held as excess capacity for four years. The purchase precluded others from using the plant. It also created the specter of significant excess capacity should a rival enter. In addition, Dow held significant stockpiles that acted like excess capacity. In the 1960s, as the threat of entry heightened, Dow preannounced capacity increments that were intended to be held as excess capacity. In one sense, building capacity ahead of demand could be seen as a way of maintaining an efficient production mix over time. The effect of the strategy, however, was also to deter entry. Holding excess stockpiles and preannouncing "phantom" capacity probably are not efficient strategies under normal competitive conditions. The strategic government surpluses in both aluminum and magnesium acted to deter entry as well.

IBM and Microsoft used preannouncement as a way to forestall entry. Their customers invest in other capital that supports the use of those computers and operating systems. A new generation of a non-compatible technology may be more efficient than existing technologies, but its adoption requires a cost in that the supporting capital may have to be converted. The longer a firm could gain the benefits of a new non-compatible technology, relative to its current old technology, the more likely it would be to cover the conversion costs. Preannouncement makes firms believe that a new generation of a compatible technology is more imminent. This reduces the expected amount of time a non-compatible new technology could generate extra benefits to the firm, which means the expected benefits relative to conversion costs are reduced, decreasing the likelihood of entry. Furthermore, the greater the lock-in to a particular technology, the greater the incentive buyers have to stay with a particular firm's technology if they believe a new version would be coming out soon. This makes preannouncement all the more effective. In both the computer and the operating system markets, preannouncement was a frequently used strategy. IBM preannounced its 360 line. Some of the products finally became available almost two years after preannouncement. Others never became available. Yet this helped IBM maintain its position in the mainframe market at a critical time. Microsoft consistently preannounced its new operating systems. Its strategic preannouncement of MS-DOS 5.0 helped repel Digital Research Incorporated's version of DOS from the operating system market. Another advantage of preannouncement was that it denied revenues to competitors when they needed them most—early in their lives. This would help force any potential competitor's early exit from the market.

Blue Cross's history of dominance is different. Many of its markets are regional. It has maintained its dominant position in some of these markets through tax policy and its relationships with hospitals. Its tax exempt status as a non-profit provided it with cost advantages relative to its rivals. Its mutually beneficial association with hospitals protected it, to some extent, from competition. Blue Cross's insurance plans effectively created few incentives for hospitals to contain costs. In that sense, actions that strengthened Blue Cross also acted to support hospitals. This created an incentive for hospitals to favor or protect Blue Cross. This protection came in the form of retaliation against doctors and other insurance plans that threatened Blue Cross's position. In some cases the fear was realized and doctors joining other plans were excluded from hospitals. Also, the clouded antitrust status of health-care providers before the *Goldfarb* case created an atmosphere where hospitals and insurance providers could collectively plan coverage into the future.

It is interesting to examine pricing strategies these firms used to hold dominance. Some, like Alcoa and Dow pursued a strategy of low prices. But both firms were extensively vertically integrated. This allowed them to set limit prices for raw magnesium and aluminum, and recover forgone profits by price discriminating in downstream markets. These strategies deterred entry and stimulated long-run demand. Both companies were very sensitive to elasticities for their various alloys when setting prices. Notice that Dow's limit-pricing strategy preannounced phased-in price reductions to likely entrants as an incentive to keep them out of magnesium production. The Dow chapter also shows that domestic prices were very near a small entrant's costs and well above world prices. This suggests that while U.S. prices may have been low as a result of limit pricing, they were not at marginal cost. Blue Cross maintained its dominance in some regional markets in part because it passed hospital discounts on to customers.

Ford passed many of its cost savings onto customers in the form of lower prices in order to stimulate demand. However, it was still very profitable during most of its period of dominance. Kodak did the same in its early years. In later years, however, Kodak earned considerable excess profits on its film. Furthermore, Kodak's integration let it cross-subsidize price wars in one regional or product market with profits from other markets. Microsoft's pricing of operating systems acted to deter entry. Its high fixed fee and large license amount acted to create a zero-per-unit fee. This created an incentive for competitive computer manufacturers to offer only Microsoft operating systems on their machines. Other provisions of the licensing agreement reinforced this incentive. Yet the Microsoft chapter shows that such a pricing scheme is not profit maximizing absent its effects on entry.

The tobacco companies engaged in selective price wars and predation to maintain their dominance. Twice they engaged in predatory price wars–once in the 1930s to get rid of low-priced cigarettes and again in the 1970s to discipline generic producers. The earlier episode also witnessed a classic price squeeze as the name-brand producers bought inferior tobacco for which they had no use, either to raise its price or to deny it to their low-cost competitors. This cost-raising action combined with a price war for the final output successfully squeezed the non-name-brand producers out of the market. AT&T and Standard Oil also used selective predation to combat competition. Standard did it to soften recalcitrant acquisition targets and to discipline competitors. This created a predatory reputation effect that worked in Standard's favor. AT&T did it to maintain dominance in some local operating markets and to thwart entry into selected cities.[1]

Federal government policy addressed dominance in several of these industries. Yet in a number of cases, the remedies did little to negate power. Antitrust policy ordered a break up of Standard Oil and the Tobacco Trust. In response, Standard Oil reorganized on paper, but the previous owners retained control. In 1911 the Supreme Court ordered the dissolution of the Tobacco Trust. Yet the resulting oligopoly soon began to coordinate the industry through strong tacit collusion. In the 1930s, the tobacco companies were again found guilty of violating antitrust laws. In that case no structural remedy was sought. Antitrust policy broke

Kodak's tying of film and photofinishing. It also forced Kodak to reveal finishing technologies. Neither had a significant impact on Kodak's overall power. Judge Hand found Alcoa guilty of monopolization. The eventual remedy, however, was meted out by the War Surplus Property Board. One case where antitrust policy may have led to the loss of power was IBM. The onus of the antitrust case against IBM made its management hesitant to respond quickly and forcefully to competition. This allowed IBM-compatible computers to gain significant market share. A Justice Department consent decree with Microsoft ended its per CPU license-pricing scheme. It is too soon to tell the impact this will have on competition in the operating system market.

One of the most obvious contrasts between the aluminum and magnesium industries was post-World War II government policy. In magnesium, the only efficient surplus war plant was sold to Dow, the existing monopolist. In aluminum, surplus war capacity was sold to create two efficient, integrated producers to compete against Alcoa. Note that entry finally occurred in the magnesium industry, but only after Dow abandoned its limit-pricing strategy in the mid-1970s. Perhaps if the War Surplus Property Board had not created Kaiser and Reynolds as integrated producers, Alcoa would have remained the dominant producer for another twenty years.

Trade policy influenced the magnesium, aluminum, and automobile industries. Dow was consistently protected from foreign competitors by a high tariff. Alcoa successfully petitioned at times for high tariffs. A consent decree halted limits to foreign competition in both aluminum and magnesium because of cross-licensing agreements. The automobile industry forced the Japanese to agree to "voluntary" restraints, in part under the threat of more serious protectionist mandatory restraints. Tax policy toward non-profits helped Blue Cross maintain its dominance in several markets. AT&T maintained its dominance through specific government policy. In exchange for regulation it was granted a monopoly over the provision of local and long-distance telephone service and equipment in the United States.

Common Factors

The common thread that runs through these studies is that firms seem to be able to hold dominant positions when they can create and maintain advantages over their rivals. The sources of the advantages can vary. A number of firms, for example, had cost advantages over their rivals. Alcoa, Dow, Kodak, Ford, and IBM invested in process-improving technologies to reduce their costs. Almost all of the firms studied in this book gained cost advantages through economies of scale. Many benefitted from learning-by-doing. Maintaining dominance through a cost advantage is an efficient form of competition. Alcoa's, Dow's, Kodak's, Ford's, Microsoft's, and at times IBM's investments in new technologies allowed them to offer better products than either actual or potential rivals. As with a cost advantage, maintaining market share through technological progressivity is an efficient strategy.

Many of these firms were vertically and/or horizontally integrated. This integration created many advantages. In some cases it helped reduce costs. In other cases it prevented the creation of secondary markets. This forced more difficult integrated entry and helped protect the firms' primary markets. The lack of a secondary service market, for example, protected IBM from entry into its primary market, computers. Slow development of photofinishing and camera markets insulated Kodak's dominance in film. Both Dow and Alcoa protected their primary metal markets through integration. Alcoa's backward integration prevented the development of input markets. Their forward integration insulated their primary metal markets. Standard Oil's vast integrated system deterred significant competition for a number of decades by allowing it to add or manipulate capacity at particular stages to deter smaller scale entry. Integration gave many of these firms more flexibility in pricing. They could shift profits downstream or upstream to protect markets. Dow and Alcoa practiced limit pricing in their ingot markets and recovered profits downstream. Other firms practiced price discrimination across markets. Apparently Kodak, AT&T, and Standard Oil used their horizontal integration across regional markets to support selected predatory campaigns and price squeezes. The Tobacco Trust used its sheer size to support two episodes of predation. Both were successful in either disciplining or eliminating rivals.

The efficiency of many of these specific strategies is hard to evaluate; however, there are some indications. In theory, limit pricing is efficient when the limit price is near marginal cost. However, in Dow's case, information indicates that its limit price was above the world price and presumably above any reasonable measure of cost. Furthermore, when limit pricing is supported by integration and price discrimination, as was done by Dow and Alcoa, its relative efficiency is more suspect. Integration supporting focused predation was a strategy used in several of these industries. There is little argument that predatory prices are efficient. Hence, integration to support predation is presumably suspect as well. Predation's inefficiency is magnified when periods of predation help enforce a reputation that deters entry during non-predatory times. Standard Oil's integration allowed it to purchase key assets of an encompassing effort to enter. If its purchases undermined entry, then the benefits to competition as a process are dubious.

Integrating to prevent the development of secondary markets is similar to tying, another strategy used by many of these firms. IBM tied its computers, peripherals, and service together. Kodak effectively tied its new films to new cameras and its film to photo-finishing. Microsoft's pricing to computer manufacturers effectively tied its operating system to computers. Tying is a controversial topic. Tying forces a customer to buy two or more goods together as one package rather than as separate goods in separate markets. In the classic tying example, if a firm has power in one market, it may be able to tie a second good from another market to the monopolized good. In this sense the firm can expand its market power into two markets. In the present analysis, the competitive effect is slightly different. If a firm with power over one good can tie it with a second good, the firm may be able to prevent the development of a market for the second good. If the lack of a market for the second good deters entry and, consequently, creation of a market for the first good, then tying can reinforce a dominant position. From a policy perspective, this may not be a problem in the sense that to overcome tying, a potential entrant may have to enter markets for both goods simultaneously. Since the dominant firm had to enter both markets, it puts a potential competitor at no relative disadvantage. However, if the dominant firm was a first mover, it may have been able to establish both of its goods as new products more easily than a second mover could establish both of its goods as alternatives.

Another factor that created advantages for some of these firms relative to actual or potential rivals was the "locking-in" of consumers. In the early computer years, customers were tied to a producer once they invested in capital that supported computing on that producer's platform. This created an advantage for IBM. Microsoft gained similar benefits with its software and operating systems. An anecdotal indicator of the advantage of lock-in is that even a company as big, experienced, and well known as IBM was afraid to develop an operating system in direct competition to MS-DOS. IBM feared it could not win because it would be hard to capture the established base of locked-in DOS users. IBM and Microsoft also had an advantage over rivals through network externalities. When lock-in, network externalities, and tying are combined, they create a strong advantage for a dominant firm.

The standard economic literature shows that an investment that reduces marginal costs will be undertaken when the fixed plus the marginal costs of the new investment are less than the marginal costs of the existing investment. Lock-in can mean significant fixed costs of switching to a new technology. In that sense, even though the existing technology may have higher marginal costs or upgrades may be expensive compared to new technologies, the new technology may not be adopted. Being a first mover creates a potentially significant advantage that may have little to do with the adoption of more efficient technologies in the future.

Alcoa and Dow attained advantages over their rivals through the strategic use of excess capacity, either through building ahead of demand, acquiring surplus capacity, adjusting to government strategic stockpiles, or manipulating secondary markets. It could be argued that in the production of goods like magnesium and aluminum where scale economies matter, planning capacity increments is important. But it is unclear whether the capacity increments of both firms followed paths that were optimal in meeting expected new demand, or were optimal in preventing new entry. The other strategy that effectively reduced the threat of entry was IBM's and Microsoft's strategic preannouncement of new technologies. If preannouncement provides accurate information, that is, if firms honestly approximate the time to introduce a new, compatible technology, it can be beneficial. However, inaccurate preannouncement does little to improve economic welfare and can significantly reduce welfare by forestalling entry.

In many of these industries, several factors combined to support dominance. Often, tying was supported by integration. Tying's effects were also sometimes reinforced with network externalities, customer lock-in, economies of scale, and learning-by-doing. Firms used capacity expansion in markets where scale economies were important. Preannouncement was used in markets with network externalities and customer lock-in. Underlying market conditions such as scale economies, learning-by-doing and network externalities are generally beyond a firm's control. Other strategies, such as capacity choices, integration, tying, and preannouncement are within a firm's control. To the extent that these latter strategies create advantages for dominant firms, they may or may not be beneficial to competition as a whole. If dominance is a problem, the policy toward strategies that maintain dominance may want to be predicated to some degree on the environment in which the firm operates.

THE LOSS OF DOMINANCE

In eight of these industries firms eventually lost their dominant positions. The Tobacco Trust and Microsoft are still dominant, the former for close to a hundred years, the letter for approximately fifteen years. The other firms lost their dominance mainly because they were not able to maintain their advantages over potential competitors.

Standard Oil maintained its dominant position for many reasons. Among them were the power and efficiencies created by its size and integrated nature, its ability to gain rate breaks from the railroads, and its ownership of a large part of Eastern refineries and scarce pipelines. Standard began to lose its dominant position as the Mid-Continent and California oil fields opened up. Large refineries were built in the Gulf region with ample access to cheap transportation and inexpensive crude. Also, the changing demand for petroleum products fostered by the growing automobile market caught Standard somewhat by surprise. Its lack of gasoline-refining capacity allowed other refiners to gain a perch in the market. Standard's strategy all along had been to acquire through agreement, coercion, or intimidation, enough properties to hold monopolies (or at least enough share to give it significant market power) where it needed to. With the discovery of oil in Kansas, Oklahoma, Texas, California, and abroad, Standard could not foreclose all of the competition. Too many firms could gain close enough cost parity and enough market share to weather any threat Standard may have imposed. In addition, the Supreme Court's decision of 1911 broke up the Standard Oil of New Jersey holding company. This does not mean the refining business became anything like a perfectly competitive market. It did mean, however, the loss of Standard Oil's monopoly on the market.

Alcoa lost its dominant position as a result of government policy. In the early 1940s it had been found guilty of monopolization. After World War II, the War Surplus Property Board created two new integrated producers. While free market entry had been attempted twice in the industry's history, it was never successful. Only integrated entry supported by government subsidy was successful. In addition, Alcoa's antitrust experience of the preceding decade may have made it hesitant to compete too vigorously against those fledgling firms. In any case,

Alcoa's cost advantage dissipated. Later, foreign entry further eroded Alcoa's market position.

Unlike Alcoa, Dow was able to acquire surplus war property and maintain its monopoly after World War II. In the early 1970s Dow changed its entry-prevention strategy. Dow limited its investments in process and product development, and also in excess capacity. At the same time, Dow abandoned its limit-pricing policy. This led to the successful entry of domestic and foreign producers and to Dow's loss of dominance. Dow is one of the few firms in this study that actively chose to relinquish its dominant position.

Kodak lost its dominant position in film processing as a result of government policy. An antitrust decree dissolved the tying of film to processing. This allowed a processing market to develop over time. Kodak eventually faced competition in its primary market, film, from Fuji, a foreign producer. Fuji entered the U.S. film market with its own brand of film in 1972. Part of Fuji's success was due to luck in that it overcame Kodak's product differentiation advantage. Its economies of scale, research and development, marketing and quality control experience in foreign markets enabled it to overcome many of Kodak's, other historical advantages. Favorable exchange rates further eradicated any cost advantage Kodak may have had. Its low costs and large capital base allowed Fuji to weather price wars. Its comparable quality made it attractive to consumers. Its compatibility with Kodak's finishing system allowed it access to Kodak's large finishing network. In short, Fuji's position as an established producer in other parts of the world gave it the ability to overcome many of Kodak's advantages in the U.S. film market.

Another area where Kodak seemed to face problems was in its managerial culture. It's management became "glacially slow, bloated, stodgy, conservative, and lacking marketing savvy."[2] Kodak apparently lost its focus on its core areas and made a number of product and diversification decisions that, in retrospect, seem ill-advised. However, Kodak is still in a strong position in this market. Interestingly, recent court decisions have allowed Kodak to resume some of the strategies that led to its holding of power through most of the 1900s. Once again it will be able to tie film to processing. Its integration through recent acquisition has also given it significant market share in the finishing market. If Kodak can respond to the blossoming market for alternative technologies it may be able to recapture its dominant position in a variety of markets.

Ford rose to power for two reasons. First, Ford was a pioneer in mass production and this gave it significant cost advantages over its rivals. Second, its cost advantage let Ford tap a blossoming market by selling a simple car at a moderate price. Eventually, however, other car manufacturers adopted Ford's production-line methods, eroding its cost advantage. In addition, Ford remained focused on process development while customers and other producers became increasingly interested in product development. Ignoring product development was an outgrowth of Henry Ford's beliefs and his autocratic style of management. Ford's product line congealed. Its cars became less and less desirable to maturing consumer tastes. With its cost and product advantages dissipating, Ford quickly lost market share to more responsive car producers.

GM lost its dominant position as efficient foreign producers entered the high-fuel-cost market of the 1970s. Their own home country production allowed foreign producers to benefit from economies of scale and learning-by-doing. Japanese producers had lower labor costs and superior manufacturing technologies. Their high-quality, fuel-efficient product line better met consumers' needs. GM management was unresponsive to this challenge. Its management had ossified. Decision making had become too centralized. The loss of divisionalization reduced nimbleness and flexibility in management. In addition, GM's cost were steadily increasing because of its extensive integration, refusal to invest in new capital, and out-of-control labor costs. In short, GM's advantages of low costs, desirable products, and responsive management had evaporated. GM and other domestic producers steadily lost market share to imports.

IBM lost its dominance because of several factors. First, government policy in the form of antitrust intimidated top management. Fear of prosecution did not allow IBM to respond to changing conditions as freely as it otherwise would have. Second, and perhaps more importantly, management grew too political and hierarchical. It had lost its entrepreneurial edge and was unable to make fast decisions and adequately respond to competition. Partly as a result of IBM's antitrust concerns and its management structure, IBM made several blunders. These included not responding quickly enough to the coming of the PC, not buying into Microsoft, not competing head-to-head with Microsoft on operating systems, and losing control of pricing of DOS for non-IBM systems. The loss of control over the licensing of DOS was a significant faux pas. This severely dissipated any advantages IBM might have had in terms of customer lock-in and network externalities. Once it lost control of DOS, the compatible market grew so rapidly, customers could get equipment that performed like an IBM, but at a significantly lower cost. They could maintain their current operating system, software, and data bases and still convert across machines. As the market for IBM clones grew, customers became more savvy buyers. They no longer needed the IBM name as a symbol of unique quality. Of course, it is easy to judge in hindsight. But the companies that remain dominant generally call the future correctly.

Blue Cross's advantage lay in its status as a non-profit provider. Initially, this gave it a cost advantage over rivals. Its close association with hospitals also gave it an advantage in that other groups were wary of competing too vigorously for fear of losing hospital privileges. These two factors, however, eventually led to Blue Cross's demise in a number of regional markets. Its non-profit status required it to be a common carrier. As other health insurers grew, they could skim lower cost patients from the customer pool and leave Blue Cross with a distribution of participants skewed toward higher costs. Its close association with hospitals created incentives for Blue Cross to stress care rather than prevention, encourage services to be provided in a relatively high-cost hospital setting and pass hospital costs on to its customers in the form of higher rates. In contrast, other insurers were writing policies to encourage preventive medicine, move service to lower cost providers, and reign in hospital costs. Blue Cross lost its cost advantage and its dominant position.

Blue Cross's organizational structure facilitated the loss of dominance in many markets. As competition increased, other national insurance providers were able to contract with large companies for health-care services on a national scale. The disaggregated nature of the Blue Cross plans made it hard for them to negotiate for services on the same scale. Yet their history of autonomy prevented them from forming a coalition to compete against the national insurers. In addition, Blue Cross plans had relatively high administrative costs.

AT&T's dominance was created by government action. It was also government action that eventually dispelled that dominance. Technological advances in the form of integrated circuits, computers, microwave transmission, satellites, digital data communications, and sophisticated terminal equipment created opportunities for firms to enter niches in the telecommunications market. AT&T fought their entry with pricing, connection, and political tactics. However, over time, the Federal Communications Commission allowed entry into an ever increasing number of segments in the market. To compete, AT&T needed more freedom and flexibility. The Modified Final Judgment of 1982 finally ended AT&T's legal monopoly.

Common Factors

The firms that lost their dominant positions did so because they lost their advantages over rivals. For example, many of these firms were able to hold onto their dominant positions because of cost advantages over potential entrants. They either held patents or had scale economies or benefitted from learning-by-doing. These cost advantages made *de novo* entry difficult. However, there was another source of entry where these factors did not create such significant advantages. This was foreign entry. Foreign producers already had established technologies. They may have benefited from scale economies and learning available from production in their home countries. If trade barriers were not prohibitive and transportation costs were reasonable, they could penetrate domestic markets on a nearly equal cost basis with domestic producers. This is exactly what happened in four of these industries. Dow, Kodak, and GM all lost their dominant positions as a result of foreign entry. Alcoa saw its position erode further as imports entered a previously tight oligopoly. In GM's case, import penetration brought in arguably better technologies as well.

Other firms lost their advantages and fell from dominance because of problematic management. In his later years Henry Ford became autocratic and his management skills and style did not fit with an integrated company and a maturing industry. Other auto firms gained cost parity and produced more desirable products. He was unable to respond to changing market conditions. General Motors fell for similar reasons. Kodak lost its management direction. IBM's management became ossified and, hampered by the ongoing antitrust suit, made some critical decisions that unlocked its customers from IBM technology.

Sometimes markets grew too quickly to retain control. Standard Oil could not buy up enough of the newly discovered crude and newly built refineries in the Gulf Coast area to stop competition. Firms in the newly developing oil regions felt the value of staying in business was greater than the value Standard Oil would pay for their companies. In part this occurred because Standard did not have enough power in those regions to credibly threaten warfare if the entrants did not sell out. As the market for health insurance exploded, Blue Cross could not maintain its advantageous relationship with hospitals and regulators. Too many firms were able to offer better plans and/or lower prices and attract enough participants to force health-care providers to recognize them. Furthermore, over time the health-care market lost some of its mystique, being viewed more and more as just another commodity. AT&T fell from dominance for the same reason. The future was too lucrative. Other firms figured ways to penetrate the market via rapidly evolving technologies.

Firms' policies toward product development also influenced their ability to hold dominance. Companies like Alcoa and Dow were responsive to customers' needs, helping consumers use their materials in a number of new applications. Kodak maintained its dominance, in part, through its ongoing development of more desirable films, cameras, and systems. Standard Oil acquired a significant advantage when it figured out how to remove the sulfur from Lima oil. Microsoft has introduced new versions of its operating system to pre-empt potential entrants. During its period of dominance, IBM was willing to scrap existing technologies for new technologies. The car companies, on the other hand, became slow in their product development. This allowed other companies with better products to gain market share and end existing dominance. IBM's fall was due in part to its unwillingness to abandon its mainframe computers to personal computers.

Government policy also influenced market dominance. Reductions in tariffs helped open the magnesium and aluminum industries to foreign competition. An antitrust suit and the policies of the War Surplus Property Board effectively ended Alcoa's monopoly. The Modified Final Judgment ended AT&T's monopoly. The antitrust suit against IBM forced its management to limit its responses to competition. This was a significant factor in IBM losing its dominance. It is asserted that once deregulation occurred, AT&T deliberately let its market share slide low enough to avoid the antitrust scrutiny that hurt IBM. These were the situations where government policy really mattered. The Standard Oil Trust of New Jersey was broken up under an antitrust decree. However, there is little to suggest this had a significant effect on operations in that industry. The Tobacco Trust was likewise broken up to no avail. It is yet to be seen what impact the consent decree between Microsoft and the Justice Department will have.

EVALUATION

What has been learned from the preceding analyses? Was the source of dominance always luck, efficiency, and/or superior management, or was something more involved? If something more was involved in acquiring dominance, was it something that acted to impede the allocation of resources across markets? Consider maintenance of that dominant position. Was dominance maintained through efficient pricing and continued progressiveness, or were anticompetitive behaviors involved? For those firms that eventually lost their dominant positions, did the inexorable flow of competition dislodge them, or did their own mistakes or perhaps government intervention cast them from power? Looking at the progression of these firms as a whole, did competition as a system work, or did dominance create long-lived market imperfections? It is to these broader questions we now turn.

These firms became dominant because they were able to create advantages over their rivals. To forge these advantages they had to do many of the things efficiency suggests. They had to actively work to reduce their costs via, for example, learning-by-doing, economies of scale, and investing in new process technologies. They had to meet consumers' needs. This meant, among many things, stimulating demand and pursuing product development. More generally they had to push technology. Many of these firms had good leadership and management. They were careful with their pricing, keeping prices low to stimulate demand and foster needed growth. But once they started to gain market share, they could do things typically thought of as inefficient to solidify their positions. Predatory price wars focused on selected product or geographic markets constituted one such strategy. Profits from other markets supported this predation. Buying key companies to diffuse an entry threat was another. Having an integrated system allowed the selective purchase of a variety of assets to prevent entry. In essence, consolidation of power allowed those things to occur.

The eleven firms considered in this book maintained their dominance as long as they were able to maintain their advantages over rivals. To do this, these firms had to keep doing some of the things market efficiency predicts. In almost all of these industries, they had to lead the evolution of technology. Two technology-related strategies were process development and product development. Process development allowed these firms to keep their cost advantages and to push scale economies. Product development allowed them to meet evolving market needs and to retain first-mover advantages. The lessons from individual industries are revealing. When IBM, for example, was willing to abandon its 1401 series computers for the new 360 line and Microsoft was willing to desert DOS for Windows, they were able to remain dominant. When IBM became reticent to replace its mainframe technology with personal computers or to invest in the 80386 line, it began to lose dominance. AT&T's struggle to prevent technology-driven entry into niches shows how important it is for a dominant firm to keep on top of technological evolution. Ford and then GM did not stay up with product development and both eventually lost their dominant positions to competitors that were building more desirable cars.

The link between dominance and technological progression varied across these industries. Near one end of the spectrum were Alcoa and Dow. They faced threats mainly from established foreign producers. As long as trade barriers protected them, they could control the evolution of technological change. Companies like IBM and Microsoft, on the other hand, have been near the other end of the spectrum. They are in technologically fast-moving markets with lots of domestic firms pushing technology. To remain dominant, IBM and Microsoft had to stay ahead of an industry-driven technology curve. Standard Oil faced a similar problem. It could not stay ahead of industry exploration and, hence, lost its dominant position. Kodak was in the middle ground. Sometimes it was first in introducing new technologies. Other times it apparently was prepared with new technology, but preferred to wait for a competitor to move first and then quickly leapfrog that competitor with yet a next generation of technology. In this sense Kodak could gain as much profit as possible from existing technologies (something IBM and Microsoft could not do) and still retain a first-mover advantage. AT&T was protected from competition by regulation. For decades it controlled the evolution of technology in its markets. Yet by the 1960s, other firms were using new technology to make inroads into unprotected niches.

In many cases, size and integration supported a dominant firm's advantage. In part they brought efficiency. This was especially true where scope and scale economies were important. But size and integration also created other opportunities to retain dominance. Size supported staying power in price wars with smaller rivals. This was seen in the oil, tobacco, aluminum, magnesium, and telephone industries. Integration helped insulate primary markets from competition by hindering the development of secondary markets. Kodak and IBM did this with tying. Dow and Alcoa did it with vertical foreclosure and price discrimination. Standard Oil stopped the development of competing pipelines, refineries, and other competitors through price wars, predation, and strategic acquisition. The acquisition of diverse capital was possible because different types of capital could be absorbed into Standard's integrated system. AT&T did many of the same things in its early history.

In some industries, underlying market conditions fostered advantages for leading firms. Network externalities in computers, operating systems, and telecommunications created advantages for the first firms to garner significant market share. Technological lock-in in the computer and operating system markets also supported the leading firm. Sometimes, however, the leading firms were able to pursue particular strategies to extend these advantages. Lease terms influenced lock-in in computers. Sales agreements with computer manufacturers and expanding into software enhanced Microsoft's network externalities in operating systems. Stopping smaller rivals early, a strategy AT&T used against local operating firms that were trying to build long-distance networks, prevented rivals from acquiring their own network externalities.

The combined effects of evolving technology and moving early further helped these firms create dominant positions for themselves. As new technologies emerged, they typically led to increases in minimum efficient scale. In markets where competition existed early on, this forced competitors to consolidate. Consolidation, in turn, meant a better chance to gain market share, especially if a firm was leading the technology wave. This happened in oil refining, tobacco, and automobiles, especially during Henry Ford's time. In markets where the dominant firm entered as a first-mover monopolist, increases in minimum efficient scale just made its advantage that much stronger. It increased the costs and the risks associated with entry. Alcoa, Dow, and Kodak, for example, became more securely established as efficient scale grew in those markets. Standard Oil enjoyed the same type of benefit with its Lima refinery. Whether a first mover or early mover, increases in efficient scale helped incumbents become more entrenched. It also made successful entry more difficult. This notion is supported in the actions of the War Surplus Property Board. The board felt that only integrated producers stood a chance of competing successfully in the post-war aluminum industry. Furthermore, it had to subsidize the creation of those competitors. Apparently, free market integrated entry was just too risky to be viable. Yet Alcoa was a very profitable company.

These dominant firms seemed to attack challengers soon after the latters' announced or actual entrance as new competitors. This lesson was repeated across many industries. Standard Oil, for example, felt it had to crush quickly the threat from the Pennsylvania Railroad-Empire Transportation Company. This was true for other entrants into refining and pipelines as well. IBM's PC operation wanted to hastily introduce an 80386 processor to stop the clones before they made heavy inroads. Kodak briskly responded to technologies introduced by aspiring competitors. Dow undertook a variety of strategies to prevent announced entry before it actually ever occurred. Alcoa stopped entry supported by Canadian hydro power before capacity was even built. Stopping competitors early made sense in that many of the dominant firms had size-related advantages. If a competitor grew, it could possibly dissipate some of those advantages. Fighting entry early also created a reputation for challenging entry. Finite period game theory suggests that such reputation creation is not rational.[3] Yet it occurred nonetheless several times across a number of these markets.

Combining the advantages of size with the advantages of stopping entry early paints an interesting picture of maintaining dominance. Size supported the dominant firms' advantages for many reasons, including those discussed above. Smaller entrants almost by definition could not match those advantages because they could not match the dominant firms' sizes. Either preventing entry entirely or retaliating early against an actual entrant made it that much harder for a new firm to build the experience, technological expertise, distribution networks, customer acceptance, scale, scope economies, network externalities, customer lock-in, vertically related markets, or other things necessary to garner parity with the dominant firm.

Were the particular strategies used to maintain dominance efficient from an economic point of view? That is a hard question to answer. From a short-run perspective, most were not obviously inefficient strategies in and of themselves (although clearly inefficient strategies like predation did occur). However, they may have been undesirable in the following sense. While it may have been inefficient in the short run to limit the use of a dominant firm's advantage in order to allow a competitor to grow, once the competitor reached parity, it would have created a long-run basis for more equal competition. It then becomes a tradeoff of the short-run inefficiencies associated with creating effective competitors against the long-run efficiencies of creating effective competition. Actually evaluating this short-run-long-run tradeoff is difficult. On the one hand, we may want to limit the things a dominant firm can do to impede competition. On the other hand, too many limitations may create powerful disincentives to undertake the potentially efficiency-creating investments necessary to become dominant in the first place.

Nine of the eleven firms considered in this analysis eventually lost their dominant positions. This occurred for a number of reasons. In some markets, foreign producers were able to negate dominant firm's cost advantages. In other cases, managements made poor decisions in evolving markets. Yet other firms lost their dominance because markets just grew too rapidly or because government intervention forced them to acquiesce to entry. Dow chose to abandon limit pricing and specifically allow entry to occur. In all of these cases, entry occurred as the dominant firm lost its advantage over rivals.

Since most of these firms did eventually fall from dominance, one could argue that the competitive process worked. In some cases it did. Ford, for example, led the market for only about thirteen years. Other car producers were quick to adopt its new manufacturing techniques and to provide goods consumers found more desirable than Ford's staid product line. In other cases, however, a closer look suggests that even if a leading firm's pricing consistently generated excess profits, the process of entry and competition moved very slowly to capture those profits.

Dow, for example, dominated the U.S. magnesium market for forty-five years. It engaged in extensive price discrimination and limit pricing well above the world price. Yet its dominance ended only by choice. Alcoa dominated the U.S. aluminum market for almost fifty years. Like Dow, Alcoa used a combination of limit pricing and downstream price discrimination to generate profits. Only direct government intervention ended its monopoly. Although Kodak eventually lost its film monopoly, it happened only after ninety years of power and excess profits. When significant entry did occur, it was in the form of about the only other well-established film producer in the world. What if Fuji had not developed as a strong foreign producer? Would a de novo entrant have been able to break Kodak's power, even with excess profits as an inducement? Previous experience suggests that it is doubtful. GM was another case where its product development and pricing became inefficient. Yet GM remained dominant for forty years. Japanese penetration was successful only after the major oil price shocks of the early 1970s.

How long would it have taken the Japanese to become successful if there were not an oil crisis?

Finally, consider the tobacco industry. They produce a product that is not technologically sophisticated. The production techniques are well known and the market for inputs could be fairly competitive. They have been among the most inefficient pricers of any industry. From the 1920s through today the industry has exhibited tacitly collusive prices, rising roughly twice a year and well in excess of any measure of cost. Yet the major U.S. producers have acted as a dominant trust and then as an oligopoly for over a hundred years. There have been only two attempts at entry over the last century, and both were successfully stopped.

Policy

Dominance has its positive and negative aspects. In its favor is the technological progressiveness that ascendance fosters. Against dominance is the power it creates. So it seems the proper policy is one that nurtures the benefits of dominance while limiting its economic costs. Of course, these conclusions are based on only ten industry studies. Further analyses may temper these findings. Overall, however, the preceding studies suggest a cautious but active approach toward dominant firms. Generally, the rise to dominance should not be discouraged when it meets two criteria. The first is that it bring some clear efficiencies to a market. These include new and better products and technologies, and more efficient production. The second is that dominance not arise out of blatantly anticompetitive means. But not discouraging the quest for dominance means not obliterating one of the rewards of attaining that goal, namely the advantages of having a dominant position. So we have to think carefully about the types of things a firm should be allowed to do once it gains an advantage in the market.

One school of thought suggests that the correct policy is to be passive. Let dominant firms generally do as they will. If they become inefficient, competition as a process will dethrone them. If they remain dominant, it is because they remain efficient. But the preceding industry analyses show that this does not always happen. Dominant firms can become inefficient, yet remain dominant for many years. Even if the firm remains efficient in a technology-production cost sense, it can price inefficiently without attracting successful entry. Furthermore, once a firm becomes dominant, its size may allow it effectively to stop the development of significant competition without necessarily engaging in actions that are clearly anticompetitive. Dominant firms may be able to create situations and do things so that they keep rivals from gaining enough critical mass to become successful. Furthermore, they may be able to do this without remaining efficient themselves. This is not an indictment against competition as a system. It does suggest, however, that a more active policy is called for.

A more reasonable policy would take a rule of reason approach toward dominance. Generally, this approach allows firms to rise to dominance and lets them engage in normal, efficient behaviors. However, in certain situations, when, because of their power, normally neutral strategies consistently block meaningful competition from occurring in a market, a closer look should be taken. In particular situations, antitrust policy should step in and prevent a dominant firm from stifling meaningful long-run competition. Things like extensive integration, tying, pricing schemes to lock customers into specific technologies, discriminatory rates for long leases, selective price wars, acquisition of key components of a competitive threat, preannouncement, acquiring strategic inventories or excess capacity, and other strategies may have to be limited within a dominant firm's strategy space.

It also seems reasonable that the decision to challenge certain behaviors would be based, in part, on underlying market conditions. Microsoft is a good example. Network externalities and customer lock-in have given Microsoft a significant advantage over its rivals. Under these conditions, close scrutiny of its pricing seems reasonable. However, as technology evolves, other competitors may think of ways to reduce those advantages. If that occurs, there may be less need to monitor Microsoft's pricing schemes. Notice also the difference between the evolution of Standard Oil and the Tobacco Trust. Both began to acquire competitors, and gain the advantages of scale economies and integration. Their sheer size created many advantages that gave the companies considerable power over their rivals. Under those conditions their pricing, capacity expansion, and acquisitions should have been watched carefully. Over time, however, Standard's underlying market changed. New oil fields were discovered and new products were demanded where Standard had little capacity. New firms were able to get into the market and get established before Standard could bring its power to bear against them. Under these latter market conditions, Standard's previous actions may have been less onerous. The Tobacco Trust, on the other hand, was pervasive enough and tobacco-growing land restricted enough so that no firm could get into a niche that was protected from the Trust's power. No firm could evade the Trust long enough to overcome the Trust's advantage. As long as these conditions remained, the tobacco companies should have been monitored in their pricing, input purchasing, and other decisions.

The results also have implications for trade policy. In a number of these industries, the only competitors able to overcome the advantages attained by dominant firms were foreign firms. They had the experience, technological know-how, accumulated learning, and product mixes to successfully penetrate U.S. markets. Furthermore, they were able to enter even after de novo domestic entry failed. This suggests that a fairly open trade policy may be one tool to limit the power of dominant firms.

NOTES

1. For a discussion of AT&T's predatory practices against smaller rival local operating companies, see David Gabel and David I. Rosenbaum, "Prices, Costs, Externalities and Entrepreneurial Capital: Lessons from Wisconsin," *Antitrust Bulletin* (fall 1995): 581-608.

2. See Chapter 6 on Kodak.

3. See Reinhard Selton, "The Chain-Store Paradox," *Theory and Decision* 9 (1978): 127-159.

BIBLIOGRAPHY

Ackerman, C. (1930). *George Eastman*. Boston: Houghton Mifflin.

Adams, W., and Brock, J. W. (1991). *Antitrust Economics on Trial: A Dialogue on the New Laissez-Faire*. Princeton, NJ: Princeton University Press.

Adams, W., and Brock, J. W. (1986). *The Bigness Complex*. New York: Pantheon.

Adams, W., and Brock, J. W. (1996). "Predation, 'Rationality,' and Judicial Somnambulance," *Cincinnati Law Review* 64: 811.

Adams, W., Brock, J. W., and Obst, N. P. (1996). "Is Predation Rational? Is It Profitable," *Review of Industrial Organization* 11: 753-758.

Adler, S. J., and Freedman, A. M. (5 March 1990). "Tobacco Suit Exposes Ways Cigarette Firms Keep the Profits Fat," *Wall Street Journal*, p. 1.

American Tobacco Co. v United States, 147 F2d 93 (1944).

American Tobacco Co. v United States, 328 US 781 (1946).

Annual Reports, Eastman Kodak Company.

"Another Outsider is Appointed at IBM," *New York Times* (6 May 1993).

Armentano, D. T. (1982). *Antitrust and Monopoly: Anatomy of a Policy Failure*. New York: John Wiley and Sons.

Arrow, K. J. (1962). "The Economic Implications of Learning by Doing," *Review of Economic Studies* 29: 155-173.

"AT&T: Will the Bad News Ever End?" *Business Week* (7 October 1996).

Bain, J. S. (1956). *Barriers to New Competition*. Cambridge, MA: Harvard University Press.

Baseman, K. C., Warren-Boulton, F. R., and Woroch, G. A. (1995). "Microsoft Plays Hardball: The Use of Exclusionary Pricing and Technical Incompatibility to Maintain Monopoly Power in Markets for Operating System Software," *Antitrust Bulletin* 40: 272.

"B.A.T. to Buy Rival American Brands' Unit," *Wall Street Journal*. (27 April 1994). A3.

Belden, T. G., and Belden, M. R. (1962). *The Lengthening Shadow: The Life of Thomas J. Watson*. Boston: Little Brown.

Berkey v Eastman Kodak. (1979). 603 F 2nd, Boston.

Berkey Photo v Eastman Kodak Co., 603 F2d 263 (1979).

Besen, S. M., and Farrell, J. (1994). "Choosing How to Compete Strategies and Tactics in Standardization," *Journal of Economic Perspectives* 8: 117-131.

"Bill Gates and Paul Allen Talk," *Fortune* (2 October 1995).

Blackstone, E. A., and Fuhr, J. P., Jr. (1996). "Monopsony Power, Funding, and Cost Containment," *Widener Law Symposium Journal* 1: 384.

Blair, R. D., and Esquibel, A. K. (1995). "Some Remarks on Monopoly Leveraging," *Antitrust Bulletin* 40: 371-396.

Blue Cross and Blue Shield Association, *Fact Book.*

Blue Cross of Maryland, Inc. v Franklin Square Hospital, 352 F2d 708 (1976).

Blue Cross of Maryland, Inc. v Franklin Square Hospital, 352 F2d 798 (1976).

Bork, R. H. (1978). *The Antitrust Paradox: A Policy at War With Itself.* New York: Basic Books.

Bork, R. H. (1978). *Concentration, Mergers, and Public Policy.* New York: Macmillan.

Bostoff, S. (8 February 1993). "D.C. Blues Slammed in U.S. Senate," *National Underwriter.*

Bradsher, K. (8 September 1996). "What's New at GM? Cars, for a Change," *New York Times.*

Brandeis, L. D. (December 1911). "An Illegal Trust Legalized," *The World To-Day* 1440-1441.

Brandenberger, A. M., and Nalebuff, B. J. (1996). *Co-Opetition.* New York: Doubleday.

"Breaking Up IBM," *Fortune* (27 July 1992).

Bresnahan, T. F. (1987). "Competition and Collusion in the American Automobile Industry: The 1955 Price War," *Journal of Industrial Economics* 35: 457-482.

Bringhurst, B. (1979). *Antitrust and the Oil Monopoly: the Standard Oil Cases. 1890-1911.* Westport, CT: Greenwood Press.

Brock, G. (1975). *The U.S. Computer Industry: A Study of Market Power.* Cambridge, MA: Ballinger.

Brock, J. (1981). "Market Control in the Amateur Photography Industry," Ph.D. dissertation. Michigan State University.

Brook Group v Brown & Williamson Tobacco Co., 113 S. Ct. 2578 (1993).

Brozen, Yale (1982). *Concentration, Mergers, and Public Policy.* New York: Macmillan.

Bulow, J., Geanakoplos, J., and Klemperer, P. (1985). "Holding Idle Capacity to Deter Entry," *The Economic Journal* 95: 178-182.

Burnett, W. B. (1994). "Predation by a Nondominant Firm," *The Antitrust Revolution,* 2d. ed. Edited by J. E. Kwoka and L. J. White. New York: HarperCollins.

Burns, M. R. (1989). "New Evidence on Predatory Price Cutting," *Managerial and Decision Economics* 10: 328.

Burns, M. R. (1986). "Predatory Pricing and the Acquisition Cost of Competitors," *Journal of Political Economy* 94: 266-296.

Carlton, D. W., and Perloff, J. M. (1990). *Modern Industrial Organization.* Glenview, IL: Scott Foresman.

Carlton, D. W., and Perloff, J. M. (1994). *Modern Industrial Organization*, 2nd ed. New York: HarperCollins.

Carroll, P. (1993). *Big Blues: The Unmaking of IBM.* New York: Crown.

Chemical and Engineering News (14 August 1967).

Chemical Engineering (14 March 1966).

Chemical Week (17 May 1969).

Christian, N. M., and Sharpe, A. (21 March 1996). "A Rich Benefits Plan Gives GM Competitors Cost Edge," *Wall Street Journal*.

Cleveland, R. G., and Williamson, S. T. (1951). *The Road Is Yours*. New York: Hawthorn.

"The Coming Telescramble: Deregulation Is Launching a $1 Trillion Digital Free-for-All," *Business Week* (8 April 1996).

Commissioner of Corporations. (1909). *Report on the Tobacco Industry*. Washington, D.C.: U.S. Government Printing Office.

"Compaq Increases PC Sales Lead," *Syracuse Post-Standard* (30 January 1996).

"Computing's Bold Alliance Falters," *New York Times* (14 September 1994).

Crandall, R. W. (1984). "Import Quotas and the Automobile Industry: The Costs of Protectionism," *Booking Review* 2: 8-16.

Cusumano, M. A., and Selby, R. W. (1995). *Microsoft Secrets*. New York: Free Press.

Darling, M. (1995). "Saturn: GM's $5 Billion Blunder?," *Stern Business* 1: 26-31.

Datamation (15 June 1993).

DeLamarter, R. T. (1986). *Big Blue: IBM's Use and Abuse of Power*. New York: Dodd, Mead.

Demsetz, H. (1973). "Industry Structure, Market Rivalry, and Public Policy," *Journal of Law and Economics* 16.

Dennis, A. J. (1995). "Most Favored Nation Contract Clauses Under the Antitrust Laws," *University of Dayton Law Review* 20: 846.

Dixit, A. (1980). "The Role of Investment in Entry-Deterrence," *Economic Journal* 90: 95-106.

Donnenfeld, S., and White, L. J. (1988). "Product Variety and the Inefficiency of Monopoly," *Economica* 55: 393-401.

"Dow Ready to Boost Magnesium Capacity," *Oil, Paint and Drug Reporter* (7 November 1966).

Epstein, R. C. (1978). *The Automobile Industry: Its Economic and Commercial Development*. Chicago: A. W. Shaw.

Estabrooks, M. (1995). *Electronic Technology, Corporate Strategy and World Transformation*. Westport, CT: Quorum Books.

Farrell, J., and Saloner, G. (1986). "Installed Base and Compatibility: Innovation, Product Preannouncements, and Predation," *American Economic Review* 76: 940-955.

Federal Communications Commission (1995). *Commission Declares AT&T Nondominant*, Report #95-60, Common Carrier Action. Washington, D.C.: Federal Communications Commission.

Federal Communications Commission (1986). *First Report and Order in the Matter of Implementation of the Local Competition Provisions in the Telecommunications Act of 1996: Interconnection Between Local Exchange Carriers and Commercial Mobile Radio Service Providers*. FCC #96-325. Washington, D.C.: Federal Communications Commission.

Federal Trade Commission (1974-1977). *Statistical Report: Annual Line of Business Report*. Washington, D.C.: U.S. Government Printing Office.

Feenstra, R. C. (1985). "Automobile Prices and Protection: The U.S.-Japan Trade Restraint," *Journal of Political Modeling* 7: 49-68.

Ferguson, C. H., and Morris, C. R. (1993). *Computer Wars*. New York: Random House.

Fisher, F. M., and McGowan, J. J. (1983). "On the Misuse of Accounting Rates of Return to Infer Monopoly Profits," *American Economic Review* 73: 82-97.

Fisher, F. M., McGowan, J. J., and Greenwood J. E. (1983). *Folded, Spindled, and Mutilated: Economic Analysis and U.S. v. IBM*. Cambridge, MA: MIT Press.

Frech, H. E., III. (1993). "Health Insurance," *Industry Studies.* Edited by L. Deutsch. Englewood Cliffs, NJ: Prentice Hall.

Frech, H. E., III. (1976). "The Property Rights Theory of the Firm: Empirical Results from a Natural Experiment," *Journal of Political Economy* 84: 149.

Frech, H. E., III, and Ginsburg, P. (1988). "Competition Among Health Insurers, Revisited," *Journal of Health Politics, Policy and Law* 13: 280.

Froeb, L., and Geweke, J. (1987). "Long Run Competition in the U.S. Aluminum Industry," *International Journal of Industrial Organization* 5: 67-78.

From Glass Plates to Digital Images: The Kodak Story. Pamphlet published by Eastman Kodak Company (1994).

Gabel, D., and Rosenbaum, D. I. (1995). "Prices, Costs, Externalities and Entrepreneurial Capital: Lessons from Wisconsin," *Antitrust Bulletin* 40: 581-608.

Gaskins, D. (1971). "Dynamic Limit Pricing: Optimal Pricing Under Threat of Entry," *Journal of Economic Theory.* 3: 306-322.

Gaul, G. M. (2 April 1996). "U.S. Healthcare's Abramson: Dedicated, Perhaps Ruthless," *Philadelphia Inquirer.*

Gelderman, C. (1981). *Henry Ford: The Wayward Capitalist.* New York: Dial.

Geroski, P. A. (1987). "The Dynamics of Market Structure," *International Journal of Industrial Organization* 5:93-100.

Geroski, P. A. (1991). *Market Dynamics and Entry.* Oxford: Blackwell.

Geroski, P. A., and Masson, R. T. (1987). "Dynamic Market Models in Industrial Organization," *International Journal of Industrial Organization* 5:1-14.

Gilpin, K. N. (April 27, 1994). "American Tobacco to B.A.T.," *New York Times.*

Ginsburg, P. B., and Sunshine, J. (1987). *Cost Management in Employee Health Plans: A Handbook.* Santa Monica, CA: RAND Corporation.

Goldbert, L. G., and Greenberg, W. (1985). "The Dominant Firm in Health Insurance," *Social Science and Medicine* 20: 720.

Goldfarb v Virginia State Bar, 421 US 773 (1975).

Graham, M. B. W., and Pruitt, B. H. (1990). *R&D for Industry: A Century of Technical Innovation at Alcoa.* Cambridge: Cambridge University Press.

Habermeier, K. F. (1992). "The Learning Curve and Competition: A Stochastic Model of Duopolistic Rivalry," *International Journal of Industrial Organization* 10: 369-392.

Haller, L. E., and Cotterhill, R. W. "Evaluating Traditional Share-Price and Residual Demand Measures of Market Power on the Catsup Industry," *Review of Industrial Organization.*

Harrington, J. E. (1986). "Limit Pricing When the Potential Entrant is Uncertain of its Cost Function," *Econometrica* 542: 429-438.

Hay, D. A., and Morris, D. J. (1991). *Industrial Economics and Organization.* Oxford: Oxford University Press.

Haynes, J. J. (1988). "Rural Hospitals: In Critical Condition," *Texas Hospitals.*

Health Insurance Association of America, *Source Book Health Insurance Data 1991.*

"Health Insurance," *Standard and Poor's Industry Studies* (2 March 1995).

Herndon, B. (1969). *Ford: An Unconventional Biography of the Men and Their Times.* New York: Weybright and Talley.

Hidy, R. W., and Hidy, M. E. (1955). *Pioneering in Big Business, 1882-1911.* New York: Harper and Brothers.

Hirshleifer, J. (1962). "The Firm's Cost Function: A Successful Reconstruction?" *Journal of Business* 35: 235-255.

Hofmann, M. A. (1 February 1993). "Washington BC/BS Plan Targeted by Senate Panel," *Business Insurance*.

Howell, C., Congelio, F., Yatsko, R. (December 1994). "Pricing Practices for Tobacco Products 1980-1994," *Monthly Labor Review* 6-7.

Huber, P. W. (1992). *Geodesic Network II: 1993 Report on Competition in the Telephone Industry*. Washington, D.C.: Geodesic Co.

Hundt, R. (4 September 1996). "Seven Habits of Hopefully Highly Successful Deregulatory Communications Policy People." London: Royal Institute of International Affairs.

Hwang, S. L. (24 April 1995). "B.A.T. Selects Nick Brookes to Succeed Sandefur as Brown & Williamson CEO," *Wall Street Journal*.

"IBM Chief Making Drastic New Cuts," *New York Times* (28 July 1993).

"IBM Foresees Benefits from Price Cuts," *New York Times* (26 April 1977).

"IBM Posts First Annual Profit Since 1990," *New York Times* (24 January 1995).

Ichbiah, D., and Knepper, S. L. (1993). *The Making of Microsoft: How Bill Gates and His Team Created the World's Most Successful Software Company*. Rocklin, CA: Prima.

Igrom, P., and Roberts, D. J. (1982). "Predation, Reputation, and Entry Deterrence," *Journal of Economic Theory* 27: 280-312.

ILC Peripherals Leasing Company v International Business Machines, 458 F. Supp. 423 (1978).

"Illinois, Texas Blues Pursue Merger," *Modern Healthcare* (5 February 1996).

Jenkins, R. (1975). *Images and Enterprise: Technology and the American Photographic Industry 1839 to 1925*. Baltimore: Johns Hopkins University Press.

Kadiyali, V. (1996). "Entry, Its Deterrence and Its Accommodation: A Study of the U.S. Photographic Film Industry," *Rand Journal of Economics* 27: 452-478.

Kadiyali, V. (1994). "Pricing and Advertising Strategies for Entry and Accommodation: the Case of the U.S. Photographic Film Industry," Ph.D. dissertation, Department of Economics, Northwestern University.

Kattan, J. (1994). "Beyond Facilitating Practices: Price Signaling and Price Protection Clauses in the New Antitrust Environment," *Antitrust Law Journal* 63: 149.

Katz, M. L., and Shapiro, C. (1985). "Network Externalities, Competition, and Compatibility," *American Economic Review* 75: 424-440.

Katz, M. L., and Shapiro, C. (1992). "Product Introduction with Network Externalities," *Journal of Industrial Economics* 40: 55-84.

Katz, M. L., and Shapiro, C. (1994). "Systems Competition and Network Effects," *Journal of Economic Perspectives* 8: 93-115.

Katz, M. L., and Shapiro, C. (1986). "Technical Adoption in the Presence of Network Externalities," *Journal of Political Economy* 94: 822-841.

Keller, J. J. (19 September 1996). "Telecommunications: The 'New' AT&T Faces Daunting Challenges," *Wall Street Journal*.

Keller, M. (1989). *Rude Awakening*. New York: William Morrow.

Kenney, G. B. (1979). *An Analysis of the Energy Efficiency and Economic Viability of Expanded Magnesium Utilization*. New York: Garland.

Kirman, W. I., and Masson, R. T. (1986). "Capacity Signals and Entry Deterrence," *International Journal of Industrial Organization* 4:25-44.

Klagsbrunn, H. A. (1945). "Wartime Aluminum and Magnesium Production," *Industrial and Engineering Chemistry* 37: 608-617.

Krouse, C. G. (1994). "Market Rivalry and Learning-by Doing," *International Journal of Industrial Organization* 12: 437-456.

Kuhn, A. J. (1986). *GM Passes Ford, 1918-1938: Designing the General Motors Performance-Control System*. University Park: Pennsylvania State University Press.

Kwoka, J. E., Jr. (1996). "Altering the Product Life Cycle of Consumer Durables: The Case of Minivans," *Managerial and Decision Economics* 17: 17-25.

Kwoka, J. E., Jr. (1993). "Automobiles: Overtaking an Oligopoly," *Industry Studies*. Edited by L. L. Duetsch. Englewood Cliffs, NJ: Prentice Hall.

Kwoka, J. E., Jr. (1994). "International Joint Venture: General Motors and Toyota (1983)," *The Antitrust Revolution: The Role of Economics*. Edited by J. E. Kwoka and L. J. White. New York: HarperCollins.

Landler, M. (23 December 1996). "A Year of Law but Scant Competition," *New York Times*.

Law, S. A. (1976). *Blue Cross: What Went Wrong?* New Haven, CT: Yale University Press.

Lazich, Robert S. (1997). *Market Share Reporter: 1997*. Detroit, MI: Gale Research.

Leeman, W. A. (1956). "The Limitations of Local Price Cutting as a Barrier to Entry," *Journal of Political Economy* 64: 329-334.

Leibenstein, H. (1950). "Bandwagon, Snob, and Veblen Effects in the Theory of Consumers' Demand," *Quarterly Journal of Economics* 64: 183-207.

"Lessons in Rebounds from GM and IBM," *New York Times* (24 October, 1994).

Levin, J. (1985). "The Potential Entrant and the Decision about Entry: The Case Studies," PhD. Dissertation, Boston College.

Lieberman, M. B. (1987a). "Excess Capacity as a Barrier to Entry: An Empirical Appraisal." *Journal of Industrial Economics* 35: 607-627.

Lieberman, M. B. (1987b). "The Learning Curve, Diffusion, and Competitive Strategy," *Strategic Management Journal* 8: 441-452.

Lieberman, M. B. (1983). "The U.S. Magnesium Industry (A), (B), and (C)," Stanford University, Graduate School of Business, case S-BP-231.

Liebowitz, S. J. and Margolis, S. E. (1994). "Network Externality: An Uncommon Tragedy," *Journal of Economic Perspectives* 8: 133-150.

Liggitt Group, Inc. v Brown & Williamson Tobacco, 748 F Supp. 344 (1990).

Liggitt Group, Inc. v Brown & Williamson Tobacco, 964 F2d 335 (1992).

Liggitt Group, Inc. v Brown & Williamson Tobacco Co., Plaintiff's Exhibit 5, 12.

Lipin, S., and Cauley, L. (26 August 1996). "WorldCom Reaches Pact with MFS in $14.4 Billion Stock Deal," *Wall Street Journal*.

MacDonald, R. M. (1963). *Collective Bargaining in the Automobile Industry*. New Haven, CT: Yale University Press.

"Magnesium Use in U.S. Seen Rising 4 Percent to 77,500 Tons in 1965," *Oil, Paint and Drug Reporter* (22 February 1965).

"Major Exploitation of Great Salt Lake Chemicals Seems to Be in the Works," *Chemical Engineering* (14 March 1966, p. 103).

Mansell, R. (1993). *The New Telecommunications—A Political Economy of Network Evolution*. London: Sage.

Mariger, R. (1978). " Predatory Price Cutting: The Standard Oil of New Jersey Case Revisited," *Explorations in Economic History* 15: 341-367.

Marmor, T. (1991). "A New York's Blue Cross and Blue Shield, 1934-1990: The Complicated Politics of Nonprofit Regulation," *Journal of Health Politics, Policy and Law* 16: 786.

Marshall, A. (1923). *Industry and Trade*, 4th ed. London: Macmillan.

McDonell, P., Guttenbert, A., Greenberg, L., and Arnett, R. H., III. (1986). "Self-Insured Health Plans," *Health Care Financing Review* 8: 1-16.

McGee, J. S. (1958). "Predatory Price Cutting: the Standard Oil (N.J.) Case," *Journal of Law and Economics* 1: 137-169.

Memorex Corporation v International Business Machines, 636 F2d 1188 (1980).

Milgrom, P., and J. Roberts. (1982). "Limit Pricing and Entry under Incomplete Information: An Equilibrium Analysis," *Econometrica* 50: 443-459.

Montague, G. H. (1903). *The Rise and Progress of the Standard Oil Company.* New York: Harper and Brothers.

Moore, J. F. (1996). *The Death of Competition Leadership Strategy in the Age of Business Econsystems.* New York: Harper Business.

"More Tumult for the Computer Industry," *Business Week* (30 May 1977).

Mueller, D. C. (1986). *Profits in the Long Run.* Cambridge: Cambridge University Press.

Mussa, M., and Rosen, S. (1978). "Monopoly and Product Quality," *Journal of Economic Theory* 18: 301-317.

Nevins, A. (1954). *Ford: The Times, the Man, the Company.* New York: Charles Scribner's Sons.

Nevins, A. (1940). *John D. Rockefeller: The Heroic Age of American Enterprise.* New York: Charles Scribner's Sons.

Nevins, A., and Hill, F. E. (1963). *Ford: Decline and Rebirth, 1933-1962.* New York: Charles Scribner's Sons.

Nevins, A., and Hill, F. E. (1957). *Ford: Expansion and Challenge, 1915-1932.* New York: Charles Scribner's Sons.

"New Wage of Change in IBM," *Business Week* (29 May 1978).

Nicholls, W. H. (1951). *Price Policies in the Cigarette Industry.* Nashville: Vanderbilt University Press.

Niman, N. B., and Irwin, M. R. (1995). "Computers," *The Structure of American Industry.* Edited by W. Adams and J. Brock. Englewood Cliffs, NJ: Prentice Hall.

Oil, Paint and Drug Reporter, various issues.

Ordover, J. A., and Panzar, J. C. (1982). "On the Nonlinear Pricing of Inputs," *International Economic Review* 23: 659-675.

Padgug, R. A. (1991). "Looking Backward: Empire Blue Cross and Blue Shield as an Object of Historical Analysis," *Journal of Health Politics, Policy, and Law* 16: 801.

Payton, S., and Powsner, R. M. (1980). "Regulation Through the Looking Glass: Hospitals' Blue Cross and Certificate of Need," *Michigan Law Review* 79: 215.

Peck, M. J. (1961). *Competition in the Aluminum Industry, 1945-1958.* Cambridge, MA: Harvard University Press.

Penrose, E. (1959). *The Theory of Growth of the Firm.* Oxford: Oxford University Press.

Perloff, Jeffrey M. (1994). *Modern Industrial Organization.* New York: HarperCollins.

Plunkett, J. W., and Plunkett, M. L. (1995). *Plunkett's Health Care Industry Almanac.* Dallas, TX: Corporate Jobs Outlook.

Posner, R. A. (1976). *Antitrust Law: An Economic Perspective.* Chicago: University of Chicago Press.

Preston, L. E., and Keachie, E. C. (1964). "Cost Functions and Progress Functions: An Integration," *American Economic Review* 54: 100-106.

"Process Changes Boost Magnesium Capacity," *Chemical and Engineering News* (14 August 1967, pp. 54-56).

Pugh, E. W. (1995). *Building IBM: Shaping an Industry and Its Technology.* Cambridge, MA: MIT Press.

Reazin v Blue Cross and Blue Shield of Kansas, Inc., 635 F Suppl. 1287 (1986).

Reazin v Blue Cross and Blue Shield of Kansas, Inc. 663 F Supp. 1360 (1987).

"RJR Leader in IBM Spotlight," *New York Times* (22 March 1993).

Roberts, P. (1995). *The Hospital Industry and Its Environment.* New York: Dun and Bradstreet.

Rosen, S. (1972). "Learning by Experience as Joint Production," *Quarterly Journal of Economics* 87: 366-382.

Rosenbaum, D. I. (1994). "Efficiency v. Collusion: Evidence Cast in Cement," *Review of Industrial Organization* 9:379-392.

Rosenbaum, D. I. (1993). "Profit, Entry and Changes in Concentration," *International Journal of Industrial Organization* 11: 185-203.

Sapolsky, H. M. (1991). "Empire and the Business of Health Insurance," *Journal of Health Politics, Policy and Law* 16: 751.

Scherer, F. M. (1996). *Industry Structure, Strategy, and Public Policy.* New York: HarperCollins.

Scherer, F. M. (1967). "Predatory Pricing and the Sherman Act: A Comment," *Harvard Law Review* 89:868-903.

Scherer, F. M., and Ross, D. (1990). *Industrial Market Structure and Economic Performance,* 3d ed. Boston: Houghton Mifflin.

Schmalensee, R. (1989). "Inter-Industry Studies of Structure and Performance," *Handbook of Industrial Organization*, vol. 2. Amsterdam: North Holland.

Schonbrun, M. (1977). "The Future of Blue Cross," *Journal of Health Politics, Policy and Law* 2: 326.

Seager, H. R., and Gulick, C. A. (1929). *Trust and Corporation Problems.* New York: Harper & Brothers.

Selton, R. (1978). "The Chain-Store Paradox," *Theory and Decision* 9: 127-159.

Seltzer, L. H. (1928). *A Financial History of the American Automobile Industry.* Boston: Houghton Mifflin.

Shepherd, W. G. (1990). *The Economics of Industrial Organization,* 3d ed. Englewood Cliffs, NJ: Prentice Hall.

Shurleff, J. L. (1975). "Review of Blue Cross; What Went Wrong?," *Hofstra Law Review* 3: 215-218.

Sloan, A. (9 December 1991). "Why Jumbo Has to Take Dance Lessons," *Boston Globe.*

Smith, G. D. (1988). *From Monopoly to Competition: The Transformation of Alcoa, 1888-1986.* Cambridge: Cambridge University Press.

Sobel, R. (1986). *IBM vs. Japan: The Struggle for the Future.* New York: Stein and Day.

Spence, A. M. (1977). "Entry, Capacity, Investment and Oligopolistic Pricing," *Bell Journal of Economics* 8: 534-544.

Spence, A. M. (1981). "The Learning Curve and Competition," *Bell Journal of Economics* 12: 49-70.

Spitz, P. (1987). *Petrochemicals: The Rise of an Industry.* New York: Wiley.

Stein, H. (1952). *Public Administration and Policy Development.* New York: Harcourt.

Stigler, G. J. (1963). *Capital and Rates of Return in Manufacturing Industries.* Princeton, NJ: Princeton University Press.

Stigler, G. J. (1965). "The Dominant Firm and the Inverted Price Umbrella," *Journal of Law & Economics* 8: 167-172.

Stigler, G. J. (1950). "Monopoly and Oligopoly by Merger," *American Economic Review* 40: 23-34.

Stigler, G. J. (1964). "A Theory of Oligopoly," *Journal of Political Economy* 74: 55-69.

Tarbell, I. M. (1963). *The History of the Standard Oil Company.* Gloucester, MA: Peter Smith.

Teitleman, R., and King, R., Jr. (10 February 1986). "Insurance Blues," *Forbes.*

Telex Corporation v International Business Machines, 510 F2d 894 (1975).

Tennant, R. B. (1950). *The American Cigarette Industry.* New Haven, CT: Yale University Press.

"Too Big Blue," *The Economist* (22 May 1993).

Travelers Insurance Co. v Blue Cross of Western Pennsylvania, 361 F Supp. 774 (1972).

Trebing, H. M. (1996). "Achieving Coordination in Public Utility Industries: A Critique of Troublesome Options," *Journal of Economic Issues* 30: 561 ̄70.

"A Tyro Challenges in Big Computers," *Business Week* (12 May 1975).

Ulhman, M. (22 May 1996). "Blue Cross Plans in NJ, DE To Merge," *Philadelphia Inquirer.*

Uhlman, M. (3 April 1996). "When Health Care Firms Marry Who Benefits?" *Philadelphia Inquirer.*

Uhlman, M., and Knox, A. (2 April 1996). "Aetna, U.S. Healthcare Plan Merger," *Philadelphia Inquirer.*

United States v American Tobacco Co., 191 F 371 (Cir. Ct., SDNY, 1911).

United States v American Tobacco Co., 221 US 106 (1911).

United States v Microsoft, No. 94-1564 (DDC filed July 15, 1995).

United States v Microsoft Corp., No. 94-1564 (DDC filed July 15, 1994). Amended versions filed with the court on July 27, 1994.

"United States v. Standard Oil Company of New Jersey" (1909) 173 Fed. 177, *Brief of the Law for Petitioner.* Washington, D.C.: U.S. Government Printing Office.

United States Government. *Minerals Yearbook* (annual issues). Washington, D.C.: U.S. Government Printing Office.

U.S. Chamber of Commerce (1986). *Employee Benefits, 1985.* Washington, D.C.: U.S. Chamber Research Center.

U.S. Department of Labor, Bureau of Labor Statistics (1994). *Employer Costs for Employee Compensation.* Washington, D.C.: U.S. Government Printing Office.

U.S. Healthcare v Blue Cross of Greater Philadelphia, 898 F2d 914 (3d Cir. 1990).

USFTC (1939). *Report on the Motor Vehicle Industry.* Washington, D.C.: U.S. Government Printing Office.

USITC (1985). "A Review of Recent Developments in the U.S. Automobile Industry, Including an Assessment of the Japanese Voluntary Restraint Agreements," Publication No. 1648.

Verity, J. W. (5 June 1995). "AT&T and Computers: Any Signs of Synergy?" *Business Week.*

Wallace, D. H. (1937). *Market Control in the Aluminum Industry.* Cambridge, MA: Harvard University Press.

Wallace, J., and Erickson, J. (1992). *Hard Drive: Bill Gates and the Making of the Microsoft Empire.* New York: John Wiley & Sons.

Ware, R. (1985). "Inventory Holding as a Straegic Weapon to Deter Entry," *Economica* 52: 93-101.

Weiss, L. W. (1989). *Concentration and Price.* Cambridge, MA: MIT Press.

White, L. J. (1972). "The American Automobile Industry and the Small Car, 1945-1970," *Journal of Industrial Economics* 20: 179-192.

White, L. J. (1977a). "The Automobile Industry," *The Structure of American Industry,* 5th ed. New York: Macmillan.

White, L. J. (1982). "The Automobile Industry," *The Structure of American Industry*, 6th ed. New York: Macmillan.

White, L. J. (1971). *The Automobile Industry in the Postwar Period*. Cambridge, MA: Harvard University Press.

White, L. J. (1975). "A Legal Attack on Oligopoly Pricing: The Automobile Fleet Sales Case," *Journal of Economic Issues* 9: 271-284.

White, L. J. (1977b). "Market Structure and Product Varieties," *American Economic Review* 67: 179-182.

White, L. J. (1986). "The United States Automobile Industry: A Case Study of De Facto Industrial Policy," *Industrial Policies for Pacific Economic Growth*. Edited by H. Muto, S. Sekiguchi, S. Suzumura, and I. Yamazawa. Boston: Allen and Unwin.

Whitehead, D. (1968). *The Dow Story: The History of Dow Chemical Company*. New York: McGraw-Hill.

Wilgus, H. L. (1911). "The Standard Oil Decision; the Rule of Reason," *Michigan Law Review* 9: 647.

Williamson, H. F., and Andreano, R. L. (1960). "Competitive Structure of the American Petroleum Industry, 1880-1911: A Reappraisal," *Oil's First Century*. Boston: Harvard Graduate School of Business Administration.

Williamson, H. F., and Daum, A. R. (1959). *The American Petroleum Industry: Volume I, The Age of Illumination, 1859-1899*. Evanston, IL: Northwestern University Press.

Williamson, H. F., et al. (1963). *The American Petroleum Industry: Volume 2, The Age of Energy, 1900-1959*. Evanston, IL: Northwestern University Press.

Williamson, O. E. (1967). "Hierarchical Control and Optimum Firm Size," *Journal of Political Economy* 70: 123-138.

Williamson, O. E. (1975). *Markets and Hierarchies—Analysis and Antitrust Implications: A Study in the Economics of Internal Organization*. New York: Free Press.

Wolfman Report on the Photographic and Imaging Industry in the U.S. (1969-1996). New York: ABC Leisure Magazine.

Womack, J., Jones, D., and Roos, D. (1990). *The Machine That Changed the World*. New York: Macmillan.

Wright, J. (1979). *On a Clear Day You Can See General Motors: John Z. DeLorean's Look Inside the Automotive Giant*. Grosse Pointe, MI: Wright Enterprises.

Yates, B. (1983). *The Decline and Fall of the American Automobile Industry*. New York: Vintage.

INDEX

ABOUT THE EDITOR AND CONTRIBUTORS

Walter Adams is a distinguished professor of Economics at Michigan State University and Trinity University in Texas. He has co-authored several books, including *The Structure of American Industry*, in its ninth edition. He has written over two hundred scholarly articles in law and economic journals.

Erwin A. Blackstone is professor of Economics at Temple University. He has written several articles and chapters of books on health-related issues.

James W. Brock is the Moeckel professor of Economics at Miami University in Ohio. He has written several books and articles related to market power and has testified numerous times before congressional committees.

Hayley Chouinard is a graduate student in Agricultural Economics at the University of California at Berkeley.

Maurice Estabrooks is chief of Regulatory Policy Analysis in the Telecommunications Policy Branch of Industry Canada. He has spent over twenty years in the fields of telecommunications, broadcasting, cable television, and information technology. He is the author of numerous publications, including the books *Programmed Capitalism: A Computer Mediated Global Society* (1985) and *Electronic Technology, Corporate Strategy and World Transformation*.

Joseph P. Fuhr is professor of Economics at Widener University. His primary research interests include health economics, an area where he has authored several papers. He has been an expert witness on a variety of antitrust matters.

Vrinda Kadiyali is assistant professor of Economics and Marketing at Cornell University. She has written a number of papers detailing the U.S. photographic film industry.

Marvin B. Lieberman is associate professor at The University of California at Los Angeles. He has extensive experience studying industries and has written numerous articles on market evolution.

Leslie D. Manns is associate professor at Doan College. He has studied a number of industries including oil refining and hazardous waste disposal.

David I. Rosenbaum is professor of Economics at the University of Nebraska-Lincoln. He has written a number of articles analyzing firm strategies and market outcomes. These include examinations of the aluminum, titanium dioxide, and brewing industries.

Rochelle Ruffer is assistant professor of Economics at Youngstown State University in Ohio. She has examined both the banking and computer operating system markets.

Harry M. Trebing is professor emeritus of Economics at Michigan State University. He has been involved with the telecommunications industry for most of his professional life and held positions including Director, Institute of Public Utilities, Michigan State University; chief, Economic Studies Division, Federal Communications Commission; and member, National Research Council Committee on Telecommunications.

Don E. Waldman is the Richard M. Kessler professor of Economic Studies at Colgate University. He has written several books and articles relating to antitrust and market power.

Lawrence J. White is professor of Economics at New York University. He has served as chief economist for the Antitrust Division of the U.S. Department of Justice. Professor White has written several books and articles on the automobile industry, including *The American Automobile Industry Since 1945*. He has also been involved in antitrust litigation involving the automobile industry.